MW01048329

ap cut
to
" Vogelstein *poem'*

A HISTORIAN'S PILGRIMAGE
Memoirs and Reflections

By Frank (U. F. J.) Eyck, 1921-2004
Edited by Rosemarie Eyck

A Historian's Pilgrimage
© Rosemarie Eyck 2009

Library and Archives Canada Cataloguing in Publication

Eyck, Frank
    A historian's pilgrimage : memoirs and reflections / Frank Eyck ; Rosemarie
Eyck (editor).

Includes bibliographical references.
ISBN 978-1-55059-383-9

    1. Eyck, Frank. 2. Historians--Alberta--Biography. I. Eyck, Rosemarie
II. Title.

FC151.E92A3 2010   971.23'007202   C2010-900239-3

Detselig Enterprises Ltd.

2I0 I220 Kensington Rd NW
Calgary, Alberta T2N 3P5
www.temerondetselig.com
temeron@telusplanet.net
p. 403-283-0900 *f.* 403-283-6947

We acknowledge the support of the Government of Canada through the Book Publishing Industry Development Program (BPIDP) for our publishing program.

We also acknowledge the support of the Alberta Foundation for the Arts for our publishing program.

SAN 113-0234
ISBN 978-1-55059-367-9
Cover Design by Dave Casey

To my sons

Andrew John Stephen
and
George Anthony David.

In Memoriam

My heart is heavy
From my eyes tears fall.
I look upon sad faces that surround me and ask
God's blessing on us all.

A smile shimmer
And memories abound.
Laughter, advice, a hug, conversation and debate.
A love never lost but always there, always found.

My heart is heavy, but lighter now.
Remembering fondly his joy of life, his joy of writing,
teaching
And his books.
Understanding kindness and so much more,
All contained in a simple but profound look.

A smile shimmers and blooms.
As from my eyes still tears fall.
His love of wife, family and friends,
Is God's blessing on us all.

Angela Eyck, December 28, 2004

Table of Contents

Preface

FOR SOME TIME MY HUSBAND, ULRICH Franz Joseph (Frank) Eyck, Professor Emeritus of History at the University of Calgary, had worked on this biography. In doing so, he had in mind not only the wish to be remembered by his family and friends, but above all to give a sincere and truthful account about his way through turbulent times as well as more quiet reflective periods. When he passed away on 28th December 2004 he left me with a good start towards this end. There are carefully sorted files on his desk and in his computer. There are letters to and from him, detailed notes, sometimes only a few words, documents he had collected and started to sort, library research lists of books he had read and planned to read. There was also the analyzed journal of his grandmother. As ours was a marriage of intense partnership I was always well informed about Frank's work, and assisted wherever I could. However, I soon realized that being informed is quite different from doing the work itself. When I found myself surrounded by all these papers I dared to attempt to bring them together, to edit as well as I could. The result is not exactly as Frank would have written his memoirs. But I stayed as close as possible to his own writing as I found it, filling in with facts where I felt the need to do so in order to provide a wider context and to cover areas I knew he considered important. In all this I had encouragement and help from our sons, Andrew and George and his wife Angela, our wider family and friends of different generations and backgrounds, members in the history department and the Library of the University of Calgary. It was not possible for me to mention the many people who touched Frank's life in friendship and scholarly exchange - often in both, deciding who should be mentioned was no easy choice.

My friendship with Frank started in 1933 when my father was transferred to Berlin and I first met Frank as my brother's friend, a friendship into which our parents soon joined. We lived through the same political upheaval, though in different quarters, but we upheld the same critical approach to the disturbance around us. Although my close family was not directly targeted, as a nine-year old girl, I remember the Nazis usurping of power as a decisive negative turn of events. There was less laughter among the adults. The sky seemed to be permanently clouded over. With any political remark you had to be careful in what you said, and to whom you said it. This is all a long time ago. We hoped that, at some stage, the problems of those days would be a thing of the past and purely of historical interest. We hoped the world would learn from history.

In his teaching and writing Frank was always keen to base the search for truth on careful and scrupulous research into the actual, as opposed to imagined or desirable facts. He had great confidence in the civilizing power of learning and understanding. He liked the stimulating personal contact with others, and he was happy if he could bring people together in things that mattered. He tried to build bridges, and to bring peace to conflicts without sacrificing moral values. Unfortunately the old difficulties surfaced again and again. That is why I think Frank's story, though a personal one, is relevant today.

Rosemarie Eyck

Acknowledgements

MANY PEOPLE personally and professionally connected to Frank and myself provided invaluable advice and encouragement in my effort to complete Frank's draft of his memoirs and reflections.

Steve Randall, Dean of Social Sciences, and John Ferris, Professor of History of the University of Calgary supported my idea to put Frank's memoirs together on the basis of his draft, memoranda, notes and letters. After reading my first effort John Ferris visited me. Sitting in the upper library of my home he gave me lots of good advice on how to handle sensitive topics. He also suggested I make use of Frank's article on his grandmother's journal. All of this and his editorial comments I gladly accepted.

Frank's schoolmate from the Collège Français, Rolf Sabersky kindly sent me the picture of the class of 1935. With his help and the good memory of Charles Cahn, Gerry Field and my brother, Wolfgang Schmidt, we were able to identify all the boys. Wolfgang also procured the details of school examinations (*Einjährige* and *Abitur*) including the essay topics of the former. Early on in my endeavour Gerry Field besides being tireless in his instigation also helped me with research. Ken Adam allowed me to quote him on his experience of Bergen-Belson. Irving Hexham, Professor of Religious Studies, immensely practical and supportive helped me to find a shortcut for the German modified vowels. He also made it possible to procure the article on nationalism in the *Flensburger Tageblatt* that Frank had long sought. His wife Karla Poewe, Professor of Anthropology, was equally supportive. My nephew Michael Alexander, Professor of History, assisted greatly with his critical reading of my draft. I thank my sons George and Andrew who listened to my progress reports and gave valuable comments.

Andrew always provided me with needed books from the University of Calgary library or from other sources and did some research and proof reading.

Other friends encouraged me and helped me with this book and I like to mention a few: Norman Denny (LCdr RNC Ret' – Canadian Navy), Carol Baldwin, Sheila Gow, Mary MaLellan, all three school teachers; Sister Mary Mcgrath; Donald Smith, Professor of History; Christel and Karl Schunicht; Dr. Otto Spika; Theo and Tea Smit, who experienced the flooding after the Dutch dykes had been dynamited; Ali and Michael Ward, Michael who never failed to aid me when I had my frequent computer problems; and Alan and Yvonne Wells who told me and gave me material about Yvonne's father Otto Lehmann Rusbüldt. Rosvita Voska of the University of Calgary Library always quickly found bibliographical details and the sources of the German quotes. Barbara Howard and Kate Mergen helped me to ready the manuscript for publication. Dave Brown at the library of the U of C and Gold Photography in Bragg Creek expertly processed the pictures.

To all of them, many are my neighbors, and to my family, I owe a lot of understanding, moral support, encouragement, and kindness; with their help I was able to complete the work on Frank's experiences, he so much wanted to share.

Introduction

F RANK EYCK WAS ONE OF THE most remarkable people I have
ever met. The impression he created was of a born and
bred English gentleman. His cultivated accent, clearly spoken
Queen's English, his gestures and mannerisms, all spoke
of someone totally comfortable in the best society. He was
educated at St. Paul's Public School, London; he served in
His Majesty's Army during World War II and went up to
Worcester College, Oxford, to read Modern History. Frank
was like a character straight out of the upper crust segments of
society portrayed in popular television series like *All Creatures
Great and Small* or *Inspector Morse*. One could easily imagine
him playing the role of a distinguished country squire or
learned Oxford Don in such a series. His sense of fair play, his
unfailing courtesy, and his decency, portraying the values of
Englishness, made him typical of the best sort of Englishman.

After my wife, Karla Poewe, and I became close friends with
Frank, and his equally charming wife Rosemarie, another side
of Frank became visible. Not only was he a perfect English
Gentleman but he was also a highly cultured German from a
distinguished Jewish family. Frank loved the music of J.S. Bach
(1685-1750), Beethoven (1770-1827) and Mozart (1756-1791),
the literature and poetry of men like Goethe (1749-1832) and
Schiller (1759-1805), he appreciated the art of Adolf Menzel
(1815-1905) and Caspar David Friedrich (1774-1840), and
valued the "human scale" of the architecture of Karl Friedrich
Schinkel (1781-1841) all of whom created the world of his
early childhood in Berlin.

At the same time he was painfully aware of the horrors of Nazism which caused so much death and suffering in his own and other families. Yet Frank did not blame the Nazis, or the Holocaust, on "the Germans." He knew only too well that many Germans, indeed many of his friends, or families of friends, also suffered at the hands of "Nazi Gangsters." Like Peter F. Drucker (1909-2006) in his classic The End of Economic Man (1939), Frank saw National Socialism as a symptom of a far deeper human malaise rooted in the loss of spiritual values. Like Drucker, Lord Keynes (1883-1946) and Jan Smuts (1870-1950) he also saw the culpability of the victorious Allies in 1918 who imposed the treaty of Versailles with its reparations, massive loss of land, glib demands for an admission of "war guilt," and Allied inaction while the monarchies and dukedoms, the stabilizing feature of German society, were removed. Frank, along with many others, realized the tragedy of "the peace of 1918" was that it was no peace at all but the beginning of a civil unrest that tore Germany apart, creating instability and the destruction of the middle classes. Into this vacuum the Nazis boldly strode, making the Jews scapegoats for all "the wrongs," imagined and real, inflicted upon the German people.

Frank vividly remembered the burning of the Reichstag and the speed with which the NSDAP (National Socialist German Workers Party) used this event as an excuse to seize power in what was effectively a coup against the existing coalition Government. He also remembered the machine-gun nests on top of prominent buildings that ensured the passage of the Enabling Act of 1933, and similar later legislations. Even as a child he knew that once in power there would be no easy way to resist the Nazis when resistance would mean imprisonment or death.

Despite his very real aversion for National Socialism and all things associated with it as an ideology and political movement, he showed remarkable sympathy to people caught up in the maelstrom. For example he remembered with a certain fondness the Headmaster at Berlin's French High School (where he was a pupil) who, although a Nazi, treated him with respect while encouraging his academic development and allowing him considerable freedom of thought and expression. He also remembered that same man sadly advised him that he and his family ought to leave Germany. As Frank observed, the Nazis were people and, like all people, some were evil, some indifferent, and many were good people deceived by evil men.

At the end of the early years of Frank's interesting life, that of a German-Jewish schoolboy, he was sent to England in 1935 to learn English and to complete his education and helped to prepare the way for his immediate family's eventual escape. Frank's new life was that of an English Public schoolboy, with all that entailed in terms of learning to live in a very strange culture. After the outbreak of war Frank experienced life as an "enemy alien" and for a short time was interned on the Isle of Man with other Jews, Germans, and some real Nazis. When this terrible blunder was recognized, Frank and many other Jewish German internees were released on condition they joined the British Army. So Frank became a soldier, eventually returning to Germany as a member of the Army of Occupation where he ended his military career by editing the newly established German language newspapers of the British Military Government, working in Hamburg and in the northern German town of Flensburg.

Demobilized, Frank recovered again the problem that he was still not a British subject. In fact, he was officially German and a former "enemy alien" who had no right to remain in England despite his loyal war service. After some time this outrageous situation (which several thousand people in the same position faced) was resolved, and Frank and other German

Jewish ex-servicemen were granted citizenship. He then began life as an undergraduate at Worcester College, Oxford, to read History and, after graduating, joined the BBC's World Service preparing German language programs for broadcast to Europe. This was an interesting time during which he resumed his contact with the Schmidt family in Berlin and eventually married their daughter Rosemarie in 1955. Soon thereafter he returned to Oxford as a fellow of St. Antony's College for post-graduate work, subsequently becoming a lecturer (assistant professor in the Canadian sense) in Modern History at the University of Liverpool before moving on to a more secure job at the newly established University of Exeter. In Exeter Frank and Rosemarie began their family and settled into English life until, in 1968, Frank was offered a full professorship at the University of Calgary which he readily accepted.

After immigrating to Canada, Frank became one of the pillars of the University of Calgary and an international authority on both British and German history. He was a delightful and highly valued colleague who encouraged younger scholars and freely gave of himself to help those around him. Remarkably, he continued his academic work until a few weeks before his death. Throughout his eventful life Frank was on a spiritual pilgrimage from secular Jew to practicing Christian. He began life in a liberal Jewish family. As a solider he converted to Christianity through the efforts of a Methodist minister in Buxton, England, where he at one time had been stationed as a soldier. Later he gradually moved towards Catholicism, while increasingly appreciating his Jewish roots and the rich spiritual heritage of Judaism.

The book you have in your hands is Frank's biography, lovingly edited by Rosemarie. Although Frank left the broad outline and all the key passages behind in partially complete form, minor changes were needed to turn his chapters into a book. It was also necessary in places to add explanations, letters and other material to make the book eminently readable and an important testimony to twentieth century history as it was experienced at the time. This is a book I highly recommend and am sure you will both enjoy and benefit from reading it.

Irving Hexham
Ph.D. Bristol University, Professor of Religious Studies at the University of Calgary, Canada.

Bibliography

Drucker, Peter F. *The End of Economic Man. A Study of the New Totalitarianism.* New York: The John Day Co., 1939.

CHAPTER 1

Helene Eyck, a fin-de ciècle Diarist.[1]

I N NOVEMBER 1938, my father Erich Eyck, the historian, and my mother, Hedwig, received their belongings from Germany which they had to leave behind slightly more than a year earlier. The property in question had been released after payment of the capital flight tax, the *Reichsfluchtsteuer*, yet still showed the labels of the earlier – as it turned out temporary – confiscation by the authorities. All the furniture and the household goods arrived, which were a great help to Hedwig in the guest-house she took over in the London suburb of Hampstead to provide the livelihood for her family. But it was the books that were invaluable to Erich Eyck in creating the historical writing that was to win him international renown.[2] The papers that arrived in London included a number of family letters and two notebooks containing the journal that Erich Eyck's mother kept in Berlin during the two decades before her death in 1898.[3] This journal gives a vivid picture of the life of an educated German-Jewish middle-class family in the German capital and throws light on the early development of their children.

Helene Veitel was born in Halle in May 1857, the daughter of a businessman Adolph Veitel and his wife Theresa née Gottschalk.[4] Early in 1877 Helene, who resided in Leipzig with her family, married Joseph Eyck[5] who for many years was a broker at the grain exchange in Berlin. Joseph had been born in November 1846 at Freystadt, *Kreis Rosenberg*, a District of West Prussia, and thus was ten years older than his wife. Helene was well educated and her first entries in the journal were made in 1876, while she was reading Johann Wolfgang von Goethe's[6] *Wahlverwandtschaften*. Goethe's writings established a strong link to German culture for educated German Gentiles and Jews. Helene's second son Erich, born in December 1878, was certainly strongly influenced by Goethe, whose works he knew thoroughly, and whom he admired deeply. There was hardly an occasion when Erich did not quote Goethe. I remember one quote that was often applied:

> How merit and luck intertwine
> The foolish men will never know,
> Had they the stone of wisdom,
> The stone would miss the wise man now. [7]

The journal was kept as a record for the development of their children, so that it my might later be consulted by them and their parents.[8] It describes in detail the story of a growing family, the development of the children, the attitude to Judaism, and relations with the Christian outside world. The first post-matrimonial entry in the journal is dated 4th June 1881, by which time three children had been born: Hans, the eldest, born in 1877, with Erich the following year, and Erna in 1881. Hans was to be a successful patent lawyer in Magdeburg; and Erna was to marry Fedor, a relative from her mother's side. Fedor was a capable architect who changed his surname from Veitel to Feit. There were three more children: Trude, born in 1883, married Arthur Nussbaum, the distinguished jurist; Ernst, born in 1886, went into business; and Lilli, born in 1893, who became a French language teacher and married the physician Hermann Pineas. There are many references in the journal to infectious diseases,[9] which, given the state of the medical knowledge at the time, could easily be fatal. Remarkably all six children survived to adulthood, but the younger two died of tuberculosis (which was endemic in the big cities of Europe), Ernst at about forty and Lilli at thirty-three.

Joseph Eyck Family. 1884

Hans (with boat), Erik (with book), Erna (left of Helene),
Ernst (right of Helene), Trude (below Ernst)

With a cook, a maid, and often a resident Governess, a *Fräulein*, for the children, the household eventually grew to eleven people, the supervision of which constituted a major task for Helene.[10] One sometimes wonders whether the pressure "to live according to one's rank"[11] was not a burden, as "one would like very much to live comfortably."[12] Certainly for her husband Joseph, the struggle to keep up middle-class standards and to secure the means of providing a cultural home for the family involved frequent worry. This is reflected both in the journal and in the letters Helene wrote to her husband from the prolonged family holidays during which he had to continue working in Berlin. Husband and wife faced their problems together, in a spirit of partnership. Obviously Helene was well informed about their situation. As early as 1884, references to monetary worries appear in her journal,[13] and later on, in 1891, to their not fragile financial circumstances.[14] However, even that year Joseph and Helene still had their holiday in Switzerland, one of the two major trips they undertook without their children.[15] The other was spent in Scandinavia in 1895.[16] In 1898, another serious monetary crisis affected the family, which led to the abandonment of all plans to go for the usual summer holidays.[17]

The following year, Joseph's appointment as manager of the Berlin brewery firm *Krugbier-Gesellschaft* brought some hope. Helene's father anticipated a splendid future for the firm, and hoped to support the enterprise by concluding agreements with the brewery and beer distributors in Leipzig, presumably in the interest of his son-in-law.[18] Helene was more skeptical, believing that for several reasons, which she did not state, the success of the company was not assured. The previous year, when Joseph had been a broker at the grain exchange, had not gone well,[19] so there was a great deal of income to be made up. Helene fully recognized her husband's efforts in earning the money needed to provide for the daily bread of his loved ones as well as the provision of their education and customary extracurricular activities, such as musical instruction. Joseph found the new job physically very exhausting.[20] Interestingly enough, Helene considered the post to be particularly burdensome because she regarded her husband at the age of fifty-one as a man of advanced years, *in vorgerücktem Lebensalter*. In response to the difficulty of making ends meet, Helene repeatedly suggested economizing, though she did not indicate where the cuts should be made. In any case, in many ways the family lived in a simple style. For the children, a buttered roll with sugar on an ordinary weekday was something very special.[21] While she felt that it would not do the children any harm if their standard of living was somewhat reduced, she regretted her and her husband's nervousness due to their financial worries and that the punishments the children received – corporal ones only as a last resort after due warning – would otherwise sometimes have been milder.

For many years the family lived in the increasingly cramped quarters in the Oranienburger Straße 59, in central Berlin (in what was to form part of the Eastern sector of the city in 1945). This was a few houses away from the liberal synagogue at Oranienburger Straße 30, which had been completed in 1866. The original design by the famous architect, Eduard Knoblauch, the synagogue had Moorish features to distinguish it from churches. At the same time the architecture demonstrated its character as a public building. It was set facing the street, whereas at one time Jews had to hide their places of worship.[22] Incidentally, the synagogue could accommodate a congregation of three thousand, about twice the capacity of the *Kaiser-Wilhelm-Gedächtnis-Kirche*,[23] the largest Protestant church in Berlin.

In spite of all obstacles, the family moved in 1893, to a "better" district in the West of the city, in the proximity of the Tiergarten. At first they lived in the Klopstock Straße but, in 1897, went to live in the rather quiet Augsburger Straße, roughly parallel to the Southern side of the Tauenzien Straße.

In the effort to bring up her children, Helene did not spare herself. The idea that her highest aim should be self-realization at the expense of her family would have been alien to her. She had a task both joyful and worrisome to which she felt that she had been called – to work together with her husband for the good of her family.[24] The supervision and the upbringing of their children were primarily left to her, but her husband, who constituted a power of last resort, assisted her. Her reward was the love and affection her family had for her and any success that her pedagogy might yield with her children over the years that followed. She was open to new methods and, in October 1882 she arranged for her children to be taught by a *Kindergarten* teacher employing the Fröbel method.[25] This model focused on the natural spontaneous development of the child, which turned out very well for her children.[26] She watched the development of her children realistically and with great care, trying to bring out positive features and correcting negative ones, such as laziness or a quick temper. Her main aim was that both the boys and the girls should one day be able to stand on their own feet as decent people. She was not overly ambitious for them in intellectual or professional respects, but she wanted them to realize their full potential for their own satisfaction. She attached great importance to getting on with other people and was pleased when her children were well liked. Helene was particularly happy at any feeling of sympathy or care for others that her children showed. She emphasized the need for good manners, especially at the table; she watched diligently over their hygiene and posture in order to ensure their good health.[27]

In many respects, the home Joseph and Helene Eyck provided for their children would have found numerous parallels in both Catholic and Protestant families of this period in Germany. Yet these similarities also raise some interesting questions about their Jewish heritage. Was there any thing characteristically Jewish about the way they lived? How did they react to the Christian society around them? How much contact did they have with it?

Joseph, more so than Helene, had received a Jewish upbringing, from parents who continued practicing their religion.[28] The District of Rosenberg, in which Joseph's birthplace, Freystadt, was situated, underwent frequent territorial changes that afflicted Prussia. In 1619, it had belonged to the Duchy of Prussia, *East Prussia,* which the Elector of Brandenburg had inherited from their Hohenzollern relatives.[29] The district was only later allocated to West Prussia, as part of an administrative re-arrangement following the annexation of that territory from Poland.[30]

Freystadt was a small township with a population of over two thousand inhabitants. Its main income came from a cattle market and the grain trade. It also had a Protestant church and a synagogue.[31] In a Jewish congregation that was small enough for all the families to have known each other, religious observance must have played a vital role. Unlike the comparative anonymity found in city synagogues, everyone in the community would know immediately if someone missed worship service. Quite generally in the Eastern territories – like West Prussia, Silesia, and Posen – strong bonds within the Jewish community must have been required as bulwarks against the more numerous ethnic Germans and Poles in the region.[32] As in other parts of the Prussian territory conquered earlier by the Teutonic Knights (the *Deutscher Ritter Orden,* which expanded Prussian territory from the twelve-century onwards) the landed nobility played a considerable part. Except for one break, the local *Reichstag* constituency, *Marienwerder-Rosenberg,* was represented by Protestant Conservative land-owners and former district magistrates, the *Landräte,* usually drawn from the nobility or from the establishment of the North German Confederation until the end of monarchy. From 1890 to 1898 the District was held by a Roman Catholic physician in the Polish interest.[33] The Neudeck estate, which was to become well known as the home of President Hindenburg, was only five kilometers away from Freystadt.[34] When Joseph grew up in Freystadt, Field Marshal von Hindenburg's grandparents still owned Neudeck.[35]

For Joseph the departure from a comparatively rural area was bound to bring challenging changes. The move from the countryside or a small township to the city, similar to the dissolution of European *shtetl,*[36] often led to the abandonment of religious customs, such as dietary laws and Sabbath observance.[37] All too easily, the greater assimilation to German culture could lead to the loosening of the ties to the faith or, at any rate, to its rites. In Berlin, from the time Joseph became more independent from his parents, he moved away from strict religious observance. Sabbath observance in the household of Joseph and Helene was not very precise, but Friday was kept as a kind of half-holiday,[38] and the children still said their prayers regularly.[39] Helene records in May 1898 that Lilli, the youngest, had got into the habit, instead of saying prayers, of reciting a poem out of a picture book. Helene felt that the poem thus received valid sanctification.[40] Biblical knowledge was also apparently imparted to the children. Helene records that once when Ernst, age four, leaned out over the side of his bed and bragged about his good behaviour, the nine year old Erna commented, "He behaves like a Pharisee. He leans out of the window and proclaims his good deeds!"[41]

Dietary laws were not strictly kept within the household as Helene makes several references to ham being eaten.[42] However, ritually cooked fish was served on Fridays[43] and there was aversion to some non-kosher food.[44] The children receive their presents on Christmas Eve, am *Weihnachtsabend*.[45] In 1882, Helene suggested having the two older boys instructed in Hebrew, partly to please Joseph's parents, but her husband would not agree and thus the project was not pursued for the time being.[46] However, they must have received some instruction later on, for both boys had their Bar Mitzvah at the customary age of thirteen. Helene thought of Hans' Bar Mitzvah with great joy. "For it was whatever one may otherwise think about religious aspects of the celebration, a real family festival."[47] Interestingly, about a year later Helene used the word *confirmation*, the German term *Einsegnung*, rather than Bar Mitzvah when recording the Erich's ceremony in her journal. The family character of religious custom is once more stressed, yet hope is expressed "that the admonition and the recollection of the day will always recall him [Erich] to his duty, more than to the threat of punishment."[48] When Joseph's father died in Berlin 1895, Erich apparently said Kaddish, a Jewish prayer praising God that is said for the dead, for the required period of nine days.[49]

It is clear from all this that the family was immersed within the ethic of Judaism, which has much in common with other monotheistic religions; indeed, this ethic was taken for granted. Thanks to their upbringing, Joseph and Helene shared Jewish moral values even as they had abandoned much of the ritual, as the great majority did when they moved away from the countryside and settled in large cities.[50] They were convinced that they could pass on this moral heritage without exposing their children to the religious observances that Joseph, at any rate, had been accustomed to in his youth. But to what extent could this particular moral heritage survive beyond the generation that had the practice of Judaism to base their convictions on? To what degree was there any prospect that the ethical code could continue beyond the next generation, in which the children had still witnessed their parents' religious observance, at least during their youth? In what measure was the move away from ritual connected with assimilation and acculturation? Was there a problem with reconciling the faith of one's ancestors with German culture?

There was no legal requirement for possessing German citizenship that depended on belonging to any particular faith or which affected the exercise of an individual's worship. Citizenship was determined by the father's nationality, not the place of birth. But the legally decreed equality between the adherents of the Judeo-Christian religions was limited in practice. Intermarriage between a Protestant and a Catholic caused even more tension than between a Protestant and a Jew.[51] Although the pogroms of Poland and Russia had not extended over the borders of Germany, it cannot be denied that during the lifetime of my father, even before 1933, a form of anti-Semitism existed in Germany. However, anti-Semitism at this time had a more religious basis than a racial one. German

Jews could not advance in the civil services and the universities, or enter an officer's career, although baptism could open some doors. All this changed through the First World War.

Within the faith, a German Jew could be anything from ultra-orthodox to the most liberal through his interpretation of the Torah. A Jew also had the right to leave the congregation and to declare himself a dissident, or to convert to a Christian denomination. It did not occur to Helene and Joseph or to any of their children to take any of these steps leading away from Judaism. They all remained and married within the faith. Ties with the extended family, which included "in-laws" were close, as is shown, for instance, by the three marriages that took place between the Eycks and the Veitels.[52]

Was there some kind of subtle pressure in the German culture to weaken the ties to Judaism? German Nationalism saw religious division more as a nuisance from the point of view of national unity. In this respect, Protestants actually often regarded Roman Catholicism as much more of a real threat than Judaism. While it is true that German Roman Catholics were branded as enemies of the *Reich* during certain periods and considered *prima facie* disloyal due to their orientation towards Rome, their greater numbers made them better able to deal with the emotional trauma they suffered than the Jewish minority.

Jewish families formed friendships mainly within members of their faith, as the journal, which goes up to 1898, and the surviving letters confirm. Among families mentioned are the Calé's, including the later poet, Walter Calé, then a boy.[53] Particularly dear to Helene was Emma Weiß, the mother of Bernard Weiß, who became Deputy Police Commissioner for Berlin in the Weimar period. Helene was deeply shaken by Emma's untimely death.[54] Erich Eyck would also form close ties with Bernhard Weiß,[55] both in Berlin and, after emigration, in London. Dr. Pelteson was the Jewish physician Helene and Joseph consulted for themselves and their sons and daughters.

However, the domestic staff, including the Home Governess, were presumably Christian. Thus, during the first years of their life, the children were comparatively sheltered from problems of contact with the Christian majority and those posed by anti-Semitism.

But this changed once they began their school education, by which time Helene was certainly very conscious of the current anti-Judaism expressed both in word and deed. Like all her generation, she was deeply shocked by the anti-Semitic outbreaks in Russia following the assassination of Tzar Alexander II by revolutionary terrorists.[56] She was obviously worried, too, by the anti-Semitic propaganda conducted by the court preacher Adolf Stoecker in Germany himself. Eventually this stirred up public opinion against him and in 1890 he was dismissed from his post.[57] However in July 1881, Helene referred in a letter to her husband, while on holiday with their children:

> Altogether the newspaper can make one ill and nervous. [There is] nothing in it but incitement against Jews, infernal machines, and bloodshed. How badly that fits with our lovely stay [here], how little one understands the hatred of human beings, you [Joseph] will know best.

She added that she would not worry about any newspaper anymore once her husband had joined her.[58] Helene thus has anti-Semitism in mind when, in September 1883, she wrote about her children:[59]

> If only one could for rather a long time preserve for them their untroubled childlike nature and their genuine cheerful spirit. If only their contact with their fellow students would not break this bloom and the delicately fragile veil of poetry, which is only found

in the soul of a child. And drive them all too soon from this children's paradise, in which they live so innocently without concern for the future and view each day as a new miracle and as a new playground.

The two elder boys had been told that, when the time came, they would be going to the *Friedrichsgymnasium* one of the leading High Schools in Berlin, to obtain a classical education:

What a role the school, which they do not know, already plays with them and with what pride they say "our school, the *Friedrichsgymnasium!*" May they find joy and happiness at school, in learning all that is great and beautiful, and may they be spared a hatred and ill-will which easily affects them as Jews; and may we as parents be allowed to surround them with love, care and everything good until they make their own way in the world, so that in their mind's eye they may see their parental home for a hundred years as a radiant and peaceful place and that they may carry within them the good seed and bring it once more to good fruition. [60]

Helene felt that childhood was too short and that school, with the considerable demands it made on children, encroached on it too early. Therefore, she decided to delay as long as possible the school entry of the girls, believing that starting half a year later would not make too much difference.[61] When the fifth child, Ernst, reached school age, Helene was not looking forward to being without him for much of the day as she loved his company. But the matter had to be settled in the spring of 1892 when there was an even weightier reason for hesitation:

From Easter onwards he [Ernst] will be going to the High School, the *Friedrichsgymnasium* to which I am reluctant to send him as at the present an indescribable anti-Semitism prevails there from which the boys of the middle form, to which Erich belongs, suffer very much. Not only do the fellow students display incredible impudence, but also the master of the fourth class of the Gymnasium, the *Untertertia* master, shows little consideration. He was led to punish more rigorously a [Jewish] boy, who defended himself by using the word '*Goy*' [a derogatory term for a Christian], than the Christian student who had uttered the most incredible insults. Additionally he more or less expressed the opinion that the Jewish students could actually thank God that through the emancipation they had been admitted at all as Germans and Prussians. Thus spoken in the year of grace 1892, fin de siècle![62]

If such sentiments were not artificially promoted from higher up, they would not exist. Of course, at a time, when the Emperor [Wilhelm II] himself condescends to give a speech in the Provincial Assembly *(Landtag)* of the *Mark Brandenburg*, we can look forward to the strangest and most dangerous developments! The disturbances in the streets have passed without special mishaps, but there, too, one tries to drag in anti-Semitism, although the masses attacked stores to be plundered without making any distinction between different religions.[63]

At the banquet of the Brandenburg Provincial Assembly on 24th February 1892, Wilhelm II had complained about those who consistently criticized the measures of the government.

He asked whether it would not be better if these discontented grumblers shook the German dust from their feet. He invoked God and expressing his own *unshakable* conviction that "our Ally of Roßbach and Dennewitz [Prussian victories over Austria in 1757 and over the French in 1813] would not forsake him. He [God] had taken infinite trouble with our old Mark and with our dynasty." Wilhelm added that he would lead his Brandenburger towards glorious days.[64]

Among those who shared Helene's concern with the Emperor's speech was the famous diarist, Baroness Spitzemberg, wife of the Württemberg minister in Berlin. She was an intimate member of the Bismarck circle and an admirer, though not an uncritical one, of the founder of the *Reich*. She recorded in her diary on February 28th: "We are all very dismayed and distressed at the Emperor's recent speech in the Provincial Diet, which up to date is the worst that he has made in this respect, and which really makes one fear megalomania [in him]."[65]

There cannot be any doubt that the anti-Semitism he experienced at school left its scars on Erich. That the experience was not unusual is clear from a statement by Walther Rathenau, the later Foreign Minister, which seems additional weighty given his place within a successful, well-connected family: "In the youth of every German Jew there is a painful moment which he remembers all his life: when he becomes fully conscious for the first time that he has entered the world as a second-class citizen and that no ability and no merit can free him from this situation."[66] However, in spite of all the turmoil in the early part of 1892, Erich, in fact did better in April than his mother and father had expected. He was promoted to the next class ranking. So far as the objectivity of the school report was concerned, Helene regarded criticism of Erich made in it, such as bad posture, as justified. She knew, as did the teachers at the school, and as Erich later freely admitted that he was at times simply lazy. However, things began to change in 1894, when he, against all odds, passed his Examination, the *Einjährige,* necessary for promotion to the upper (eighth and ninth) grades, the *Obersekunda* and the *Prima,* which carried with it a reduction of the period of compulsory military service to one year. Helene recorded with delight that the school Principal, Professor Vogt, had spoken favorably of Erich and had called him a "very gifted boy" and expected that during his last two years at school he was certain to acquire the serious attitude toward study that he presently lacked.[67]

By 1896, the parents already benefited from the moral support they received from their oldest child. Hans, nineteen years old, received the praise of his mother for the high quality of his sound and solid character, *"treu wie Gold"* [As true as gold]. She adds:

> He feels and thinks with us. He surrounds us with the most caring love and is very perceptive to the worries that burden us, particularly his father, at the present time. [68]

Helene was convinced that Hans would, in due course, make good in his chosen profession. Erich, too, was beginning to make his way. For many years, the parents showed doubts about the endurance and diligence of the two elder boys. But towards the end of his schooling, Erich was beginning to show sound knowledge and great intellectual gifts:

> Erich has read extensively, a great deal of good [books], and his historical and literary knowledge is very significant, and his wish would be to study these subjects, but as a Jew and as the son of parents of limited means he is prevented from doing so and has to follow the well-trodden path of jurisprudence.[69]

Erich could have followed his own inclination and studied history instead of the law, but at that time a university career progressed very slowly, if at all. There were comparatively few paid professorial posts in a subject like history, and while waiting for one of these to come up, there was usually a prolonged period of service as an unsalaried lecturer, *Privatdozent*. The possession of private means was, therefore, almost a necessity for the academic aspirant. For example, Arthur Nussbaum, the future husband of Trude Eyck,[70] was thus enabled to risk the long wait required before receiving a salaried position. In Nussbaum's case this was liable to be even longer as he was also a Jew. During the time of the Empire, the promotion of Jews to full professor, *Ordinarius*, was a rarity. In 1914, the Berlin University appointed Nussbaum university lecturer, *Dozent*. He became honorary Professor, *titular Professor*, in 1918 and Associate Professor, *außerordentlicher Professor* in 1921. He was dismissed in 1933, and from 1934 to 1950 was Research Professor of Public Law at Columbia University, New York. Nussbaum acquired an international reputation as a scholar whose work ranged widely over many aspects of the law. He died in New York in 1964.[71]

The journal does not chronicle daily events and is not primarily concerned with politics, except where, as we have seen, general events affected the family. The reference to Emperor Wilhelm II in 1892 is negative. Joseph and Helene appear to have inclined towards Left-Liberalism, in the sense of the German Party of Progress, the *Deutsch Fortschittspartei*. The early death of Emperor Friedrich III in 1888 after a reign of only ninety-nine days was perceived as a severe blow for the whole country. Friedrich's proclamation to my people, *"an mein Volk"* – with its liberal constitutional message – apparently had a place of honour in the home. Helene was certainly devoid of any strong German nationalist feeling. A few weeks after the ratification of the treaty with Great Britain which ceded *Heligoland*, the small island slightly North-West of the estuary of the Elbe River and Hamburg, to Germany, Helene expressed her regret not to have visited the island earlier while the English governor and English coast guards controlled the island: "Who knows, whether it will later still have its charm, when a 'German representative' has hoisted his flag." She added that she found the reports in the press altogether quite abominable, that they abounded in accidents and crimes.[72]

Looking back on the journal and the surviving letters, it is often difficult to distinguish Jewish and German elements, as they were so closely interwoven. The family life that emerges from these records is impressive in that it combined both. It reveals close bonds to the German culture without surrendering the spiritual Jewish heritage. Family life was intimate. The sense of justice and duty, combined with the importance of caring for others and mutual respect, was emphasized.

Helene made the last entry in the journal on 4th September 1898. She was full of joy over the development of her youngest child, Lilli, who was then five years old. She felt that she was re-experiencing her youth along with her daughter.[73] Helene was deeply thankful for her daughter's quick wit and affection, which she warmly reciprocated. Incidentally, although he was fifteen years older, the relationship between Erich and his youngest sister Lilli was also particularly close. After many years of worrying about her second son, Helene now gave him the highest praise:

> Erich has become good and capable, his character is industrious and frugal, and if he continues to utilize his fine gifts so felicitously, something will become of him (according to his father). His health has benefited from his stay in Freiburg, where he was studying law, and this independence had done him good.[74]

Helene died on December 26th in the flu epidemic of 1898 at the age of forty-two. It was Hans, the eldest, who helped his desolate father by reporting the death to the authorities at the registry office, the *Standesamt*. Husband and children were shattered. Helene may have had a premonition that she would pass from this earth before her time. In September 1883 she confessed her fears for the future of her children in the journal. She hoped to be able to complete the education of the children at her husband's side.

> But if things were ordered differently . . . would I know anybody to whom I would want to entrust my place, of who I would believe that he [sic] could continue in my sense the work that has been started? I believe not, for – though there may be many women who would be better at educating, would they bring along the mother's heart, the acquaintance with the potential, characteristics, faults, which rest in *our* children? No and a thousand time no.[75]

When Helene died, a void was left in the family. Naturally, the younger children were affected with particular severity, possibly Trude most of as she was an adolescent of fifteen years of age at Helene's death. All the children held the memory of their mother very dear.

Joseph did not remarry and was eventually looked after by a housekeeper. For a time, he was Berlin representative of a number of business firms with their head offices elsewhere.[76] He was apparently a director of the Victoria Mühle, a highly respected feed-and-seed business corporation. Although Joseph never did brilliantly in business, unlike his brother-in-law Ludwig Stein who took over the delicatessen firm Rollenhagen, [77] he seemed to have commanded a great deal of respect among his peers. He was elected president of the Greater Berlin branch of the Hanseatic League for Trade, Commerce and

Industry, the *Hansabund für Gewerbe, Handel und Industrie.*[78] The preponderantly liberal *Hansabund* was founded in 1909 as a counterweight to agrarian, particularly large land owning interests, represented mainly by the Conservatives. In the 1912 parliamentary *Reichstag* election, this organization scored, up to a point, considerable successes against those groups. The organization, which was dominated by an oligarchy of banking, wholesale, and industrial circles, had close links with the Liberals of both the Right, the national liberal Party, *Nationalliberale Partei,* and the Left, the German liberal party, *Freisinnige Partei.* The policy of the *Hansabund* was largely determined by the National Liberal *Reichstag* deputy, Jakob Riesser, who was president of the central association of German bankers. Riesser, a Protestant, belonged to a prominent originally Jewish family closely connected with the emancipation movement in 1848.[79] Berlin, where the *Hansabund* was founded, remained its focal point. Joseph Eyck was elected chairman of the Berlin branch, which honored him at the celebration for his seventieth birthday in November 1916, at which Riesser spoke. [80]

The most useful source on the last decade of Joseph Eyck's life proved to be Hermann Prineas,[81] the husband of his youngest daughter, Lilli. I remembered him from occasional meetings with my father in the *Tiergarten*, when at that time gentlemen demonstrated their mutual appreciation by shortly lifting their hats to each other in greeting. To my great joy I was still able to visit Herman Pineas in 1988 in New York where he lived alone, but was looked after by two African American ladies. These women were full of deep admiration and devotion for him, whom he jokingly called his harem. Hermann Prineas even then gave advice to the Jewish medical center. He spoke with great love of his first wife. He had been born in Düsseldorf in 1892 and served as medical officer in the German army during the First World War. He was at first stationed on the Eastern front, but spent time back in Germany as he was ordered by the army authorities to take his final medical examination there. During his stay in Berlin for his studies, he got to know Lilli Eyck whom he married in July 1918. Dr. Leo Baeck,[82] who had taught Pineas about Judaism while he was a schoolboy in Düsseldorf, officiated at the wedding, which took place in Joseph Eyck's apartment at Passauer Straße 26 in the Charlottenburg district the old West of Berlin. Erich Eyck was among those who held the *Huppah* at the wedding, a canopy symbolizing the future home. Leo Baeck, who stayed on for the wedding meal after the ceremony, had arranged for the bride to be given some religious instruction before the wedding, as he found she had quite a few deficiencies in this respect. Pineas himself was a practicing Jew.

Joseph Eyck was a member of the *Jüdische Gemeinde zu Berlin*, belonged to the synagogue in the Oranienburger Straße. However, at that time he no longer fasted or attended the synagogue on the High Holy Days. He gave his admission tickets for the synagogue services to Dr. Pineas, who attended with his wife. For Joseph there were no longer special arrangements for the Sabbath in his home. He had for many years a Christian housekeeper, Fräulein Fischer, who was much loved and became part of the family; the younger generation called her "Tante Fi." She later returned to her hometown in the *Harz* Mountains where I sometimes visited her on short holidays, and was most taken with her rabbits. My suggestion to have a rabbit of my own on our balcony in Berlin, however, did not find the hoped for response.

The Eyck's exhibited a strong family spirit and Pineas expressed special gratitude to his wife's older sister Erna and her husband Fedor Feit for arranging his transportation to Berlin from the military hospital in Weimar. He had been treated there after being severely wounded on the Western Front in mid-October 1918. The Feits were also most generous and helpful to other members of the family. It is interesting to note that Helene Eyck spotted some of these features in Erna quite early, when her daughter was only nine:

> Erna . . . shows extraordinary goodness to her fellow
> creatures, especially towards subordinates and gives
> away everything without a moment's consideration,
> in order to give joy to somebody. [83]

In general Helene Eyck was quite shrewd in her positive observations on her children, loving but not uncritical. Negative comments mainly applied to phases of gradual development.

During the early days of their marriage, Hermann and Lilli Pineas regularly dined with Joseph Eyck, since Hermann's earnings as a physician were meager at the beginning of his professional career. Lilli taught commercial French at a school of commerce, a *Private Handelsschule,* on the Wittenbergplatz, a square on which they also had their apartment. Sadly Lilli died in the mid-1920s of acute tuberculosis which brought some estrangement from the family. Alas, tuberculosis at that time, in whatever form, was endemic in the big cities and without assured treatment. Dr. Pineas served last in the neuro-psychiatric department of the Jewish hospital in Berlin when in 1943 when he and Herta, his second wife, went underground in various pastors' homes of the Confessing church in Swabia, Southwestern Germany.

By the time of Lilli's wedding, Joseph Eyck had retired from the Berlin grain exchange, but still acted as a referee in disputes there. This activity, like that in the *Hansabund*, reflects an unbiased recognition from the non-Jewish community in Berlin. Incidentally, Joseph returned temporarily to his West Prussian birthplace in July 1920. When he voted in the plebiscite on the future of the territory, he presumably lent his support for its continuance with Germany and rejecting its transfer to the re-established Poland. As a result of the overwhelming majority for Germany in the plebiscites in the region, the status quo was maintained.

In 1921, Joseph celebrated his seventy-fifth birthday with his family. They looked to him as a wise and loving patriarch. The children performed a skit and the adults gave speeches after enjoying a festive meal. To all the ladies Joseph presented a three-quarter carat diamond gem. Joseph died peacefully of old age in Berlin in his apartment in Passauer Straße on 17th November 1925, honoured by his children and grandchildren. By the time of his death his children were all well established.

Endnotes

1   I gratefully acknowledge here the financial contribution of the expenses for the work on the journal given to me through a research grant from the University of Calgary, using funds provided by the Social Science and Humanities Research Council of Canada. My thanks go also to my sisters Mrs. Irene Reuter and Mrs. Eleanor Alexander, as well as to my cousins Dr. F. Günther Eyck, Mrs. Marianne Scheck née Nussbaum, Mr. Gerhard Rosenberg, and Dr. Pineas for the information on the family history they supplied.

   Chapter one and parts of chapter two were originally published as *A diarist in fin-de-siècle Berlin and her family, Helene, Joseph and Erich Eyck*, (London: Secker & Warburg, the Leo Baeck Year Book XXXVII, 1992), pp. 287-307. The article is dedicated to Dr. Arnold Pauker, a long-time friend, in gratitude for his outstanding contribution to the development of the study of German-Jewish history.

2   See inter alias William H.Maehl, *Erich Eyck*, in S. William Halperin ed. *Essays on Eminent Europeans, Some 20th Century Historians*, (Chicago: University Press of Illinois, 1961), pp. 227-253. Also Hans-Ulrich Wehler und Klaus Hildebrand, eds., *Deutsche Historiker*, on *Erich Eyck*, (Göttingen: Metropol Verlag, 9 vols. 1971-1982), vol. II., pp. 98-119.

3   The papers of Erich Eyck, including his mother's journal and letters, are in Frank Eyck's possession, copies of many of them are deposited in the Bundesarchiv in Koblenz. In due course, the remaining papers will be deposited after the publication of this book.

4   Most of the details concerning the birth and descent, etc. of Joseph and Helene Eyck are taken from the information kindly supplied by the Standesamt Charlottenburg in Berlin.

5   The date emerges from Adolph Veitel's letter from Leipzig 3rd January 1877 about the readings of the bans.

6   J. W. von Goethe, a lawyer and Prime Minister of the Grand Duchy of Saxe-Weimar-Eisenach, Thüringen, was a literary genius who applied the vitality of concrete experience to the ideas of the mind. *Die Wahlverwandtschaften*, the title means kinship by choice, and deals with relationships. Goethe and

Friedrich von Schiller, Professor of History in Jena are the most famous German authors representing the European classicism, the age of reason, at the turn of and into the first half of the nineteenth century. *Goethe's sämtliche Werke, Jubiläums Ausgabe* in 42 vols. Eduard Heinrich von der Hellen und Konrad Burdach eds., (Stuttgart: Cotta, 1902-1907).

7   *J. W. von Goethe, Faust II, Act 1, Saal of the Throne, Mephisto vers 6061.* After the Emperor, on Mephisto's advice, had assignation [paper money] printed he called for a carnival.

8   Journal, 4th June 1881.

9   They were tonsillitis, whooping-cough, measles, German measles, scarlet fever, diphtheria (that was treated with serum).

10 Journal, 7th October 1895.

11 "Man mußte standesgemäß leben." This characterizes the financial pressure on higher officialdom in the period, Ernst Heilborn, *Zwischen zwei Revolutionen*, vol. II, (Berlin: Elsner, 1929), pp. 214, is quoted in John C. G. Röhl, *Kaiser, Hof und Staat. Wilhelm II. und die deutsche Politic*, (München: C. H. Beck, 1987), p. 153.

12 Journal, 7th October 1895.

13 Journal, 2nd June 1884.

14 Journal, 1st January 1891.

15 Journal, 18th and 22nd July 1891.

16 Journal, 26th August 1895.

17 Journal, 17th July 1896.

18 Adolf Veitel to Joseph Eyck, 21st September 1897.

19 Possibly this may have something to do with the severe decline in grain prices. See J. H. Clapham, *The Economic Development of Germany and France 1815 to 1914*, (Cambridge University Press, 1961), pp. 211ff. Erich Eyck, *Das Persönliche Regiment Wilhelm II. Politische Geschichte des Deutschen Kaiserreiches von 1890 bis 1914*, (Erlenbach-Zürich: Eugen Rentsch Verlag, 1948), pp. 68, 77. Neither vol. 3 of *Bismarck*, nor vol. 1 of *The Personal Regiment of William II* have been translated.

20 Journal, 26th November 1897.

21 Journal, 6th September 1883 and 20th October 1884.

22 Veronika Bendt, *Wegweiser durch das jüdische Berlin. Geschichte und Gegenwart*, (Berlin: Nicolai, 1987), pp. 108ff. I owe the gift of this book to

the *Informationszentrum Berlin* on the occasion of an invitation by my native city for its 750th anniversary in 1987.

23 Ibid, p. 92.

24 Journal, 10th June 1891.

25 Journal, 15th April 1883.

26 Journal, 21st April 1882.

27 Journal, 31 December 1888, 2nd January 1891, and 17th July 1896.

28 Apparently Jakob Eyck, Joseph's father, commissioned a Torah which was destroyed in the November 1938 *Kristallnacht*.

29 Early in the Nazi period, the presence of the Eyck family on German territory was traced back to 1685.

30 Paul von Hindenburg, *Aus meinem Leben*, (Leipzig: Hirzel Verlag, 1929), p. 4. The preface to this later edition is dated September 1919.

31 These details are taken from E. Uetrecht ed., *Meyers Orts und Verkehrs-Lexikon des Deutschen Reiches*, vol. I.(Leipzig: Biographisches Instiut, 1913),. p. 512.The population of Freystadt is given as 2,607.

32 The Polish presence did not necessarily impinge strongly on Freystadt itself.

33 Max Schwarz, *MdR. Biographisches Handbuch der Reichstage*, (Hannover: Hannoversche Druck- und Verlagsgesellschaft GmbH. 1965), p. 146, detailed biographies of members.

34 Meyer, Joseph, *Meyers Orts- und Verkehrs Lexikon des Deutschen Reichs: Mit 51 Stadtplänen, 19 Umgebungs- und Übersichtskarten, einer Verkehrskarte und vielen statistischen Beilagen*, Bibiographisches Institut, (Leipzig: Biographisches Instiut, 1913), vol. II. p. 260.

35 Some time after the end of the First World War, the estate passed out of the possession of the Hindenburg family. But in 1927, as a present for his eightieth birthday, the *Feldmarschall* and *Reichspräsident* received the gift of the former family home purchased with the money provided mainly by the German industry. Erich Eyck, *Geschichte der Weimarer Republik*, pp. 333-334, which also describes the motives of the leader of the East Prussian agrarian lobby, von Oldenburg-Januschau, in initiating the gift, as well as some dubious tax aspects of the transaction on President Hindenburg's part, *op.cit.* pp. 4-5.

36 Shtetls are Jewish quarters, often enclosed settlements in the towns or villages of Europe, "protected" but with a due to the Emperor. Shtetls were socially

stable, and for many centuries unchanged, communities where Jews lived in their traditional pious way till after the end of the seventeenth century despite frequent outside attacks. See ample literature on this theme and the musical *The Fiddler on the Roof.*

37 Monika Richarz ed. *Jüdisches Leben. Selbstzeugnisse zur Sozialgeschichte im Kaiserreich*, (Stuttgart: Veröffentlichung des Leo Baeck Instituts, 1979), esp. pp .48ff.

38 Journal, 2nd January 1891.

39 There are references to this in the journal on 21st February 1884, 2nd January 1891, and 16th May 1898.

40 Journal, 16th May 1898.

41 Journal, 2nd January 1891.

42 For instance, Helene's letter to Joseph of 9th August 1878 from Arnstadt.

43 Journal, 2nd January 1891.

44 There are references to the purchase of kosher sausages: "I do not like to eat the others any more." Helene to Joseph from Arnstadt, 20th July 1878.

45 Journal, 2nd January.

46 Journal, 9th October 1882.

47 Journal, 17th January 1891.

48 Journal, 4th January 1892.

49 Recollection of Erich Eyck, the prayer was written in the thirteenth century by Or Zarna inspired from Ezekiel 38:23.

50 Monika Richarz, ed., *Jüdisches Leben. Selbstzeugnisse zur Sozialgeschichte im Kaiserreich*, op.cit. p. 48.

51 Walter Laqueur, *Generation Exodus*, (Walham, MA: Brandeis University Press, 2000), Ch XII, pp. 243, 231, 275, 287-288.

52 Besides the two mentioned in the text, there was a marriage between James Eyck and Anna Veitel in 1880, which broke up around 1902 (Erich Eyck papers).

53 In a letter from Helene to Joseph from Friedrichroda of 4th August 1890, Helene described Martin Calé, Walter's father, a *Kaufmann* as an educated, fine man. See *Walter Calé* in Theodor Lessing, *Der Jüdische Selbsthaß*, (Berlin: Zionistischer Bücher-Bund, 1930), with an essay by Boris Groys and later editions (Berlin/München: Matthes & Seitz, 1984, 2004), pp. 152-166. This citation does not necessarily imply that the present writer agrees with

Lessing's categorization of a brilliant young poet, who took his own life in Berlin in 1904, at age twenty-three.

54 Journal, 28th March 1892.

55 Werner Röder and Herbert A. Strauss, eds., *Biographisches Handbuch der deutschen Emigration nach 1933/ International Biographical Dictionary of Central European Emigrés 1933-1945*, 3 vols. (München: Saur) vol. I. p. 809; Bernard Weiß remembered. A Courageous Prussian Jew, see in *AJR information*, November, 1981. Dietz Bering, Isidor - Geschichte einer Hetzjagd. Bernhard Weiß, einem preußischen Juden zum Gedächtnis, in *Die Zeit*, 14th August 1981; and see also, *Der Name als Stigma. Antisemitismus im deutschen Alltag, 1812-1933*. Stuttgart 1988 passim; translated by Neville Plaice, (Ann Arbor, MI: University of Michigan Press, 1992).

56 This happened in March 1881 on the very day the Tsar, who during his reign had freed the serfs, had signed the first democratic constitution. The assassination was carried out by members of the "peoples' will" group demanding land reform, who were close to Marx's ideas.

57 Erich Eyck, *Das Persönliche Regiment,Wilhelm II*. p.69.

58 Helene to Joseph from Friedrichroda, 29th July 1881.

59 Journal, 6th September 1883.

60 Ibid.

61 Journal, 26th January 1886.

62 Probably a reference to the accusation of theocide.

63 Journal, 6th March 1892.

64 A.O.Klaußmann, ed., *Kaiserreden. Reden und Erlasse, Briefe und Telegramme Kaiser Wilhelms des Zweiten. Ein Charakterbild des Deutschen Kaisers*, (Leipzig: J. J. Weber, 1902), pp. 400-402.

65 Rudolf Vierhaus ed. *Das Tagebuch der Baronin Spitzemberg. Aufzeichnungen aus der Hofgesellschaft des Hohenzollernsreiches*, (Göttingen: Vandenhoeck & Ruprecht, 1960), p. 297.

66 Walther Rathenau, *Staat und Judentum. Eine Polemik* in Gesammelte Schriften,. vol. I, (Berlin: S.Fischer, 1918). Quoted in Richarz, ed., *Jüdisches Leben, Selbstzeugnisse. Im Kaiserreich*, op. cit., p. 38.

67 Journal, 8th January 1895.

68 Journal, 29th December 1896.

69 Ibid.

70 Nussbaum met his future wife through the lawyer Curt Rosenberg, who attended an economics seminar at the University of Berlin with Erich Eyck. The husband of his cousin, Rosenberg introduced Eyck to Nussbaum. See Curt Rosenberg, *Jugenderinnerungen*, in Richarz, ed., *Jüdeisches Leben. Selbstzeugnisse im Kaiserreich, op .cit.,* pp. 303-304. Rosenberg married Else Stein, Helene's niece. His piece contains many interesting insights into the German-Jewish relationship.

71 Röder and Strauss, eds., op. cit., vol. II, pp. 689, *New York Times* obituary, 22ⁿᵈ November 1964.

72 Helene to Joseph from Friedrichroda, 9ᵗʰ August 1890.

73 Journal, 16ᵗʰ May 1898.

74 Ibid.

75 Journal, 6ᵗʰ September 1883.

76 Adolf Veitel to Joseph Eyck, 22ⁿᵈ April 1902.

77 The husband (owner of Rollenhagen, Berlin's famous delicatessen shop), of Helene's younger sister, Louise ("Lieschen"). Louise, desperate, and not seeing any way out of the situation in Nazi Germany, took her own life.

78 On the occasion, see Siegfried Mielke, *Der Hansabund für Gewerbe, Handel und Idustrie 1909-1914,* (Göttingen: Vandenhaeck & Ruprecht, 1976).

79 In the constitutional debate in the Frankfurt Parliament during August 1848, Gabriel Riesser cited the discrimination he had himself suffered, in his speech supporting the removal of legal restrictions for Jews. See Frank Eyck, *The Frankfurt Parliament 1848-1849,* (London: Macmillan, 1968), pp. 242-243.

80 This is a cutting from an unidentified monthly journal of November/December 1916 in Erich Eyck papers which contains material on the arrangement for the celebration. I had the pleasure of meeting the former Executive Director of the *Hansabund* in the decade up to 1933, Professor Hans Reif (by then a *Freie Demokratische Partei* deputy in the Bundestag) in 1954. Reif remembered Joseph Eyck from his work in the *Hansabund*.

81 By chance I stumbled on the piece by Hermann Pineas in the section *Überleben in Deutschland 1941-1945,* in Monika Richarz, ed., *Jüdisches Leben in Deutschland, Selbstzeugnisse zur Socialgeschichte 1918-1945,* pp. 429-442, while working in the Staatsbibliothek in München in 1986. Fortunately Dr.

Fred Grube of the Leo Baeck Institute New York was able to confirm that Dr. Pineas was still alive and I was able to have a three-day discussion with him. Dr. Pineas died in 1988. I also want to thank Dr. Michael Riff, formerly of the Leo Baeck Institute, for allowing me to consult him while I was in New York. I thank the Department of History and the Faculty of Social Sciences of the University of Calgary as well as the Institute of Humanities, for financial aid and encouragement. Dr. Gordon Hamilton gave me much useful advice while we were fellows at the institute during the academic year 1985-1986.

82 Rabbi Leo Baeck, 1873-1956, stayed with the remaining Jewish congregation, was in contact but not active with conservative resistance circles; interned in Jan. 1943 until the end of the war in the Theresienstadt Concentration Camp. From 1933 on he worked on his Manuscript: *Die Rechtsstellung des Deutschen Judentums,* see Arnold Paucker, *Deutsche Juden im Kampf um Recht und Freiheit,* (Berlin: Hentrich & Hentrich, 2004), p. 315-118. Leo Baeck, *Das Wesen des Judenums,* Sonderausgabe 1985, (Darmstadt: Joseph Melzer Verlag, Sonderausgabe 1985).

83 Journal, 2nd.January 1891.

Chapter 1

CHAPTER 2
Berlin 1921-1936

D URING THE AFTERMATH FOLLOWING THE FIRST World War, with its unrest and run-away inflation,[1] I was born in my parents' apartment of Luther Straße 40, Berlin, on 13th July 1921. I was welcomed into the peaceful and loving home of a German-Jewish family as the youngest child of Erich Eyck and his wife Hedwig née Kosterlitz. I was named Ulrich Franz Joseph; Ulrich in case I grew fat, Franz in case I was thin, and Joseph after my paternal grandfather.

My father, born in 1878, grew up in Berlin, a city to which he was very much attached. His family, while maintaining a bourgeois living standard, was not particularly well-off financially. My father would have preferred to read history as his main subject but the means to follow this career were not at his disposal. In the nineteenth century, university study was still only pursued by a small minority of young people. To try to follow an academic career was even more difficult and this applied to anybody, Jews or Gentiles, but more so to Jews. It required independent financial resources since the University lecturers, *Privatdozent,* had to work for many years without pay. A university education that led to practical careers was more likely to achieve relatively early financial independence.

My father's second choice therefore was the study of law. The obstacles to a Jew in the legal profession were comparatively few. Legal careers had been followed before by other Jews, who could therefore be consulted and might provide employment in their partnerships. There may well be another reason for the attraction the legal profession had for the Jews. They had an advantage having imbibed some training in legal concepts through biblical studies with their emphasis on the Torah.[2] After finishing their primary education at a high school that was teaching classical languages, a *humanistisches Gymnasium*, both my father and his older bother Hans were able to study at the *Königliche Friedrich Wilhelm Universität zu Berlin*, which in later years was renamed the *Humboldt Universität*. Erich enjoyed one term away from home at the University of Freiburg, Breisgau. He was able to combine his interest in law with those in history, politics, and literature.

Following the left-liberal leaning of his parents, he became associated with the German Peoples Party, the *Deutsche Volkspartei*,[3] which had its adherents mainly in southern Germany. One of its leaders was Leopold Sonnemann,[4] a publicist who became the founder and owner of the *Frankfurter Zeitung* in 1856. There my father made his debut as an author around June 1899 with a pamphlet on unemployment and unemployment insurance published under the auspices of the German Peoples Party.[5] It is thus not surprising that he chose for his doctoral dissertation the topic of the origin of the German workers movement: *Vereinstag Deutscher Arbeitervereine 1863-1868*,[6] dealing with the early attempt to form a workers' union.

As a result of the industrial revolution in the nineteenth century, a new social class had emerged quite different from the artisans with their century-old guilds. He examined the movement's development to provide an alternative to Ferdinand Lassalle's programme which under August Bebel,[7] a leading Social Democrat, merged into the Social Democratic Workers Party. Sonnemann strongly opposed the class struggle concept of Ferdinand Lassalle on the one hand and of Marx and Engels on the other.[8] He believed that the problem could be solved by co-operation between the bourgeoisie and the workers, and emphasized the importance of self-help and individual responsibility.

Unfortunately, the new movement was short-lived. It was taken over in 1868 by supporters of the class struggle who in due course, proceeded to form the Social Democratic Party, the *Sozialdemokratische Partei*.[9] From 1871-76 and 1878-84, Sonnemann was a member of the Imperial Diet, the *Reichstag* representing the German People's Party.

Sonnemann, whose attention Erich had already attracted through his treatise on unemployment,[10] became a kind of patron for my father.[11] He received Erich when he came to Berlin and later when he visited Britain. From about 1900 on he agreed to publish Erich's reports in the *Frankfurter Zeitung* whenever possible. Erich Eyck defended his doctoral thesis before four distinguished examiners, the philosopher and pedagogue Friedrich Paulson, the economists Gustav Schmoller and Adolf Wagner, and the historian Hans Delbrück. He regarded Delbrück as a model scholar because of the independence and candor he displayed.[12] Erich Eyck received his Doctorate in Philosophy *cum laude* in 1904 at the University of Berlin.

During some longer visits to Great Britain, my father was deeply impressed by what he saw of the operation of parliamentary government. He was particularly fortunate on his first journey, when he witnessed the Liberal landslide at the general election of January 1906.[13] It gave him the chance to form some lasting friendships with British Liberals, especially with the journalist Harold Spender,[14] his wife Violet née Schuster, and with the historian G. P. Gooch, who had just gained a seat in the House of Commons.[15] Increasingly, Erich Eyck judged the German political system by the extent to which it fell short of the standard of parliamentary responsibility set in Great Britain.

Thanks to great determination, seemingly boundless energy, and generally robust health, my father was able to combine his legal work with a host of other activities, first concentrating on his career in law in order to make it a success and then also focusing on writing and politics. He completed the obligatory period of court service in articles as a *Refrendar* in Luckenwalde, a small town just south of Berlin, which he enjoyed and after which he was promoted to *Assessor*, and thereby entered the legal profession. In 1906, he established himself as a lawyer in Berlin, at first taking a job in a partnership of lawyers who were also Jews. However, in 1910, his colleagues were displeased with him and terminated his partnership because they had not been invited to celebrate Erich and Hedwig's wedding at a civil ceremony on the 12th of May. Consequently he set up in practice of his own. His experience as a lawyer taught him well to weigh of evidence in interpreting documents and helped him acquire evaluation skills through written briefs, *Schriftsätze*, and court pleadings. He was admitted as a lawyer to the Supreme Court of Prussia, the *Kammergerichtshof*, in Berlin, and eventually appointed notary public.

In time, my father became an accomplished writer and speaker, immersing himself in the contemporary political scene, adhering to a left-liberal stance. *Wilhelmine* Berlin offered wonderful opportunities to a young man eager to find things out for himself. He took advantage of this, and often watched debates in the Imperial Diet, the *Reichstag,* and the Prussian State Diet, the *Preußische Landtag.* It is worth noting that during the German Empire these bodies did not grant its members a stipend or compensation, *Diäten,* for daily expenses.[16] Thanks to his knowledge of shorthand, *Debattenschrift,* he was able to practice alertness by taking the proceedings down in this special type of shorthand. Of the speakers, he was particularly drawn to Theodor Barth,[17] one of the left-liberal leaders, and editor of the weekly journal *Die Nation*, to which his father Joseph Eyck had been a loyal subscriber, and which Erich had begun to read during his school days. He himself contributed to the journal from 1902 onwards.[18]

As a university student, my father consulted Theodor Barth on an economics paper he was attempting to write. He was impressed by Barth's friendliness and by the absence of any air of superiority towards a much younger person. My father was privileged to be entertained by Barth in a small circle at his Tiergarten residence in Berlin and frequently met Barth at various political functions. Barth warned against inciting people into extreme nationalism and racial anti-Semitism, and in powerful speeches he pleaded for international understanding. To the end of his life, my father regarded Barth as one of the two great masters of politics at whose feet he had sat; the other one being Friedrich Naumann.[19] For many years, this parliamentarian – with his free trade view, his opposition to all forms of state tyranny, and his support for and openness to the Social Democrats – best represented Erich's own views.

My father fully recognized the outstanding parliamentary expertise and strength of conviction of Eugen Richter,[20] leader of the German Party of Progress, *Deutsche Fortschrittspartei*, and later of its successor the German Liberal Party, the *Deutsche Freisinnige Partei*.[21] He was an exceptional parliamentarian who could cross swords with Bismarck. However, my father disapproved of a certain rigidity in Richter's ideas and tactics. Above all my father was critical of Richter's conduct in 1893, when he insisted on the expulsion from the parliamentary group of those *Reichstag* deputies who had broken ranks by voting in favor of Chancellor Caprivi's army bill. This split the left-liberals, because the expelled deputies formed their own party the German Liberal Party, which Barth joined despite voting against the bill.

All this was past history when my father began to take an active part in political life at the turn of the century, but undoubtedly it influenced his attitude. He opposed a further splintering of the liberal forces and attributed the decline of the left-liberals mainly to their divisiveness.[22] In retrospect, and from a historical perspective, he also questioned the wisdom of the liberal opposition to the government of Caprivi who had taken over from Bismarck. At any rate, Erich began his political work for the German Liberal Association of Barth,[23] rather than for the German Liberal Party of Eugen Richter.

It was through Barth that my father got to know his other political teacher, Friedrich Naumann. The reasons for Erich's attraction to Naumann are not quite as obvious as those that connected him to Barth. Indeed, it may appear strange that Erich was influenced by a Protestant pastor, who had collaborated with the anti-Semitic Court Preacher of the Emperor, the *Hofprediger* Adolf Stoecker. Stoecker had become politically involved and, in 1896, had to withdraw from the Conservative Party when it became public knowledge that he had tried to sow discord between Bismarck and the young Wilhelm II.[24] But Erich emphasized in an appreciation published in 1924 that Naumann had come quite a distance since the turn of the century from the somewhat narrow Christian-Social views of his youth. By way of his intermediate programme of reconciling monarchy and social democracy,[25] he was trying to draw attention to the needs of the working class, changing in his mature days to embrace liberal-democratic ideas. As a young man, my father must have been profoundly impressed by Naumann's charisma. He regarded Naumann's death in 1919 just after his election to the leadership of the German Democratic Party (DDP) as the successor of the Empire's left-liberals, to be a grave loss for the new regime. However, he believed that Naumann's ideas had a deep and lasting general effect on both the left and the right, and was not in any way confined to those who followed his banner. My mother shared this high esteem for Naumann.

My father's introduction to Hedwig came through two of her friends, two sisters, Trude Goldschmidt and Agnes

Riegner née Arnheim, both married to lawyers, so the law proved useful in more ways than one. As to my mother's side of the family, her father had also moved to Berlin from further east of Prussia, like so many other Jewish families at that time. Adolf Kosterlitz with his wife, Dora, and their four children hailed from Pless in Upper Silesia, part of the Prussian Province of Silesia, which then still belonged to the German Empire. My maternal grandmother Dora was a née Liebes, a member of a remarkable family that had migrated from the Prussian province of Posen to trade with El Salvador and Guatemala through offices in Hamburg. They became quite wealthy and lived in the prestigious Harvestehude district, where I visited them and remember a wonderfully carefree time.

The Liebes family helped Adolf Kosterlitz to resettle in Berlin, where he ran a demolition business. He was a kindly man of great warmth and considerable merit. He provided financial support to his younger brother Theodor for his studies as an ophthalmologist. Dora, possibly due to an illness in her childhood that had left her handicapped, did not display quite the same ability as her siblings. But there was a lot of talent among the four children she bore.

Hedwig, born in 1887, hardly had the educational opportunities offered to later generations of women. However, she went to a *Höhere Töchter Schule,* a secondary school for daughters of middle-class families in Hanover (*Hannover*),[26] where allegedly the best German was spoken. There she received a more limited academic education than contemporary boys did, but she gained practical skills and some economic instruction to prepare for marriage and motherhood. Her father noticed that she had certain business abilities and asked her to look after an apartment house he owned so that she could gain personal experience in how real estate property was to be run and, above all, learn how to achieve a fair price for tenants and owner. She often said that a business agreement is only

Erik Eyck, 1910

good if it is good for all parties involved. She frequently voiced the wish that her epitaph should be "I never had an overdraft," a motto which indeed she followed carefully and in difficult circumstances. Her experience is quite exceptional at a time when young women from good families were supposed to be

Hedwig Eyck, 1910

merely "decorative."

As my grandmother did not always find it easy to supervise the household, my mother assumed additional responsibility in the family home. She was a great source of strength to her father, who loved to look up to her in the gallery where the women were segregated from the floor of the synagogue reserved for the men. Although only twenty-one when my mother got engaged to my father in March 1910, she had already gained a practical experiences and wisdom that would place her in good stead throughout her life.

In 1921, a plebiscite was held in the small disputed territory of Upper Silesia.[27] My mother traveled while six months pregnant to Pleß and voted for the German side, although she believed that quite a few ethnic Germans voted for Poland because they did not think much of Germany's prospects after the lost war. As expected, Upper Silesia was conceded to Poland and the small town of Pleß was thereafter renamed Pszczyna.

Each of my mother's three brothers survived front service in the German army during the First World War. The eldest, Georg (Jorg) Kosterlitz, was severely wounded, and only saved from the amputation of his leg by his younger brother Erich, a medical doctor; however, Georg limped for the rest of his life. After his father's death in 1925, Georg went on running the demolition business, but in the early thirties immigrated to Santiago de Chile where he founded a successful business producing and selling safes. In 1939 he still was able to bring Dora, his mother, to Santiago and he looked after her until her passing. On one of his visits to London he gave Hedwig a large Chilean Peso gold coin, which she gave to me to have made into our wedding rings when I married Rosemarie Schmidt in 1955. There was enough gold left for two engagement rings, as well. Erich, my mother's, second brother, emigrated during the 1920s to the USA where he practiced medicine. He was very intelligent but somewhat of an outsider (ein Sonderling). When we met well after the Second World War, he spoke about his emigration, saying that he had the vague feeling that something did not feel right in Germany. He gradually had lost confidence in the fatherland, a rare attitude among German Jews. An assimilated German Jew, like my father however, he identified himself with Germany and culturally felt a deep bond to her. Her literature, above all Wolfgang von Goethe, played an important role. Martin, the youngest brother of my mother was also a lawyer in Berlin. I remember my mother telling me that all her eight male cousins served in the German army during the First World War; only half of them returned.

Only my maternal grandfather – unlike the paternal one – was still practicing Judaism. Adolf Kosterlitz was initially not entirely happy with the religious background of his son-in-law, but time was a great healer and Hedwig's family was won over by the happiness of the young couple.[28] The two families were well integrated into Germany. Altogether their background was a felicitous one with its family members presenting a sound combination of professional, academic, and commercial careers. My mother's intelligence, her understanding for others, as well as her gentleness and sensitivity melded beautifully with my father's learning; she always considered him her great teacher.

I had an idyllic childhood during the first eleven and a half years of my life. Our loving and stimulating parents, my two older sisters – Irene, born in 1911, Eleanor born in 1913 – and I, the youngest, formed a closely knit family. Our father had a good legal practice. He had been invalided out of the army in his younger days as a conscript because he had collapsed on parade-ground and was not considered fit enough to serve during the First World War, although there were periodic medical examinations to check up about this. Nevertheless, he went on to develop a great capacity for intellectual work. In 1915, he had joined the German-Jewish publishing firm Ullstein as law correspondent, *Juristischer Mitarbeiter*, for *Die Vossische Zeitung*. This publication was the oldest daily newspaper in Berlin and was highly respected. In outlook the publication was closest to the German

Democratic Party. Erich founded the paper's law section *Recht und Leben*, Law and Life (*Recht* refers to both law and justice). From 1916 on he contributed articles on a whole range of legal, political, and historical subjects, paying particular attention to Great Britain, which he continued to look on as a model for parliamentary government. In his writing he emphasized the importance of assuring that every person, including Jews, was treated fairly by the justice system.[29] He played a leading role in the Central Society of German Citizens of Jewish Faith (*Centralverein deutscher Staatsbürger jüdischen Glaubens*), known as the CV.[30] Members of the CV saw no insuperable obstacles to combining loyalty to Germany with the Jewish faith. He was a lifelong opponent of Zionism for, among other arguments against it, he believed it would undermine the position of Jews in the country in which they lived, to which they belonged and felt loyal to. For several years from 1912 on he had been an executive of the anti-Zionism committee, incidentally together with our family physician *Geheimer Sanitätsrat* (confidential member of the board of Health), Dr. Pelteson[31] and Bernard Weiß,[32] deputy chief of the Berlin police.

Most of my father's energy was spent on the general defense of the rule of law and of the parliamentary and democratic system, to which he devoted a pamphlet on the crisis of German justice in 1926.[33] When, in December 1932, the National Socialists agreed to have their theory of criminal justice debated they faced Eyck as a speaker defending the rule of law. The National Socialist lawyer, a member of the *Reichstag*, Dr. Hans Frank (Frank II)[34] was to propound Nazi ideas. The lawyer and writer Ernst Feder noted the following in his diary on 12th December 1932:

> [I went] to the *Oberverwaltungsgericht* [High-Court of Administration] in the evening where the National Socialist theory of criminal law was to

be discussed. Frank II [who was to speak from the Nazi point of view] bolted. Fabricius [another Nazi Reichstag member] deputizing for him spoke miserably in the discussion. The speech by Eyck is good. The hall was overcrowded. Many young lawyers [were present][35]

From 1915 to 1920, Erich served on the council of the Charlottenburg Municipal Assembly, *Stadtverordnetenversammlung,* before its incorporation into Greater Berlin. A fellow councilor was Oskar Meyer,[36] a prominent member of the German Democratic Party, in the Weimar period. From 1928-1930 Erich served on the Berlin Municipal Assembly at a critical time, earning the friendship of men like Oskar Meyer and Ernst Reuter,[37] later to become the first mayor of West-Berlin from 1947-1953. My father also helped as secretary and played an important part in the running of the Democratic Club in Berlin (1919-1933) where he himself often gave talks. The club was a social centre for politically interested people. It attracted excellent speaker and animated discussions frequently carried on late into the night. When my mother thought it was getting rather too late, there was a phone call with an indisputable interpretation; the butler discretely whispered to Dr. Eyck: "*Frau Dr.* is on the phone!" The quarter of an hour's walk to our home in the large apartment of the Magdeburger Straße 5 then late at night with the certains drawn back and lit windows to warn him of his wife's displeasure awaiting for him.[38] The apartment was part of the "old West" close to the Landwehrkanal, the Ministry of defense, *Reichswehrministerium,* and the Tiergarten. The latter was a large park with a lake and beautiful old trees on the southerly bank of the Spree River stretching beyond the Sieges Allee and to the Brandenburg Gate, often used for excursions by people from other parts of the city.

Unfortunately, after a good initial showing the German

Democratic Party (DDP) saw its parliamentary strength dwindle. In 1930, Erich Koch-Weser, the party leader, was Minister of the Interior and previously had been Minister of Justice. My father knew Koch-Weser well and held in high regard both inside and outside of the *Reichstag*.[39] He agreed with Chancellor Gustav Stresemann in October 1929 to stress the common interest "of all groups opposed to the misdirection of national feelings."[40] Koch-Weser believed that the only way to arrest the decline of his party was to broaden its base. He therefore proposed amalgamation with the Young German Order, the *Jung Deutsche Orden*, which had moved from a position on the Right to a position of greater acceptance of the democratic republicanism. Many of the older party members, including my father, had grave doubts about the new party, but they accepted the fusion with the Order under the name of the German State Party, *Deutsche Staatspartei*. This desperate step did not bring its reward in the Parliamentary Election of September 1930. The number of seats shrank and the deputies drawn from the Young German Order soon seceded.

When I asked my father many years later about the Young German Order he simply replied that they were anti-Semites. Actually, I later met a member of the Young German Order, who like myself had been a student of the French Gymnasium, and who told me that he and others of the Order were arrested by the Nazis and treated very harshly. August Weber,[41] a close friend of my father who succeeded Erich Koch-Weser as leader of the State Party was faced with an almost hopeless task. In a parliamentary debate he stated that the National Socialists had traveled the route of political murder. This remark caused such a wild uproar on their part that the session had to be adjourned. On request by the *Reichstag's* speaker, Bernhard Weiß had the culprits arrested. As Weiß was a Jew, he soon became the target of "Nazi justice." Not discouraged by a street-brawl, Weber gave evidence that among their deputies was a convicted murderer, whereupon the Nazis just walked out.[42]

My father served on the committee of the CV.[43] Here Alfred Wiener was secretary and legal representative, *Syndicus*[44]. In order to keep a record of the values that keep a pluralistic and democratic society alive, he started an important collection on the Nazi movement, anti-Semitism, and Fascism, which grew to about 40 000 volumes. Just before the outbreak of the war he managed to evacuate this library first to Amsterdam and then to London.[45] This library became very useful for my father's later research. In a letter to my father from 5th April 1961 Alfred Wiener writes:

> In the changing situations of my life I always tried to do my duty; especially after all hell broke loose in Germany. Even though I had the most bitter experience in my family, I myself on the whole remained spared. It was this knowledge which obliged me to fight [in] any way I could against this hell. If the Wiener Library in its modest way was helpful to you, this is as it should be. It was always a joy to talk to or hear from you.

My father's various activities harmonized well with each other and provided him with a wide experience; they were highly stimulating and earned him general respect. He was an avid reader beyond the fields of law and politics, and particularly enjoyed reading history. He loved sharing what he read and what he experienced with his family. On many walks through the Tiergarten, and on excursions to places outside the city, such as Frederick the Great's Palace of Sans Souci in Potsdam, he told us about historical events and the great figures of German literature. The news of the day always had held an immense fascination for me. I remember when I heard the newspaper being dropped through the letter slit in our front door, I rushed to cycle along our long corridor (so typical for Berlin apartments) to get to the paper before my father could reach it. He was an excellent teacher. I also knew that however busy my father was, he always had time for his wife and his children. He was very close to us and we felt great warmth towards him.

Outside of our home I had joined the youth wing of the CV affiliated to thc *'Wandervögel'* (literally: birds of passage, a youth organization engaging in hiking, camping, games, singing folk songs) led by Werner Rosenstock.[46] We went for walks in the countryside and enjoyed boyish games. I attended a camp on the Schocken Estate near Berlin.[47] In the Jewish Cultural League, the *Jüdische Kulturbund*, we discussed Gotthold Ephraim Lessing's *"Nathan der Weise"* ("Nathan the Wise") wherein a man with an experience like Job's did not dwell on hate or revenge but overcame these destructive emotions through loving action, leading to his inner peace, and reconciliation with God and between men. Nathan's fable of the three rings introduced us to religious tolerance. Lessing lived in the eighteenth century; he was an enlightened, successful writer and thinker who advanced the German prose style with his sparkling and clear language. During the Nazi regime performance of this play was prohibited.

In my youth, members of the bourgeoisie, who like us were not particularly wealthy, had resident domestic staff as a matter of course. This allowed my mother to keep abreast of what was happening in my father's law office, which was in our apartment. She also shared in his wide activities and interests and provided an open table for the many visitors of all ages that came to our home. My mother had plenty of time for me in particular as my sisters began to be more independent. Together my parents developed a circle of intimate friends from various walks of life, lawyers predominately, that my sisters and I always had a chance to share. It was a great privilege for me to grow up in this circle of acquaintances and friends whose humane and cultural qualities surrounded me, an experience I rarely met with later on.

As my father practiced at the Supreme Court of Prussia, some of the lawyers there and their wives, as well as some lawyers accredited to other courts, became close friends. Among those who were Jewish was Heinrich Riegner, who in addition to being a lawyer was also an expert in art history. It was through his wife Agnes and her sister that my parents had met. The Riegner's son, Gerhard, was a rare example of a Zionist in our circle. During the Second World War he worked at the listening post in Geneva at The World Jewish Congress and played an important part in trying to save Jewish lives. Until his death in 1998 he was General Secretary of the World Jewish Congress.[48] The friends among my father's lawyer-colleagues included Richard Calé, whose brother Walter made a mark as a brilliant poet, but sadly died early. Richard Calé and his wife Alice were gifted musicians. Heinrich Veit-Simon, an exquisitely refined person in the best sense of the word, was a member of a leading Jewish family in Berlin and a practicing Jew.[49] His wife Irma, raised as a Christian, adopted her husband's faith. Rudolf Isay, a patent attorney, had converted to Protestantism from Judaism as an adult,[50] and later married Isabella ('Bella') Trimborn, a member of a leading Catholic family in the Rhineland.[51]

Those who retained the religious affiliation of their families did not necessarily observe Jewish practices. My father had received his Bar Mitzvah but was not a regular participant at the synagogue; the various dietary, hygienic, and Sabbath restrictions were not observed in our home and my father in fact objected to them. Some friends kept the high festivals.

Looking back at our friendship circle after all these years, even those who practiced Judaism still respected conversion to Christianity or intermarriage.[52] Although I could not have worked this out for myself as a boy, I would now say that by the 1920s, at any rate, highly educated German Jews were generally beginning to show greater tolerance for these decisions. For them, the bond with Judaism was not necessarily broken by conversion to Christianity or inter marriage.The strong ties created by the shared Jewish descent and the centuries of persecution remained. This mutual acceptance had not always prevailed. My mother told me how shocked she was when one of her uncles severed all contact with a son who had married a Christian woman. Often anti-Jewish or anti-Christian opinions were in part incited by the "snail's pace of integration" as many in the Wilhelmine era "looked to integration to remove friction between Gentiles and Jews."[53] Did this perceived torpid integration reflect the reality of German-Jewish life at that time, and if so, was it applicable to the two generations of the Eyck family? So far as the well-educated Jews were concerned the very opposite was usually true. In our families the speed of assimilation was often increased by the move westwards from eastern territories of smaller towns of the Prussian monarchy. In the proceeding paragraphs I seek to record aspects of the life of a group of well-educated Jews, who achieved high ethical and intellectual standards, marked by true tolerance attained without compromising their moral values.[54] They had adopted the general ideal of the well-educated bourgeoisie, the *Bildungsbürgertum*.

Sometimes, the Jewish friendships dated back to our grandparents' generation, on my father's side of the family, to the days of residence in the area close to the synagogue in the Oranienburger Straße in the northeastern part of Berlin. But my parents also had intimate Christian friends. To the Friedrich Naumann circle my father owed one of his close and enduring friendships, that with Theodor Heuss,[55] later to be the first President of the German Federal Republic, and his wife Elly,[56] the daughter of the economist Georg Knapp at the University of Strasbourg. Naumann, originally leader of the German Democratic Party, and many of his followers joined the German Liberal Association, the *Freisinnige Vereinigung*, in 1903 under Theodor Barth. In order to bring the two groups together, a fortnightly gathering was arranged in an inn. Theodor Heuss was a close collaborator of Friedrich Naumann and later his biographer.[57] He became his aide on the journal The Help *(Die Hilfe)*, to which my father contributed from 1906 onwards. As Heuss described in a volume of his memoirs, "[Erich] Eyck turned up as a follower of Barth, a soft, not yet firmly drawn personality."[58] Elly Heuss was incidentally very active in women's causes. She became a mother not long before Hedwig and taught her how to swaddle a baby. My parents were particularly impressed by the way Elly came to the rescue when the Nazis deprived Theodor Heuss of their livelihood. She pioneered and developed an advertising business, writing appealing verses or lines that were imaginatively broadcast and became very popular. I still remember Elly Heuss demonstrating her advertising techniques, which provided for them and helped them to survive.

Through his political work, my father also met and became well acquainted with the Secretary of State *(Staatsekretär)* Fritz Kempner of the Weimar period and a left-liberal, high official named Vossberg, who unfortunately died early. Kempner was also a friend of the Vossbergs. Incidentally, Kempner was involved in the 20th July plot of 1944 against Hitler. Oberst Claus Schenk von Stauffenberg had managed to plant a time fuse bomb hidden in a briefcase close to Hitler during a strategic conference *(Lagebesprechung)* at the Head Quarters in Rastenburg, East Prussia. Somebody inadvertently pushed the bag under the heavy oak table, so that the explosion missed its target.[59] The Nazis staged a merciless persecution of all the people and their families involved in the plot.

Vossberg's widow, Editha, later married a senior civil

servant, *Ministerialrat* Rau. Editha Rau, a Prussian officer's daughter from a Protestant background, was a person of rare distinction, wonderfully literate even in her speech; she was an author, and her letters are a pleasure to read. She and her husband detested the Nazis.[60] With Frau Rau, as with Theodor and Elly Heuss, my parents shared a close relationship of great mutual warmth.

We often traveled as a family, frequently abroad, to the Netherlands or Switzerland. Occasionally, separate holidays were arranged for me. My parents thought it would be helpful for me to be together with children of my age. In my fourth year, they sent me to a children's holiday home, a *Kinderheim*, in Kipsdorf not far from Dresden, run by *Diakonissen*, a Protestant women's order. I was not happy there and my father's unexpected visit on my birthday was a welcome relief. In 1928, my parents joined a tour of German lawyers to the United States and I was" parked" in Frankfurt am Main with close friends of theirs, the lawyer Max Maier,[61] and his wife Mathilde 'Titti',[62] an expert gardener with a doctorate in botany. She is the author of *All the Gardens of my Life.* The Maiers had a beautiful home whose atmosphere reflected their inner harmony. Max Maier had fought at the front in the First World War and, on being demobilized, at once resumed his legal practice.

In his book *Memories of Germany*[63] he distinguished between the often, in his opinion, emotionally overvalued concept of citizenship, and the belonging to a community of cultural values. He was one of the most Irene [isenic], peace-loving persons I have ever met.

Through friends in Berlin, we heard about a farm in Pomerania that took in paying guests for vacationing. This was Emilienhof in eastern Pomerania not far from the Polish border. It belonged to Heinrich Kaphan, a Jewish farmer who had fought in the First World War. Jewish farmers were a comparative rarity, because for centuries Jews had not been allowed to own land. His wife Käte belonged to the Manasse family, some members of which had acquired academic renown; Käte's brother, Ernst Moritz, followed in these footsteps and became a philosopher.[64] From about the age of eight on, I spent many holidays at Emilienhof with numerous other children who were also guests. I also enjoyed the friendship of the Kaphan children, who were slightly younger than I. Growing up in a big city, seeing the work of an experienced farmer like Heinrich Kaphan, whom I much admired, provided an excellent balance. I befriended many of the horses and did some riding, mainly on ponies, as well as a lot of cycling around the countryside and swimming in nearby lakes. In the evenings, Käte Kaphan, who combined all the skills of a farmer's wife with an excellent education and great sensitivity, introduced and read German literature to us children. I still remember the vivid manner in which she recited an account of the actions of Napoleon's Marshal Grouchy in the campaign, which culminated in the battle of Waterloo, from Stefan Zweig's *Sternstunden der Menschheit*.[65]

I think it was at Emilienhof that I began to be acquainted with the kind of serious problems facing many Germans, though these did not appear to me at the time as a threat to German Jews in general. The Kaphan's, like other farmers, were hard hit by the world economic crisis, which had begun in 1929.

The German government was trying to help the farmers, but their programme, called *Osthilfe*,[66] which was meant to assist smaller land-owners in the eastern parts of the country, got bogged down by the opposition of major agrarian interests. In any case, I still remember a conversation with Käte Kaphan when she told me that they might lose the farm. Fortunately, they received some help and were able to keep their farm. Both my sisters and our parents were also frequent visitors to Emilienhof. *Osthilfe* was carried out under the chancellorship of Heinrich Brüning, appointed by the Agricultural Minister Hans Schlange-Schöningen, who was himself a large estate owner but, as leader of the People's Party *(Volkspartei),* supported the smaller estates. In 1932, he developed a plan for German settlers in the tropical forest of Parâna, Brazil. There it was possible to buy land through the British Parâna Railway Company, who bought their heavy machinery in Germany. By investing in the German equipment companies and thereby using the German currency, one could thus make full use of German capital and avoid the Flight of Country Tax *(Reichsfluchsteuer).* This tax had been introduced by Chancellor Brüning in 1931 to avoid tax evasion by rich people who took their money out of Germany in order to put it into tax-free havens, as there was then no tax due in Germany.

The exemption from the *Reichsfluchtsteuer* meant that full use could be made of one's assets. In this way, the British Land Development Company under the directorship of Mr. Thomas was able to finance and develop a railway system to open up the wilderness of Parâna. The Kaphan's and many of our friends, both Jews and Christians, took this chance to leave Hitler's Germany at his rise to power in 1933. At the end of 1935, my sister Eleanor (Lore) sailed with them in order to teach their children and stayed with them for a year. After several weeks of traveling by ship and trains the families arrived in Rolândia,[67] named so by Erich Koch-Weser, who emigrated soon after 1933. He had been a long-time resident and Lord Major of city of Bremen, Germany, and this was his way to remember the Knight Roland, a hero of the epic cycle around Charlemagne. Rolândia would eventually grew into a lively city, it began as a hamlet consisting of small huts with streets of red soil that were either dusty or muddy. The Kaphan's lived in a house that was left empty when the Isay's moved onto their own land. The house was a square box with walls dividing it into four rooms and a kitchen. Windows had only shutters and no glass. Besides beds, large boxes served as furniture. There was a bathhouse and toilets in a little hut a few meters away, but neither running water nor electricity. Eleanor wrote to our parents: "I was perfectly happy with our new life, but probably no one else in our family would feel that way."[68]

The development of the Brazilian community to which the Kaphan's emigrated provides a helpful example of the history of Germans who left their country because of the Nazis. Erich Koch Weser and his family had immigrated in 1933 and soon after had a productive *fazenda*, the Portuguese word for plantation. Directly or indirectly, many of the newcomers knew each other. There was a lively exchange of experience as well as of farm products among the people who had previously arrived. The only mode of transportation was the horse, rarely a horse-drawn carriage. Heinrich Kaphan had chosen the land about eight miles into the jungle from Rolândia. In dividing the land up, the Company had taken care to do it in a way that every parcel had its own water source. After three months of extremely hard work and risks for everybody cutting trees and burning brush, Henry had opened up part of his virgin forest, assisted by a hired local family with two sons and two daughters, the latter to help in the house. Gradually their land was turned into a successful *fazenda*. The Kaphan's and Maier's had moved into their new farmhouses, growing first rice, coffee, cotton, and corn wheat and now mainly orange trees. At times they engaged in mixed farming with fowls and cows. The Jaù, a creek passing quietly through their land, could soon generate electricity and run a mill. To clean the coffee beans from the dusty iron rich soil, Rudolf Isay invented a machine making use of magnets which saved a lot of manual sifting. Lore, as a teacher and general helper, took part in this early development and gave a colorful description of the life on the developing *fazendas*. In spite of very basic living conditions or perhaps because of constant improvising and careful planning, there was an optimistic atmosphere among those mostly young people of similar background. There were about eighty families of refugees settling in this area. They were all starting a new life in a new country with little more than an abundance of hope, exchange of practical knowledge, and *joie de vivre*.

In a much later period of my life, I received a surprise visit by Käte's son Klaus, now Claudio Kaphan, and his wife Ruth while they were in Alberta to enjoy a helicopter tour of the Rocky Mountains. Following this pleasant surprise, we visited Käte and Titti in the spring of 1990. To our regret their husbands had already passed away.

On the day we arrived, Brazil suffered one of her many currency reforms. Our traveler's checks could only be exchanged weeks after we arrived. So we stayed on the beautiful Jaú with the many luxuriant flowering trees and shrubs that grew in the Kaphan's *fazenda*. During the first years after settling the area, many had left some of their virgin forest untouched, but when taxes were levied on all their land, any reminder of the jungle disappeared. Ruth, who owns one acre, now tries to let plants grow wild to see whether some original vegetation will come back. The Jaù is now without its own electric installations as all the *fazendas* connect to the general electric grid. The drive to their bungalow farmhouses led under eucalyptus trees, large hedges of poinsettias, trumpet vine, philodendron, and bougainvillea, just to mention a few of the botanical delights. Among others there grew an enormous avocado and star fruit tree in Käte's garden surrounded by fertile fields. We got close to the three generations of the Kaphan family and their friends, and celebrated Käte's eightieth birthday. She still had her old guest book, from the time at *Emilienhof* and showed me my farewell entry of 19th Oct 1935; translated it reads:

I was here often, and often did I experience lovely holidays at Emilienhof. Now, when I have to think

Ullo (U.F.G. later Frank) Eyck. 1935

that this should be the last time, that in future someone else should own Emilienhof, a stranger, that Uncle Heinrich and Aunt Käte will be separated from us by a journey of several weeks, I pause in awe of the terrible fate that by capricious decree [*Willkür*] life has thus been transformed. I wish Uncle Heinrich and Aunt Käte that they establish a new home in Brazil, that within the family circle they will lead a joyful – if difficult – life, the way they had done here during the first eleven years of their marriage.

Ullo Eyck

At the time of our visit to Brazil all emigrants were well settled and we received generous hospitality from the Kaphans, their friends in town, and their neighbors. We visited many nearby *fazendas* and to our delight, they were all different from each other. There were the *fazendas* of Kurt and Magdy Ullstein, Hans and Hildegard Kirchheim on Fazenda Bimini. The drive to their home was unlike others, as it led between the austere beauty of jucca trees to a spacious house surrounded by a park-like garden. By 1936, Hans Kircheim had to sell his father's prosperous textile factory for which he had been a widely traveled salesman. Hildegard had been a medical doctor. We met among others Joachim Schlange-Schöningen, the son of Hans; Inge Rosenberg,[69] whose husband had taught in the Jewish Groß Breesen agricultural teaching farm in Silesia near Breslau; and the von Treuenfels family who run a plantation for Boehringer, the German pharmaceutical firm. The conversations were always intensive, covering past and present.

By 1990, the railway tracks were overgrown and abandoned. Rolândia had developed into a town, and was no longer reached on horseback or by train, but on well-paved roads by a car running on corn-alcohol. Ruth had long organized and run a school for workers' wives where they could learn to read and write, sew and knit, and bring their children and babies along. She also gave imaginative English lessons to a group of housewives using everyday activities or cooking special dishes, which never failed to be a feast for her students. With her we visited the spectacular Iguazù falls. Claudio administered his mother's and Titti's farm as well as his own. After he managed to exchange our traveler's cheques we visited Bel Horizonte of the state Minas Gerais, the once gold and precious stone capital of Brazil. This journey was one of our most memorable holidays, but we found the obvious class distinction troublesome – even if maid service was indeed a welcome relief in the Brazilian heat. In the correspondence that ensued, Käte wrote about the sorry plight of the Brazilian economy due to inflation and corruption, but also joyfully about her large family of four generations. However, old scars still break open easily. Käte sent these words to me after another person gave her books on the Jewish situation during 1933-1945.[70] In translation, her letter reads:

> The photos, I cannot bear to look at. Surely I cannot thank the person, who sent them to me. Why does anybody send me those books? I am not able to read the text.

In her last letter on 10th January 1993 she ponders the strikingly strange fate of her family. Their new home in Brazil gave her husband Henry the chance to display abilities that he could not have developed in Germany, but to see any redeeming consequence in the cause of their emigration can hardly be endured.

> Do you remember Emilienhof? To think that we could have concluded our life on Emilienhof . . . but to flee from the terrifying Jewish fate to a far away foreign world and build a new life and develop Henry's gifts, which otherwise would have remained unknown. Very incomprehensible these simultaneous occurrences. To think about it makes one doubting and despairing.[71]

These terrifying events were still only vague premonitions when my parents, as good democrats, sent me to a state run elementary school, the local *Volksschule*. Many of their friends put their children into private elementary schools, which saved one of the four years normally required. I seemed to have been quite bored in my Elementary School. I had to undergo an examination during the third year in the Elementary School to see whether I could omit the fourth year, which I promptly failed. My father, who was forty-two years old when I was born, feared that he would not live long enough to see me "get somewhere." But my father never gave up. So I went on to the fourth year of the Elementary School, now with the idea of skipping the first year of the French High school, the *Französische Gymnasium or Collège Français.* This was all the more difficult, because the school selected for me required some knowledge of French, which I did not have.

The school's history goes back to 1685 when the King of France, Louis XIV, revoked the Edict of Nantes, the concessions his predecessors had granted their Protestant citizens, the Huguenots. Many of them fled to other countries. In the autumn of the same year, Friedrich Wilhelm, the Great Elector of Brandenburg, granted many refugees asylum and protection in his own domain and, for children of the refugees in Berlin, he founded the French School in 1689. Facilitating the integration of the refugees into their new country was a highly successful political move that would benefit the Mark Brandenburg and later on the Kingdom of Prussia. As the refugees brought their traditional skills with them, which were new to the country in which they had now settled, they helped to develop a number of novel industries. Following the French Revolution of 1789, Prussia, and with it the school, had again welcomed a new generation of refugees, this time mainly Roman Catholics, to continue in sharing in the French culture and language carefully maintained at the school, which was wholeheartedly supported by the Hohenzollern rulers.[72] French was then after all still the language for diplomacy and the ruling aristocracy.

During the last year of the Elementary School, I had to take regular lessons in French in another part of Berlin from a Huguenot descendent, Mademoiselle Tournier. These private lessons had to be kept secret, as somehow the whole *manoeuvre* of skipping the first year of the high school was not being handled quite according to the rules. For a time, we also had a "Mademoiselle" staying with us in our home. With her, my sisters and I had to converse in French, which to our shame we did not always do so willingly.

Fortunately the effort paid off and in the spring of 1931, I would take the first of many walks to the classical school building of the French High School. It took me about fifteen minutes to walk along the Tiergarten, and under the chestnut trees of the *Reichstags Ufer,* an arm of the Spree River, and past the still-intact Parliament Building. But my walking peacefully past the Parliament quite suddenly changed two years later when armed guards would sit on the roof tops of adjacent buildings. I entered the *Quinta* of the French High School or fifth school year (under the North American system this equals the sixth year of school). Some teaching already took place in French in that grade, with more subjects gradually being added. Eventually Latin and Greek, for example, had to be translated into French; history and geography were also taught in that language. Religion was another obligatory subject taught according to the student's denomination, separate but at the same class time. My father had me exempt from much of the religious teaching, so to my regret I did not learn Hebrew. A later attempt to do so did not succeed. However, I was fortunate with my new school, in which I had excellent teachers and intelligent, friendly schoolmates.

A happy, sheltered childhood ended abruptly on the 30th January 1933 with Adolf Hitler's and the Nazis' ascent to power. With one third of the popular vote in favor of them, they had become the largest party in the *Reichstag.* I remember the day well. Nobody remained unaffected by it. Many years later, I was sometimes asked to summarize my impressions of this period. I responded that I knew that all conversations on political topics had to be conducted with great prudence, and that from this day onwards, I felt that my parents could no longer protect me. The carefree atmosphere of childhood had gone. Nothing could be taken for granted. So far as I can reconstruct events more than two-thirds of a century ago, this is how I felt at the time. There was a sudden negative change on that particular day. In a relatively short time, things got even worse than the pessimists in our circle of friends imagined. So far as my family was concerned, the new situation affected my parents, my sisters, and me in different ways, in my case particularly in relation to my position at school.

My father had been a respected member of Berlin society. I still remember the celebrations on his fiftieth birthday in December 1928 in our apartment. I was eager to help with serving the food and remember climbing under all sorts of tables to do so. The Calé family, who were very musical, gave a performance of Bertold Brecht's Three Penny Opera, *Dreigroschenoper,* based on the Beggars Opera, with adaptations of the libretto to the history of our family. The press publicized the event. Good wishes were received from many personalities prominent in the various fields with which my father was connected, especially from lawyers, judges, public prosecutors, ministers, public officials, newspaper publishers, and journalists.[73] Now, in a process beginning only four years later, my father as a Jew – a "non-Aryan" – was shunned by people he had known well.

He witnessed the gradual destruction of his professional position and of his earning capacity. As a result of the systematic exclusion of Jews from public life, he lost his position as a notary public *(Notar),* this was an official position representing the state, which Jews were no longer allowed to hold.

He retained his position as lawyer but, in common with his Jewish colleagues, had to put up with a great deal of chicanery, both official and unofficial, interfering with his practice. Soon the journal of the lawyers' association refused to publish the names of Jewish lawyers. My father wanted to fight some of these measures, but was fortunately dissuaded by a colleague who recognized the hopelessness of the situation. His clients rapidly diminished him from their employ since being represented by a Jewish lawyer was not considered particularly helpful. My father had a frightening experience in his legal practice during this period. One day, when he was acting for the defense, his client though acquitted, was nevertheless arrested outside the court-chamber by the Secret Police, the *Gestapo,* immediately after the verdict. As a Jew my father also had lost his position as law editor of the *Vossische Zeitung.* The paper soon afterwards, being a liberal and Jewish-owned newspaper, was ordered to cease publication.[74]

A boycott of Jewish businesses by order of the authorities began on 1st April 1933, on which day my father was physically prevented by SA troopers (Storm Troopers, the "brown-shirts") from entering the *Kammergericht*, the court to which he was accredited. We spent the day in fear. One of our friends, an official of the Prussian Ministry of the Interior, who attended his office as usual that same day, was arrested and sent to a concentration camp apparently on Göring's, the Minister of the Interior, orders. He was never the same after his release. In the end the boycott was called off after a day. The only ray of sunshine in a desperate situation was the visit of my parents' first maid. My parents had employed the woman in earlier days before World War I. During this time, my mother had noticed that the young woman was frequently sick in the morning Not knowing what to make of this, my mother had taken her to see the family doctor who suggested the girl might be pregnant. My mother in disbelief stated it could not be and she said that she would put her hand in the fire for her. But with a smile Dr. Pelteson said, "Mrs. Eyck, don't do that!" Soon his suspicion was proved to be correct, and the young woman was helped by my parents to smooth things over.

Now married for a long time and with a family, she came to our home on 31st March, the birthday of Irene my elder sister, when the boycott had already been announced. The visit was a simple gesture of solidarity and humanity we never forgot.[75]

In the night of 17th February 1933, the *Reichstag* was set on fire allegedly by the deranged and rather psycopathic Dutchman Marianus van der Lubbe, a member of the Communist Party.[76] When Göring learned about the fire, he gave orders to delay the fire brigade. The Communists were very quickly blamed for the destruction, which they rightfully denied vigorously. The Nazis used this opportunity to act against all their adversaries on their well-prepared list, just waiting to be implemented at a given opportunity. The very next day an emergency decree was proclaimed that annulled every important fundamental right of the German citizens. The infamous Law of Empowerment, the *Ermächtigungsgesetz*, was then initiated, overruling any opposition and legalizing indiscriminate imprisonment.[77] The Enabling Law was soon to follow. Within two months the SA killed between 500 and 600 people and 100 000 Communists, Social Democrats, Jews, civil servants, and other undesirable from the Nazi point of view were arrested by the police.

Ernst Reuter and his co-worker, Otto Lehmann-Russbüldt, a family friends, were arrested in the same night and were imprisoned for a time in the notorious Alexander Platz Prison of Berlin and in Spandau. Lehmann-Russbüldt was a freelance writer, a sage of the German Peace Movement. Through the Union New Fatherland, established in 1914, he was an ardent supporter for the idea of the United States of Europe and founded the League of Human Rights. He did not belong to any particular party or religious persuasion, but he could gather and had been supported by people of all shades of German society, including diplomats, statesmen, soldiers, scientists, authors, and journalists. He influenced people as diametrically opposed as Karl Liebknecht, Hans Delbrück, Fürst Lichnowsky, and Albert Einstein. Lehmann-Russbüldt managed to flee to Holland and from there to England by feigning to be severely physically and mentally deranged and in the company of Catholic clergymen, he walked across the boarder. He published and informed the British Government about the development in Germany, the Nazi atrocities, and rearmament that would lead to war. After the war he returned to Germany. For his intense work for peace, he was awarded the First Class Order of the German Federal Republic in 1953.[78]

All Jewish as well as quite a few Christian editors like Theodor Heuss in *Die Hilfe* and Gustav Stolper, both members of the *Reichstag* lost their jobs.[79] The latter was the editor of the *Deutsche Volkswirt,* 1926-1933. Gustav and Toni Stolper enjoyed an intimate friendship with Theodor and Elly Heuss. Close acquaintances of my parents were interrogated by the *Gestapo.* Georg Bernhard,[80] the colorful Vice President of the *Vossische Zeitung,* a member of the Economic Council of the State (the *Reichswirtschaftsrat),* and a democratic Member of Parliament who worked in the German Foreign Office, had to flee via Copenhagen to Paris where he established the *Pariser Tageblatt.* Julius Elbau,[81] Deputy Editor of the *Vossische Zeitung* became editor in the New Yorker *Staatszeitung.* Bernhard Weiß,[82] Vice Chief of the Berlin police, had to hide under the coals in his cellar while his house was searched by the Gestapo. He managed to flee via Prague to Great Britain. Carl Eduard Misch, assistant editor of the *Vossische Zeitung,* was taken into protective custody *(Schutzhaft).* After release, he immigrated to Paris and worked with his old boss Georg Bernhard for the *Pariser Tageblatt,* the successor of *the Pariser Zeitung.* Bernhard, after being interned by German troops in 1940 at Marseille, was able to immigrate to the United States and became Professor at an American university. He died in 1944. Carl Misch returned to Germany after the war and worked from October 1945 on for the cultural-political monthly paper *Der Aufbau*, the Restructure.[83] Ernst Reuter was twice arrested because of communist affiliation and spent some years in the Lichtenberg concentration camp.[84] He immigrated to Turkey where he was appointed traffic minister and Professor in the Academy for Management and Administration. After the war he returned to Germany and was twice elected mayor of West Berlin, 1947-1953.

The Democratic Club, which had provided so much intellectual stimulation for my father, was closed. I remember going there with him when the books of the library were sold off. For balance and comfort my mother sometimes attended the services at the *Kaiser Wilhelm Gedächtnis Kirche* to listen to Pastor Jakobi, a member of the Confessing Church, opposed to the Nazi regime. The large neo-Romanesque Church at the junction of the Kurfürstendamm and the Tauentzien Straße was built in 1891-1895 by the Emperor's leading Architect *(Königliche Baurat)*, von Schwechten. It had a rich interior of mosaics, statues, and colored windows, and a seating capacity for a 1500 people. It was always over full when Pastor Gerhard Jakobi held the service.

My father went through a severe health crisis that affected his eyesight, and had to have books and articles read to him for some time. Fortunately, he rallied and began to embark on an important new career as a modern historian. He started work by dealing with the history of England. With her effective parliamentary democracy buttressed by the rule of law, the country represented a political model that he wished that Germany had followed. He wrote a biography of Gladstone, whom he admired as a liberal parliamentarian inspired by a profound sense of justice. With a dwindling and gradually disappearing income that left them drawing on their savings, my parents moved to a smaller apartment of the Dörnberger Straße in the same area of Berlin in which they had been living, and my mother rented out rooms.

From 1933 on, our harmonious family was scattered. My two sisters, to whom I had been very close, emigrated. Irene, the elder one, had qualified as a librarian while Lore had to terminate the medical studies on which she had embarked. Initially they were in France, but after a time they went on to England. They often had to content themselves with *au pair* positions providing domestic service, as work permits were practically impossible to obtain. At great risk, Lore, the younger of my two sisters came home to read aloud to my father when he had trouble with his eyesight. On at least one occasion, the authorities, probably the Gestapo telephoned our home to inquire whether my sister was still there; she had just left. We were not sure whether our telephone was bugged. Telephones could only be rented from the Telephone Company, and, unknown to the user, could have had listening devices installed. It became quite customary also for our Christian friends to plug the telephone into another outlet, as by law it had to stay connected; this put this device well away from the living room to allow a free conversation behind closed doors.

German-language newspapers like the *Basler* or *Zürcher Nachrichten* could still be obtained. But that avenue to independent news was also soon closed off. Joseph Goebbels, the Minister of Culture and Propaganda held tight control over the press and radio. Hitler had stated in *Mein Kampf* that:

> With skill and continuous application of propaganda
> it is possible to make the people consider even heaven
> as hell and also make them consider the heavenly –
> the most miserable existence. [85]

It could be dangerous to listen to the British Broadcasting Corporation, and after the beginning of the war, when it became a criminal offence, it was punishable by death. [86]

In 1940 alone nine hundred and ninety six people were arrested and some of them executed for this "crime."

Lastly, there was my position at school. Certainly the Nazi regime wrought considerable changes there. As schools were part of the state system, its teachers were civil servants. Some teachers and students appeared in Nazi uniform. For a short while the gifted Jewish language teacher Kurt Levinstein could still stay on at the school.[87] Studying Friedrich Schiller's *Wilhelm Tell*, he made the boys argue a case for and against tyrannicide. He and his Aryan wife survived the Third Reich in North Berlin. Dr. Ansorge, the son of a famous concert pianist and very cosmopolitan in outlook, was delegated to teach racial theory, *Rassenkunde*.[88] In his subtle ironic way, he would take pleasure in demonstrating a typical Nordic skull by measuring the head of our fellow schoolmate Hans Hollander, tall, blond, and blue-eyed, who was the only really orthodox Jew in our class.

The teacher most responsible for the liberal atmosphere at the school was Ernst Lindenborn.[89] The experience of his military service in the First World War had turned him into a pacifist. He had studied theology and philosophy and taught German, French, Latin, and Greek at the school. After the dismissal of the rabbi in 1935, he supervised the Hebrew lessons for the Jewish and any other interested students in the students' homes; previously through Headmaster Roethig's effort the Hebrew lessons could be taught at the school covered up as evangelical theological studies, which was a language requirement. Because of Lindenborn's perfect French he also taught history, biology, and geography. He was not a dried up scholar, humor was a special feature of his teaching. Very deliberately, he provoked his students to laughter and reflection. He was kind, charitable, and wise. He did not leave much doubt about his attitude towards the Nazis and their racial theories; under the guise of the foreign language he called it the *maladie*

French Gymnasium, the class of 1935

(left to right)

Top Row
· Ernst Günther Kahlmann, Udo Derbolovsky,
· Gerd Freuthal (Gerry Field)(*Jewish*)

Second Row
· Herbert Jadrech, Heinz Schiel, Rolf Sabersky(*Jewish*),
· ? ? ? Strauch, Alexander Ringer(*Jewish*),
· Mr. Janke(teacher), Willi Bekker, Günther Levi(*Jewish*),
· Wolfgang Friedrich Schmidt

Third Row
· Ernst Günther Brosius,
· Ulrich Franz Jospeh (Ullo) Frank Eyke
  nom de guerre, Frank Alexander(*Jewish*)
· Dietrich von Otterstedt(*Jewish mother*)
· Hans Hollander(*Jewish*)

Front Row
· Anne-Het Bouché-Deckert, Frank Otto Alexander Budy

contagious (infectious disease).

For the 250 anniversary of the Post dam Edict he wrote the Huguenot play "Faithfulness" *(Glaubenstreue)* that was performed in the French Cathedral *(Französische Dom)* by the students at the school. His historical novel *Coligny, Der Schwertträger Gotte* (God's Carrier of the Sword) dealt with the persecution of the Huguenots. In true Huguenot tradition, he became a Calvinist pastor to serve his spread out congregation in the French Dome. Eventually he was denounced by a "nice colleague" and interrogated several times by the Gestapo; for a while he was not allowed to teach. Among the teachers, Kurt Levinstein was respected but Lindenborn gained the love of his students.

In 1933, Headmaster Dr. Gerstenberg,[90] a scion of a baptized Jewish family, was demoted from his position as a 'non-Aryan' and became a teacher at another school; he eventually immigrated to England to teach at a Public School there. His successor was Max Roethig, a former teacher at the school who had fought in the First World War. As a Government employee he was forced to join some Nazi association and chose the NSKK, *the National Sozialistische Kraftfahrer Korps*, which had the appearance of a motorbike sport's club but was eventual "equalized" (merged) into the NSDAP; some people might have joined both. The *Nationalsozialistische Arbeiter Partei* was the only party anybody could and, most often, had to join. Roethig became controversial, particularly during the war, when he seemed to have definitely turned militaristic if not excessively nationalistic.[91] My own memories of Roethig are far more positive. He took a great interest in me and entrusted me with our class when he was detained by administrative business. The school had a high proportion of Jewish students and those of partly Jewish descent; they all, including the Aryan students, accepted my delegated authority without any problems.

I never had any trouble with my school mates.

When I had not done my homework, which was not a rare occurrence, I could rely on the intelligent students who had conscientiously done so. I managed to stay with the syllabus without getting me into trouble. The standard of the school was high because of the quality of both teachers and students. School hours ran from 8 a.m. to 2 p.m., except one afternoon when we went rowing. There was homework, but the free afternoon and evening gave us ample time for activities of our choice. Often we visited each other in our homes.

The teachers allowed us plenty of scope to develop our talents. Thus, some of us were asked to give lecturettes. I gave a presentation on the Alsace-Lorraine, the long and bitterly disputed strip of land between Germany and France. I reached this conclusion that these border territories had always been German to my own satisfaction. Naively, I simply equated the Holy Roman Empire of the German Nation with the modern German Empire. I have learned better since, as some of my books show.[92] Somehow the performance was remembered later. Lindenborn referred to it in a letter to me after the war and our family doctor, who had fled to the Netherlands and survived underground, recalled that my talk was greeted with applause.[93] It is interesting that I still looked at German history from the German point-of-view when I gave this talk in 1934 or 1935 in spite of the policy of the new regime that stated that a Jew or of Jewish descendent could no longer be a German. I do not think that I had to come down so firmly on the German side; probably a mixed verdict would not have gotten me into trouble. I believe that I said what I thought at the time, not what I was expected to say.

Two of my schoolmates left Germany already in 1934 for racial reasons. Charles Cahn and his parents went to Oxford where he continued school.[94] During the British indiscriminate internment period he was transported to Canada, a country he learned to love in spite of the hardship of the circumstances that led him there. After the war, he studied medicine in Oxford and eventually became director of the Douglas Hospital of McGill University in Montreal as a psychiatrist. To honor his many achievements, the library carries his name. Klaus Adam and his family also left early; because of the boycott they had lost their very elegant sports and fashion house in the centre of Berlin and settled in London where their mother ran a guesthouse in Greencroft Gardens in Hampstead. Klaus became a Production Designer whose films *Dr. Strangelove, Mad King George, Around the World in Eighty Days*, and *Barry Lyndon,* among many others brought him two Oscars and as Sir Ken Adam a knighthood.[95]

By the 1935/36 school year, there were seventeen boys and one girl left in my class. A girl could be admitted to the school if she was a foreign national or could prove Huguenot descent but very few could and did do so. To follow the official racial division, our class had nine Aryan boys, one Aryan girl, one of the boys was a Dutch citizen and seven were Jews or of Jewish descent. By the time of the final examination in the spring of 1938, the class had fourteen students and all passed the final examination, the *Abitur.*[96] Four were Jewish: Gerd Freuthal, Hans Hollander, Alexander Ringer and Rolf Sabersky.[97] 1938 was the last year Jewish students and those of Jewish descent were admitted to the final examination, after that year even attending a high school was prohibited to them. Those who had already progressed to the higher levels of schooling were expelled. There were, however, a few schools in Berlin who did not follow this rule, and even admitted half-Jewish students.

Not long after the *Abitur* at the French High school the four Jewish students left the country. Following the November pogroms in 1938 and the Night of Broken Glass, the *Kristallnacht*, Alexander Ringer and his family escaped to the Netherlands.[98] After the war broke out, they went into hiding until they were found out and deported to Bergen Belsen concentration camp where he taught music to his fellow prisoners. Miraculously, the whole family survived, and Alexander was able to start his musical career, which eventually brought him to USA and earned him international renown in musicology and musical education. He taught at many USA and German Universities as well as at the University of Jerusalem. As a devout Jew he served as a Cantor and is buried in Israel. Rolf Sabersky built a successful career in the USA.[99] He studied at the California Institute of Technology where he acquired a Bachelor of Science and a Master's degree. He worked for Aero Jet, was awarded a Ph.D. at Caltech, and joined their faculty as Professor of Mechanical Engineering. He did important research in heat-transfer, while remaining a consultant at Aerojet. Hans Hollander went to Israel and was killed as a colonel in the war of 1967.

The remaining eight Aryan young men served half a year in the *Reichsarbeitsdienst*, the compulsory labor-service, to be followed by a two-year service in the various branches of the German Military of their choice. This was an inescapable prerequisite in order to get permission for entry into university studies. They had already served one year, when World War II broke out. Udo Derbolowsky, Günther Kahlmann, Heinz Schiel, and Wolfgang Schmidt survived the war; Frank Otto, Alexander Budy, Hans Werner Canon (who was always called by his last name), and Ernst Günther Brosius did not. Willi Bekker, a Dutch citizen, returned to his country and died early, but not before he witnessed the overrunning of Holland by German troops and their ensuing cruelty.[100] Of the schoolmates who remained in Germany, Udo Derbolowsky became a Neurologist and Psychiatrist combining western and eastern medicine.[102] He got involved in the resistance and helped Jewish fellow citizens to hide. For his far-reaching scientific and humanitarian work, particularly the help he gave to his fellow Jewish citizens as well as the educational work for underprivileged and disabled youths, the German President

Rosemarie and Wolfgang Schmidt 1935.

honored him in 1984 with the first class Order of Merit of the Federal Republic *(Großes Bundersverdienstkreuz)*.

As Doctor of Engineering, Günther Kahlmann held a leading and decisive position in the *Heidelberger Printing Machines* and stayed in close contact with the firm after retirement. Günther and Udo both died in 2005. Anne-Het Bouché married Hans Jürgen Deckart, who had a controlling position in the *Reichsbahn*, the German railway.[103] She was as a loving and wise woman the center of a large family, and died in 2004. Among my schoolmates, close friendships endured outside Germany with Charles Cahn, Gerry Field (formerly Gerhard Freuthal), Rolf Sabersky, and in Germany with my later brother-in-law Wolfgang Schmidt, a Chartered Accountant in Cologne.

In 1933, Wolfgang had gone to Berlin a term ahead of his family and stayed with the Schlochow's, who were old friends of the Schmidt's. The Schlochow's lived in the same apartment house of the Luther Straße like our friends the Calé's, and we met there even before the beginning of the school year after Easter. When in the autumn of the year Dr. Erhard Schmidt was transferred to the head-office of the Deutsche Bank, he and the rest of the family moved to Berlin and we frequently visited each other's apartments. Wolfgang introduced me to his family calling me his new friend with three mothers, obviously impressed by a demonstration of the maternal instinct of my two sisters. Our parents soon shared in this friendship. [104] This happened in spite of the political situation and division of the German People into Aryan and Non-Aryan. A new friendship under these conditions was quite rare if not to say singular. Wolfgang was confirmed by Pastor Martin Niemöller in the spring of 1935 in the Jesus Christus Kirche in Berlin-Dahlem.[105] Niemöller had been a U-boat officer and after World War I became a Protestant pastor. I attended the ceremony and took part in the festivities at their home in Berlin-Grunewald, Hubertusbader Straße

16 where I also got to know the wider family including both grandfathers. On Wolfgang's table of gifts, I remember seeing Niemöller's book *From U-Boot für Kancel*. The family Schmidt belonged to the Dahlemer Congregation of the Confessing Church and enjoyed friendly relations with Martin Niemöller, who is often quoted, having stated:

> First they came for the Communists, and I did not speak up because I was not a Communist. Then they came for the Socialists and the Trade Unions, and I did not speak up because I was not a Trade Unionist. Then they came for the Jews, and I did not speak up because I wasn't a Jew. They came for the Catholics, and I didn't speak up because I was a Protestant. And when they came for me, there was no one left to speak up for me.[105]

Niemöller soon came in conflict with the Nazis and in 1937 was taken prisoner. 1938 in legal proceedings he was declared innocent and set free, but was immediately detained by the Gestapo and taken to the concentration camp Sachsenhausen near Berlin. From 1941 on he became the personal prisoner of Hitler and was transferred to the Dachau Concentration camp.[106]

The connections between Wolfgang's family and notable religious teachers were extended by his sister Rosemarie. To prepare for confirmation, a course of weekly lessons over two years, Wolfgang's sister Rosemarie was first instructed by the erudite assistant to Niemöller, Pastor Franz Hildebrandt, a close friend of Dietrich Bonnhöfer.[107] Hildebrandt gave interpretations of Biblical texts to a group of twelve-year-old girls, sometimes while sitting on the sunny lawn outside the Dahlem parish hall. Once on their request to study a particularly difficult text, Hildebrandt had chosen the prologue of the gospel of St. John: "In the Beginning was the Word . . . " He certainly didn't spare them from learning difficult theology. How much more difficult is it to understand God's words when even the words of people have such unknowable effects? Starting the confirmation lessons Hildebrandt gave an introduction to the books of the Old and New Testament, and told them to read one chapter of the Bible a day. But he was taken prisoner in the summer of 1937, and after release, being racially Jewish he fled to England with the help of the Bonnhöfer family and received much help from Bishop Bell of Chichester.

Among Rosemarie's other teachers was Otto Dibelius, who had been Superintendent of the German Protestant Church, the highest administrative position before Ludwig Müller was appointed *Reichsbischof*.[108] At that time Dibelius had been banned from public speaking (*Redeverbot*) which meant he could not conduct any church service or lead a congregation. He started classes with a joyful hymn playing the piano with great passion. Among the students he was referred to as Otto the Great. [109] His instruction of how to handle pride still comes to mind. After the Second World War he became Bishop of Berlin-Brandenburg and president of the World Council of Churches. Rosemarie was confirmed in 1939 by Pastor Helmut Gollwitzer, a gifted theological teacher, later Professor for Theology in the department of Philosophy of the Free University in Berlin. [110] But at that time he deputized for Martin Niemöller.

Although a degree of academic freedom existed at my school that was rare in Nazi Germany, there was also definitely a limit to what the school could do to curb the Nazi influence. Teachers were, after all, civil servants. Sometimes, the school simply had to fall in with directives; such as when it was decreed that Jewish boys were no longer allowed to take part in rowing exercises or to participate in the several day-long excursions on the scenic Havel River flowing through the many vast lakes west of Berlin. All that Headmaster Roethig could achieve here was to gain exemption from this prohibition to those whose fathers had been in active service during the First World War, for which I did not qualify. This was a hard blow to me. I had always particularly enjoyed the rowing tours and the contact it gave me with fellow students and teachers. The tours had their moments, because the waters around Berlin could be quite turbulent. Thanks to good direction and teamwork we managed to keep afloat. The physical exercise and the outdoor activity, which I now had to miss, had previously balanced the academic pursuits.

The anti-Jewish measures affecting my life at school strengthened my willingness to emigrate. With great kindness and insight Headmaster Roethig counseled my parents about my future. At first he advocated keeping me at the school, but at some stage during 1935, probably when the Nuremberg laws were proclaimed,[111] he advised my parents to send me to a school abroad as soon as possible. These "Laws" deprived Jewish people of their citizenship: Jews no longer had the right to vote or hold a public office; they were not allowed to employ German nationals; and intermarriage was prohibited in order to "preserve the purity of the German blood." Many years later when I worked with Headmaster Christian Velder (1975-1979) for his book *300 Years Französisches Gymnasium Berlin* as a historical adviser, I wrote: "I owe among others to Roethig's care my timely move to England where again in St. Paul's I was privileged to attend a first-class school."[112] Roethig was not only helpful to me alone. Through my advisory work for the school's history, I learned that Roethig had obtained a scholarship for Hans Schwab-Felisch, a student two classes higher than I, to enable him to finish the High-school with the *Abitur* while his father Alexander Schwab, a Jewish medical doctor, had been arrested. [113] Dr. Schwab died in prison (*Zuchthaus*) in 1943. After serving in the war, Hans became a leading figure in the German publishing world.

I stayed in contact with happenings at the school through the *Collegianer Verein* (Alumni Association). When I found out that Mr. and Mrs. Roethig had planned a visit to England, my wife and I invited them to stay with us in Exeter, where we had moved to in 1959. Unfortunately Max Roethig died before a visit was possible. I called on Mrs. Roethig in the 1970s in Kiel, when I was on business in Hamburg, and befriended her. To close this controversy about Roethig I would like to say that although he belonged to the NSKK to the NSDAP, the school was a far-reaching isle of asylum in those terrible times. To achieve some limited liberty, his membership of the Party did help perhaps for a while. Harmut von Hentig speaks of the large number of Jewish schoolfellows who up to 1938: "Through the Directors's internationalism and morality found protection under the cover of his party-badge."[114] Our physical education teacher Rudolf Hartmann was not a great light, and stood well below the educational level of most of the other teachers. He was an ardent Nationalsozialist and anti-Christian. Remarks he made during class invited two parental complaints. Headmaster Roethig succeeded in settling the matter internally among the teachers with Hartmann consenting that he would desist from remarks of that kind in future.[115]

I left the school at fifteen years of age after passing the middle school examination, the *Einjährige*. Here are the essay themes for the German language class that we were given to think and write about during a three hour class:

- A human fate that particularly affected me.
- Thoughts about traveling—traveling thoughts.
- For a tree to grow strong, it must develop strong roots around hard rocks. (Nietzsche).
- My attitude to nature, a contribution to the development of my mind.
- For while misfortune follows crime, yet

more frequently crime follows misfortune; (Grillparzer).

- He who plays with life will not succeed; who does not harness himself will stay downtrodden. (Fontane). [116]

During part of the summer of 1935, I attended a term at the English preparatory school in Beaumont House at Heronsgate, Rickmansworth Herfordshire near London. There I began to learn to speak English, which had not been taught at the French High School. I still remember not knowing how to spell "yes" (which I rendered with a "j") when filling in the immigration form on my first journey to England. But during a very happy time at Beaumont House, which in J. H. Keating had an excellent headmaster who took a great interest in me, my English improved and I took an examination at the end of the term.[117] If my memory is correct, I passed the examination, which was a prerequisite to entering into an English public school. On coming home for the rest of the summer people remarked that I spoke French with an English accent.

It was fortunate that my sisters were still in London during 1935. I frequently traveled to London to see them and sometimes I stayed with one of them at the home of their friends. They introduced me to their circle, which gave me a network of support when I started regular schooling in London just after Easter 1936. My elder sister, Irene, had a friend, a young biochemist, Fritz Reuter (Reu), also a refugee. When I returned home, my mother asked me whether there was anything serious between the two of them. At age fourteen, I did not spot anything but some months later Irene and Fritz were engaged. I made up my mind that I was never again going to be so oblivious to matters of love.

When Reu was awarded a Carnegie scholarship at

Sydney, Australia, they got married in February 1936 at the Barnet Registry in London with Erich Eyck and Henry an uncle of Reu's, as witnesses. After a drawn out farewell in London and Paris and Berlin where they met family and friends, they sailed and arrived on a fine May morning in Sydney. Reu worked at the University there and during the war started to build a successful food technology department. He and Irene had two children Dorothy and Peter. Irene gave much support to the University socially and financially through organizing an annual book sale. Reu died in 2001 and Irene in 2004, both well over ninety years old.

When my younger sister, Lore, received a letter from a friend, the Byzantinist Paul Alexander in the United States, I at once asked her whether she was going to marry him. She did so in due course, but via a good year in Brazil, when she helped the Kaphan's to establish their new plantation. Paul and Lore lived in Ann Arbor, where he became Professor of History at the University of Michigan. Before that he taught at Hobart College in New York and Brandeis University in Waltham, Massachusetts. His final call was for a Professorship for Byzantine history at Berkeley California, until he died rather early in 1977. They had three children Ann, a musical festival organizer, Larry, a lawyer married to Kay, a photographer, and Michael, a Professor in Classics in Chicago, married to Jean, a librarian. Our family was dispersed over vast distances, but we stayed in contact through letters and in person on sabbaticals and professional travels whenever possible.

The rest of the summer 1935 and the summer of 1936 I was still able to spend at home in Berlin, often visiting the Schmidt's. Rosemarie told me that I looked smart in my long black trousers and a white shirt that was part of my school uniform. To wear uniforms was not a custom in Berlin schools, where the boys wore knickerbockers suits and usefully patterned shirts with pullovers or jackets of their mothers' choice. She was surprised, but did not say so at the time, that I wore my pocket watch on a First World War iron chain. It had war-dated links 1914, 1915, 1916, 1917, and was a substitute for a gold chain which had been officially collected from the German citizens, in an effort to support the war, called *"Gold gab ich für Eisen"* that translates into: "I gave gold for iron." Looking back at the watch I have to wonder about what was I thinking. Had not my German citizenship been taken away from me? Or was I honouring my uncles who had taken part in that war? Regardless, Wolfgang, Rosemarie, and I would often bicycled through the Grunewald, a forest not far from the Schmidt's home, around Lake Grunewald or going further under the Avus, the famous car-race track, up and down steep little hills to the Havel River. On one occasion when Rosemarie was out of breath, she pleading us to push her bike up the little hill, which I did, while her brother insisted that she was just showing off. Not surprisingly, she still thinks of this memory with a great deal of fondness.

The autumn of 1936 brought me back to England. With the help and advice of G. P. Gooch, my father's friend whom Fritz and Irene had consulted, they recommended to my parents, that I should attend St. Paul's School in London, Hammersmith. I also received an invitation to tea from Gooch that year and I remember I was ushered in to be with Gooch in his large library in his Kensington House.118 He wept in response to his questions when I told him about things in Nazi Germany. Later on I would meet him regularly either in London or at Upway Corner in the country where he was more relaxed. During the early years, he always paid my fare when I came out to Chalfont St. Peter. He was deeply interested in everything I did and helped me with testimonials and references at various stages of my career.

Endnotes

1   Erich Eyck, *History of the Weimar Republic*, (Cambridge, MA: Harvard University Press vol. I, 1962 and vol. II, 1963), pp. 962.

2   Faulhaber, Kardinal Michael von, *Judentum, Christentum, Germanentum, Adventspredigten*, (München: A.Huber, 1933), pp. 1-76.

3   This party was quite distinct from that founded by Stresemann at the end of 1918.

4   Klaus Gerteis, *Sonnemann, Ein Beitrag zur Geschichte des demokratischen Nationalstaatsgedanken in Deutschland*, vol. 1 (Frankfurt/Main: Waldemar Krämer, 1969). Handbuch der Deutschen Geschichte, 1960, vol. III, p. 177.

5   Erich Eyck, *Die Arbeitslosigkeit und die Grundfragen der Arbeitslosen-Versicherung*, (Frankfurt/Main: Sauerländer, 1899).

6   Erich Eyck, Inaugural Dissertation, *Der Vereinstag Deutscher Arbeitervereine 1863-1868*, Georg Reimer, Berlin, 1904.

7   August Bebel (1840-1913), Leading Social Democrat in the 1870s his party gained twelve seats in the Reichstag, Handbuch der Deutschen Gerschichte, 1960, vol. III, p. 219f.

8   Handbuch der Deutschen Geschichte, vol. II, pp. 347f. Kleine Brockhaus vol. II, p. 11.

9   While recognizing many of the merits of the Social Democrats during the Empire, Erich Eyck criticized their dogmatic bias and class isolation. See E. Eyck, *Die Sozialdemokratie*, Berlin, 1912, which came out under the imprint of the book-publishing firm of the journal *Die Hilfe*.

10 See Erich Eyck's letter to Carlheinz Gräter of 6th January 1962 (Erich Eyck papers). Eyck received a personal copy of Heinrich Simon, *Leopold Sonnemann, Seine Jugendgeschichte bis zur Entstehung der Frankfurter Zeitung, zum 29th October 1931*, privately printed at the Frankfurter Societät-Druckerei.

11 Letter from the Frankfurter Societäts-Druckerei to Erich Eyck of 7th October 1898.

12 Erich Eyck to the Dean of the Faculty of Philosophy, Freie Unversität of Berlin, 3rd April 1964.

13 Erich Eyck had the honor of an invitation to the National Liberal Club in

February 1906 where he met the new Prime Minister, Sir Henry Campell-Bannerman, delivering the address, Erich Eyck papers.

14 Frank Eyck, *G. P. Gooch, A Study in History and Politics,* (London: Macmillan, 1982), pp. 261-262, 295-296.

15 Frank Eyck, *G .P.Gooch*, chap. 7.

16 Erich Eyck, *Auf Deutschlands Politischem Forum, Meine politischen Lehrmeister*, p. 47, Deutsche Parlamentarier und Studien zur neuesten Deutschen Geschichte, (Erlenbach-Zürich: Eugen Rentsch, 1963), which came out thanks to the initiative of his publisher Dr. Eugen Rentsch and appeared the year before Erich Eyck's death in 1964.

17 Ibid, p. 65ff.

18 I am greatly indebted to Dr. Helmut Goetz for the bibliography of Erich Eyck's works compiled by him; the list totals 280 items.

19 Erich Eyck, *Auf Deutschlands Politischem Forum*, pp. 69-72.

20 Ibid, p. 47ff.

21 *Freisinnige* literally translated, it means free-thinkers.

22 Erich Eyck, *Das Persönliche Regiment Wihelm II. Politische Geschichte des deutschen Kaiserreiches von 1880 bis 1914,* (Erlenbach-Zürich: Eugen Rentsch, 1948), p. 71. Erich Eyck called the left-liberals' division of 1893 a suicide.

23 Erich Eyck, 6th January 1962 to Karlheniz Gräter, who was then working on a dissertation about Theodor Barth, Erich Eyck papers. Carlheinz Gräter, *Theodor Barth's politische Gedankenwelt: Ein Beitrag zur Geschichte des entschiedenen Liberalismus*, Ph.D. dissertation, Würzburg 1963.

24 Erich Eyck, *Bismarck*, vol. III, p. 550, and *Wilhem II*, p. 156.

25 Erich Eyck, *Auf Deutschlands politischem Forum*, op. cit, pp. 69-72.

26 Irene Reuter née Eyck, *Memories of a Childhood and Youth 1911-1933*, Frank Eyck papers.

27 Bruno Gebhart, Handbuch der Deutschen Geschichte, (Stuttgart: Kletter & Cotta, XXIV vols. ongoing to 2007), vol. IV, pp. 121.

28 I owe this information to the late Erika Suchan, a close friend of the family, who was told by Hedwig that at the bridegroom's wish, there was only a ceremony at the registry office.

29 Erich Eyck, *Die Krise der Deutschen Rechtspflege*, (Berlin: Verlag für Kulturpolitik, 1926).

30 Arnold Paucker, *Der Jüdische Abwehrkampf gegen Antisemitismus und*

Nationalsocialismus in den letzten Jahren der Weimarer Republik, (Hamburg: Leibnitz Verlag, 1969). Arnold Pauker, Barbara Suchy, ed., *Deutsche Juden im Kampf um Recht und Freiheit: Studien zu Abwehr, Selbstbehauptung und Widerstand* der deutschen *Juden seit Ende des 19. Jahrhunderts,* introduction by Reinhard Rürup, (Berlin: Heinrich & Heinrich, Publication of the Leo Baeck Institut, 2001).

31 Many titles of honor were conferred to people during the German Empire 1871-1918. Medical practitioners and members of the board of health were called Sanitätsrat and Geheimer Sanitätsrat; outstanding teachers were Professors, like Prof. Levinstein, etc.

32 Erich Eyck, *Weimar Republik*, vol. II, p. 358-359, 414.

33 Erich Eyck, *Die Krisis der deutschen Rechtspflege.*

34 Frank II (family name) was Governor-General of Poland during the war and was executed as a war criminal in 1946.

35 Arnold Paucker, *Searchlight on the Decline of the Weimar Republic. The Diaries of Ernst Feder,* (Leo Baeck Institute, Leo Baeck Year Book XIII 1968), p. 233.

36 Oskar Meyer was advisor to the Berlin Chamber of Commerce, Prussian state secretary and Reichstag representative. Biographisches Handbuch der deutschen Emigranten nach 1933, *International Biographical Dictionary of Central European Emigrés 1933-1945.* (Röder and Strauss eds., 3 vols.) München: Saur, vol. i, op. cit. vol. I, p. 498; Schwarz op. cit. p. 714.

37 When Ernst Reuter, by then Mayor of West Berlin, came to London not long before his death in 1953, he invited Erich Eyck to dinner, to which I accompanied my father as the only other guest.

38 This story was often told in the family circle, also that his friends were gently teasing him on their way home. Frank Eyck 23rd August 2000 to Johannes Mikuteit. Curtains were drawn at dark for privacy as well as

39 Erich Koch-Weser served as a Reichsminister in the Weimar Republik. Himself a Protestant, he came under the Nazi's racial laws because of Jewish descent on his mother's side. He immigrated to Brazil and helped to develop the plantation settlements near Rolândia, where he was joined by Rudolf Isay, Max Maier, and Heinrich Kaphan among many others. For Koch-Weser see Röder and Strauss (eds.), op. cit. vol. I, p. 378.

40 Erich Eyck, *Weimar Republic*, vol. II, p. 212.

41 August Weber, a brave opponent of the Nazis, after several Gestapo interrogations he immigrated to Britain in 1939 and settled in London. Earlier on he had incidentally been on the board of the Hansabund, Roeder and Strauss (eds.) op .cit. vol. I,. p. 798.

42 Erich Eyck, *Weimar Republic*, vol. II, p. 358-359.

43 *Juden in Berlin 1671-1945 Ein Lesebuch* mit Beiträgen von Annegret Ehrmann, Rachel Livné-Freudenthal, Monika Richartz, Julius H. Schoeps, Raymand Wolff, pp. 144-146.

44 Manfred Durzak, *Die Deutsche Exilliteratur 1933-1945,* (Stuttgart: Philip Reclam jun. 1973), p. 138.

45 Ben Barkow, *Alfred Wiener and the Making of the Holocaust Library,* (London: Vallentine Mitchell, 1997).

46 Werner Rosenstock, secretary of Jüdischen Jugendoraganisation, (Jewish youth organisation) a branch of the CV, immigrated to Britain: *The Refugees, some Facts and Britain's New Citizens,* in Durzak, *Die Deutsche Exilliteratur* 1973, pp. 135 and 143. In 1941 as secretary he published the small AJR letter, Association of Jewish Refugees circular to keep the immigrants in England informed generally and also about each other; after 1946 it became the AJR Journal.

47 Anthony David, *The Patron:* A *life of Salmon Schocken, a complex institution builder, 1877-1959,* (New York: Metropolitan Books, 2003). Obituary, TLS, 27th February 2004.

48 Gerhart Riegner, *Ne jamais désespérer, soixante années au service du peuple juif et des droits de l'homme,* (Paris: Cerf, l'histoir à juif , 1998). The World Jewish Congress (WJC), is a voluntary organization that was established 1930; it alerted the world to the dangers of Nazi anti-Semitism. Its first president was Edgar Bronfman and Gerhart Riegner became Secrètaire Genèneral in Geneva until his death in 2001, see Geneva Briefing Book on WJC. When working in Geneva for my Gooch research in 1979 I visited with Gerhart. He told me that in 1942 when he first received the news about "the final solution" for the Jews how difficult it was for him to believe it. On informing the Vatican, the British Foreign office and other Jewish and Christian organizations, he encountered the same reaction. Because of its enormity it took time for this information to be verified and accepted. Frank

Eyck to Gerhart Riegner 31st July 1979, 31st May 2000. Gerhart Riegner to Frank (Ullo) Eyck, 14th April 2000.

49 Ernst G. Löwenthal, for H.Veit-Simon, *Juden in Preussen*, Biographisches Verzeichnis., ein repräsentanter Querschnitt, (Berlin: D. Reimer, herausgegeben vom Bildarchiv Preußischer Kulturbesitz, 1981), p. 232. See also *Herrmann Veit-Simon. Zum Gedächtnis, 8th May 1856 to 16th July 1941,* privately printed, Berlin, 1945.

50 Rusolf Isay, *Aus meinem Leben,* (Weinheim/Bergstr.: Verlag Chemie, 1960).

51 As a boy I was familiar with what I describe in this paragraph with the possible exception of Rudolf Isay's conversion to Protestantism.

52 Arthur Koestler, *The 13th Tribe, Race and Myth*, Random House, 1976, p 181. Brian Mark Rigg, *Hitler's Jewish Soldiers,* (Kansas City: University Press of Kansas, 2002), pp. 107-108, 156, 299-301.

53 Donald L. Niewyk, *Solving the "Jewish Problem" – Continuity and Change in German Antisemitism 1871-1945*, (London: Secker & Warburg, 1990), in the Leo Baeck Institut, Yearbook XXXV, 1990, p. 335 ff.

54 I want to especially thank my wife Rosemarie, who, coming from a different background, has been able to enter into my family's German-Jewish heritage through her sympathy and understanding. Much of the preservation of my father's books and papers, as well as making archival material available to others, has been due to her unstinting efforts.

55 Theodor Heuss correspondence with Erich Eyck papers.

56 Elly Heuss, *Ausblickck vom Münsterturm,* (Stuttgart/Tübingen: Rainer Wunderlich Verlag, 1934). *Bürger zweier Welten* (Stuttgart: Rainer Wunderlich, 1961).

57 Theodor Heuss, *Der Man, das Werk, die Zeit,* (Stuttgart & Tübingen: Rainer Wunderlich Verlag, 1934 and 1947).

58 Theodor Heuss, *Vorspiele des Lebens, Jugenderinnerungen,* (Tübingen: Rainer Wunderlich Verlag, 1955), pp. 281-282.

59 Freiherr Fabian von Schlabrendorff, *Offiziere gegen Hitler,* (Zürich: Europa Verlag, 1946.).

60 Editha Vossberg-Rau, *Namenlose (Nameless) Roman,* (Suttgart Engelhorn 1926; Engelhorn Romanbibliothek 997/998).

61 Max Hermann Maier, *Ein Frankfurter Rechtsanwalt wird Kaffeepflanzer im Urwald Brasiliens, 1938-1975,* (Frankfurt/Main: Josef Knecht Verlag,

1975).

62 Mathilde Maier, *All the Gardens of my Life*, (New York: Vantage Press, 1983). It has also a German (Frankfurt/Main: Verlag Joseph Knecht, 1978) and a Portuguese edition.

63 Max Hermann Maier, *In uns verwoben tief und wunderbar, Erinnerungen an Deutschland*, (Frankfurt/Main: Joseph Knecht, Carlus Druckerei, 1972), p. 171.

64 Ernst Moritz Manasse emigrated and became professor of philosophy in USA, *Historical Miniatures*. Viking Press 1940, vol. VIII, p. 245.

65 The title translates literally: "Zenith of Mankind," meaning turning points in history. In the English translation the title is given as: *The Tide of Fortune*: *Twelve Historical Miniatures*, (New York: Viking Press 1940), vol. VIII, p. 245.

66 Erich Eyck, *Weimar Republik*, vol. II, p. 342. Also on Hans Schlange-Schöningen, Max Schwarz, Verlag für Literatur und Zeitgeschichte GmbH, 1965, *Biographisches Staatshandbuch* vol. II, p.1975. Er war ein entschiedener Gegner des Nationalsozialismus (a resolute opponent to nationalsocialism) 1945 in leitender Stellung in Agrarwirtschaft, 1951 Deutscher Botschafter in London, England.

67 Erich Koch-Weser, explains the name Rolândia: "Roland der Riese am Rathaus zu Bremen," in memory Roland the Giant from the epic circle of Charlemagne his statue stands in effigy in front of the city hall of Bremen. Also see Biographisches Staatshandbuch, vol. II, p. 697.

68 Eleanor (Lore) Alexander née Eyck, *Stories of my life*, private publication 1989, p. 46, Frank Eyck papers.

69 Inge Rosenberg and her husband Hans were among those who emigrated to Parâna, and developed a successful *fanzenda*. With the Kaphan's they tried to build a small agricultural school for Jewish refugees similar to the Lehrgut Groß Breesen in Silesia, due to the outbreak of war it never materialized. We stayed in the student residence during our visit.

70 Ingeborg Hecht, *Als unsichtbare Mauern wuchsen. Eine deutsche Familie unter den Nürnberger Rassegesetzen*, (Hamburg: Hoffmann und Campe, 1984). Gerhard Schönberner, *Der Gelbe Stern, Die Judenverfolgung in Europa 1933 bis 1945*, mit 202 Bilddokumenten, (Hamburg: Rütten & Leaning Verlag, 1960).

71 Käte Kaphan to Frank (Ullo) Eyck, 10th January 1993.

72 Christian Velder, *300 Jahre Französisches Gymnasium Berlin*, (Berlin: Nikolaische Verlagsbuchhandlung, 1989).

73 Erich Eyck papers on fiftieth birthday celebration; see also The History Place, Holocaust Timetable 1933, 1938-1945. In October 1933, Jews were prohibited from being newspaper editors.

74 From October 1933 onwards Jews and "undesirable" German writers from the Nazi point of view, were prohibited from being newspaper editors or contributors.

75 Irene Reuter née Eyck, *Memoirs of a Childhood and Youth 1911-1933*, private publication 1996, Frank Eyck papers. Monika Richarz, *Jüdisches Leben in Deutschland 1918-1945*, (Suttgart: Deutsche Verlagsanstalt, Veröffentlichung des Leo Baeck Instituts, 1982), p. 112, 119, on Boykott Tag 1st April 1933, Kurt Sabatzky, p. 293-298.

76 Joachim C. Fest, *Hitler*, (New York: Vintage Book, Random House, 1975), pp. 395.

77 Ibid, pp. 396-401.

78 I owe this information kindly granted to me by his daughter Yvonne Wells neé Russbüldt. N.A. Furness, Otto Lehmann-Russbüldt (1873-1964), Forgotten Prophet of a Federal Europe, in: *England? Aber wo liegt es? Deutsche und Oesterreichische Emigranten in Grossbritanian 1933-1945*, by Charmian Brinson, Richard Dove, Marian Malet and Jenifer Taylor, (München: Iudicium Verlag, 1995), pp. 59-75; also articles, *The House at 3 Regent Square*; by N. A. Furness, *Otto Lehman Russbüldt: Forgotten Prophet of a Federal Europe*, Frank Eyck papers. Manfred Durzak, *Die Deutsche Exilliteratur*, p. 555.

    Charmian Brinson, *Im politischen Niemansland der Heimatlosen, Staatenlosen, Konfessionslosen, Portemonnaielosen, Otto Lehmann Russbüldt, In British Exile, German-speaking Exiles in Great Britain*, (München: The Yearbook of the Research Centre for German and Austrian Exile Studies), vol.1, 1999, pp. 117-144.

79 Toni Stolper, *Ein Leben im Brennpunkt unserer Zeit*, (Stuttgart: Rainer Wunderlich, 1970).

80 Exil-Literatur 1933-1945, Ausstellung der Deutschen Bibliotheken, Frankfurt/Main 1965 Monika Richarz, on Georg Bernhard, pp. 112-118,

note 6.

Modris Ekstein, *The Limits of Reason, the German Democracy and the Collapse of the Weimar Democracy*, (London: Oxford University Press , 1975), pp. 117-122, 290.

81 Monika Richarz, ibid. on Julius Elbau, p. 116-119, and Modris Ekstein, note 70.

82 Werner Röder and Herbert Strauss eds., *Biographisches Handbuch der Deutschen Emigration nach 1933 Internationale Dictionary of Central European Emigrés 1933-1945*, Institut fur Zeitgeschichte, vols. III (München, Saur,1980-1983), vol. I, p. 809; *Bernhard Weiß remembered. A Courageous Prussian Jew*, in AJR Information, November 1981. Dietz Bering, *Isidor - Geschichte einer Heztjagd. Bernhard Weiß, einem deutschen Juden zum Gedächtnis*, (in Die Zeit 14th August 1991). Dietz Bering, *Der Name als Stigma. Antisemitismus im deutschen Alltag 1812-1933*, (Stuttgart: Klett-Cotta 1988*)* passim.

83 Handbuch: *Deutsche Presse*, (Bielefeld: Deutscher Zeitungsverlag GMBH, 1951), p. 134. Johannes Mikuteit, *Der steile Aufstieg führte in die Villen im Westen*, zur Gedenktafel für Georg Bernhard am DGB-Hochhaus (Deutscher Gewerkschafts Bund), 24th October FAZ (Frankfurter Allgemeine Zeitung) 2000, Berliner Seiten. Also Adriano Cocozza, *Georg Bernhard "volkstümlicher" Handelsteil prägt die Morgenpost*, 20th October 2000, Berliner Morgenpost.

84 Biographisches Staatshandbuch: on Ernst Reuter, p. 1928.

85 Adolf Hitler, *Mein Kampf*, US edition, 1976, p. 32.

86 Joseph Müller and Ulrich Chaussy, *The White Rose: the resistance by students against Hitler*, München 1942/43, (München: White Rose Foundation, 1991). Helgo Ollmann, *Die Rundfunk Situation in der Bundesrepublik Deutschland Vergangenheit, Gegenwart und Zukunft, Kap.1+3* Rundfunk im 3. Reich. (online publication: Zu Helgo Ollmann, Listening to the BBC under Nazi dictatorship, *http://helgo-ollman.de* (1997). In 1942 alone 985 people were condemned to death under this "Law."

87 Kurt Levinstein, Festschrift, *Zur Feier des 260th Jährigen Bestehens des Französischen Gymnasiums. Fondé 1689*, (Berlin: herausgegeben vom Leiter und Kollegium der Schule, Graphischer Betrieb W. Büxenstein GmbH, 1949).

88 Gerry Field to Rosemarie, 10th Aug. 2005 about Dr. Ansorge, Frank Eyck papers.

89 See Christian Velder, on Ernst Lindenborn, pp.448-456 and 530. *Coligny*, written between 1938 and 1945 was at first as private publication, in 1985 published by Quadriga Verlag J..Severin. It was a *Schlüsselroman*, i.e. a novel where people and a past situation stand for the present difficulties. This was quite a common literary device at the time for those who knew and wanted to know what was happening in Germany. See also his *Résisté*. Both novels deal with protest against excessive state power, about resistance to it, persecution of people of different faiths, and physical elimination; but also with the conquest of hate, survival, the victory of tolerance, and the triumph of love (agape). *Collection of Sermons*, among others for the 256th Anniversary of the Edict of Potsdam. See also Nachruf von Jürgen Reiss, Vorsitzender des Collegianervereins, Collegianerverein und FG-Nachtichten Berlin 1964.

90 For Teachers and Student of the French Gymnasium see Christian Velder.

91 Wolfgang Schmidt, my brother-in-law, was very upset about the tendencies in the pamphlets Headmaster Roethig sent to his former students serving at the front.

92 Frank Eyck, *Religion and Politics in German History*, (New York: Macmillan and St. Martin's Press 1998).

93 Lindenborn, 13th January 1964, and Dr. Gottschalk, 10th February 1969 to Frank Eyck.

94 Charles Cahn in conversations with Rosemarie Eyck 2005/6. Charles died in April 2008.

95 Klaus Adam, Sir Ken to Rosemarie, 17th January 2006. Christopher Frayling, *Ken Adam the Art and Production Designer*, Faber & Faber. Rolf Sabersky to Rosemarie, 10th September 2005.

96 The Abitur lasted about three months: A homepaper in January, to be followed by 6 hourly papers in class, German, French, Latin, Greek, Mathematics and Biology, followed at the beginning of March by oral examination for each subject lasting up to 1 hour per student and subject. A detailed report was kept at the school. Wolfgang Schmidt, 8th August 2005 to Rosemarie Eyck, F. Eyck papers.

97 Rolf Sabersky to Rosemarie Eyck, 28th November 2007, Frank Eyck papers., "Yes, of course, I feel honored to give permission to use the the photograph of our class in 1935."

98 Alexander Ringer musicologist 1921-2002.

99 x missing g Fieed's note.

99 Rolf Sabersky to Rosemarie, 10th September 2005.

100 I owe this information about Willi Bekker to his mother, who on her visit to the Schmidt family in the winter of 1942 told Rosemarie about Willi's distress when civilians who had fled to the fields were shot by low flying German fighter planes. He seemed to have died suddenly of a brain aneurism.

101 Udo Derbolowsky, see *300 Jahre Französisches Gymnasium*, p. 553-560. He served in the German Air Force, was ordered to study medicine, and as medical Doctor combined the disciplines of neurology and psychiatry adding chiropractics, psychoanalysis, therapy of breathing techniques, and acupuncture. His medical documents and books number more than 100 and are in the Lindenborn-Memorial Library of the French Gymnasium. The German President honored him in 1984 with the Großen Bundesverdienstkreuz.

102 The information on Kahlman and Bouché was kindly given to me by Wolfgang Schmidt, see Frank Eyck papers.

103 Dr.rer.pol, Erhard Schmidt, banker, director in the Zentrale der Deutsche Bank in der Mauer Straße, Berlin, specialized in bad debts. In 1932 giving a talk in the Deutschen Demokratischen Klub in Köln/Rhein dealing with war-reparations, had called the Nazis "a bunch of criminals."

104 Martin Niemöller, *Vom U-Boot zur Kanzel.* Autobiography, (Berlin: M. Warneck, 1934).

105 There exist various versions for this quote, the one used here is the one that appears on the stone tablet of the Holocaust-Memorial in Boston. Niemöller's remark stems from his response to a question in a discussion after his address 1933, wherein he mentioned the political relevance expressed by the opposing forces i.e. the Communists, Trade Unionists and Social Democrats. About the later addition referring to the Jews, Niemöller would certainly have had no principal objection. Klaus Gottstein letter to Rosemarie, 27th March 2006. Dr Heinz Hermann Niemöller kindly gave Rosemarie the original version in his letter of 10th April 2006:

Als die Nazis die Kommunisten holten, habe ich geschwiegen, ich war ja kein Kommunist. Als sie die Sozialdemokraten einsperrten, habe ich geschwiegen, ich war ja kein Sozialdemokrat. Als sie die Gewerkschafter holten, habe ich geschwiegen, ich war ja kein Gewerkschafter.

Als sie mich holten, gab es keinen mehr, der protestieren konnte.

The letter also stated that any assertion that early on Niemöller had given anti-Semitic sermons is "absolutely wrong. All the sermons that have survived do not support the slightest evidence of this."

106 The connection between Church and State was administratively very close. Hitler tried to gain control of the Evangelical Churches and to use them as an instrument of Nazi propaganda and politics. The state appointed *Reichsbischof* was Ludwig Müller. His *Deutsche Christen* denied the authoritative position of the Scriptures, confessional writings of the Reformation, eliminated all Jewish themes, and replaced Christian and Jewish ideas with racial theories. In 1933 Karl Barth, Professor of Theology in Göttingen, Hanns Lilje, Martin Niemöller, and many others resisted these teachings as un-Christian. They drew pastors and congregations from the various Protestant Denominations together, and formed the independent Confessing Church (*Bekennende Kirche, BK)* that was not recognized by the state. The Synod of Barmen in May 1934 and, at the end of the year of Dahlem gave a clear declaration of the Faith, based on Holy Scripture. Members of BK actively opposed euthanasia and the persecution of the Jews. There were numerous arrests, and by 1937 many members were forced to go underground. In the Wednesday prayer services in Dahlem, well over fifty pastors' names were mentioned. See John Leith, *Creeds of the Church*, 3rd ed. (Atlanta, John Knox, 1983). In 1948 the BK ceased to exist when the territorial Evangelical Churches were reorganized. Niemöller became bishop of Hessen, and Lilje of Hanover (Encyclopaedia Britannica online pp.1-2).Karl Barth thereafter taught and lived in Basel, Switzerland.

107 Franz Hildebrandt who after 1937 became the Methodist Minister in Cambridge, where he closely cooperated with Bishop Bell, England, to minister to Protestant refugees. Later he went to Drew University, USA, as professor of theology, specializing in studies of Luther and Wesley. Amos Cresswell and Maxwell Tow, *Dr. Franz Hildebrandt. Mr Valiant-for-Truth*, Smyth & Helwys publishing, Georgia.

108 Otto Dibelius, (1881-1967), Autobiography, *Ein Christ ist immer im Dienst.* (Stuttgart: Kreuz Verlag, 1961), As Superintendent of the United Church of Prussia, which was created by Friedrich Wilhelm III decree of 1817 to unite

Lutherans and Calvinists, he gave a speech in the Reichstag in 1933, though a proud German, he cautiously stated that dictatorship is not according to the will of God. He played a leading role in the Confessing Church, concentrating on the struggle for freedom of religious expression.

109 Otto I, the Great of the Saxon Dynasty 936-973, Frank Eyck, *Religion and Politcs*, p72-82.

110 *Helmut Gollwitzer, und führen wohin du nicht willst*, (München: Beck, 1952, Gütersloher Verlag 1994), after his release from a Russian prisoner of war camp, discussed Marxist-Leninist communism. In his book *Krummes Hols Aufrechter Gang*, (München: Beck,1970). He held an ambiguous position towards communism and is critical of inhuman capitalism. See Christa Halm, *Essay on Helmut Gollwitzer. Professor für Systematische Theology,* Universität Bonn and Freie Universität West-Berlin. Ausgewahlte Werke, ed. bei Friedrich Wilhelm Marquart, *Weg und Werk, 1988,* w.u.Bd. 10, pp. 49-179.

111 Nürnberg Laws, 15th September 1935.

112 Frank Eyck in Christian Velder, *300 Jahre Französisches Gymnasium Berlin*, p. 565.

113 Velder, pp. 554 ff.

114 Hartmut von Hentig, Velder, p. 582-586.

115 Rudolf Hartmann, Velder, p. 582.

116 The essay topics translated in the main text are given here in German: Ein Menschenschicksal, das mich besonders ergriffen hat; Reisegedanken – Gedankenreise; Das ein Baum groß werde, dazu will er um harte Felsen harte Wurzeln schlagen; Mein Verhältnis zur Natur, ein Beitrag zu meiner Seelenentwicklung; Denn wenn das Unglück dem Verbrechen folgt, folgt öfter noch dem Unglück das Verbrechen; Wer mit dem Leben spielt, kommt nie zurecht, wer sich nicht selbst befiehlt, bleibt immer Knecht.

117 Frank Eyck papers, letter from J. F. Keating, 21st April 1940 and 10th February 1940.

118 Frank Eyck to Charmian Brinson, 26th January 1997.

CHAPTER 3

St. Paul's School, London, England 1936-1940

AT THE AGE OF FOURTEEN, I entered St. Paul's School, a public school – in the English sense – and lived as a boarder in Colet House. Such schools are elite and not run by the state but funded by a private trust and supervised by a board of governors. They are usually several centuries old and derived from monastic institutions. In 1505, on inheriting a large fortune from his father, John Colet,[1] Dean of St. Paul's Cathedral London, founded St. Paul's Boys School in 1509 for 153 boys to improve the knowledge and morals of the clergy, which he found lacking. In 1518, he put the School under the management of the Mercers Company, a step of decisive importance, as it was one of the first examples of a lay-managed educational institution. The Mercers still govern and look after this school today, besides other schools and properties they acquired over time.

There are some negative aspects to this system of schooling, but at their best the public schools of England as well as the universities of Oxford and Cambridge are superb institutions. In the first half of the twentieth century, what one might call the British establishment was still comparatively centralized, probably to a greater extent than was the case in other large countries such as the USA, Canada, or Germany. Integrating factors for the establishment – besides the dominance of London – were particularly the public schools and universities, especially Oxford and Cambridge. Like most schools at that time, they were single-sex schools catering generally to students aged between 13 to 19, usually with a preponderance of boarders who lived in the school's houses during term-time and were at home mainly in the school holidays. For the past hundred years, a sparate St. Paul's School for Girls has also been open. The public schools devoted a great deal of attention to training young men for leadership positions in Britain, the Empire and Commonwealth, both in regards to the civil and the military service. Besides a high academic standard, the "right spirit" was inculcated in the boys, which had the effect of isolating them from "ordinary people." They aimed at promoting a strong corporate spirit. For boarders in particular felt the influence of parents and home was considerably diminish, at least in term-time. The emphasis in these schools was on endurance, rules, and team spirit, practiced endlessly in all sorts of sport and games; on social polish and self-assurance; on loyalty to King and Country; and on a 'muscular Christianity'.

There was a strict hierarchical system in force, with masters delegating to senior boys, usually called prefects. Junior boys had to "fag" for these elder ones (i.e. to run errands and provide some personal services like cleaning shoes, etc.). The prefects enforced rigorous punctuality and numerous rules, sometimes exacted by ritual beatings, occasionally in circumstances that can only be called obscene. One had to learn the hard way how to fit in while also developing self-reliance and keep one's counsel. It was not proper to "rat" on any member of the group, not even if the bullies made one's life a misery. One either adapted to or was broken by the system. Obviously, the more sensitive suffered particularly. Homosexuality was rampant in the boys' public schools. Many of the boys may have found the behavior of their homosexual contemporaries odd, but they would not normally give them away at school or later. There was a certain conspiratorial or "secret society" atmosphere about this, particularly in view of the fact that homosexual acts were still a criminal offence at the time. All this carried over into Oxford and Cambridge. Naturally, an entirely different spirit dominated the "red brick"

Frank Eyck, getting a hand at Cricket, 1937

secular universities created in the 20th century like Manchester or Liverpool. Whereas Oxford and Cambridge had a monastic origin with their buildings made of ancient stone.

I was stimulated and happy at the school, but not so at Colet House with its unexpected "Prussian discipline." To escape this place I spent many weekends at the home of Gretl and Kurt Hübschmann,[2] relatives of my elder sister's husband and gifted photographers. Early in 1930, Kurt had contributed to a German photo agency, the *Deutsche Photodienst*. After he and Gretl immigrated to England in 1934, he sold his pictures back to Germany until war broke out. He became a respected photojournalist covering events in a restrained and unobtrusive way for which he was famous. When King George VI was asked on one occasion which photographer he preferred, he answered "that quiet German." Under the editorship of Stephan Lorant,[3] the former chief editor of the *Münchner Illustrierte*, Kurt and Gretl provided material for the *Picture Post*, a highly successful weekly paper until the advent of television decreased its popularity. Kurt worked for it until it ceased to exist in 1957.

After a term or so, I became a boarder in Greencroft Gardens, Hampstead, in the friendly and well-run guesthouse of Lilly Adam.[4] With her husband Fritz and their four children, she had immigrated in 1934 after their clothing business had folded because of Hitler's measures against the Jews. I renewed my friendship from my time at the Collège Français with the Adams' boys. Klaus, who had been in my class at the Collège Français, was also at St. Paul's, but in the modern section rather than the classical section where I studied. I also had a very good English friend named Hugh Myers, the gentlest person you can imagine. Taking the bus through Kilburn, a working-class district, to Hammersmith in our identifiable public school uniform – black trousers and jacket and a straw hat or cap – we were happy chatting young adolescents. On one occasion, he introduced me to the finer points of the

English language by telling me about the difference between a quick and a fast woman. He later studied at Balliol College, Oxford and became a language teacher

Fortunately, my father was able to transfer money legally from an account in Switzerland to England for my education, so long as some funds were repatriated to Germany.[5] By chance in October 1937, my parents had received some money as compensation for an accident my mother had suffered in a public bus that had turned over. At the time, there were restrictions on the amount of money that could be exchanged into foreign currency. But it was still possible to exchange this money into Lire allowing my parents to take a holiday in Taormina Italy in December 1937. It gave them the opportunity to observe developments in Germany from a distance. They had not quite made up their minds to emigrate, but they wanted to go to England if things got any worse in Germany. While they were in Italy, they received a postcard from friends back home warning them that the passports of Jews returning from abroad would be confiscated at the border. On this information my parents decided to emigrate, which was easier said than done. My father found it more difficult than my mother to sever ties with Germany, particularly with Berlin, where he was born. It was an emotional and hard decision because of their deep roots in the German culture. My mother's fine instinct for the danger in which her family found itself correctly interpreted the insight my father had through his wide professional experience and great intelligence. She made up her mind that they had to leave, whatever might await them abroad, and in a first instance suggested opening an espresso bar. The combination of my parents' qualities saved the family from the terrible fate awaiting untold numbers of German and other European Jews.[6]

Apart from other obstacles, my parents would have to find a country willing to admit them. As my father had visited England in his youth, and in the years after the collapse of his legal practice had written a biography of William Ewart Gladstone (1809-1898), four-times Prime Minister, England was therefore the most appealing choice to him for a new start late in their lives. They were fortunate that they also had friends there who had immigrated earlier providing support, which not everybody could claim. When my parents arrived in Great Britain, the Immigration Officer asked my father if he was coming only to visit or whether he planned to immigrate. Afraid that his entrance might be denied, my father answered that he only came to visit. However, the situation was later successfully straightened out so that my parents were able to stay in England.

The Gladstone family appreciated my father's biography of their famous ancestor. They were most helpful and financed the English translation of the Gladstone biography published within a year in 1938. My father had dedicated the German version to me, which is translated here:

> To his beloved son Ulrich [Frank], that he shall pay respect to the dreams of his youth when he will become a man.
> Erich Eyck, August 1938
> The first year of exile, or the new homeland?

For the translation of his book he offered the inscription:

> To my Hedwig, the always loving and brave companion in good and gloomy days, without her I could not have written this book.

He went on to quote Gladstone's description to his own wife:

> "It would not be possible to unfold in words the value of the gifts which the bounty of Providence has conferred on me through her."

London 12th May 1938, our 20th Wedding Anniversary "

To honor the English publication, the Gladstone family invited my parents to their annual celebration in the Library of Harden Castle in North Wales. In conversation with Lady Gladstone, Isla Margery, my mother mentioned that I would have to spend the summer holiday at their home in London. With great kindness Lady Gladstone arranged for me a holiday with her friends, the Maxwell Garnett's, who had children of my age. At Seaview, their summer residence on the Isle of Wight, I thoroughly enjoyed their home life as well as a range of activities like swimming and sailing. Mr. Garnett was an educationalist with high ideals.[7] His own subjects were mathematics and engineering. He was a devout Christian serving on many boards and as secretary of the League of Nations Union.

Years later when I had expressed my condolence to Lady Gladstone on her husband's passing, she answered on 5th November 1969:

> I am still re-reading the wonderful letters I had when my husband died. This is to thank you so much for one written on May 19th and to ask you to thank your mother too.
>
> It is strange how some memories remain always with one and I shall, I hope, never forget the remarkable and touching one of your father sitting on the drawing room floor . . . playing with our then little children, and the wonder of joy he expressed that such simple real pleasures remain in such a (particularly for him) torn and horrible world of bitter experience. So that is what he did for me and your letter recalls the experience in depth.[8]

My father had also since died and I sent a copy of this letter to my mother adding: "The impressions we have of 'Vati' remain with us and I think they get even stronger over the years. It is wonderful what we, you, Irene, Lore, I and Rosemarie owe him."

Many Jewish immigrants kept close and helpful contact with each other. The vast majority of Jewish immigrants arrived during 1939, and finding a way to survive in the new country was often very difficult.[9] Through the initiative of Werner Rosenstock, the Association of Jewish Refugees, AJR, published a modest but informative circular to keep emigrants in touch with each other and offered helpful indications to answer and solve current questions and problems. [10]

Starting to settle in England, Hedwig Eyck first rented out rooms in their apartment. In order to have their belongings shipped to them, the Flight of Country Tax, the *Reichsfluchtsteuer*, had to be paid to the German authorities. They had taken the view that my parents had in fact emigrated, therefore confiscated our belongings and levied the appropriate tax which was based on the capital my father had possessed several years previously, but which in the meantime had been spent. Erich no longer had the resources to pay the taxes and had to borrow the 1000 *Reichsmark* from his older brother, Hans.[11] He was still in Germany and was able to help out, and in his kindness paid the tax. In restitution proceedings, some time after the war, my father received compensation for this unjustly levied tax. The belongings arrived in London soon after the Munich Agreement, about the same time that we heard about the November pogroms of 1938. In these Hans, who had fought for Germany in the First World War, was imprisoned in a Nazi concentration camp, from which he eventually somehow got freed. His wife Erna, née Kallmann, who had received a visa to Sweden where she had relatives, was arrested just before she could make use of it. She perished, probably, in 1943 during the battles in the Warsaw Ghetto.

Hans was able to obtain a ticket on a boat and arrived in Shanghai with 10 Marks in his pocket.[12] Having worked as a patent attorney he had a lot of practical knowledge that eventually proved useful for earning his daily living. One of his jobs was in a photolaboratory developing films. Between late 1938 and 1941, Shanghai was the only remaining place still open for refugees that did not require an entrance visa. The train or ship ticket sufficed for entry. Shanghai was legally a no-man's land; officially it belonged to China, but it was now occupied by the Japanese, besides having extraterritorial concessions belonging to France, Great Britain, and USA. It was the "last hour place" for 20 000 refugees.[13] By the end of the war, Hans had saved enough money to take a boat to New York, where he arrived in May 1947. For five years he stayed with his sister Trude and her husband Arthur Nussbaum working as a researcher with the metallurgist Klaus Goetzel, who was married to a cousin on his mother's side.[14] After his retirement in 1952, he joined his daughter Vera in Corpus Christi, Texas, where Vera and his son-in law Philip Rosenheim, a medical doctor, had settled. Hans died there a year later. [15]

Though my father read English without difficulty, he was at first not so fluent in writing or speaking the language. His expertise in German law did not enable him to practice as a lawyer in England. After the arrival of the furniture and the library in November 1938, my mother took over and ran a boarding house that was also in Greencroft Gardens Hampstead for Dr. Hilde Maas.[16] She was a psychoanalyst and her husband a psychiatrist who, in Germany, had been the medical director of a mental health hospital near Berlin. With their small son, they were already well established in London. My mother saw to it that my father could concentrate on his writing. He regularly attended the reading room in the British Museum. Although my parents emigration to England was a struggle at times, I could not be more satisfied. I no longer had to be a boarder; I could now live at home.

But the financial situation of my parents would not enable me to stay at the school without my obtaining a scholarship. I worked and sat for the examination. Unfortunately, my name did not appear on the scholarship list. Some days later, however, on the 18ᵗʰ July 1938, a letter arrived addressed to my father:[17]

Dear Sir,

A vacancy having occurred in the number of senior Scholars, it has been decided to award it to your son commencing from the beginning of the next term. Will you kindly inform me if you wish to accept it?

Yours faithfully

R.L.L.Braddell
Bursar.

This offer brought great relief to my parents and myself. It was decisive for my later career. I could now remain at the school as a day-boy. It did not take long to find out that the winner of the scholarship came from a family of independent means. He had accepted the honor, but declined the financial support of £33 per term.

I became very attached to my new school and am deeply thankful for the excellent standard of its teachers. History under Dr. Philip Whitting was my favorite subject.[18] In later years, whenever Old Paulines of the "History VIII" class met, we talked with great esteem and gratitude about Philip Whitting, F. G. S. Parker, and W. H. Eynon Smith. They were friends and a good thing too. After evacuation Parker and Smith took their classes in opposite ends of a large room at Easthampton Park. They compelled attention; being men of wide culture they made their lessons interesting, never raised their voices and created an atmosphere of intense concentration. They were hard taskmasters and assigned a lot of work which nobody dared to do badly. In schoolboy fashion, we had called them "the three headed monster," but their teaching was important for our development and a guide in our lives. They were, in their different ways, awe-inspiring; nobody tried to fool around in their classes. Parker taught French but beyond the language, he introduced us with sardonic affection into the French way of life. Eynon Smith was our teacher for Latin and General Studies. He could also be provocative in his remarks. Latin had to be translated as if reading an English text, he would be standing close by and if one was, when translating, slowing down one received a painful thump on the back. The method brought results, but today would hardly be acceptable. General Studies was an exciting time. He started to teach us systematic working methods, how to read swiftly and effectively, how to organize material and time. After that there would be discussions using articles of *the Spectator, the New Statesman, the Economist*, famous quotes or even provocative statements of his own. Using the Socratic Method he made us think and express ourselves clearly. He showed us how to use the Decimal classification system of public libraries.

Whenever possible I stayed in contact with my contemporaries. Rolf Blumenau became Professor of Philosophy in University of London. Being younger than I, it is amusing to remember that I helped him out with mathematics. Karl Leyser,[19] already a brilliant student under Whitting in the History VIII's, became an erudite Medievalist at Magdalene College Oxford and was appointed to the Chichele chair there. Sir Derek Mitchell, at Christ Church College, became a high-ranking civil servant. While in the British Embassy in Washington, DC working for the

Economic Ministry from 1969 on, I often saw him and his wife Miriam and enjoyed their generous hospitality whenever I attended historical conferences or did research for my biography on Gooch. He held many important positions, and was Principal Private Secretary to Prime Minister Harold Wilson. Hugh Myers taught English as a second language and Egon Hanfstängl, engaged in the family tradition of art publishing, named one of his sons Eynon in honor of our outstanding master – Eynon Smith.

Egon was the son of Ernst Hanfstängl (a giant of a man with the nickname *Putzi*, which may be translated into Tiny), who was the Nazi Chief of the Foreign Press.[20] When I first met Egon in 1937 I was not sure what to make of him, and I wasn't alone in my reservations. Beginning in 1922, Ernst Hanfstängl, who belonged to the famous art publishing firm in Munich, had helped to make Hitler acceptable to the established society, *machte ihn hoffähig* (acceptable at Court) by aiding him in various ways, socially, financially, and emotionally. On request, Hanfstängl often played the piano for Hitler, giving his interpretation of Franz List and, above all, of Richard Wagner's operas. Notably the Prelude of the *Meistersingers* and the *Liebestod* from *Tristan und Isolde* had a special calming influence on Hitler.[21] Ernst Hanfstängl with his American wife and his knowledge of England and the USA was very useful to the Nazi government. However, Putzi became disillusioned and by the mid-1930s he also had fallen out of favor with the leaders of the Nazi regime. In order to try to kill him, they tried to parachute him over the communist part of Spain involved in civil war. Ernst managed to dissuade the pilot who himself did not like the order and faked engine trouble so Ernst could escape. He gave Egon an agreed-upon sign that allowed them to meet in Switzerland. From there, they proceeded to London. By that time, his parents had divorced, his mother eventually becoming a housekeeper for wealthy men in the USA. At the outbreak of war, Ernst was interned and sent to Canada. The USA was interested in him and he became an exchange prisoner of the USA and advisor to President Roosevelt on Nazi affairs and ideology. In the meantime, Egon, being an American citizen, became a soldier in the American army and was one of the guards for his father. Many years later, while researching in Munich, Philip Whitting initiated our re-acquaintance. He was also still in contact with Egon and a warm friendship between he and his wife, Rosemarie, and myself was sparked. We spent many evenings in their beautiful home wherein we shared our experiences and had searching discussions about those terrible earlier years. Even then, the shadow of his father still loomed heavily over Egon.

For a few months in the spring of 1939, I had a lively exchange of letters – first in German, and after September 1939, in English – with Gerald (Gerd) Fränkel, whom I had met at *Emilienhof* and had often visited in his Berlin home.[22] Gerald had studied at an agricultural school for Jewish young men, the *Lehrgut Groß Breesen* in Silesia not far from Breslau. For a short time, he was in a German concentration camp. After his release, he obtained a managerial position on a farm in Kenya through the British Plough Settlement Association where he felt happy and useful. He very much hoped to get his parents to join him. For good reason he got very worried about the European situation and described in his letter the Kenyan plans prepared for the outbreak of war. His employer, a British officer from the First World War, had to report for military service within thirty days should hostilities break out. He tried to get Gerald mobilized into his own battalion as he desperately wanted to avoid Gerald's internment. Gerald's own application to be registered in the Nominal Roll was rejected, because he could not supply the necessary letters of recommendation to join any military unit due to the limited time of his residence in Kenya. Gerard suspected that his rejection from the ranks was partly due to allegations that some refugees were spies. In a letter he states that "one knew that spies existed among the refugees; [but] of this unproved allegations the refugees themselves did not know anything." A request was forwarded by Gerald's employer to have Gerald placed in charge of the farm, which would become an evacuation point for women and children of the neighboring farms, if he was not able to mobilize with the English soldiers. This request was also denied. According to this plan, however, he might have found himself in the position to use force against possible attacks or insurrection by the Africans and this possibility troubled him deeply.

But nothing prevented his arrest on the 4th September 1939. He stayed interned for a fortnight, after which he returned to the farm. He had this to say about the experience: "Believe me; it gives one a funny kind of feeling to be imprisoned twice before one year has passed. Though the treatment in those camps [in Nairobi] was much better compared to what they did to us in the German concentration camps." Just having received the latest news, he added: "The endless lies the Germans produce about Poland make me furious, *ich koche vor Wut*, [which translates I am boiling with rage], and I can do nothing else but sit by the radio and listen." In another letter he writes: "In my opinion there is little chance for Germany to win the war but all chances to lose it like the last one. I only wish I could do my share and have my revenge on those Nazis. This also expresses the wish of many other refugees who I know." Miraculously, his parents survived persecution and air raids in their own unharmed house in Berlin.[23]

In January 1939, a change took place at St. Paul's School that had a profound effect on the future of the institution and on me personally. Walter F. Oakeshott, only in his mid-thirties, who had taught at Winchester College, took over as High Master of St. Paul's, succeeding John Bell after an interregnum of one term.[24] At the request of Archbishop William Temple, Oakeshott had played a leading part in the unemployment inquiry culminating in the report to the Pilgrims Trust, *Man Without Work,* published in 1938.[25] He carried within himself a deep yet practical concern for his fellow men.

Meanwhile the Munich agreement lost more and more credibility. Prime Minster Chamberlain's "Peace in our Time," had conceded the *Sudetenland,* the part of Czechoslovakia with a German minority, to Hitler. But this agreement became nothing more that fading piece of paper as the whole of Czechoslovakia was subsequently occupied by German troops. There was fear of war. In Britain, general plans were made for an evacuation of children from the large cities in case war should break out. In addition, the authorities informed St. Paul's School that the Hammersmith building, dating to 1884, would be requisitioned. Indeed, the probable closure of the school for the duration of the war was announced to the parents a day before the Munich agreement. This was dire news for the new High Master, who was determined to avoid having to close the school. About his teaching method, the school paper of 1939 reports that through his strong optimism and a combination of steel and velvet he managed to bring out the best in each boy and staff, and his determination may have saved the school.

On assuming office W. F. Oakeshott was helped by his devoted staff in investigating the possibilities of evacuating the school from London. In particular, Maurice Tyson, who had been acting Head Master the previous term, and Alan Cook, a future Surmaster or a second master, aided him in making these excellent arrangements. The school was to be housed in the spacious lodge of the seventh Marques of Downshire and the Dowager Duchess at Easthampstead Park in Wokingham, Berkshire. After some reluctance, the Dowager Duchess realized the advantage of having studious Paulines rather than rampaging evacuees in her "house of only ninety-four rooms" and conceded one wing of the Park as classrooms, but no lavatories. For £80 the Mercers secured the option of a lease, in the event of war, at £250 per annum. Nearby, another leading public school, Wellington College, made some old laboratories available for restoration by St. Paul's as they had just built new ones. Bank loans were negotiated and granted for the lease of houses in Wellington to be used as hostels. Against a bank loan the High Master bought one house that also doubled as hostel. These houses had space but no beds. The Mercers Chairman was charmed into authorizing £26 5s to provide camp beds for the boarders, and £33 5s for construction. The parents contributed £50, £1 per head, for timber stored in the Park. Crowthorne, a small neighborhood town, was prepared to billet further boys. Some of the town's fields were rented to grow crops. These three locations in the country were within easy cycling distance, roughly five miles of each other. In case of overcrowding of railway stations and trains, it was advantageous that Crowthorne, some 35 miles from London, could also comfortably be reached on bicycles. On 17th February 1939, I joined a rehearsal for the evacuation by bicycle; it went smoothly.

The school was thus prepared when in the summer of 1939 war threatened again. The only uncertainty was about the number of boys who would be evacuated. As the crisis intensified, the school issued instructions to those boys whose parents had subscribed to the evacuation scheme to cycle out to Crowthorne early on 1st September. Hugh and I did so, carrying with us enough provisions to keep going for a short while until our belongings could be sent to us. About half way on our journey, when we paused at a road-side café for refreshment, we heard on the radio that Germany had started to invade Poland. We were apparently among about 150 boys who cycled out on that day. By late October, some 570 Paulines had assembled in the Crowthorne. I seem to remember that just before the war the school had about 800 boys in Hammersmith. Certainly not everybody moved out to Wellington or

Crowthorne.

On arriving in Crowthorne on 1st September, as directed, we reported immediately to the billeting office. We were very fortunate to be allocated to the home of Mr. and Mrs. Lightfoot, who owned Lightfoot's Garage, a local filling station.[26] Mrs. Lightfoot at once gave us a warm welcome. She asked us what our first names were. There was no problem for Hugh to answer but for me this normally simple question was problematic that day. The answer "Ulrich," a difficult name for an English tongue, would at once have given me away as somebody who automatically would become an enemy alien the moment Britain declared war on Germany, as happened on 3rd September. So I quickly adapted my second forename, Franz, by anglicizing it to Frank.

To prepare the school for term everybody lent a hand digging trenches for the latrines. The Chaplain led a party of boys to convert the stored timber into classroom furniture and bicycle stands. Others did the plumbing, carpentry and painting needed in the old Wellington laboratories. A third group set about to cultivate the rented field (at £15 p.a.) to plant potatoes for us hungry boys. Later we added hens and pigs to a little farm. Our uniform was adjusted to suit the daily bike rides; black jackets and trousers, and bowler hats for senior boys would not have done. Corduroys, sports jacket, a cap and, when needed, a rain cape fitted the new situation better. The initial confusion around the bicycle stands was solved when a senior boy complained to the Headmaster about it. The boy was promptly given responsibility to organize supervision, to arrange lessons for those who could not ride, and above all allocate prescribed routes so to avoid annoyances to local farmers. In the Ballroom, renamed The Hall, school started at 9:30 a.m. with prayers that were said in Latin or Old English, many dating back to before the Reformation. This was followed by readings from the Bible or some other sources from English literature and singing of English hymns before making our way to classes. Lunch break stretched over one and a half hours so that we could cycle back to our various lodgings, which gave us plenty of exercise and fresh air and easily made up for the lack of the ample sports facilities we had earlier enjoyed but left behind. In due course, some parents commented that we looked very healthy and showed more self-reliance.

On the 17th September, Soviet troops invaded Eastern Poland and Hitler entered into a non-aggression treaty with Stalin's Russia. But for me that day is memorable because I had to appear before an Alien Tribunal.[27] These tribunals "were appointed by the government to investigate the case of each refugee and to decide whether he should be interned, or classified as a refugee from Nazi oppression and freed from the restrictions placed upon 'enemy aliens'."[28] I cycled some twelve miles over to Reading, found the tribunal very understanding, and was classified as a refugee from Nazi oppression. In the jargon of the time, I became a "friendly enemy alien." But generally I was very unhappy about the position of German refugees, as a letter I wrote to the *London Times*, published on 18th September 1939, shows. It appeared anonymously under the heading:

REFUGEES, A YOUNG MAN'S PLEA. [29]

Sir, As a young German refugee just of military age who has been at an English public school for over three years, the regulations concerning 'enemy aliens' came to me as a great blow. Once more, with the declaration of war, I, like many others was confronted with the refugee question.

As the Master of St. Paul's has pointed out in your columns, it is possible to this country under the age of 16 to acquire an English background much as the children of English parents do. I am certain I am one of the many who not only regard this country as theirs, but consider discrimination against them, or any special treatment, as a setback to their earnest endeavours to become good Englishmen. The process of assimilation ought to be recognized by the Government, which had time to consider the question in all its aspects. Young refugees who have been educated in this country desire to share the burden – as well as the privileges – of British citizenship, and a generous gesture, such as their naturalization after a period of years, would be a great encouragement to them. I feel assured that all those of my age will be glad to serve King and Country in any way they can, answering the call when it comes in exactly the same manner as their British-born friends.

Among the general public there is, as is perfectly understandable, little appreciation of the intricacies of the position of refugees. There is little realization among them that the war is ours in two ways, and not only in one, as in our case. We shall sacrifice our lives if necessary in the struggle to uphold Western Civilization, remembering the inhuman suffering of those who are so dear to us.

Yours faithfully

A YOUNG GERMAN REFUGEE

I understood how difficult it was for British people, with their settled history, to appreciate that a German Jewish refugee no longer could consider himself to be German in any meaningful sense. At this stage, the authorities adopted a reasonable approach. The Tribunals were appointed to interview refugees and to put them into one of three categories. Those in 'A' were to be interned; those in 'B' escaped internment, but were to be restricted in their movements; and those in

'C' were recognized as victims of Nazi oppression and could remain at liberty, with minimal restrictions. The vast majority of German Jews or non-Aryan refugees, including my parents and me, were placed in category 'C'.

On returning from my excursion to Reading, I told Mrs. Lightfoot my story. By that time, she had come to know me and we had formed a good relationship. She was very sympathetic to my situation. Soon after, my mother was able to visit and the two ladies got on very well with each other as they also shared experience as landladies. After I left her home, Mrs. Lightfoot wrote regular letters to me full of warmth and genuine interest in the happenings in my life. She always thought I would become a Professor. She kept the other boarders and me informed of each other and wrote about "the sorry plight of evacuees from London who were bombed out and their difficulties to find new lodgings." She inquired about my parents, also referring to the terrible fate of "their people in Germany," and was glad when my parents had moved out of London. In a restrained way, she also mentioned their own business difficulties because of petrol rationing and when private cars had been taken off the roads as a measure to save petrol.

I felt that it would do me good to have some experience as a house prefect and, after a term, I moved out of the Lightfoot's home in January 1940 to join Mr. and Mrs. Monk-Jones at Green Hedges, a house for fifteen boys. I learned a lot from Arnold Monk-Jones about educational questions,[30] such as handling discipline problems that arose with the boys at the house. His attitude was humane, patient, and understanding without being complacent. He was a just man. His wife, a nurse was most helpful too, and I was delighted later to be able talk to her at meetings of the Council of the Association of University Teachers at the Home University Conference of 1963. At this conference the University extension was discussed and the thorny subject of the balance between administration, teaching, and research was debated.[31] Mrs. Monk-Jones represented the London Medical Schools and I was a delegate of the University of Exeter. I am thankful for the warmth I received from my hosts during these two terms.

Philip Whitting, my history master in Hammersmith, stayed behind in London with the fire-fighting services.[32] He was enlisted to help protect St. Paul's Cathedral, which won him the George Medal that King George VI instituted in 1940. Later he served in the Royal Air Force. I was taught well by his replacement, a younger man, Leslie Herne, whom I was to meet later on while I was serving as a member of the Pioneer Corps; as a conscientious objector he had joined the Non-Combatant Corps.[33]

Eynon Smith, our much venerated master, was killed at the beginning of March 1944 during a London air raid by a V1, the infamous Weapon of Retaliation (*Vergeltungswaffe).* W. F. Oakeshott wrote to the *London Times*:[34]

> The younger generation of Paulines will greatly regret to hear of the death of Mr. Eynon Smith, who had been a master at St. Paul's for 19 years. Form Modern Special was pre-eminently his creation, and to his insistence on the need for clarity of thought and intellectual honesty, and his shrewd, often professional, analysis of psychological difficulties many boys owed a balanced mind that they would not otherwise have acquired. It is partly because of his own shyness, and his determination to overcome it, that he was able to help many boys so much. Mr. Eynon Smith was 42.

I found the atmosphere in Crowthorne more congenial than in Hammersmith, but for some of the older boys it seemed too informal. One of them complained on 12th June, after the fall of France, because the High Master went twenty minutes overtime discussing Thucydides' "Melian Dialogue" and whether this justified Hitler or whether we had right on our side in this war.[35] At another time, the High Master, and on his own expense, took some of us on an excursion to see the illuminated Winchester Bible and had tea with us. Relations with the Masters were more relaxed and natural, without sacrificing any of the respect we had for them. Perhaps as the architect of the evacuation scheme, and the one who implemented it, Oakeshott made the most important contribution to this success. To the range of problems that confronted him, he gave vent in October 1940 in a letter to his wife Noel:

> There are a good many things on one's mind just now, what with [sister] Maggie's overdraft and the Governors trying to insist that I should put a number of the servants (who've been with us twenty years or so) on half pay, and cases of chicken pox that Longdon [a teacher] is fussing about (naturally, I suppose), and a representative of the Country Gentlemen's Association coming to make trouble about the Mansion, and parents writing to say that their boys are living in unsanitary conditions (something in it sometimes) – not to speak of the failure of 140 parents to pay billeting-fees – and all this makes a highly complex situation in the midst of which I'm expected to decide the rights and wrongs of Mr. Swain's row with the photographic society, to teach people Tacitus and to drop on boys for poaching rabbits . . . I am amazed by enjoying it all prodigiously.

A lot of his energy was spent on diplomacy. Nevertheless, in the winter 1940-41 he found time to write a narrative of the English maritime and overseas enterprises during 1550-1616: *Founded upon the Sea*, which was much appreciated and widely read.[36] Surprisingly, the positive reviews did not mention that his writing could easily have been chauvinistic, yet on the contrary it reflected a great achievement of Western civilization. In it Oakeshott discussed Raleigh's splendid 'prospectus' to plant a colony in Virginia and showed that the Pocahontas story had a French, German, and Latin edition. The seamen's calendars and astronomical tables were printed in Germany or Italy. The difference was only that with the English the seamen's achievement became part of the British national tradition, while on the continent countries were getting involved in the Thirty Years War.

Amidst all these activities, Oakeshott always remained calm, never raised his voice and stayed very approachable. One could talk to him freely while cycling to school, which he did regularly in all weathers, quite deliberately, I think, to stay in touch. I certainly felt that there was something special about him. This was not due to his status, because – perhaps unfairly – I had not been that much impressed by his predecessor John Bell, who looked at the ceiling when he taught our class. There was a certain excitement about Oakeshott's teaching. He fostered analytical thinking supported through discussion. Moreover, he added intellectual stimulation from outside the school's walls by having visiting speakers. William Temple, then Archbishop of York, and C. S. Lewis, Fellow of Mary Magdalene College in Oxford known mostly for his Christian writing, came to preach at morning prayers. T. S. Eliot, the famous poet and critic,[37] Harold Laski, a brilliant political scientist and Labour Member of Parliament, and Rudolf Wittkower, a German-British art-historian, talked to select groups. Clearly Oakeshott was interested in the development of his charges and always attempted to encourage without trying to push anyone in a particular direction. I also felt I could rely on him. Whenever I contacted him, he responded promptly. I made several attempts to secure an award at Oxford and Cambridge, but, unlike most of my classmates, I did not succeed. Therefore, I decided to leave school at Easter 1940 and, to attempt to secure an appointment as a junior master at a preparatory school. Oakeshott was kind enough to give me a favourable testimonial on 18th April 1940 showing how much care he took over his school-boys and how well informed he was about them:

> U. F. J. Eyck has bccn at this school since May 1936 and has held a scholarship at it. He is the son of a distinguished historian from Germany, and the line in which he has specialized here has been history. Many of us expected him to secure some award in history either at Oxford or Cambridge, and we have been disappointed that he failed to do so. Certainly his work has come very near scholarship standard. He is keen and industrious, and what he does, he does do thoroughly.
>
> He can be most warmly recommended. His manner is pleasant and confident without being over confidant. Those who have had to do with him here liked him, and there is no doubt that he would be liked by his colleagues wherever he went. He is deeply interested in things English, and it is probable that one of the factors which told against his securing a scholarship was the effect which the experiences of his upbringing in Nazi Germany had on him. He will be a loyal citizen of this country and provides one of those many examples of the loss which Germany has sustained through its racial policy.

I kept in touch with Oakeshott after leaving school and occasionally met him on visits to Crowthorne. One conversation with him later on in the war remains vivid in my mind. As an army education instructor, I had to lecture on the Beveridge Report of 1942, which recommended a social system that attempted cradle-to-grave protection for its citizens.[38] I suppose, in Oakeshott's opinion I was somewhat too uncritically enthusiastic about it. Although the Beveridge Report drew on Oakeshott's pre-war examinations of unemployment and his involvement in the report *Men Without Work*, he was – rightly – keen to develop my critical judgment. He only raised some questions about the Beveridge Report without attempting to convince me one way or another; he just wanted me to give further thought to the problems involved. The excellent biography by John Dancy, in fact, states that "by 1948 Oakeshott had distanced himself at least from the naïve forms of idealism" and presumably he felt I was being somewhat simplistic in my attitude to the question of social reform.

Oakeshott did not "show off" to the boys. He had no need to do so. I knew about some of his wide interests. He served on the Board of the Mercers Company. Under the chairmanship of Sir Cecil Clement, Oakeshott found the encouragement and support for his planning and strengthening of the school for wartime survival and postwar growth. He suggested a wider opening of societal doors to make it more democratic, to serve a larger spectrum of talented boys, so that those who thought with their hands would also have access to higher education. He proposed to attach a preparatory school to St. Paul's through financial help to the parents obtained from the London City Council.[39] He spoke about "the social cleavage in education" doing "at least as much harm to the boys from the comparatively sheltered and well-to-do home as to the boy who does not share these apparent advantages."[40] Social reforms remained of deep concern to him.

In a letter to the *London Times* in 1940, never doubting that Britain would win the war, he argues against imposing excessive sanctions on a defeated Germany, lest it might lead to unemployment in the victorious country. He must have had in mind that the excessive reparation demands of the

French after the First World War caused loss of work and unemployment in that country. With the present war intensifying, he felt disconcerted that he was living in Crowthorne as in an oasis, in a reserved occupation, among boys. He would read to them at prayers from Drake or quote Milton "I cannot praise the fugitive and cloistered virtue." Many of the young men he instructed would go off to serve, some of them to their death, leaving him to write consoling letters, to take his turn at roof-top watch in London, and to sit on Admiralty interview boards. In a report to his Governors he describes the two attitudes the boys took to the war:

> There are those who are deeply interested by the technical developments of war and who read all that there is to be read about new weapons, new methods, and the lessons of campaigns already fought; and there are those who regard all this as a necessary evil and look forward to the post-war world and its problems as the thing which should be their main concern . . . There is much to be said for both.

In a more personal reflection on war, he thought it a mistake to think about it as a dilemma: to either glorify war in the way of the Nazis, or go to the other extreme to confess to pacifist solution. In his job as a teacher of young boys neither was acceptable to him.

> If they left school at age 18 and had gone to serve, life would be intolerable for them had they been taught that war was wrong in all circumstances; that it was uninteresting, and destructive of all good qualities in man's nature. It may mean some of it, but it means too the emergence of other qualities . . . It may be that I glorified war too much (I do sometimes find it most desperately interesting). If so, I've made a bungle.[41]

His contact with the Admiralty, after they wisely refused his joining commando raids, brought him on merchant convoys as an observer in order to write a pamphlet for the Ministry of War Transport. Having done work on unemployment and with it on working conditions, he concentrated on the seamen and compared the Norwegian and American ships to the British. He called for rising of standards of accommodation and wages in British ships, adding "some British ships are among the slums of the merchant fleets in the amenities they provide for seamen, and there is some justification in the allegation that this represents not chance, but policy." Needless to say, the report was unacceptable and never published.

I knew about Oakeshott's friendship with Archbishop William Temple, and about his work for youth movements, so long as these could be kept out of misuse for political purposes, such as in Nazi Germany with the compulsory Hitler Youth and Labor Camps, *Hitlerjugend* and *Reichsarbeitsdienst*. The latter was originally designed as a voluntary service to cope with unemployment, dating back to ideas in the late 1920s established in Germany under the Chancellorship of Heinrich Brüning.[42] Oakeshott's proposal for a kind of compulsory youth service involved him in a distressing controversy that brought him to the absurd accusation of supporting Fascism when attending a Conservative Party Committee in 1942. There had been long discussions about the wording of the report. In the public opinion at the time, "compulsion" had a strong affiliation with dictatorship that made it unacceptable, whereas in education it was known as a rudimentary principle and common fact.[43] It is noteworthy, too, that a man who was so critical of Conservative social policy in the pre-war period was prepared to serve on a committee of that party. As a pragmatist, he was ready to work with any political party or grouping that might advance the social objectives he regarded as desirable.[44] Feeling deeply offended and getting away from "all this nonsense of Fascism" he concentrated more on his work on the illuminated Winchester Bible which he had started in 1939. It brought him in contact with scholars in the field and allowed him to publish the small but trailblazing volume *Artists of the Winchester Bible* in 1943.

Without necessarily belonging to any congregation or denomination, he regarded himself as a "convinced Christian." One side of him that I did not see was his ability as a homilist. As a Jew, I missed his sermons, which not surprisingly for a man of his intellectual range, wide reading, deep thought and magnificent style were quite exceptional.

Reading the Dancy biography, one is saddened to learn that somebody who had so much to give both to the individuals with whom he came into contact and to society in general was given to bouts of depression. He was plagued at times by self-doubt. Oakeshott, who was conciliatory in judging others, clearly applied a too critical standard to himself. These self-doubts came through as a remarkable humility, which warmed his relationship with his schoolboys, who were growing up in an uncertain world. It did not prevent him from being unusually effective in the high posts he had held: that of Head Master of Winchester from 1946 to 1954 and of Rector of Lincoln College, Oxford, from 1954 to 1972, together with that of Vice-chancellor of the University from 1962 to 1964. He was, in the variety of his pursuits, a true Renaissance man. He made important bibliographical discoveries, such as that of the somewhat forgotten manuscript of Sir Thomas Mallory's *Morte D'Arthur* which he found hidden in the Fellows' Library at Winchester College pre-dating Caxton's printed edition of 1485.

The wide range of his stimulating writings and his contribution to society were marked by two significant honors. In 1971, he was elected to a fellowship of the British Academy and, late in life, a knighthood was bestowed on him in 1980.

He died in1987. I am sure that I am only one of many who think of Walter Oakeshott with affection and gratitude.

Over the years I stayed in contact with the school enjoying the "News of the Old Paulines." I met Walter Oakeshott during my fellowship at St. Antony's College 1956 to 1958 and as a senior fellow 1972 to 1973 in Oxford when I was on sabbatical. On our visit to London in 2002, I gave a talk at the school to a lively class about my memories on life at St. Paul's and my experience during the war.[45] By then the school had long moved out to Barnes, near London. My wife and I were both impressed by the excellent academic atmosphere at the school, and by the relaxed demeanor and interchange between boys and masters. Compared to the more formal terms that had prevailed at Hammersmith, the ease with which student and teacher would interact was refreshing. The facilities for music and art are first class – and there is the chapel as of old. Like everything in the building, the Walker Library is welcoming as the staff is friendly and helpful; for some reason I had felt inhibited entering the Walker Library in Hammersmith.

There is also now a period in which the boys attend meetings of their choice. The sighting of the school, surrounded by ample playing fields, close to the Thames with easy access to rowing boats is superb.

Although I had an offer to enter the University of London after finishing my education at St. Paul's, it became necessary for me to earn my own living. I applied for a teaching job for which I had the support from Oakeshott and Gooch. It afforded quite some paperwork at the Home Office. [46] The Headmaster of the school wrote to me on 23rd April:

I have today been in touch with the Police here and

I am informed that if you take this letter to your Local Employment Exchange they will give the necessary permit to take up your post here on my staff next week.

Dear Sir,

I shall be glad if you will kindly authorized U. F. J. Eyck to come to Norfolk House next week as a member of my teaching staff

Yours truly,

C. M. Glover, M.A., LL.B.I.

On 26th April I called at the Edgware Rd. Labour Exchange and my case was referred to the Home Office. I also called at the Ministry of Labour where my request was referred to the HO. On the 30th April the document reads:

[the] Department has no obj[ection] to alien's appointment to the teaching staff of Norfolk House Prep. School. Beaconsfield. Signed

And on 6th May it reads: T.R.C.

Support app[roved] no action necessary, signed

At the Jewish Refugee Committee, E. N.Cooper on 2nd May wrote:

I am enclosing a letter addressed to Ulrich Eyck by Mr. C. M.Glover Headmaster of Norfolk House

School Beaconsfield, Bucks. He is anxious to engage Ulrich Eyck to teach French and one or two kindred subjects. As a matter of fact I have seen a letter written by Mr. Glover to Eyck himself in the most glowing terms and he is obviously most anxious to have him as a member of his staff. He will pay him £90 per annum plus board Lodging and Laundry during term time. Ulrich Eyck came here as a student and has been educated at St.Paul's for the last 4 years. Prior to that, he was at the French Gymnasium in Berlin, so his knowledge of French is very complete.

The Labour Exchange, on production of the attached letter, would not give the necessary permit because they say, quite rightly, that as he was a student he must have a Home Office permit.

Mr. Glover wants Eyck to start on Friday, May 3rd, so I do hope you will be able to authorize a permit right away.

On the 9th May I received a letter at my parents' home at 65 Greencroft Gdns, N.W.6:

Sir,

With reference to your call at the Department on the 26th ultimo, I am directed by the Secretary of State to say that he does not desire to raise objection to your appointment to the teaching staff of the Norfolk House Preparatory School, Beaconsfield.

I am Sir, Your obedient Servant.

I was offered and accepted the position as a junior master in the Preparatory School at Norfolk House in the summer term of 1940. In the pleasant rural setting, I enjoyed teaching the lively boys who in turn helped me when I had to supervise English games I had not experienced myself.

However, my life there was rudely ended as part of the Government's action when the police arrested me on 4th June 1940 and I was transported to the Isle of Man for internment.

Endnotes

1 Chamber's Encyklopædia, vol. III, p. 722f.

2 Kurt and Gretel Hübschmann, renamed Hutton during the war. From 1957 on they covered the Aldenburgh Festival. After the war, their son Peter and his family emigrated to live in Australia, see Frank Eyck papers.

3 Stephan Lorant, *I was Hitler's Prisoner*, (London: Victor Gollancz 1934/35). Manfred Durazak, *Die Deutsche Exilliteratur 1933-1945*. (Stuttgart: Philip Reclam jun. 1993), pp. 139, 557.

4 Fritz Adam died in 1936 disillusioned and unable to find a new use for his skills.

5 Frank Eyck papers, Worcester College Record, Oxford 1995, p. 70.

6 Ibid, p. 71.

7 Dictionary of National Biography 1901-1960, pp. 392ff.

8 Frank Eyck papers, Lady Gladstone to Frank Eyck, 5th November 1968.

9 Over the years many personal stories are reported in the Leo Baeck Year Books. Monika Richarz, *Jüdisches Leben in Deutschland 1918-1945*, (Stuttgart: Deutscher Verlagsanstalt, 1982). Mark M. Anderson, ed., *Hitler's exiles: personal stories of the flight from Nazi Germany and Austria,* in Central European History, (New York: The New York Press, 1998), vol. XIV, pp.354.

10 Werner Rosenstock after 1941 became the 1st Secretary of the Association of Jewish Refugees, Information letter (AJR) renamed in 1946 AJR journal, which still publishes today.

11 At that time 1 Pound = 13 Reichsmark.

12 Frank Eyck papers, Hans Eyck letter to the family from Shanghai, 24th January 1941.

13 Kultur Chronic 2, 2001, pp. 9-10.

14 Frank Eyck papers, Günther Eyck to Frank Eyck, 2nd March 2005.

15 I received this information from my cousin Vera Rosenheim née Eyck of Corpus Christi, Texas. She has her own story of survival; there are in the Frank Eyck papers two CDs recording an interview on 11th March 2007 by Helen Wilk, who worked for the Jewish Historical Society of Southern Texas. Well in her

nineties she still volunteers on week ends at the local hospital, and works as treasurer at the local temple; she sadly passed away age 97 on 6th May 2008.

16 Dr. Hilde Maas became a friend; she often worked together with Anna Freud.

17 Erich and Frank Eyck papers.

18 Frank Eyck papers, correspondence with Philip Whitting. The £33 scholarship of 1936 would be equivalent to £3000 in 2008 A.D.

19 Frank Eyck papers, Karl Leyser to F. Eyck, 3rd June 1986. Frank Eyck to Karl Leyser, 25th June 1986, and 12th August 1991. K. Leyser to Frank Eyck, 29th August 1991. F. Eyck to K. Leyser, 15th September 1991 18th December 1991.

20 Ernst Hanfstängl, *The Missing Years*, (London: Eyre & Spottiswood, 1957). *Zwischen Weißem und Braunem Haus: Memoiren eines politischen Außenseiters*, (München: Piper Verlag, 1970). Egon Hanftängl, *Erinnerungen von Egon Hanfstängl*, in his private papers (München).

21 Lothar Machtan, *The Hidden Hitler*, (New York: Division of the Perseus Book Group, 2001).

22 Frank Eyck papers, Gerd Fränkel to Frank (Ullo) Eyck, 8th May, 20th August, and 1st October 1939.

23 I owe this information to Inge Rosenberg, who was so kind to let me have some correspondence of the Groß Breesen students. Gert Fränkel tried to be naturalized but, there was no interest of the British authority to do so, in fact he talks about rising anti-Semitism in Kenya. He continued working on the farm but, after the war worked in the pharmaceutical wholesale trade in Nairobi, married in 1951 (*'holte sich eine Frau aus Berlin'*). He has one daughter and returned in 1973 to live in Berlin.

24 John Dancy, *Walter Oakeshott, A Diversity of Gifts*, (London: Michael Russell 1988), p. 92-139.

25 Ibid, p. 88 ff.

26 Frank Eyck papers, Lightfoot letters 8th May 1940 to 8th January 1948.

27 Home Office Document, HO 405/12352 258266, Tribunal 26th October 1939: Whether exempt from Article 6(a) and 9(a): Yes. Whether desired to be repatriated: No.

28 Norman Bentwich, *I understand the Risks. The story of the refugees from Nazi oppression who fought in the British Forces in WWII*, (London: Victor Gollancz, London 1960).

29 Frank Eyck Papers, *London Times*, 18th Sept 1939.

30 Frank Eyck papers, Arnold Monk-Jones, 21st April 1940, 29th January 1963, Mrs. Monk-Jones, 4th December 1964, after her husband's death.

31 Report of the Home University Conference 1963, excerpt in Frank Eyck papers.

32 Frank Eyck papers, Philip Whitting letters to Frank. He was always encouraging me, particularly when I served in the Pioneer Corps. During his retirement he specialized in Byzantine history and assembled a substantial numismatic collection of that period. He gave lectures in schools and adult education centers. He died in 1986.

33 Frank Eyck papers; also Old Pauline Notes, the Staff 1953, p. 95.

34 Frank Eyck papers, W. Oakeshott's short obituary on Eynon Smith, in *London Times*, 1944.

35 John Dancy, *Walter Oakeshott*, pp. 92-139.

36 Walter F. Oakeshott, *Founded upon the Sea*, CUP 1942.

37 T. S. Eliot, *Idea of a Christian Society*, 1939; Chambers Encyclopedia vol. V, p 142 ff.

38 Beveridge Report of November 1942 presented to Parliament by Command of His Majesty, HMSO, CMND 6404, recommending a society system that attempted a cradle-to-grave protection for its citizens. Many of these ideas were adopted in the first post war Labour Government.

39 John Dancy, *Walter Oakeschott*, p. 122.

40 Ibid, p. 112.

41 Ibid, pp. 124, 126, 129.

42 Brüning, Chancellor of the Weimar Republic, at the time of high unemployment authorized on 5th June 1931 the creation of a voluntary national service called *Freiwilliger Arbeitsdienst* (FAD). In 1934, Hitler gave orders to make it, as RAD, compulsory and used it to indoctrinate Nazi ideas, which gave it a bad name; see Jason Pipes, *Reichsarbeitsdienst*, 1995.

43 John Dancy, *Walter Oakeshott*, p. 119.

44 Ibid, pp. 106, 111, 113.

45 Old Pauline News 2002, p. 11, also 2005, p.34.

46 The National Archives, Kew, London, kindly copied for me seven documents referring to my first employment. HO 405/12352 258266.

Chapter 3

CHAPTER 4
Isle of Man 1940

AFTER THE GERMAN OCCUPATION OF THE Low Countries, as well as Denmark and Norway, even people officially recognized as "victims of Nazi oppression" were no longer safe from internment.[1] There were widespread rumors, later clearly disproved, that Holland had a fifth column.[2] But Viskun Quisling in Norway,[3] a Nazi leader, had betrayed his own country. As England had given shelter to approximately 75 000 aliens, mainly refugees from Germany and Austria, there was fear in Britain that they included active supporters for Nazi Germany or German fifth columnists.

Although support for appeasement had not suddenly disappeared by September 1939, fringe political peace groups were carefully watched as they still favored a settlement with Hitler.[4] But after Hitler broke the Munich Agreement with the invasion of Czechoslovakia, Prime Minister Chamberlain and Foreign Minister Lord Halifax realized that the appeasement policy had failed. Hitler simply could not be trusted. Suspicions also pointed to a few private individuals of high standing in British society – both those who sympathized with Hitler and those who viewed Russian communism too favorably. The government felt uneasy about such possible threats.

Early in 1939, the Defence of the Realm Act was drafted. It allowed the indiscriminate internment of questionable people, on the premise that they might be harmful to the country. The Defence of the Realm Regulation 18 Code A allowed the implementation of internment during peace time, but if war were to break out, and the Defence of the Realm 18 Code B allowed, by the order of Council, detention without trial of anybody, including foreigners. Selective internment had already taken place in the autumn and winter of 1939. On May 23rd, it led to the imprisonment in Brixton Prison in South London of Sir Oswald Mosley, leader of the British Union of Fascists, BUF, and of his wife Lady Diana in Holloway, the prison for women.[5] In 1918, Mosley had started his career as a Conservative MP, became independent after, then joined the Labour Party in 1924. He later started his own party, the BUF, far to the right of the Conservatives. In its prime, the BUF had some 20 000 members. Mosley, a nationalist, visualized himself leading a corporate state. As an anti-Semitic, he had strong personal and political affiliation with Hitler and Mussolini. In 1936, Sir Oswald's married Lady Diana with Hitler and Joseph Goebbels present – in fact it was a private ceremony held in Goebbels' living room. Before the war, Mosley had published a plan to co-operate with a victorious Germany in case Britain was conquered. However, after hostilities between Britain and Germany started, he strongly advised his followers not to do anything that might harm Britain. In due course, his party officials and members, as well as collaborators and general sympathizers of his ideas, were detained. On May 25th, his party was declared illegal, and within the following days all of the party's publications were prohibited.[6]

William Joyce, who was more politically extreme, had already moved himself to Germany at the start of the war. There, he carried on treasonable activities through a clandestine shortwave radio station where he transmitted Nazi propaganda from somewhere north of Berlin, pretending to broadcast from Scotland. His programme was popular, even if not taken seriously, partly because of its obvious bias.[7]

Pacifist and other peaceful movements were closely watched by MI5. These included the Quakers, the right wing non-political Peace Pledge Union, PPU with its 136 000 members, and the appeasement faction of the conservative party and the Communist Party of Great Britain. Yet nothing discriminating could be found or even assumed through any of their activities.[8]

When Chamberlain resigned, King George VI appointed Winston Churchill Prime Minister on 10th May 1940 to form the Wartime Coalition Government. In addition, Churchill took over the Ministry of Defence. He assigned the position of Foreign Secretary to Anthony Eden and put his friend Lord Beaverbrook in charge of the Ministry of Aircraft Production. Lord Halifax stayed in the Foreign Office; Sir James Griggs became Under-Secretary in the War Office. Ernest Bevin became Minister of Labour, Clement Attlee the Lord Privy Seal. Sir Stafford Cripps was appointed Speaker of the House of Commons, but soon after was sent as ambassador to Moscow.

On 13th May 1940, Churchill gave his first speech in the House of Commons, warning that he had nothing to offer but a fight that would cost "blood, toil, tears, and sweat." At a time when Britain's situation looked grim, Churchill instilled hope with convincing exuberance through his proclaimation on 19th May: "Conquer we must, conquer we will." At the time, the British attempt to keep a foothold on the European Continent had failed. The retreat from Dunkirk, on 29th May, ended with a great loss of life and as well as a loss of much of the military equipment. German guns fired across the Channel, and German fighter planes were seeking air supremacy. An invasion of the British mainland seemed imminent; Hitler had ordered and planned an invasion under the code name of Operation Sealion to commence on 15th August, 1940.[9] On 4th June, Churchill rendered his most famous speech:

> We shall fight on the beaches, we shall fight on the
> landing grounds, we shall fight in the fields and the
> streets, and we shall fight in the hills. We shall never
> surrender! [10]

In truth, Britain was ill equipped and utterly unprepared for war. Britain also stood alone: Russia was still allied to Germany after Hitler and Stalin had divided Poland between them, and the United States of America was still neutral at this part of the war.

It is not surprising then, particularly during the spring of 1940, that panic, fear, suspicion, and general mistrust of foreigners – sometimes mixed with a certain amount of anti-Semitism – tended to get out of control. An intensive search for subversion or participation in anything that looked like a fifth column started with renewed impetus, culminating in a call for indiscriminate internment. The notion of internment was reflected by part of the press and some British authorities; however, the main support for internment came from the security service, with its intelligence arm, MI5.[11] There were two incidents that sparked the MI5 to lead what was thought to be the discovery of a wide field of adversaries against Britain. The first was a cipher clerk, a US citizen named Tyler Kent, who the MI5 had found passing the American code and other information to a foreign country from the US Embassy in London. Another was Anna Wolkoff, a woman of Russian origin, as well as Captain A. H. M. Ramsey – both were found working with Kent.[12] Having part of the public opinion on their side, the MI5 put enormous pressure on the British Government to take action. Home Secretary Lord Anderson, though skeptical about further findings, nevertheless for reasons of political expediency finally gave way: the Emergency Power (Defence) Act 18 B (1A) became law.[13] This allowed for the arrest of anyone that could be argued likely to "endanger the safety of the realm" without trial.[14] Churchill, although also skeptical, agreed to the move and told the House of Commons on 4th June:

> There is, however, a class, for which I have not the slightest sympathy. Parliament has given us the power to put down Fifth Column activists with a strong hand, and we shall uses those powers, subject to supervision and correction of the House without the slightest hesitation until we are satisfied . . . that the malignancy in our midst has been effectively stamped out.[15]

This measure was directed against the refugees, and affected people between 16 to 60 years of age. It gave the British government a power that, by its definition, was equal to that of a totalitarian state's exercise. Initially, Anderson aimed to detain some forty-five people, but soon this number escalated to 2000 detainees. Additionally, planned internment of enemy aliens amounted to 567 people, but by October, this number had grown to 30 000 men, women, and children.[16] It no longer mattered which refugee status one had been given by the tribunals: people assigned category 'A', 'B', or 'C' were all regarded as enemy aliens. Both the soldiers and the police in charge of executing these orders were poorly briefed. Everyone foreign was considered to be a threat. This policy remains a dark chapter in British history.[17]

Although the relevant documents of the National Archive in Kew have been opened to the public since 2000, the record of the camps themselves are practically impossible to find.[18] In the chaotic situation of quickly interning foreigners, documents were deliberately or accidentally destroyed, or simply lost.

From the end of May, Austrian and German refugees, as well as other foreigners stranded in Britain at the beginning of the war, were indiscriminately interned. After Italy declared war on 10th June, indiscriminate internment also affected Britain's resident Italians and Anglo-Italians. Most of them had lived in Britain for many years, working mainly in Soho, London, in the culinary industry. A few were third generation residents. The internment camps were hastily made, and the facilities were badly overcrowded and often inadequate. The camps were scattered all over the British Isles, in prisons, racecourses, condemned buildings, tent-camps, and vacant and dilapidated rat infested cotton mills without plumbing. Almost any building would serve as an internment camp. As a result, out of those interned, the elderly and chronically ill suffered the most.

When I was hastily arrested, I managed to take a few necessary belongings with me. I was then transported to the Military Rock Barracks in Reading,[19] and from there, joined by an ever increasing numbers of internees, arrived at Bury, Lancashire, and placed into a temporary camp in a dilapidated cotton mill.[20] There, I remember I had a strange and disturbing encounter with Nikolaus Pevsner, an art historian who had been a lecturer at the University of Göttingen before he was dismissed by the Nazi regime in 1933.[21] Born in Leipzig, in 1902, he was of Russian Jewish decent, but had converted in 1921 to Lutheran Protestantism. Since the early 1920s he had welcomed Nazi ideas. Even Hitler's *Mein Kampf* could not deflate his enthusiasm for Nazi ideals as he saw the book as only a little piece of irrelevant propaganda. British officials did not know about this when Pevsner arrived on their shores. With a grant to study English architecture in Britain, Pevsner had an easy entry to immigration in 1934. He also obtained a teaching position at the University of Birmingham, while at the same time applying for a job in the German Ministry of Culture.[22] In his field, Pevsner was a thorough and prolific researcher, writer, and teacher. He was naturalized in 1946, and eventually gained a Professorship at the Cambridge, Oxford, and London Universities. In an interview he gave to Francesca Wilson in 1933, his positive views on Hitler were quite apparent:[23]

> I love Germany. It is my country, and in spite of the way I am treated, I want the movement to succeed. There is no alternative [to it] but chaos . . . There is much idealism in the movement much that is puritan and moral . . . Hitler is planning to cure the unemployment problem . . . For fifteen years we have been humiliated by the outside powers. No wonder that Hitler appeals to the youth!

Germany had four victorious wars in the nineteenth century, which had led to Bismarck's foundation of the Empire in 1871. This convinced a wide part of the German population that losing a war was inconceivable. So, after the loss of the First World War, many Germans bore great resentment. They felt that their pride had been deeply hurt; they as a nation had been humiliated. The infamous war guilt clause in the Peace Treaty of Versailles put the blame for the war on Germany. Which added to this sentiment, as did the Reparation Policy. The *Dolchstoßlegende*, or "Stab-in-the-back Legend," a notion that the people at home had sabotaged the German military fighting in the field, was widely believed. The runaway inflation in the early 1920s did not help German morale either. All this had a blinding effect on people's judgement, including on some German Jews. There exists a fine line between the natural love of country, one's motherland, and uncritical nationalism, particularly when it takes politically extreme egotistical forms. A similar distinction exists in the often privately discussed relationship between art and state.[24] On this point, Pevsner was in agreement with Josef Goebbels: both thought art should be subservient to the state. It is not difficult to imagine that on these topics Pevsner and I did not find any common ground.

But it proved to me that the convictions and the political insight of my family and of our circle of friends, the atmosphere in which I grew up, was indeed rare and exceptional. Compared to the overwhelming number of Germans who were led to trust and believe the Nazi ideas while ignoring, not knowing or not wanting to know, anything about the Nazi deeds, I feel deep gratitude for my upbringing. It was particularly painful for me to see somebody of my own persecuted minority fall into this diabolic trap.

Not long after this talk with Pevsner, I was further transported, with many other internees, to the Isle of Man. There, holiday resorts were requisitioned and turned into internment camps, as had happened during the First World War.[25] Additionally, quite a number of internees were transported to Australia and Canada.

In peacetime, the Isle of Man had offered pleasant and popular holiday resorts which provided the Manx's, as the residents of the Island are called, part of their livelihood, while the other part came from agricultural activities. The Manx's enjoyed a quiet, mainly rural life. They were now overwhelmed by refugees and a military presence, which used the area for guarding the internees and for their own training. By August 1940, an estimated 9700 to 10 024 internees were on the Isle of Man. They were of Austrian, British, Italian, Japanese, German, and Turkish descent.[26] Some of these people may have been considered undesirable, but no spy was found among them. Although the Home Office was responsible for their detainment and internment, the transportation and guarding of the internees came under military command.[27] To prevent the diverse groups of internees from fighting amongst each other, gradually care was taken to separate German Jews, usually pro-British, from German and British Fascists, who were pro-German.

Among the internees, there were leading academics and economists, engineers, scientists, and artists.[28] Just to mention some of the more prominent people interned: Alex Alexander, later to be the chairman of Lyons, a British popular food-chain; Hans Krebs, a physiological chemist, discoverer of the Krebs-circle (acetic-acid circle) for which he got the Nobel Price in Medicine; Otto Kahn-Freund, Professor of comparative law; Claus Moser, working in higher administration, patron of the arts and chairman of the Royal Opera House; Professor of Physical Chemistry Michael Polani, who later turned to economics, philosophy, and social science in which he received the Nobel Price; Ronald Grierson later one of the directors of General Electric; Lord Weidenfeld, famous in the publishing world; Charles Forte, founder of an international catering enterprise. In later years, some of these prominent people had knighthood bestowed on them. There was the well-known artist, Kurt Schwitters, and the concert pianists Landauer and Marian Rawicz. There were authors, journalists, and even distinguished chess players; there were musicians later to join well-known orchestras – the Amadeus Quartet originated in one of the internment camps. There were Rabbis, Catholic Priests, and Protestant Pastors among the interned. There were simple folks. All of these diverse and gifted people were placed together in camps across the island.

I spent time behind barbed wire in the Peveril Internment Camp, located in Peel on the West Coast of the Isle, in one of the requisitioned guest-houses at the end of the promenade.[29]

Many of the internees at Peveril were suspected to be Nazi sympathizers. The camp also had a high proportion of detainees. It came under direct supervision of a senior officer of the Royal Army Medical Corps (RAMC). Although Sir Oswald Mosley was widely rumoured and believed to have been on the Isle of Man, he in fact never was.

On the more positive side, in an otherwise disheartening situation, the Peveril camp housed the distinguished Professor Gerhard Bersu and his wife. Both of them were archaeologists. Hitler's measures had dismissed Bersu in 1935 from his position in an important German archaeological centre in Bavaria. Three years later, he was in Wiltshire excavating an Iron Age farmstead. After the beginning of the war, Bersu and his wife were arrested as enemy aliens and interned. Despite this, they obtained a grant and permission to supervise excavations of Celtic roundhouses and a fort. They were both so immersed in their exploratory works that they did not apply for release. Quite oblivious to the happenings in the world, they stayed on the Isle of Man till the end of the war. To anybody involved in their team, the Bersu's "embodied the permanent things of peace."[30]

Because of the nature of camp life, a lot of time was taken up with often needless regimentation all through the day. The camp officer, usually a veteran who could no longer take part in active service, set the rules. The individual houses had their own hierarchy. *Reveille* happened at 7:00 a.m., with a roll call twice a day, punctual meals, and the lights were out by 9:30 p.m. The day's activities included escorted physical exercises, which consisted of walks along barbed wire fences. The lucky ones were escorted to do farm work. Household duties were organized from within the individual house community and shared on a rotating basis. There was cleaning, the collection of daily provisions, and meal preparation. The rationed food was modest, but owing to ample rural produce of the Island, often better than on the mainland. We wore our own civilian clothes. These were primitive living conditions with extreme overcrowding.

The experience of internment was far from pleasant.[31] The living conditions combined with the mindless bureaucracy we experienced made life miserable. The feeling of wretchedness and frustration was never far off in the camps. The more sensitive among us suffered the most. A lot of people felt demoralized and depressed as a result of their internment. Some of the internees went insane; others committed suicide.[32] To further complicate matters, our armed sentries did not know what to make of us, and lacked any understanding or briefing about the difference between the Nazis and the refugees from Nazi oppression. In the camps, one was cut off from news. Our letters were carefully censored, and took an inordinate time to arrive. Any activity outside of the camp was always guarded by the military. There was an intense feeling of powerlessness among the internees. For many years, it was not a time I wanted to talk about. I felt that to intern victims of Nazism in a war against Nazism was a deplorable and senseless act. And I have not changed my mind on this since.[33]

Gradually, this policy came under strong criticism and was modified, though not before the SS Arandora Star en route to Canada with German and Italian internees was sunk on 2nd July 1940. The ship was attacked by a German U-boat and many lives were lost – out of a total of 1200 people only 530 would be saved.[34]

In this situation, there were only two options given to us: either to stay interned or join the British Army. I registered for the latter.[35] The Home Office had issued a White Paper with eighteen elaborate clauses to be answered.[36] My release from internment came on October 8th, 1940. In the release, the note of the Superintendent, Central Register of Aliens, reads:

> The above named alien [Eyck, Ulrich Franz Josef]
> joined the Pioneer Corps on 9.10.40 and is therefore
> exempt from registration as an alien whilst serving
> H. M. Forces.[37]

At that time, as an alien volunteering for the British Army, I was only able to get into the Auxiliary Pioneer Corps, popularly called "the pick and shovel corps." As a group of ex-internees, after signing an order not to talk about our internment either to family members or anybody else, we embarked from the Isle of Man to the mainland. There, we travelled by train to the training centre at Ilfracombe, Devon in the southwest of England.[38] During the transit, in Liverpool, we saw from the press that the indiscriminate internment of German and Austrian refugees from Nazi oppression had incurred strong criticism from a number of prominent British personalities. Letters and articles appeared in the *Times,* the *Manchester Guardian,* the *Spectator* and the *New Statesman and Nation* pleading for the refugees' release.[39] In July, there had been a debate in the House of Commons on the issue. At the end of August, Dr. G. H. A. Bell, the Bishop of Chichester, who had a close and helpful connection with the German Confessing Church, had visited some camps on the Isle of Man. He was noticeably extremely upset, and published a report of his findings. Pastor Franz Hildebrandt describes his visit at Douglas camp:[40]

> We were all drawn up to receive him . . . accompanied
> by Bishop Sodor and Man and the Major of Douglas,
> he [Bishop Bell] could scarce reply to our cheers and
> at first could only stammer.[41] It was an unforgettable
> moment. The sight of these refugees was just too
> much for him.[42]

Bishop Bell commented on the conditions in the camp, stating that some of Hitler's leading antagonists wasted away their time in them. Sadly, 150 of the internees had already been in Nazi concentration camps. He was astounded and dismayed about the great number of qualified men all waiting to work for Britain, for freedom and justice. His report was not well received, particularly not by the authorities, nor the people of the Isle of Man.[43]

In overcoming the shock of internment, I was greatly helped by several letters I received that expressed relief at my release. Among them was one by Walter Oakeshott, High Master of St. Paul's:[44]

> What good news that you are out of that camp at last. There have been the most awful mistakes made. All one can claim is, I think, that there were a few people who lost their heads, and that the general public on the whole kept theirs fairly under control. I have great hopes that the immense potential advantage to be gained from our aliens are now thoroughly embedded in people's mind and that if we have to go through a very difficult time indeed (which we may have to do, and goodness knows it is tough enough already for our friends in London) this notion will persist.

Philip Whitting and G. P. Gooch also came to the conclusion "that our 'friendly aliens' have been abominably treated, owing to a foolish panic."[45]

In the autumn of 1940, I put some of my thoughts about my internment experience together and circulated them. This was a method to both remember and to analyze what had happened – something that became a habit of mine. The first typed iteration of these writings – single spaced and without a margin – gave indication to the growing scarcity of paper at that time. My thoughts of indiscriminate internment are given here in full:[46]

This article is the appeal of a young German refugee who loves this country and is proud to being able to wear the King's uniform. It is addressed to all, to the ministers responsible for the 'aliens' question, the government departments which have to deal with it, and above all, to the humanity and common sense of 'the man in the street'. Recrimination over the past mistakes is useless and harmful, unless a lesson is learnt from them. Surely the time for the formulation of a new policy has come, for a constructive plan which, while preserving for this country its traditional reputation as a place of asylum for refugees, would make available to the national war effort men and women whose past experience qualifies them well for any tasks.

Unfortunately, the real issue in the past has been shirked. With one or two honourable exceptions, official policy had not addressed the internment. This is not to say that up to May 1940, either the officialdom or the public lacked any sympathy for the German and Austrian refugees who came to Britain to find peace. Many of these refugees, notably Germans prosecuted by the Nazis, had faced the horrible experience of imprisonment inside the German concentration camps.

I had been fortunate to go to an English school, and had known England in the leisure of peacetime. The majority of refugees came in 1939, in the months between the Munich agreement and the outbreak of war. After the outbreak of war, their treatment as 'enemy aliens' had unfortunately formed the bulk of their outlook on life in Britain. Only few Englishmen probably considered the feelings of the refugees and their varied experiences. Although we realized that the war would complicate our position, most of us were, nevertheless, glad that the Nazis were being stopped. Many of us did get a fair deal from the tribunals set up at the beginning of the war. Unfortunately, from that time onward, the fact that we could be considered as the most violent enemies of the Nazis anywhere in the world was more or less forgotten.

The fact that we were 'enemy aliens' was increasingly stressed. Employment restrictions were relaxed, and care was taken that these 'aliens' should not come too close into contact with the war machine itself. We were banned from the fighting services, with one exception – the Pioneer Corps. All these policies showed the timidity of the British government. To join a non-combatant unit, with no chance of promotion, was not a very inspiring call. In spite of this, many of us joined the Pioneer Corps, often leaving well-paid jobs behind. But in reality, it was no wonder that the figures were much lower than they would have been had the British government enlisted our help fully.

An important problem had not been addressed: the possibility of refugee soldiers falling into the German hands as prisoners of war. By a stroke of luck, none of the Refugee Pioneers were captured in France, although it had been admitted by the War Office that they fought – and fought well. This is my personal view: if a man is considered reliable enough to fight for a country, he should be given the opportunity of becoming naturalized. The possibility of solving the problem [of citizenship], from the point of view of international law has been conveniently ignored in the various press notices appearing on this subject recently. But it is surely criminal negligence to indicate one's nationality in all army identification papers.

Mr. Morrisson's appointment as Home Secretary, which succeeded Sir John Anderson in the position, was a great improvement for the British internees. But the question of what to do with aliens was only one of many he had to consider; Morrison had to restrict his task from the very outset to a gradual clearance of the internment camps. The practical result of this new policy will be that, in several months, the great majority of the refugees will be released from internment – and perhaps even brought back from the 'prisoners of war' camps in Canada and Australia to which they had been deported. Alas, unless the refugee fell into one of very stingy and arbitrary defined categories – ie that he can prove himself as useful – he had to join the Pioneer Corps or remain interned. The utilitarian principle was thus retained, and the case of an interned refugee is only considered on its own merits if he was not eligible for the Pioneer Corps due to reasons of age or health. Thus a man would then remains a Home Office 'case', and as the Home Office was overwhelmed with work, it was purely luck if a case was dealt with quickly.

The new policy was a really shortant [sic].[47] It was an attempt to secure the benefits of acquiring refugee skill and labour without taking the least notice of the moral aspect of their treatment. The civil servants in the Home Office and the War Office could not be expected to consider the human side of the question, unless the ministers responsible for the policy issue directions of a general nature. The reaction of people concerned – the refugees themselves – was never taken into account. What bewildered them the most was that the many changes in official policy had never been due to their own behaviour. Mr. Osbert Peake, the Under-Secretary at the Home Office, admitted that there were no incidents, and that the refugees lived up to what was expected of them. Surely the provocation for an incident was great enough. Cut off from the outside world, left to fend for themselves, internees were left to guess who was responsible for the prosecution that they were suffering from, at the hand of a supposedly friendly country. Or was the outcry of German concentration camps not genuine? These, and similar questions were bound to be asked by those interned. People, who like me, were not only strongly anti-Nazi, but also very fond of Britain, felt the blow doubly.

There was undoubtedly a change in public opinion. The last

word has not been written about how, and by what methods public feelings against the 'enemy aliens' was worked up. It was never revealed who was responsible for the press campaign, "intern the lot." Powerful forces were at work against us. The British public had a lot of political common sense, so propaganda in our favour would have been effective. All that would have been necessary to do would have been to remind the people that we were the actual victims of the Nazis. We wanted to help the war effort and our records had been carefully checked. In the House of Commons on 10th July, the government spokesperson said that he "wished we knew half as much about neutral aliens and some British subjects as we know about enemy aliens now in this country." Indeed, the various catch phrases about "not being able to take chances," etc., could have been easily and conclusively dealt with in a twenty-five line-advertisement.

Thus, should the government have ever came to the conclusion that it would be advantageous for Britain to use and trust its 'friendly enemy alien' refugees, it would have been essential to enlighten the country about the real issue in question. Furthermore, the malicious and underhanded propaganda which had been going against us could then have been stopped for good. The government could have said that it regretted the mistake, and that in future the refugees would get a fair deal. In the atmosphere of distrust, Britain [could] have reaped the full benefits from the manifold talents of its numerous refugees. There had been some annoyance that the refugees could profit from their foreign status and keep their jobs while British people were called up for war. This was not the fault of the refugees, and the position had actually been reversed.

After the wave of internment, even the objection of a man being in a reserved occupation was swept away in the case of the refugees. The position was that the vast majority of men between the ages of 18 and 50, in so far as they were not 'prisoners of war' and British internees, should have been serving in the Pioneer Corps of the British Army. The one measure which would have convinced all of us that the British Government had decided to trust us and treat us well, would have been an offer of nationalization to all who submitted to the conscription. There were thousands of us stationed all over Britain as members of H. M. Forces. This would have ensured that the refugees could not have escaped any obligation which a British subject incurred. There is absolutely no excuse to leave the parents and wives of refugees interned, 1) unless the intention was to use us as a controlled Labour-Corps similar to what the Nazis were doing with their French prisoners of war.

A word about the official promises given to refugees enlisting in the Pioneer Corps: These were few and none could be called extravagant. Every promise which could have been broken, was broken. Wives of members of the B. E. F [British Exploratory or Expeditionary Force] who fought on the continent had again been put under severe alien's restrictions. 2) Refugees who joined the Pioneer Corps from internment were promised to be able to leave after 3-4 weeks. Instead of this, they frequently had to wait nearly 4-5 months, and never got a leave before three months as this is contrary to Army-Regulations! The result is that many of us had not seen our families for half a year. Having been interned often at a few minute's notice, we had no time to settle our private affairs.

To crown all this, certain aliens' restrictions were being revived for our leave, in spite of the definite statement that our status would be that of a member of His Majesty Forces and not as that of an aliens. 3) The excuses for this last action in particular were weak. All those who still trusted the promises officially given, could not help feeling that somebody – or several people – in one of the government departments concerned, is still obstructing us. The crying need was for a man of humanity and firmness to co-ordinate policy. This man would have to be in a position to be able to make decisions and to advise government departments when they were concerned with the Refugee problem – committees are not enough. A Home Secretary and a Minister of Home Security could not be expected to formulate a clear new policy. Perhaps the tide could then turn in our favour.

However, after my release, I soon found that the government had been concerned for us, and, in nearly every question period some of my questions had found a voice. But according to *Mass Observation*, after a nearly six-hour-long Commons debate about the enemy aliens on 10th July 1940, fifty per cent of MPs still favoured an all out internment. Only twenty-five per cent were in favour of a more discriminating policy towards internees.[48] Part of the King's speech was devoted to the internment policy; Major Victor Cazalet had called it "a bespattered page in our history."[49] He, and many other MPs, argued against the Government's decision. Even if an initial excuse could be made because of Britain's precarious position at the time, the policy was wasteful and unjust. Of the two people who dissented, Mavis Tate stated:

> One only has to say the word Jew and certain members of the House lose all sense of reason. I sympathize with the Jews, but Germany has learnt to make skilful use of them. It is no good saying that because a person is a refugee or a Jew, he may not, nevertheless, be a danger to this country.[50]

By the first week in August, only thirty three per cent of MPs approved of policy to "collar the lot."[51] At the end of July, Churchill had become increasingly skeptical about the existence of a fifth column. Having access to 'ultra' decrypts he was better informed than Morrison.[52] Hidden in the rural setting of Bletchley Park, half way between Oxford and Cambridge, the people of MI5 were working on Enigma – the German secret code. Churchill personally never quite believed in the existence of a fifth column of military importance. In fact, he wrote on November 21ˢᵗ, 1940, to Morrison from Egypt, as the tide was turning in Britain's favor:[53]

> The power of the Executive to cast a man into prison without formulating any charge known to the law, and particularly to deny him the judgement of his peers, is in the highest degree odious and is the foundation of all totalitarian governments whether Nazi or Communist.

In July, Churchill asked Attlee to consider the whole problem of internees. Attlee wrote:

> The situation poses a more far reaching problem. In a war of ideas every effort should be made to enlist on our side all those opposed to the Nazis and use their service to the fullest extent against the common enemy.

Attlee submitted his memorandum on 17th July, and it was discussed in the Cabinet.[54] On 18th July, Lord President of the Council Neville Chamberlain, reported that he had received numerous complaints about conditions in the camps. A consensus emerged that refugees of category 'C' should be released as soon as possible.[55] Given the large number of people involved, and the organizational demands on the Government bureaucracy, only slow progress was made in this regard. Yet, in spite of other pressing questions and decisions concerning the war, the British Parliament and Cabinet frequently discussed the problems regarding internment. Written recommendations and White Papers were passed around, and arguments were made between the various Government Departments and MI5. Implementation involved the Foreign Office under

Lord Halifax, aided by Under-Secretary Sir Edward Griggs, the War Office under Sir Osbert Peake, the Home Office with Sir John Anderson, and later the Minister of Labour Herbert Morrison – as well as their civil-servants, numerous committees, and above all, the CIC's MI5.

When the release for internees started to be organized, each individual case was investigated in numerous committees and subcommittees. Sometimes well-known and trusted German refugees were asked to assist. Dr. Otto Kahn-Freund, Professor of comparative law, and himself a refugee (and for a short time an internee), was asked to assist as chairman of an advisory panel. He offered scrupulous comment on individual applications.[56]

During question period, the refugees' internment was frequently debated, but it was rare that question of the refugees' nationalization came before the House. On 23rd January, Major Wedgwood voiced that in most countries, notably the USA, members of the armed Forces were preferentially nationalized. Morrison declared this could not be done in wartime conditions. Aneurin Bevan avowed on 31st July that people who were prepared to serve Britain, and by doing so risked their lives, were surely particularly desirous to become British citizens. Yet he received the same negative answer as Wedgwood.[57]

My father, fortunately, was saved from the experience of internment. When an official came to my parent's home, my mother was able to prevent my father's internment by showing letters from David Lloyd George and other prominent liberal politicians addressed to my father. They dated back to my father's contacts from his visit to England in 1906.[58]

In the meantime, my mother had rented Chilswell House – a large residence of the Poet Laureate, the late Lord Bridges, on Boars Hill near Oxford.[59] She had been looking for a suitable place, for both my father and her guests; a place which would let my father carry on his historical work with easy access to a good library. The Chilswell House and the Bodleian Library in Oxford had become the answer to her search. Surrounded by a big garden and a wood, the house served as a comfortable

Erich Eyck, 1954

Hegwig Eyck, 1954

place for guests, and enabled my mother to run a profitable holiday retreat. Lady Bridges was so impressed by my mother that she gave her the keys to the house without having her signing an inventory. This stately home provided its own fine Library. It was in this graceful setting that my father, from his liberal progressive point of view, completed his three volumes on *Bismarck* that were published in 1941, 1943, and 1944, followed by one volume on the *Emperor William II* in 1948.[60] For this work, he received the *Große Bundes-Verdienstkreuz* (the highest order of Merit of the German Federal Republic) in 1953. The ceremony, which my mother and I attended, was conducted in London by the Ambassador Hans Schlange-Schöningen, who had come back from the "jungle turned *fazenda*" of Parâna Brazil, and was authorized by the *Bundespräsident* Theodor Heuss; they were both old friends from before the First World War. Based on insight and merit, these friendships ran very deep. In 1962, Erich dedicated the English translation of the *Weimar Republik* to "the friends who never failed, to Theodor Heuss on his 70th birthday and George Gooch on his 80th birthday." Any time the names of these friends came up in a conversation, I could hear a warm melodious tone in my mother's voice which was never so warm as when she said: "*Ja*, Schlange"(Yes, Schlange-Schöningen).

On Boars Hill, my parents' neighbors were eminent scholars. It was a lively and helpful community with stimulating conversation. Whenever I had the opportunity, I was particularly keen to visit my parents there.

It was with great determination and effort, and even during the air raids, my mother succeeded in buying a large house in London. At that time, and for many years, one could secure a mortgage from a bank that only charged interest. It was a leap of faith that paid off. She first rented out rooms in 12 Lindfield Gardens, Hampstead, and later had the house converted into apartments. To shop for supplies and to be able to administer the two properties, she frequently travelled between Oxford and London. We were very fortunate that the property did not suffer any damage: bombs destroyed the nearby library and fell on several houses on their street, as well as on the general Hampstead neighbours.

Endnotes

1   Miriam Kochan, *Britain's Internees in the Second World War*, (London: Macmillan, Press, 1983).

2   Louis de Joung, *German 5th Column in the Second World War*, (London: Routledge and Kegan, Paul, 1956).

3   Viskun Quisling was sentenced to death on 10th September 1945, and executed by firing squad on 24th October.

4   A.W. Brian Simpson, *The Highest Degree of Odious*, (Oxford: Clarendon Press, 1992), p. 96. See note 11.

5   Ibid, chapter 9, pp. 4-5, p. 172ff.

6   Ibid, pp. 162-16.

7   Ibid, pp. 172 and 222.

8   Ibid, p. 189.

9   On 16th July 1940, Hitler issued the Directive No.16: "As England, in spite of the hopelessness of her military position, has so far shown herself unwilling to come to any compromise, I have decided to begin to prepare for and if necessary to carry out, an invasion of England . . . and if necessary the Island will be occupied." Under the code name "Sealion" the date was set for 16th August 1940.

10 Sir Winston Churchill wartime speeches, found at the Churchill Centre.

11 A. W. Brian Simpson, pp. 163, 172.

12 Ibid, pp. 147, 159ff.

13 Ibid, p. 163.

14 Ibid, pp. 5-9 Ch. 9, p. 172. See also Defence of the Realm Act.

15 Parliamentary Debate, HV, Vol. 378 c 787-796.

16 A. W. Brian Simpson, p. 162-163, 174.222. Connery Chappell, *Isle of Barbed Wire*, (London: Robert Hale; paperback 2005), p.21-22. The number of detainees and internees vary, as documents are not always available or have been lost. See also Warren Perry, *A Biography of Professor Richard Samuel, 1900-1983*. (Melbourn: University of Melbourne Press, Australia, 1997), p. 107.

17 Ibid, pp. 189, 245-247.

18 The documents kindly sent to me by the National Archive in Kew, London, contain only dates of release from internment and of entry into the Pioneer Corps, as well as several applications for British citizenship. The Archive in Peel, on the Isle of Man, no longer has any documents from the WWII internment period.

19 Doc. HO 405/12352 258266, Report of Internment reason, e.g. Stage 2 circular 29/6/40.

20 Connery Chappell, *Isle of Barbed Wire*, (London: Robert Hale, 1988).

21 Nikolaus Pevsner, *Pevsner on Art and Architecture: Radio Talks*, Edited and with an introduction by Stephen Games, (London: Methuen, 2002).

22 Pevsner had a certain justification for his hope for obtaining this job, as Hitler and Göring were known to and in fact did decide who was a Jew and who was not. Bryan Mark Riggs, *Hitler's Jewish Soldiers*, (Kansas City: Kansas University Press, 1984), p. 29-30.

23 The Radio Talks, Interview of Sir Nikolaus Pevsner by Francesca Wilson for the Birmingham Post, 1933.

24 Nikolaus Pevsner concludes in his 1934 piece *"Kunst und Staat*, that the demands of the State took priority over art."(BBC: Radio talk 26). Here Winnifred Wagner and Leni Riefenstahl come to mind: Jürgen Trimborn, translated by Edna McCow, *Leni Riefenstahl, A Life*, (London: Faber & Faber, 2007). Steven Bach, *Leni The Life and Work of Leni Riefenstahl*, (München: Adolf Knopf, 2007).

25 Isle of Man Prison Camps, http.//timewitnesses.org/english/Isle of Man, (3rd November 2005).

26 Connery Chappell, *Isle of Barbed Wire*, p. 43, 57ff, and Ch.7.

27 Ibid, Ch. 7, p. 59 ff.

28 Ronald Stent, *A Bespattered Page*, (London: André Deutsch, 1980), p.12.

29 Ibid, p. 158. Also Frank Eyck Papers, Worcester College, (Oxford Record 1995), pp. 69ff.

30 Miriam Kochan, *Britain's Internees in the Second World War*, pp. 98-99.

31 Peter and Leni Gillman, *Collar the Lot! How Britain Interned and Expelled its War Time Refugees*, (London: Quarter Books, 1980), p. 189 ff. Diary of Hans Gál, *Internment, Music behind Barbed Wire: A Day of the Summer 1940*, copyright Anthony and Eva Fox Gál, York 2001. www.hansgal.com/biography/19-interment.html, (3rd November 2005). David Baddiel, *From*

Fantasy to Family, 6th Aug. 2004, Interview with Matthew Juergen Reisz *about the importance of (sometimes) being ernest*, Independent online edition, (http:enjoyment.independent.co.uk/books/interwies/story,jsp?story 548311; 3rd November 2005). The Amadeus Quartet had its origin in those camps.

32 Connery Chappell, *Isle of Barbed Wire*, p.79.

33 Frank Eyck papers, Worchester College Records, Oxford, 1995, p.73.

34 Ibid, p. 28. Also Ronald Stent, *A Bespattered Page*, p. 39, 100, 109, 114.

35 Ronald Stent, *A Bespattered Page*, p 243.

36 Ibid, p.234.

37 HO 405/12352 258266 Correspondence Card, 8th September 1940.

38 Ronald Stent, *A Bespattered Page*, p. 234.

39 Ibid, p. 200-202.

40 Franz Hildebrandt had got to know Bishop Bell in 1934 when he went to England but was asked by Martin Niemöller to return in 1937 to help out in the administration of the Confessing Church and parish work. 1937 after release from imprisonment in July he fled again to England. Ronald Webster, *Non-Aryan German Theologians and their Lives in Exile since 1933*, (Toronto: York University, 1995).

41 The diocese of Sodros and Man was founded in 1265AD.

42 Ronald Stent, *A Bespattered Page*, p. 240; Roland Jasper, *George Bell*, op. cit.

43 Connery Chappell, *Isle of Barbed Wire*, p. 66. Ronald Stent, *A Bespattered Page*, p. 241.

44 *A Bespattered Page*, Frank Eyck Papers, W. Oakeshott and P. Whitting, letters, Oct. 1940.

45 Frank Eyck, *G. P. Gooch, A study in History and Politics*, (London: Macmillan, 1982), p. 429.

46 Frank Eyck Papers, memorandum of some of my thoughts about my internment on the Isle of Man, Ch 4, pp 103-107.

47 This is an unusual term for a "shortcut," meaning here, taking advantage of cheap labour.

48 Ronald Stent, *A Bespattered Page*, p. 200.

49 Ibid, p.200, the quote of the motto page, see p.201.

50 Mavis Tate, MP of Frome.

51 Ronald Stent, *A Bespattered Page*, p. 200.

52 A. W.Simpson, *In the Highest Degree Odious*, p. 248-249.

53 Ibid, p. 391.

54 Ronald Stent, *A Bespattered Page*, p. 202.

55 Ibid, p. 203.

56 Ronald Stent, p. 12; p. 209-210.

57 Ibid, p. 248.

58 Erich Eyck papers, letter of Lloyd George 1906.

59 Some years after the end of the war my parents closed their business and left Chilswell House, which stood empty for a long time but it is now a nunnery.

60 Erich Eyck, *Bismarck*, Three Volumes, *Das Persönliche Regiment Wilhelm II*, (Erlenbach-Zürich: Eugen Rentsch, Switzerland), followed by Two Volumes of the *Weimar Republik* in German 1952, 1956, (Erlenbach-Zürich: Eugen Rentsch 1952 and 1956), the English transl. by Harlan P. Hanson and Robert G.L. Waite, (Cambridge, MA, Distributed in Great Britain by Oxford University Press., London),Vol. 1 published 1962, Vol. 2 in 1963.

CHAPTER 5

Pioneer Corps of the British Army, 1940-1942

A RRIVING IN ILFRACOMBE, DEVON, I was allotted to the 219 Company of the Auxiliary Pioneer Corps of the British Army. The number of men that had passed through the No. 3 Training Centre in 1940 was 9 490, forming twenty-eight Companies. Of these companies, fifteen were British, ten were comprised of aliens and refugees mainly from Germany and Austria, two were Czech, and one was Spanish. The Spaniards had already fled to France from Spain after the end of their civil war, before having to flee to Britain following the fall of France. Because of the chaotic atmosphere of unfamiliar tongues – something like the Tower of Babel I imagine – the Czechs and Spaniards had to have their own companies. The whole of the British Army Auxiliary Pioneer Corps counted some 65 000 enlisted men, and this did not include the Forces in Palestine. After Dunkirk, the non-British Pioneers were allowed to carry arms. A school of instruction was set up to give some pretty basic military training, including rifle practice in the military centre of Ilfracombe, lasting about a good month. Our function in the Pioneer Corps was supposed to be light engineering, which was somewhat liberally interpreted.[1]

My unit was employed in a whole number of navvy jobs, from loading and unloading railway trucks to building Nissan huts, and any other kind of construction including pouring concrete. There was always the usual military drill. On one occasion, our NCO (Non-Commissioned Officer) reprimanded our unit for used too much water. I dared to take the liberty to say that this did not necessarily reflect badly on us, which he obviously considered damned insolence.

Frank Eyck, entered Pionieer Corp of HM Army 1940-42

I was told with a stern disapproving voice: "Have a hair coot!" When I said that I had just had one, the order sounded: "Have another one!" Our Unit was moved quite often.

From the middle of December 1940 on we were stationed near Hexham Northumberland engaged in forestry works under the direction of Royal Australian Engineers.[2] These fellow-pioneers were wonderfully built, strong forestry workers. By Christmas we were in Long Eaton near Derby, supplying labor for the Royal Ordinance depot at Chilswell Nottingham. There was something quite satisfying about heavy physical work despite the boredom. The situation was eased by having in the ranks a number of highly educated and well-qualified men, mostly German Jewish or non-Aryan refugees. There was a Methodist Canteen for the Forces that gave the chance for informal gatherings and offered recitals and theatre performances, etc. It was an opportunity to socialize, and there I came to know Ken Green[3] and his future wife Helen[4] who had joined the Women's Auxiliary Territorial Services. They had met at a Mozart recital. The three of us gathered as often as possible and enjoyed stimulating conversations and musical concerts, starting an enduring friendship.

Soon Ken was called up and moved to the Middle East, a different landscape. He served as a Sapper in the Royal Engineers, getting very experienced in finding and drilling for water; he asked me to look after Helen. At that time he had not been sure about his relationship to her; however, that changed through a lively exchange of letters between them later on. In the summer of 1941, his first letters reached me after he had two water-related spells in hospital due to irritable contaminates. Not being able to say anything about his actual work, he instead described his surroundings:

Our location is a rather monotonous expanse of sand, dunes, pebbly desert and a blue sky. Native villages are dotted here and there – naturally where water is available. But I am afraid 'primitive' would be much too superlative to describe their daily life. Water being the Alpha and Omega of existence . . . It is used when in the form of a stream as the local lavatory, water receptacle for putridity of all varieties, washing place, and of course drinking water!! Apart from this rather lurid form of local colour we have numerous kinds of lizards, snakes and mosquitoes and countless hordes of flies; the battles we have with them are often interrupted by young cyclones that threaten to tear your accommodation up by the roots for a few seconds, then pass by covering everything with the dust, they trail up to the sky, and in spite of all this we survive… Besides the monotony life is pleasant and interesting. The inhabitants are the most amazing people. I have concluded they must have corrugated iron tummies!.. [Watching the development of the war he wondered, and asked]: Will the Russians finish the job . . . to bring about the internal collapse of the Nazi fabric? If this is going to happen I think a not too distant date we will see the end . . . Then we will sit together once again – probably guzzling 'Liebfrauenmilch' and 'Rummel'[sic] [5] instead of Long Eaton tea. …

As most of us Pioneers had lively minds, we relieved the monotony of our daily work and contributed to the other evening activities by giving lectures. Among the refugees was Dr. Richard Samuel, who had taught German literature at the University of Cambridge.[6] He was about twenty years older than I, and worked as a clerk in the company office. We became good friends and we had many interesting talks. Eventually we decided to put on a course of Modern English History, beginning with the Tudors, in our spare time. We lectured alternately, taking a century at a time; I believe I started with the sixteenth century. Many men in the company generally had only recently come to England, and were highly educated; some were university students, others were members of professions, but they had not received an education in English history, so the course fulfilled a real need for them. As for Richard and me, this activity was a tonic for our morale. I especially enjoyed recalling my excellent instruction under the tutelage of Philip Whitting at St. Paul's School, for it reminding me of those times. We had a wonderful audience, as there were many doctors, lawyers, diplomats, and so on among the non-British navvies. The teaching gave us a change from routine, tedium, and hard physical work in my case. Soon my kit bag, which I had to carry to the point of transportation on our frequent moves, was filled mainly with books and other historical material. Helen reminded me with amusement that on our long walks, come rain or shine, I tried out my lectures on her. However, the more I have learned about history the more I realize my incredible rashness in holding forth as well as I did. [7]

That winter I also contracted measles and was placed in the local children's hospital in the isolation ward for a while. As on a matter of principle, the army always sleeps under canvas; it was a great treat to be covered by clean white sheets in a proper bed and with solid walls around me and a roof over my head. Additionally, I was pampered by pretty nurses who enjoyed gently teasing me. Helen often cycled over to the hospital to visit but we had to communicate through a glass screen.

Gradually a feeling arose not only among the members of the Pioneer Corps, but also among the people outside, that navvying work, that is, unskilled labor, was a misuse of manpower when it was done by people with qualified skills. The majority of the refugees, being Jewish, knew that in Germany their race was being exterminated. The average intelligence of the refugees was very high, and they were burning to contribute more positively to the war effort. Their employment in the Pioneer Corps was a waste of human resources, particularly ill affordable in time of war.[8] Ken Green and I often discussed this topic in our letters, it went like an Ariadne-thread through the war period, although it was not necessary followed by an abundance of action. But, again I received support from my old High Master W. Oakeshott, when he wrote to me on 24th May 1941:

> Here is your OCTU (Officer Selection Training Unit) form. I do hope that you get the transfer soon to the intelligence or some similar job. There's some indication I believe that the authorities are now beginning to see what splendid reserve of ability they have in some of the aliens in England. [9]

There were influential people intervening on our behalf. Sir Herbert Emerson, the High Commissioner of the League of Nations for Refugees was concerned with the refugees in England. He insistently pressed the War Office and other authorities to make fuller uses of these "enemy aliens," who were more determined than the British conscripts to take their part in the bitter conflict against the Nazis. Professor A. V. Hill, a giant in exercise physiology,[10] as a member of the "Academic Assistance Council," had helped Jewish scientists in their flight and relocation to the West. Eleanor Rathborne, MP, who created the Parliamentary Committee for Refugees, was a social reformer.[11] Josiah Wedgwood, who was a member in the House of Commons, pointed out that the present war was not a war of nationalities, but of freedom against dictatorship.[12] The Chairman of the Jewish Refugees Committee, Otto Schiff, who for thirty years had been devoted to the cause of refugees and enjoyed the confidence of the Home Office, was another agent to help break down the barriers.[13] Those who were able to "escape" the Auxiliary Military Pioneer Corps owe a debt of gratitude especially, and above all, to Dorothy Buxton, the most ardent of all the fighters for the aliens.[14]

Dorothy Buxton, the sister of Eglantyne Jebb, who founded the International Union of the Save the Children Fund in Geneva, in 1920, had married Charles Roden Buxton, a Liberal and later Labour Member of Parliament.[15] Charles was the brother of the better-known Lord Noel-Buxton.[16] During the First World War, Charles and Dorothy Buxton had joined the Society of Friends, the Quakers. For some time during the early 1940s Dorothy Buxton, in association with other prominent personalities, lobbied the War Office to permit enemy alien soldiers to transfer out of the Pioneer Corps into other units in which they could be more useful. To obtain precise information and to substantiate her case to the War Office, she chose correspondents in each Pioneer Company to whom she sent her questionnaires.

I was privileged to be one of these helpers for a time, thanks to Lady Mary Murray, the wife of the classicist Gilbert Murray, Regius Professor of Greek at Oxford, who lived close to my parent's house in Boars Hill just outside Oxford. Lady Mary née Howard was a daughter of the ninth Earl of Carlisle and a strong, if somewhat eccentric, personality. The Murray's had voiced their strong objection against the internment policy and personally did a lot of good to others; a well-known conductor and his wife, both Austrian refugees, lived for free in the cottage on their property and the Murray's befriended them. I had my ups and downs with Lady Mary Murray. One of my sins was that I had dared to raise the question in conversation as to whether the Soviet Union, who had become our ally, was a democracy. After Hitler had broken his agreement with the USSR and invaded Russia on 22nd June 1941, the British ambassador in Moscow, Sir Stafford Cripps, had concluded a mutual Assistance

Treaty with her on 12th July. While I was having tea with the Murray's, and voiced my controversial question, Lady Mary went for me – how could I question an ally? It required the intervention of Professor Murray to restore peace. He said very quietly and slowly: "What Mr. Eyck means, is . . . " and then explained the point I was trying to make. At any rate, in November 1942, around the time I was posted out of the Pioneer Corps, I must have been in her good books. I had told the Murray's that many of the aliens were just wasting their time in the Pioneers and had put some of the information at my disposal into a kind of report. Lady Mary replied to me on 15th November 1942:

> Thank you for your detailed letter – I am very sorry indeed there should be so much misjudgement and prejudice. 'Pick and Shovel' work seems to suit some of my fellow-pacifists but not, of course, young men who want to fight. A great deal of what you say I agree with and some I know, though the unfairness is new to me. [17]

Lady Mary added that she had sent my communication and a letter she had received from Dorothy Buxton to a Mr. Hart at the War Office, who had also recently visited them, and who "prognosticated changes" in the policy relating to the employment of enemy alien soldiers. Not much later, and with the help of Richard Samuel, I had left my Pioneer Corps and soon got attached to the Army Education Corps. Richard by then was engaged in secret work, I guess, connected to Bletchley Park.[18] From time to time, we met in London to have the much needed talk about current events; on parting company, he became very secretive and seemed to have a secluded exit somewhere through the chemist shop of Boots. At my new Army Education Corp I received a letter from Dorothy Buxton dated 30th November: [19]

Lady Mary Murray has given me your address and tells me you would be willing to help me. For some time past I have been trying to promote interest in the troubles and problems of the Pioneer Corps among a number of MPs, some of whom have already bestirred themselves a bit.

With a view to this it is of course essential to be well equipped with information, and also as comprehensive as possible. This is not altogether easy. For one thing the conditions vary so greatly from one company to another that it is rash to generalize. However, I enclosed a few notes indicating some of the lines of enquiry. If you could give me information relating to the company (which was it?) which you have recently left, I should be most grateful, especially if I could get it soon. With best wishes for your new work,

Yours truly, sincerely

Dorothy F. Buxton

While the accompanying letter was hand-written, the attached memorandum, entitled Pioneer Corps Problems, was in typescript:

There are <u>so</u> <u>many</u> serious problems in connection with the Pioneer Corps that it is difficult to deal with them in writing, but I should be very glad of notes on <u>any</u> of them which you feel strongly about. I know of course that one of the most serious and urgent problems is the matter of Pioneer Corps members, more especially of aliens of 'enemy origin,' who are liable to be sent overseas. They do so at the awful risk of falling into the hands of the Germans – where they would be outside the protection offered by the

International Conventions on Prisoners-of-War, i.e. they would be treated simply as traitors. Moreover their relations, still in Germany, would be endangered. At one time volunteers for the Pioneer Corps were asked at the time whether they were <u>willing</u> to go overseas, but this has now been waived, and <u>all</u> are liable. Naturally, this is resented by those who volunteered on the <u>opposite</u> assumption. I am trying to collect information as to the present attitude of members of the Pioneer Corps about it. Some of the <u>younger</u> <u>unmarried</u> men are I know willing to accept this peculiar and very awful risk. Could you tell me anything about the attitude to it in your company?

Secondly I am collecting material on the injustice and <u>waste</u> of keeping the square peg in the round hole, e.g. regarding the doctors, dentists, engineers etc. etc. who are still being used for heavy manual work (suitable for 'navvies'). In <u>theory</u> transfer is allowed, but in practice it seems to be beset with difficulties, sometimes owing to the hostility of officers, or to a blocking policy on the part of someone higher. Similarly with the matter of <u>promotion</u> (nominally allowed), I should be glad to be told any striking examples of the above. Further I would be glad to know your opinion on such points as: whether the military training given (in your experience) is of any value for practical military purposes; whether there are any <u>special</u> <u>causes</u> for the best not being got out of the men, e.g. misunderstanding of the position of 'aliens' (and of the causes which brought refugees to this country) on the part of officers or NCO's (and other causes, too).

Conditions, of course, vary enormously from one company to another. There are, however, a number of British people, some of them in positions of influence, who are dissatisfied with the situation of the Pioneer Corps, and are doubtful whether it should really be continued in its present form, or whether an effort should be made to attach the men who want to fight to British units; and use those who do not want to go overseas for special to serve in the Royal Engineer, Royal Army Service Corps and Royal Army Ordnance Corps units for service in this country.

I would be very glad to know your opinions and to pass them on to MPs and others who might use the information; but of course I will make sure that the source of the information I am given should not be made known.

In the circumstances, I decided not to keep copies of my replies to Dorothy Buxton, who thanked me on 14th December for my

most useful letter all the more as you managed to do it so promptly. It is a valuable contribution to my material.

Unfortunately my husband has become rather seriously ill so that my time is much taken up, but I shall continue to do all I possibly can to get these many urgent problems considered afresh. With warm thanks, . . .

Actually Charles Roden Buxton died two days later, on 16th December. I wrote a letter of condolence on 28th December, for which Dorothy Buxton thanked me on 6th January 1943. I obviously raised the question as to whether I should bother her with the affairs of the Pioneer Corps (PC) at this time of her bereavement:

Thank you very much for your kind note. But please do not think you will be bothering me if you send me 'more details'. I am hoping to send in notes as full as I can to a number of MPs before Parliament meets, and shall welcome any further material you would like to send me.

A P.S. added: 'Of course I have a lot of private affairs to see to, but my husband is the last person who would have wished me to slacken any attempt to help our refugee friends.'

I received several further letters from Dorothy Buxton, including one on 4th March:

I wonder whether you will have heard that in the House of Commons on March 2nd, in answer to a question, Sir J. Grigg [Under-Secretary in the Ministry of Information] stated that "all arms" (Signal Corps excepted – which is a pity!) are now to be open to members of the PC. This means a big move on! I only hope that the policy will not be too badly blocked in the administration of it.

Also it comes when 5 or 6 PC Companies have been mobilized for overseas, and one wonders whether the men in them will have any chance of transfer.

Will you kindly help me about the following matter? On the M.o.S. film "Lift up your heads!" (About the PC) a doctor inter alias is upfronted doing digging!![sic] One of my M.P. correspondents is very interested in "the scandal" of doctors being used in this way at time of such serious shortage as now prevails in our country. He asks me for names and addresses of doctors in this position. Are there in fact any doctors, or dentists in your Corps ? My information had been that they had now been transferred.

I believe however there are quite a number of medical students in the P.C. who had nearly completed their training on the Continent before coming here or were in a position to take their final exams. Could your give me any information about this too?

In another letter of Dorothy of Buxton of 11th March she wrote:

You are right that it is necessary to suspend our judgement about the 'New Deal.'

I will be glad if you could tell me a little more about the Alien Medical Students....Whether the R.A.M.C. [Royal Army Medical Corps] could if they would give them a chance to help in the medical profession perhaps in some inferior position?

I recently circulated a memo on the PC to a number of MPs. One result of this is that my statement is queried by the "higher authorities" that any volunteer for the PC were ever told they would never be sent overseas. I know that it applies only to some of the earlier volunteers; but have heard over and over again that they felt rather bitter about it when, (I think in 1942) in disregard of this original promise it was announced that all PC members were liable for overseas service.

In her last letter at the end of March 1943 in answer to some of her questions and impressions I had given her she replied:

I would be grateful if you would let me know . . . whether anything has been done in your Company to give effect to Sir J. Grigg's statement?

From one company I hear that there is an ACI [Army Council of Instruction] disallowed transfers from Companies mobilized for overseas (which of course is nullifying the apparent concession); from another Company I hear there is an ACI to the opposite effect, i.e. allowing transfers from mobilized Companies!

I am very interested that you find the sergeants in a British unit compare favourable with the British sergeants appointed to the Alien units. . . . A British officer has been indignantly denying to me that the Pioneer Corps (British or otherwise) has a lower status in practice or public opinion than the rest of the British army. But I thought this was a matter of common knowledge.

Dorothy Buxton was very pleased with the space The London Times gave to the question of enemy aliens in their correspondence column. She added: "It is useful to see what the stupid people are thinking." On March 4th she had already sent me extracts from Hansard outlining changes in army policy concerning the employment of enemy aliens:

Some part of what we have been striving for appears now to have been achieved! I think every step will probably make the rest easier, so that we may hope for continued progress.

Dorothy Buxton certainly continued to observe the situation, to seek information about anything still amiss (from me among others) and to ensure that the undertakings given by the government were honored. Her work bore fruition. Transfers and promotions, including commissioning, certainly became easier as time went on.

I never personally met Dorothy Buxton, but this

correspondence revealed her to me as a person with a very strong commitment to help others, as somebody who knew how to get things done in politics, but who did not shirk the work and continued effort required to obtain results. Dorothy Buxton drove herself very hard, periodically to the point of breakdown. Reading about the Buxton brothers for my biography of G. P. Gooch, I learned that Dorothy undertook a visit to Nazi Germany in 1935 to appeal to Hermann Göring, at that time Minister-President of Prussia. Göring was initially responsible for the Gestapo and, therefore, the concentration camps. Dorothy came to Berlin to plead with him to stop the horrors of the concentration camps. However, the effort of the visit to Berlin was too much for her and she suffered a collapse, yet she went ahead with the arranged interview with Göring. At the beginning of the interview, as Dorothy Buxton recorded,

> Göring treated me with a magnificent and stately air of royalty. . . . What did he say? What did I say? I was in far too ill a state to be able to remember any of it afterwards in detail. At least my remarks went home to the extent that he became very angry and excited; the dignified mien was dropped and he gesticulated furiously, waving his arms over his head. I felt that my mission was hopeless. Failure once more . . . [20]

After the interview, Dorothy's husband took her back to bed, in the room of the Elisabeth Krankenhaus [hospital] where they had been given hospitality.

It cannot be overstated or repeated too often how members of the British society, of whom Dorothy Buxton is a splendid example, have engaged themselves in fighting for the aliens in their midst, particularly those serving in the PC. She was one of the most indefatigable of all. Before the war, she had written together with Sir Norman Angell,[21] an international economist and Commissioner for refugees in the League of Nations, a book *You and the Refugees*, pleading for sympathy with strangers at our gates. Although a Quaker and convinced pacifist, she threw herself whole heartedly into the fight for recognition of the alien soldiers. She knew the ardor of the men to fight Hitler and was convinced that she could make a contribution. So she set about the work in a systematic way learnt in long years of party agitation for other causes. She chose correspondents in each Company to whom she sent questionnaires, and then tabulated the answers, and composed memoranda, sending them to the War Office, the High Commissioner of the League for Refugees, to MPs, and to the Press.

In the end she convinced them. Hundreds of men wrote to her, about their individual cases and she answered them all personally. In many, she restored the belief, threatened by frustration, in the honesty, fair play, and kindness of the British people. She helped the Government to understand the aliens, and to the pioneers she brought understanding of the British form of government and restored the refugees trust and belief in the British officials. Ken Green also wrote to me from the Middle East on 26th May 1943 that the refugee question had come up in the *King-Hall letter*, a weekly publication sent out to the troops.[22] William Stephan King-Hall, MP, Minister of Aircraft Production in the Ministry of Fuel and Power, remarked "it is very true German and Austrian refugees want to fight [the Nazi regime]" to which Ken added that "I trust that the authorities will be able to provide the wherewithal." By 1943 many hesitations and misgivings were removed.

Endnotes

1   Norman Bentwich, *I Understand the Risks*: *The story of the Refugees from Nazi-oppression who fought in the British Forces in the Second World War*, (London: Victor Gollancz, 1950), p. 189.

2   Warren Perry, *A Biography of Professor Richard Samuel 1900-1983*, (Melbourn: University of Melbourne Press, 1997), pp. 107-111. Frank Eyck papers, Frank Eyck to Major Warren Perry, 31st October 1988.

3   Frank Eyck papers, Ken (Kenneth) Green to Frank Eyck, 17th and 27th August 1941.

4   Frank Eyck papers, Ken Green to Frank Eyck, 8th September 1942; about Helen, "she is the best friend I ever had." 5th and 26th May 1943.

5   An allusion to the well-known German wine and the German Fieldmarschal Rommel.

6   Frank Eyck papers, Helen Samuel to Frank Eyck, 29th October 1986 and 4th July1988; Frank Eyck to Helen Samuel, 6th November 1988.

7   Ibid.

8   Norman Bentwich, *I Understand the Risks*, p. 72.

9   Frank Eyck papers, Walter Oakeshott to Frank Eyck, 24th May 1941.

10 Professors Hill and Meyerhof received the Nobel Prize for their discovery of the aerobic and anaerobic metabolism in 1922; Hill, MP, 1940-1945.

11 Eleanor Rathborn, *Concise Dictionary of National Biography*, p. 359.

12 Josiah Wedgwood, *Concise DNB*, p. 461.

13 Norman Bentwich, *I Understand the Risks*, p. 72.

14 Ibid. p. 73.

15 Victoria de Bunsen, *Charles Roden Buxton, A Memoir*, (London: George Allen & Unwin, 1948), p. 113.

16 Edward Noel-Buxton, politician and philanthropist, 1930-1948, *Save the Children Fund*, Endowment of the Noel Buxton Trust for public and charity purposes, Baron 1930, *Concise DNB*, p. 323.

17 Lady Mary Murray to Frank Eyck, F. E., 15th November 1942.

18 Frank Eyck to Helen Samuel, 6th November 1988; Bletchley Park the place

where Enigma, the German secret code was discovered.

19 Letters by Dorothy Buxton to Frank Alexander (my nom de guerre), 15th November 1942 to 30th March 1943.

20 Victoria Buxton de Bunsen, *Charles Roden Buxton, A Memoir*, (London: George Allen & Unwin, 1948), p. 161.

21 Norman Angell (High Commissioner of the League of Nations, Nobel Peace Prize in 1933) and Dorothy Buxton, *You and the Refugees*, (London: Penguin Special, paperback, 1939).

22 Ken Green to Frank Eyck, 26th May 1843.

CHAPTER 6

British Army Education Corps, 1942–1944

THE FATEFUL EVACUATION OF BRITISH TROOPS from Dunkirk in the summer of 1940 prompted the army authorities to pay considerable attention to maintaining the morale of the large number of troops stationed in Britain. In response, they turned their attention to army education. In 1941, the Army Bureau of Current Affairs (ABCA) was set up to provide booklets for the teaching of current affairs. As the resources of the Army Education Corps were insufficient to provide all the instruction required, regimental officers and outside lecturers were enlisted. In addition, there were calls for some teaching relating to citizenship, and this led to the introduction of a course called *The British Way and Purpose* (*BWP*) as part of an intensive scheme initially limited to the winter of 1942/43. This was to be taught not only – so far as available – by Army Education Corps instructors, but also a host of outside instructors: civilian lecturers provided by the Central Advisory Council (an organ of the civil adult education movement) officers and other ranks in the military units themselves, and Members of Parliament.[1] Through a fortunate combination of circumstances, an opportunity arose for me to participate in the new programme.

Richard Samuel,[2] while only a private in the army, was well connected and helped place me in a course held at Hertfordshire to train instructors for participation in the new programme. Leading authors lecturing in the conference covered a wide variety of subjects past and present, including the political history of thought in the relevant parts of the world at the moment. They included Professor A. L. Goodhart from Oxford, who expounded on Anglo-American relations and the devastating impact of Pearl Harbour. Dr. G. P. Gooch, editor of the Contemporary Review, spoke on English History and Germany from 1806-1933, covering and analyzing a variety of subjects related to her history and political thought. Dr. Stirk introduced the subject of German culture and civilization using Walter Flex's *The Traveller Between Two Worlds*, the Prussian spirit, Goethe's *Faust*, Nietzsche's statement that there is no such thing as progress to illustrate his comments. He elaborated on Goethe's and Nietzsche's attitude to Christianity and on Oswald Spengler's historical philosophy, which depicted man as a predator, and interpreting his important work: *The Decline of the West*.[3] Dr. Otto Kahn-Freund, under a pseudonym, talked about comparative law and Dr. Hawgood spoke about various aspects of German history and politics. The question about fighting a war of ideologies was raised in Major Hall's booklet: *What is at Stake?* Unfortunately, he was tempted to answer with personal opinions, which was not the thing to do in the army, and which later on got him into trouble. Talks were given about USSR and Nazi economics, the British Colonial Empire, India, China, and Shanghai. These lectures were always followed by discussions.[4]

In November 1942, I was attached for instructional work to the Army Education Corps detachment operating from the Northampton barracks, whose activities covered the county of Northamptonshire. The staff consisted of a lieutenant, a regimental sergeant major, and a number of sergeants, the rank to which I was appointed on an acting basis. We travelled all over the country on motorcycles. On one of my routes I was thrown off the bike when an Anglican parson emerged out of a country lane without first looking, but we both were none the worse for it, only now in my eightieth year do I have some discomfort in the affected knee. As instructors of the Army Education Corps (AEC), we were allocated to different units. As the winter wore on, the scheme of a one-hour instruction devoted to citizenship was extended. The class was given during the soldiers' training and working time, and attendance was compulsory. I remained attached to the AEC for a period of fifteen months, until February 1944. My task was to lecture to the troops on The British Way and Purpose. This rather amused my former masters at St. Paul's School when I told them.

While attending to the correspondence with Dorothy Buxton, I was also busy learning my new job as an instructor in the course. As background, we were supplied with booklets issued by the Directorate of Army Education at the War Office, which appeared in three sequences. These were *Soldier-Citizen* (booklets 1-5, November 1942 to March 1943), *Report on the Nation* (booklets 6-12, April to October 1943) and *Today and Tomorrow* (booklets 13-18, December 1943 to May 1944). Each booklet contained four chapters. They dealt with such subjects as what was at stake in the war, the British governmental system, and public services, the Empire, British relations with other countries, the economy and labor relations, health, education, family life, and the future international order. The basic pattern started with an account of the existing situation and proceeded to a discussion of what was desirable for the future.

The staff of the Directorate of Education at the War Office partly produced the material, apparently with the help of specialists, and partly commissioned out to experts in the various fields. The standard was generally high and provided a reasonable balance between various political points of view. In the judgement of the anti-authoritarian author, Anthony Burgess, the *British Way and Purpose* chapter was "embarrassingly die-hard" in places,[5] while at the same time "promoting a sort of cautious egalitarianism whenever possible."[6]

Outside authors included such well-known authorities as Reginald Coupland, Beit Professor of Colonial History at Oxford, who lectured on India; Denis Brogan, Professor of Political Science at Cambridge, on the USA; Sir Bernard Pares, formerly Professor of Russian History, Language and Literature at the University of London, on Russia; and A. D. Lindsay, Master of Balliol College, Oxford, on *What More Is Needed of the Citizen*. Altogether the outside writers, with some lesser known and ideologically not so profiled names, were drawn from a variety of political outlooks. Not surprisingly, in view of British admiration for the heroic fight of the Russian people against the Germans, Sir Bernard Pares' piece on Russia is in retrospect the weakest of all. The chapters praise the achievements of the Soviet regime in general and of Stalin in particular.[7] In Britain at the time, any negative reference to the Soviet Union was liable to be interpreted as an attack on the Russian people. Other surprising passages include Brogan calling the "Holy Alliance,"[8] agreed to after the Napoleonic Wars, "the equivalent of the modern Axis."[9] More worrying for me was an in-house piece on Germany talking about "the façade of democratic government from 1919 up to 1933."[10]

In fairness, it should be pointed out that this statement was part of a thesis that the old ruling forces in the country retained a controlling influence in the Weimar Republic. In the same booklet, the text of the chronology of the maps on Germany's domination in Europe also left something to be desired. The total explanation provided for the Locarno Treaty of 1925 consists of the following: "French and British statesmen turn blind eye on German re-armament." Moreover, the evacuation of the Rhineland by the French in 1930 was "done as appeasement; and resulted in strengthening the Nazi Party."[11] But these negative points are outweighed by the meticulous care generally taken. The relevant government departments normally vetted the text. Instructors did not have to follow the booklets strictly. They were regarded as background material, and I certainly found them a great help. Instructors were, indeed, officially encouraged to frame their own courses of instruction.[12]

Thus, I see from my notes that in lecturing on "The

Information Services" I went somewhat beyond the carefully balanced piece by the editor of the BBC's publication *The Listener*.[13] I expressed the opinion that ownership of the press was confined to a narrow circle, and that this was of disadvantage to some of the parties, like Labour. I suggested the need for improved standards among journalists and for a better handling of news, as well as a reform of the libel laws. In the sessions on The Responsible Citizen, I largely followed the pattern set in the booklet on the subject by Barbara Ward and A. D. K. Owen, Stevenson Lecturer in Citizenship, University of Glasgow.[14]

But I took the opportunity when lecturing to address my listeners directly with the question on how seriously they themselves had taken their duties as citizens in a democracy: "How active have you been? Did you vote in the general election of 1935, assuming you were eligible to vote? If so, did you vote in full knowledge of the facts? How did you set about keeping up-to-date with political information?"

Throughout my activities as an instructor in Army Education, I did my best to oppose the tendency of seeing problems primarily in materialistic terms, of emphasizing the diseases of the body to the exclusion of those of the mind and spirit. I pointed out the drawbacks of a purely economic interpretation of history which did not pay sufficient attention to what man could do himself to put things right. In a later booklet: *What More is Needed of the Citizen?* A. D. Lindsay dealt with this question.[15] He argued that while we do want a decent standard of living, "if most people think only of the material conditions, if they think that being rich, and getting all the things which you can buy with money, are the only things worth thinking about, we shan't ever be really satisfied." On this topic, Aldous Huxley's book *Brave New World* provided a grave warning.

I felt that there were a number of improvements that could be made in our instruction and organization, but my detachment was not responsive to any suggestions, particularly after we lost our friendly and approachable officer following a motorcycle accident. Leadership was mainly in the hands of a regimental sergeant major, a school teacher by profession, who liked to play it safe. Fortunately, I had the company of a Scottish schoolmaster John Taylor, who was highly cultured; his letters to me are a literary treat.[16] In addition, we had the composer Alan Rawsthorne with us for a time: a wonderful conversation partner with a cosmopolitan outlook.[17] But I had the impression that neither Taylor nor Rawsthorne were in a position to achieve very much innovation in the branch. John Taylor wrote to me 13th March 1944:

My dear Frank,

I can detect a distinct undertone of disquiet in your illuminating letter . . . It would seem that culturally you are in the backwaters of civilization. But hark! The whole set-up is purely temporary . . . You are at that well known transitional stage of the nomad, where the tents are folded, the trappings and hangings are put away, and await the call of: "On comrades, into the dawn!" Then I fancy you will scurry away from the caravanserai and plod on the trail alone. After all, despite the lukewarm reception (which you may even have anticipated), it is only a matter of time before you go to WOSB [War Office Selection Board] . . . I should infer from the information you've given me that the folks around you will be only too pleased to let you go further.

After writing to him about being engaged in the instruction of BWP and international affairs for a year, I had put my ideas to paper and circulated them to anybody who might be interested; I received another letter from John on 29th March:

There is no doubt . . . that the resumption of a more natural life will serve you well . . . It is entirely wrong and misguided of you to think that your work in taking ABCA, etc. within the unit will pass unnoticed. For my part, I should fancy that particular attention will be paid to your effort by your officers, unless they are blind to the intellectual side of the unit's activities.

As for this part of the world – we are still groping among the clouds and shadows of the dim, dim world – BWP; and wrestling Truth in all her beauty from the chains that bind her to the rock of Ignorance and Lassitude. Each one of our band . . . is a Perseus in quest of his Andromade, and who is Andromade but this maiden Truth?

My memorandum, which ran to about five full-scape pages, proposed beginning a citizenship education with a short Basic British Way and Purpose course.[18]

I have presented several of my ideas from this memorandum below to illustrate the thoughts of the soldiers during the war and to portray the character of my life in these years. Though the existing BWP programme was well planned and contained a number of excellent booklets, it had unfortunately been unable to overcome the fundamental prejudice on the part of the soldier that "it is all propaganda." In my opinion, there were several reasons for that. Apart from an inadequate co-ordination between Army Education Corps personnel, civilian lecturers, and unit instructors, this was due to the booklets not taking the materialistic outlook of the soldier sufficiently into account; lecturers and audiences usually started from different premises, which kept them apart. There was an unfulfilled need for continuity of instruction. It was important to get hold of every soldier for one period a week in those units, which consistently ran the programme.

The BWP programme was not above the heads of soldiers. All the subjects chosen were topical and could be made interesting. The ordinary soldier did not suffer from lack of intelligence and common sense, or even of a certain interest in politics. But being an adult he had his fixed ideas, which had to be taken into account. Astonishingly, the same arguments recurred in one unit after another: These centred round a few slogans such as class distinction which, freely repeated, would win any constituency in the first general election after the war. Any discussion running open and unhampered by interference from a discussion leader would merely repeat these slogans and undigested arguments. In Harold Nicholson's words in a Current Affairs booklet, these stock phrases derived "from sources other than the person's knowledge, thoughts or feelings."[19] This state of mind prevented the ordinary soldier from adding new information obtained in lectures to his existing knowledge.

In my memorandum, I proposed right at the beginning of the course that these attitudes should have been brought to the surface in discussion, so that soldiers could examine them and make up their own minds as to their validity. It may take several heated discussions under strong leadership on the part of the lecturer to reach a certain number of general conclusions, but it is only then that one could prevent discussion from always returning to catch-phrases of the "capitalism and class-distinction" brand. Then the opportunity to get one's information and arguments across would open. Certainly any attempt at standardized thinking of the Nazi type of regimentation should be avoided. The soldier should be encouraged to give vocal expression to any disagreement or doubt, and should be made to feel that his reactions and responses are as valuable as the part played by the lecturer.

I put down several key topics both as an outline of a tenable point of view for a lecturer and the kind of reaction encountered in response. Naturally, democracy often came up in lectures and discussion. An instructor would suggest, for example, that while – like any other system of government – democracy could not provide absolute equality, its indispensable aim was to progress towards greater equality of opportunity. Democracy was based on the realization that changes will always be necessary and, therefore, provided the machinery to make these changes out without the intervention of force.

What they did with democracy was up to its rulers, the people. A certain degree of national educational standards were therefore of great significance for the performance of the electorate.

How did the soldiers receive this kind of analysis? In my memorandum, I summarized reactions to the topic of democracy as follows: "This country is no democracy (in fact, loud laughter every time the word is mentioned); the system of election is all wrong. The soldiers would then provide several ideas at to why democracy didn't work: (i) there should be the right of recall; (ii) there is numerical unfairness; (iii) the system favors the Conservatives; (iv) the parties are in the hands of the wrong people or parties should be abolished. The leaders of democracy, those who rise to the top are all corrupted by the system, look at Jimmy Thomas (the trade union leader and labour politician, who joined the National Government in 1931 and had to resign office for having made "unauthorized disclosure" of budget proposals in 1936)! What right has Herbert Morrison (a Labour politician and member of the war cabinet) to talk, was he not a conscientious objector in the last war? The House of Lords is an obstacle to people getting their way. Why should Ramsay MacDonald [three times Labour Prime Minister] have been allowed to stand for a safe seat after being defeated in another constituency [in 1935 defeated in Seaham, and re-elected in the Scottish University].[20] Why should some people have several votes? (Universities and the business premises vote).

What can the ordinary man do? (i) He is far too busy with his struggle for a living. (ii) He has not got the knowledge. There is bullying on the part of the employer (e.g. the big landowner): (iii) Have a pint – you know you have to vote Conservative; or (iv) if the Conservatives lose this seat, I shall have to close down (and YOU will lose your job). THEY have always been afraid that we should get too educated. They are afraid we might get the wrong opinion that is why you have been sent here, to talks [sic] us out of it. There is a law for the poor and a law for the rich. The press is in the hands of a few people; therefore, democracy is a farce.

All talk of money immediately led to class distinction. To the soldiers, capitalism was the cause of all evils: "Capitalism caused unemployment, exploitation, and starvation. If you could cut out profits and spread them over the masses, you would solve your standard of living problem." There was reference to quite unnecessary poverty in the midst of plenty (fish and grain being thrown into the sea). There were demands for cutting out the middleman. "State control would solve all our difficulties. Cartels were the root of the trouble. Monopolies should be abolished. Why should somebody do the work and another person make [sic] all the money? Capitalism forced people to walk over dead bodies."

When it came to the causes of the war, the solders felt these had something to do with Germany challenging Britain's trading position. The soldiers felt that Germany was forced to go to war for economic reasons, to secure raw materials, because of the pressure of surplus population, and to obtain markets for her goods. The ordinary man did not want this war; working class people all over the world are the same. This is not our war: it is fought for capitalism. Vested interests caused this war (e.g. armament manufacturers). Some of our people had money invested in Germany. The names of Neville Chamberlain, Stanley Baldwin [three times Conservative PM] [21] and sometimes Asquith [twice Liberal PM] were freely mentioned.[22] There were vague references to cartels. The prize answer was: "in the last war we were told that was the war to end wars. This time we are told it is a war for democracy. That is bound to be a lie. It is just a blind (i.e. it does not sound nearly as convincing as the usual "economic" explanation). The present economic system is the cause of all wars.

When it came to the Nazi system, the reaction was: "How do we know that all the atrocity stories are true?" Communism appeared to be heaven. When it came to imperialism, the view was put forward that the Nazis were only trying to grab now what we got by force years ago. There were misconceptions about the status of the Dominions. There was little realization of the ideals on which the British Commonwealth of Nations was based. The question was raised "why India wasn't given its independence according to the Atlantic Charter? What about Ireland and the Boer War?" Finally, when the question of how to abolish wars as a means of settling international disputes came up, the view was expressed that: "there will always be wars."

Many of the points raised by the soldiers were excellent, especially those concerning class-distinction and the unequal franchise in Britain. Several of the points put forward in discussion, such as the references to government ministers like Jimmy Thomas, Ramsay MacDonald, and Herbert Morrison show that at least certain aspects of politics were followed with some interest. But the views were often incoherent and ill-informed. So there was a lot of work to be done to help the ordinary soldier to move beyond suspicion to a more constructive attitude that would enable him to understand better the issues for which he was fighting and to play his part in British democracy after the war.

Teaching the elements of citizenship to the ordinary man would have had a better chance of success prior to the war, when there was a clear field for a sincere attempt to spread knowledge for the sake of knowledge and not for any ulterior purpose. If such a time were possible, the instruction of citizenship would happen best when the mind of the individual had not yet been poisoned by knowledge used for political ends, when the ordinary man still had faith and a certain fundamental belief where now there is nothing but suspicion.

Any lecturer, who believes in the possibility of democracy, finds that he is speaking a language his audience is too prejudiced to understand. The basis and the root of these prejudices stem from the materialistic or economic interpretation so clearly seen in all the quoted statements. Pamphlet No.12 was a fine attempt to create a different standard, but would only be successful if first the economic conception is proved wrong.

A basic BWP Course would therefore have had to aim at creating a common background and to deal with the prejudices, as outlined in my memorandum, describing the soldiers' basic proved and unproved assumptions. It would not have to be planned to the last detail in fact, it might have more success if it were handled as informally as possible, taking advantage of the certainty with which unmistakable trends of the arguments could be predicted. It is the method that counts and how far the basic assumptions are firmly shared by the audience at the end of the course.

Unfortunately, Judeo-Christian tradition no longer has the hold over the masses it used to have; consequently, the democratic idea is more and more separated from its religious roots. The ordinary man today has no allegiance to a spiritual ideal beyond the narrow confines of nationality, as A. D. Lindsay sees very clearly. At present, the teaching of history offers the only hope of the return to a moral interpretation. To do so, one must first disprove all other possible interpretations. Then the detail of British and Empire history should be taught, because there are facts that cannot be doubted. To teach history without boring one's listeners is no easy job, but guidance could be given to the lecturer in Pamphlets and those trends stressed that have born fruit. It is impossible to know what this country stands for and what we are fighting for, without having heard of Gladstone's pamphlet against the Bulgarian Atrocities of 1876 [The Bulgarian Horror and the Question of the East],[23] or Pitt's "Stop the War with America" speech in 1777.[24]

Beyond sending this memorandum to my officials, I also sent my report to people I knew well and to my old friend Ken Green, with whom I shared the interest in analyzing the political scene from the British perspective.

He replied to me 15th March 1942:[25]

Possibly, as you say, the men that are fighting this war will realize that their responsibilities do not finish with the end of the war. It will at least be apparent to many more people that some sort of national reform is necessary together with what is so vaguely termed by both main belligerents of this war as a 'new-world order.' The Grey's, Russell's Wellesley's etc. did turn out some amazing men, but personally I don't think they were greater than some thousands of men nowadays. They lived in times when everything accompanied by them was loudly praised by their equals – the masses just brayed their huzzahs most volubly, but without a lot of understanding. In the last twenty-five years a new type of man has arisen in England – one who wants to be progressive but who becomes despondent when everything is sat on by a lot of old fogies who rely on professional advisers and permanent under-secretaries to shape the beginnings of a policy. Party politics have only served to strengthen the grip of the latter and if this war had not come we were in great danger of having a government consisting of a select clique of closely related men in 'safe' seats. The individualist . . . did not matter a lot to the adults whose minds were swamped and befuddled by masses of 'party' propaganda: in fact the group with the most money usually got away with the prize. In the last major election, however, people began to take an interest in the people who represented them. The fear of war with another martial Germany was growing . . . But even then Parties were strong enough to sway Parliaments in their vote of confidence in such things as the 'sealed-lip's' policy of Baldwin and 'appeasement-policy' of Chamberlain. I am glad that Churchill became PM. He may have been the only eligible. But he knew his history and world-politics . . . Although he did criticize, he knew when to shut up.

While his unit was successfully drilling wells, which he found increasingly interesting, Ken had the bad luck to spend several months in a Jerusalem hospital with a painful skin disease. Unfortunately, my letters to him did not survive, but Ken gave some further answer to our exchange of thought on 26th May 1943:[26]

Your work in the AEC rather interested me, although as a Britisher I am not exactly proud that our people should have to be taught the rudiments of Parliamentary Government. In fact I think it is disquieting that so many people who live on those Isles should need educating in such subjects as the Empire. I expect many will have a bad shock when they realize what our commitments under the Atlantic Charter may cost us nationally. Perhaps those pamphlets you mention, written by experts and not by Officials, will do a lot of good.

I had kept in touch with Dr. Maxwell Garnett who, with his wife, had so kindly hosted me during the summer holidays on the Isle of Wight in 1938.[27] The Garnetts had now moved to Oxford and I visited them when I was home on leave with my parents at Boars Hill. I sent my memorandum to Dr. Garnett, who wrote back that he had read it with deep interest, and had been discussing it with his son Michael, a Captain at the headquarters of the 1st Airborne Division. Captain Garnett confirmed practically all I said about the mental background of the average soldier. Dr. Garnett thought that the memorandum might be of interest to J. B. Bickersteth, the Director of Army Education at the War Office, whom he knew. Dr. Garnett sent the memorandum to him and arranged that I should see Bickersteth when he lectured to the London International Assembly meeting. Bickersteth wrote to me on 14th February 1944:

I have now read your memorandum with care. It is an extremely interesting survey of the difficulties we are up against in attempting to put across what we have genuinely done our best to make impartial and factual treatment of domestic, imperial, and international problems. I believe your main thesis to be right, namely that, until we can rid the mind of the ordinary man of the preconceived ideas and prejudices which he holds little constructive work can be done. We are, of course, well aware of the imputation on the part of the troops those BWP booklets (issued by the Political Warfare Executive) and indeed the entire lecture programme and much else which is done from the War Office is one vast system of clever and insidious propaganda.

Your idea of a basic BWP course is one which we have already considered in connection with the intakes in PTWs (Powered Two Wheelers which ran on diesel or paraffin); although so far it has not been possible to proceed with this proposal. Much of what you write has a bearing on various ideas we have been discussing with regard to the educational programme in the demobilization period, i.e. from the armistice until the soldier is out of uniform.

I was very glad to make your acquaintance the other day at the London International Assembly meeting and wish I had read your memo before meeting you. I think you said your attachment to the AEC is shortly to end and that you are returning to your unit. I am passing your memorandum to Major I R. L. Marshall of this Directorate, who will be most interested in reading it and would, I know, like to get to talk with you. Could you let me know when you are likely to be in London so that we can have a further discussion about these matters? I am sending a copy of this letter to Mr. Maxwell Garnett so that he will know how much we appreciate his sending me your memo.

Particularly due to the lukewarm reception my suggestions had received in Northampton, I was delighted with the open-mindedness I found at the very top of the organization. Naturally, I was pleased to have my observations on soldiers' attitudes confirmed by the Directorate of Army Education. Professor Gilbert Murray commented that he found the paper very interesting and rather disturbing: "It is so difficult to reach the background of uneducated and ill-educated people." Dame Ellen Pinsent, to whom my memo was also passed on, and who is described in The *Concise Dictionary of National Biography* as a 'pioneer worker in the mental health services' wrote back to me that

> The paper interested me more than I can say, and gave me some idea of what the soldiers are thinking. I wish it were possible to do away with their suspicious attitudes, though one can't be surprised at it. However with all our faults we as a nation had raised the standard of living higher for working men than any other European country before the War. There is one consolation, i.e. that the men with grievances are always more vocal than the men with sturdy common sense and I hope that you have many of these latter among your audiences as well.

I would have liked to have stayed with the Army Education Corps, and Walter Oakeshott nearly made an effort to intervene with the new Director-General at the War Office, Philip R. Morris, whom he knew, but in the end decided not to do so.

After being superseded, partly in response to urgent appeals from Toronto to resume his duties at the University, Bickersteth resigned as Director of Army Education and returned to Canada in the late summer of 1944. I still regret not being able to see him again. After the war, he helped me by writing a testimonial in 1949 when I was looking for a job while in the process of graduating from Oxford. In the testimonial Bickersteth wrote:

During the period I was Director of Army Education at the War Office (1942-1944) it was my duty to read many reports from officers and NCOs in the Army Education Corps. I was particularly struck by a report on the reactions and prejudices of the man in the ranks concerning domestic and international affairs in which the War Office publication – *British Way and Purpose* – was trying to interest him. This report was by Mr. Eyck, who at that time was a sergeant in the Army Education office at Northampton.

Early in 1944 I had the opportunity of meeting Mr. Eyck, who at my request expanded the report which was found of much value by those at the War Office responsible for producing *British Way and Purpose*.[28]

Recently I have tried to find out more about Bickersteth. I knew that he was Warden of Hart House in the University of Toronto, but I was hazy about his duties there. He wrote to me in 1949, when I asked for the above cited testimonial, that he had returned to Canterbury, where his mother lived and where his brother was Canon Residentiary and an Archdeacon. When I expressed condolences on the death of his mother in 1954, he sent me a fascinating note on his family. Apparently his mother, the daughter of the first professor of Sanskrit at Oxford, belonged to the group of little girls surrounding Lewis Carroll.[29] Bickersteth wrote, "The similarity between the photographs he took of her and the Alice as portrayed by Tenniel is striking." She married Samuel Bickersteth, son of the Bishop of Exeter, the hymn writer, who became a Canon-Residentiary at Canterbury. J. Burgeon Bickersteth, the Director of Army Education, was one of six sons of this marriage.

Thanks to the help I received from friends and colleagues, I now know more about this remarkable man who showed much kindness to me. When finishing his degree at Christ Church, Oxford, Bickersteth was recruited for the Anglican Western

Canada Mission. Capable of great physical endurance, he spent two years in Alberta, from 1911 to 1913, often in quite primitive conditions, never considering the roughest and meanest work beneath his dignity as a lay missionary. The University of Toronto Press published his letters to home in 1976 (with a new introduction by the author) under the title *The Land of Open Doors.*[30] During the First World War, Bickersteth enlisted in the Royal Dragoons, initially in the ranks, was commissioned and received the Military Cross and Bar.[31] He returned to Canada after the war. At first teaching at the University of Alberta for a time in Edmonton, he found his niche at the University of Toronto as Warden of Hart House, the community centre and debating forum of the university open to all men and eventually also to women from faculty to undergraduates.[32] There he excelled in organizing a wide range of activities with a minimum of authority through his notable ability to get on with people, based on genuine interest in them. In the 1930s he frequently travelled to Germany, and even attended a staged invitation to the Dachau concentration camp, which he found somewhat incomprehensible and "grotesque." About a hundred half-naked, well-spoken men standing around him only answering trivial questions. He talks about the "bitter hostility to the Jews," who lived from hand to mouth. He saw the Nazi's conflict with the churches; Cardinal Faulhaber, Archbishop of Munich, preaching to huge audiences about the [Nazi's] denial of Christ's Jewishness.[33] He witnessed the Nazi media-control and was certain of an immense, inarticulate liberal-minded majority in Germany who would speak up if they only dared. Bickersteth regarded the Nazi dictatorship with "distaste and suspicion." But he invited German exchange students, the brightest, selected by the Nazis, to take part in discussions in Hart House, even when they did not waver in their enthusiasm of their Regime. Birckersteth was Warden of Hart House from 1921 to 1947, with the interruption of his service in the Second World War, first as education adviser to the Canadian army and then as Director of Army Education at the British War Office from 1942 to 1944. This unusual man, whom I remember with gratitude, died in 1979.

Further to my job at Army Education, I gave some instructions to the ATS "Girls," a branch of the British Army. Altogether about 74 000 women were enlisted in the Women's Auxiliary Territorial Services and distributed over the various war theatres. They were a gifted and committed group of people filling in at home and abroad wherever they could to replace men so as to free them for more active service. In a mixed group discussion, the question was raised what the position of women should be after the war. The first problem considered was that of a couple with a child. Most ladies were definite that no employment would be practicable in these conditions. One man suggested that privacy is necessary to maintain freedom and that women can fulfil themselves in the tasks at the home. Patience and tolerance would be destroyed if children were to be left elsewhere while the mother worked; coming home she would be tired and the child or children would suffer. A proposal was offered that women should enter a profession on equal footing with men, but there should be no compulsion applied. The idea of part-time work was introduced in the discussion as an important consideration for a compromise. Others wanted to see a law passed that if there was not enough work for men and women, men should be the first choice. This was modified to preference for the breadwinner. To employ trained and well-educated people to look after children in day nurseries was another suggestion to offer relief for the working mothers. But there was no consensus, and the questions were thought to be premature as one did not know what the situation would be after the war.[34]

I also taught classes in remedial English and Literature. I vaguely remember that I even had the audacity to give homework. It did not make me popular with my audience.

This led one of the men to offer me a partnership in his egg-distribution business in exchange for agreeing to stop teaching and prodding him, but with a smile and in good humour I declined both.

One event on the domestic front drew considerable public interest in 1943, namely the release of Sir Oswald Mosley and his wife, Lady Diana from imprisonment.[35] They had been closely associated with the Nazis. Sometime earlier, he had been moved from Brixton into a small house of Holloway Prison to join his wife. They were allowed to grow a garden and employ other prisoners for services. The minister of Labour, Sir Herbert Morrison stated in his autobiography that the decision for release was taken on a doctor's advice,[36] as Mosley suffered from phlebitis, which had the potential to kill him:

> The quandary was whether to free this fascist . . . or whether to have a British subject die in prison without trial. Apart from such blot on history going back to the Magna Carta, martyrdom is the source of profound strength. My task was to decide what the right thing to do was.

I expressed my observation and thoughts in a letter 12th December 1943 which I sent among others to Heinz Alexander, a correspondent to various British and foreign papers: [37]

As the news of Mosley's release was easier to understand for many Britons, it rivalled the importance of the surrender of Italy, the Cairo and the Teheran meeting, the vague principles of the Atlantic Charter, and the geographical importance of the Azores. Next to Churchill, Mosley was the best-known politician. By the troops, he was as much hated as Montgomery was admired. Morrison had to answer the question as to whether Mosley's detention was still necessary, which was a matter of opinion. Most people had made up their mind against the release because Mosley was a man of obvious unpatriotic and treacherous views and intentions. It seemed Morrison was taking unnecessary chances; there was the feeling of insecurity and of fear. There was objection against the privileges the Mosleys received at Holloway. The medical reason given was considered a pretext. The ordinary man had made up his mind and the tide of public opinion turned against the Home Secretary. For Morrison, the attack against the *principles* of Defence Regulations 18B,[38] simply to defend Mosley's imprisonment in the face of his death, reduced the praise of British principles of justice and democracy to mere lip service for the purpose of government baiting. Morrison expressed his doubts as to whether there was a genuine universal belief in the country in the importance of freedom of speech and freedom from arrest. Too many people wanted to see the power of the government used against those who are unpopular. This incident raised the concern that the liberal idea was dead among the masses, and replaced by a purely materialistic outlook.

Heinz Alexander answered from London on 22nd December, 1943. He did not think the article could still be published in the daily press, as too much had already written about the case, but he tried to contact the Economist:

> I found some of your remarks extremely interesting, though I do not agree with part of your attitude regarding Mosley . . . I feel it is wrong to treat enemies of democracy in a democratic way – too many continental democracies have perished that way. I do not advocate unconstitutional means but the phrasing of 18B would certainly have allowed for continued detention of Mosley, even if he died in prison, only those who would have considered him a martyr are Fascists anyway.
>
> In one point I do not believe Morrison. I am sure, charges could be brought against him [Mosley]

before the court, which would have condemned him as an ordinary criminal . . . But I feel that he could tell so many dirty stories on persons still enjoying some public respect that the cabinet does not like to have Mosley prosecuted . . .

Thanks for allowing me to see your exposé. Though I disagree on some points, I found it most instructive to see what people in general think about it. I was also much interested in your concluding remarks about lack of concern on constitutional questions and questions of liberalism and personal liberty.

In 1943, I was posted back to the Pioneer Corps at Buxton, reverting to rank of private, and the "delights" of the parade ground. Given the opportunity to apply for other postings, I survived the Alpine Rope Climb, but nearly broke my neck in a fall. The army authorities wisely decided to earmark me for special employment rather than to attempt to make an infantry officer out of me. In the run-up to D-Day, we were given the facility for a change of name "to meet military requirements," and I opted for the nome de guerre, the surname Alexander, though it was in fact that of my brother-in-law now living in the United States who was also a German refugee. However, the name would, at first sight, appear to be a British one. Our army numbers were also changed, as the current prefix indicated membership of the non-British Pioneer companies. One thus had a somewhat better chance in case of capture.

Soon I would be formally mobilized for overseas service. In this situation, I felt that I had the right to make a decision on my religion. As I had not attended Jewish classes at school or learned any Hebrew, it was difficult to connect with Judaism in a religious sense. At the Pioneer Corps in Buxton, another soldier had put me in touch with a Methodist Minister, Tom Sutcliffe.[39] With his wife Mollie, he regularly invited members of the Forces to his home, so

I also attended his small study circle. Tom Sutcliffe baptized me at a meeting of the local synod on D-Day plus one. On 7th June 1944, after long planning from the massive invasion into Europe, the Allied Troops had started and advanced rapidly. My mother stayed with the Sutcliffe's from just before my baptism, and Tom predicted a long pilgrimage for me. During my many moves, I worshipped with the Anglicans in London, Oxford, and Liverpool, with the Methodists in Buxton and Exeter, and with the Lutherans in Calgary, Canada. My wife Rosemarie and I later entered in communion with the Catholic Church, celebrating Mass in the small missionary chapel in Bragg Creek nestled in the foothills near Calgary. To the great regret and disappointment of the hundred families worshipping there, the mission, like many others in rural Alberta, was closed.

So far this was the outwardly visible "pilgrimage." Inwardly, I had for some time the desire to find the truth for life's basic questions. I had felt a void that could not be filled by rationality and secularism. To face the current maelstrom of moral decisions, this step provided me with the spiritual conviction and clarity of purpose to allow me to carry on with the work at hand. It was a long and richly rewarding process. As in the days of Christianity's beginning, I consider myself to be a Jewish Christian.[40] Over the years, we stayed in contact with the Sutcliffe's and visited each other whenever possible. Even my father respected Tom. When my mother was widowed, he visited her in 1970; they felt close enough for him to ask her for "her definition of what her religion was." She respected him enough to answer, and after some thought she answered: "The happiness of my children," which Tom thought was rather good.[41]

On this important step Richard Samuel wrote to me on 18th May 1944:[42]

Your spiritual decision is a very grave one and I think you are absolutely right feeling as you do. The Christian Churches all over the world will have a tremendous task after the war and need all sincere forces. I hope they will play an important part to stand Germany on her feet again after the war by providing international collaboration and strip themselves of the narrow nationalism and reactionary flavour they suffered from so long. There are many hopeful signs. Read the Sermon on the Mount (Matth.6-8) ten times over and you will discover the essence of the Christian homily; and how the 10 Commandments are developed (and not denied) by Jesus Christ. The Jews can and will be helped in this spirit only; they would be totally lost, if it did not exist.

To my regret, owing to the posting and to the further moves which followed, I did not have an opportunity of seeing Bickersteth again nor the chance of meeting Major Marshall, the editor of the *British Way and Purpose* booklets, but I did correspond with him. I wrote the second paper on Army Education "Basic Citizenship," which included some further suggestions running to fourteen pages, while I was at the Buxton training centre. To begin with I added a number of observations about the soldiers' opinions: [43]

There was a recurring reference to, 'they' did not make provision for the soldier after the last war, 'they' do not want to implement the Beveridge Report, 'they' are going to prevent international co-operation and full employment and have done so in the past. Also 'they' did not re-arm in time, carried out an appeasement policy, do not want to see us educated and will not get us decent housing. Interestingly, at a time when everything traditional is attacked, there is a marked abstention from saying anything derogatory about the royal family. There was still strong attachment to the Duke of Windsor in many quarters. The typical working-class soldier did have some realization of his own shortcomings, referring to the apathy of the working man. "I expect we will get back to business as usual after the war." There was also a feeling so long as somebody had enough for himself; he did not care about anybody else. The Jews were widely identified with big business, and with the capitalist system. I came to the conclusion that 'anti-Semitism' is strong in the army today. Some soldiers even go so far as to justify the way the Nazis treat the Jews. Some will swear that all bus companies, railways, banks, the whole of industry, etc., are owned by Jews. There are such statements as: "You have never seen a poor Jew or a Jew work." Also there are allegations that Jews have tried to evade military service by obtaining medical certificates on false pretences. Any Jewish participation in the Black Market has done the Jews a lot of harm. Generally, many men find complete satisfaction in the analysis that what is wrong with the world today is science and machines.

This theory is applied to explain, among other things, the outbreak of this war and the unemployment problem.

On conscientious objectors, while there was wide objection to them ('they should be shot'), at the same time they were praised as the only people who have guts. As to foreigners serving in the British Army, the insufficient use of non-British personnel is criticized, but on the whole the 1940 propaganda that "you cannot trust a foreigner" has been very effective. There is comparatively little actual friction between British and non-British personnel, but it would be an exaggeration to say that the ordinary soldier is very fond of foreigners, although with certain exceptions.

Winston Churchill had tremendous authority with the troops, as an opponent of appeasement, and, above all, for having won the Battle of Britain. However, he is considered a war-leader rather than a peacetime prime minister. Passages in his speeches dealing with home affairs are quoted as evidence to show that he wishes to ensure his continued presence at 10 Downing Street after the end of the war. In contrast, the 'Men of Munich', like Sir Samuel Hoare,[44] Sir John Simon[45] and Lord Halifax are remembered unfavourably. It would seem that Eden has lost some of the popular appeal he had in 1938 and 1939. As to the political parties, the Conservatives were regarded as the party of vested interests. Whenever the Tory reformers appear, they are suspected of being official party propagandists who try to make the Tories popular, without actually being representative and having any influence in the party. None of the Tory leaders, with the exception of Churchill and Eden have ever caught the eye of the public. The Labour Party benefited from the economic interpretation being in vogue. Socialist ideas have filtered through to the ordinary man to a greater extent than any other political doctrines. In the opinion of the present writer, the Labour movement, through the Trade Unions, and through the Workers' Educational Association, was the only political body which took any trouble to train ordinary men. Labour would thus spread their ideas where it was bound to have the greatest effect, in ordinary everyday life. Though the Trade Unions in a way gave the Labour movement its strength, in another way they weaken it. Trade unionism is bound to encounter, and encountered, many enemies. It certainly is not popular with every worker.

As to the other parties, the Liberals are hardly considered among younger men. Their idealistic interpretation is considered out of date. It was too early to judge how the Commonwealth party would do; the Independent Labour Party was not too well known. As to the Communist Party, in spite of all the admiration for Russian Communism, there is still a certain uncomfortable feeling about trying the thing too close to one's home, it might explode.

In the Middle Ages the world order was based on the ability of the local priest controlling the many functions of a community; that included education, health and 'unemployment relief'. For a long time people accepted his authority without questioning. They were not supposed to think or challenge dogma. With the Reformation and the invention of printing press more and more people learned to read and write. Though today we have no obvious fetters, yet, we too, are tied, and our ability to think is affected adversely by the appearance of a large unskilled proletariat. The willingness to think has suffered owing to the wealth of technological refinement, the cinema where you watch a 'straight' story in a comfortable seat, the type of newspaper you can read by looking at the headlines and cartoons, the wireless which you can just switch on for 'background music'. Life moved so quickly that one has little time for thought.

The influence of the Army on the soldier's psychology is immense. Whether the apparent necessary preaching of the idea of 'doing as you are told' can be robbed of its disastrous long-term effects on the power of men to think is a matter of dispute. The present writer does not take the gloomy view that Army Education is a contradiction in terms. In a way the weekly talk perhaps provides a welcome relaxation from the discipline which is so important from a military point of view, as it provides a safety valve and diverts some of the spirit of opposition which would otherwise cause trouble in the internal running of the unit. In the post-war period, the vast majority wanted security of employment, 'a living wage', old age pensions, cheap entertainment and decent houses, there was an objection to flats (apartments) owing to the perceived danger of regimentation. They wanted to avoid violent changes, ups and downs. They did not want to be 'got at'. There was a general belief in transferring industry very largely from private enterprise to state ownership, without consideration of the consequences. Capitalism is the scapegoat and state-control the New Messiah.

Unfortunately, my report then went on to argue that there was an incompatibility between the materialistic interpretation of history and politics on the one hand, and religion and democracy on the other. It seemed doubtful as to whether a reformist programme of the Labour Party could be carried out within the framework of capitalist democracy. I did not know enough about Labour Party politics and was obviously proved wrong by events. I had been strongly influenced at that time by a book by Gustav Stolper, in collaboration with his wife Toni: *This Age of Fable. The Political and Economic World We Live in.*[46] Stolper, a leading writer on economics, had been a member of the *Reichstag* between 1930 and 1932 representing the *Deutsche Staatspartei*, the successor party to the left-liberal *Deutsche Demokratische Partei*, like our mutual friend Theodor Heuss. As his wife Toni was Jewish, the Stolper's had to emigrate and in 1933 found refuge in the United States.[47]

The book was completed in September 1941, about half way between the German invasion of the Soviet Union and Pearl Harbour.[48] It was a fervent appeal to public opinion in Western countries not to give up faith in liberty, democracy, and private enterprise and to resist the allure of the claims of economic achievement by the totalitarian regimes. The tract included a brilliant polemical analysis of pervading attitudes to current political and economic questions in the world at that time. The fables or myths Stolper criticizes are the oversimplifications then in vogue, such as the notions of a perfect capitalism on the one hand and of perfect planning on the other. As to the former, in many European countries capitalism had, indeed, already been limited by a considerable degree of public ownership, without ceasing to be capitalist countries, to "both the outside world and their own socialist parties."[49] As to the latter, he warned against a socialist faith in perfect planning and asserted that "National Socialism in Germany and Fascism in Italy were never anything but socialist orders, all Marxist diatribes to the contrary notwithstanding."[50] A socialist order, including that of the Soviet Union, "by necessity must encroach upon the remotest abodes of private life, must become and remain totalitarian."[51] What probably led me astray was the rather sweeping use of the term "socialist" in these theories. I did not pay sufficient attention to the fact that Stolper indeed exempted the Labour Party, the Trade Unions (after 1926) and the co-operative movement in Great Britain from his general strictures on socialism.[52] But he was deeply worried about the radical left-wing influence Professor Harold Laski of the London School of Economics and Political Science exercised not only in Britain and on the Labour Party, but also on public opinion in the United States.[53] In any case, I infringed a code of conduct in which I very much believed and which I did my best to practice as an army education instructor, namely to leave it to the listener to draw his own conclusions as to the party political implications of any subjects discussed.

As I was mobilized for overseas service in the summer of 1944 and could not always myself write and receive letters, my father in Boar's Hill helped me to keep in touch with my correspondents, particularly in the Oxford area. In reply to my second memorandum, Dr. Garnett wrote to my father in July 1944 and stated that I had set down with admirable brevity and lucidity the opinions of the soldiers I had met.[54] He added he felt sure that Mr. Bickersteth and others concerned with education in the Services would appreciate my valuable work in this field. But he strongly – and rightly – criticized my speculations about the Labour Party, which were my "personal opinions – neither observed facts nor reasoned deductions from such facts."

In July 1944, Dr. Garnett mentioned that Mr. Bickersteth was giving up his post at the War Office: "Perhaps the appointment of P. R. Morris as supreme Director of Army Education made him feel that he himself had become redundant." Favourable responses on my report came from professors Gilbert Murray and Reginald Coupland in the Boars Hill neighbourhood. Gilbert Murray wrote that the report on my teaching observations

> confirms what I have already heard from other sources, and is certainly rather alarming. I think, however, that a great deal of the cynicism and pessimism is a sort of psychological self-defence. The men are conscious of their ignorance and do not like to profess belief in anything. On the other hand, they do really believe in their own leaders, as your son's men do in Churchill. A man who has been dealing with the Guards told me their attitude was a great disbelief in all political parties and Government.[55]

Professor Coupland also said that the report confirmed what he had heard from other quarters.[56] Walter Oakeshott in his letter of 29th November 1943 thanked me for my two memos but preferred the original document of the 'anonymous civilian', and asked me for my permission to use it in his teaching, which I was certainly pleased to give.[57]

I had sent my second memorandum to Heinz Alexander.[58] On 7th March 1945, he suggested minor alterations and contacted the *British Survey* published by the British Association for International Understanding and edited by Mr. Eppstein, probably a pseudonym of Sir John Smithers MP, who was interested and prepared to read my report. He answered the following day:

> My chairman Mr G. M. Young and I were much impressed by Mr Frank Alexander' s [Eyck's] paper

on 'Basic Citizenship.' There are one or two points
where one would like to join issue with him but on
the whole I feel that the analysis is correct. We could
not, I am afraid, publish the report as it stands. It is
mainly in the form of advice given to those who are
in control of Army Education. . . . Our surveys are
read by all ranks and I am not sure how far it would
be wise to purvey this kind of candid criticism to our
general reader.

They suggested I try publishing the memo as a pamphlet in
the Spectator under the title "What the Army Thinks." Heinz
Alexander thought their decision was understandable, but
"apart from the disappointment the letter is highly satisfactory."
However, further attempts did not lead to publication either.

Philip Whitting pointed to my apparent Conservative
prejudices. Actually, I do not think that I had formed clear
views by this time as to how I stood myself in relation to the
political parties. It is true that for a time I thought that Labour
planning and democracy were not fully compatible, but this
phase in my development passed quickly. As a soldier, I was
not particularly drawn towards the Conservative Party. After
all, issues of foreign policy had been paramount for some
time, particularly so for a German Jewish refugee. The mainly
Conservative National Government had carried out a policy
of appeasement that I thought was mistaken, though I did not
sufficiently realize at the time that left-wing pacifism, which
Baldwin and Neville Chamberlain had to take into account,
was also very much to blame.

Though Gustav Stolper's *This Age of Fable* had alerted me
to some of the pitfalls of economic planning, some of the
wartime measures, such as clothes rationing, had a certain
appeal to him in advancing greater equality. On a visit
to St. Paul's School on leave from the army, I got to know
Mr. Usborne, a new master at the school who had rather left-

wing views. He found my outlook to be close to the Fabians. Serving in the ranks, I shared an unmistakable opposition to authority with many other soldiers, though the sergeant majors rather than the officers were liable to make life difficult for me. I was critical of many of the rather aloof officers, some of whom seemed to me – perhaps quite unfairly – to owe their commissions simply to having been to the right school. I hope this was not a form of jealousy on my part for not having been commissioned. At any rate, what I regarded as a system of class distinction did not make me predisposed to the Conservative party, any more than their policy towards Nazi Germany in the pre-war period.

Finally, there is the question whether army education, such as the activities of the Army Bureau of Current Affairs and the *British Way and Purpose* booklets helped the Labour Party to victory in the General Election of 1945. Numerically, the vote of the service did not determine the election result, though obviously their feelings may well have influenced the civilian vote of relatives and friends. My own knowledge only relates to "other ranks," that is, those below commissioned rank, that I encountered as an army education instructor. Army Education had to deal with soldiers who were, so far as one can generalize, mainly guided by three factors. In the case of members of the working class and to some extent of the lower middle class, their attitudes were strongly influenced by their perceptions of how they and their families had fared during the world economic crisis and its aftermath, especially concerning the serious effect of unemployment. Secondly, there was the effect of their uprooting from civilian life. They were taken out of their normal social relationships, including the texture of their local society with their place in it. Many reacted against some aspects of their new unaccustomed environment by adopting what the troops called "bolshie," that is somewhat rebellious attitudes.

They disliked excessive discipline, which often included an element of arbitrariness and mindless routine. During comparatively calm moments, they detested having to go through the "spit and polish" routine. Discipline was mainly enforced by the sergeant major and it was he who was liable to arouse the greatest dislike, while the officers were more remote in periods of calm, though they would determine the fate of the soldier put on a charge. One of the best descriptions of the ordinary soldier's attitude to military authority I have seen is Anthony Burgess' autobiography *Little Wilson and Big God. The First Part of the Confessions.*[59] Although the British Army would not have emerged on the side of the victors if it had been quite as inefficient as Burgess claimed, and even if he likely did not emerge quite so victorious from his various encounters with sergeants as he states, he does catch the atmosphere of relations between privates and NCOs. Reading his account in my early eighties, I found myself roaring with laughter. Though no longer under the thumb of sergeant majors, I only realized then, through the relief I gained from the reading Burgess, that I had not quite got over my experiences in the army, even after nearly sixty years. To the more radical, the army with its promotion of "public school boys" to commissions only seemed to perpetuate the system of social discrimination to which they had objected in civilian life. Sergeant majors and sergeants vented their resentment of what they regarded as class distinction on "public school" boys serving in the ranks. I can testify to this in the case of several sergeant majors.

Thirdly, there were the lessons which individuals drew from the changes that had taken place in wartime. Not all these were considered negative. While food rationing limited the ability of the better off to obtain more to eat, attention also focused on those at the bottom of the economic scale who had been undernourished and were now encouraged to adopt basic nutritional standards. While not likely to lead to the adoption of an economic interpretation of history and politics, concern for social conditions can easily, but not necessarily, lead to the questioning of some features of capitalism. Well before the First World War and before he became Archbishop of York 1929-1942 and Canterbury 1942-1944, William Temple was engaged in social reform, inspired by the desire for social and national righteousness and Christian Unity.[60] He presided over the Workers Education Association and played a leading part in the unemployment question and the Ecumenical Movement. On the political front, Clement Attlee was similarly involved in social questions.[61] He was a social worker before the First World War in which he served in the Tank Corps and retired from the Army as Major in 1919. He was Under-Secretary of State in the Labour Minority Government of 1924, leader of the Labour Party from 1935–1940, and joined the Coalition Government in 1940. With a landslide victory, he won the 1945 election and carried out many moderately balanced social reforms.

What was the effect of all this in terms of party politics? There was a reaction against the traditional establishment, against privilege and elitism – rightly or wrongly – considered insufficiently mindful of the interests of the vast mass of the population. Clearly, the experience of unemployment outweighed some of the achievements of the National (mainly conservative) Governments, for example in the field of house construction. The increasing care necessarily taken by the authorities of all sections of the population in time of war had certain appeal to the soldier and made him more amenable to state intervention and to its continuation into peace-time, with some "planning." Much of this pointed to the Labour Party. In contrast, the Conservatives were often seen as responsible for the bad times, or for not dealing adequately and swiftly with the problems that arose from them.

Bearing in mind that not all service personnel were covered at all times, what was the effect of Army Education programmes, such as ABCA and *the British Way and Purpose*, on these attitudes on the part of the troops? Clearly in the case of *BWP*, the general approach was often to give a critical assessment of the existing situation in a particular field and then to ask "how can we create a better world?" This favored "planning" and the position of the reformers among whom the Labour Party was regarded as the foremost, though in fact Conservative governments had frequently carried out reforms. Furthermore, the focus on the deficiencies of the past militated usually against the party in government, effectively the Conservatives. But in no way was this method, which was adopted to stimulate the interest of the troops, a deliberate attempt to favour Labour. It was the best way to gain and keep the attention of listeners.

An alternative approach might have been along historical lines, to demonstrate the gradual development of, for example, the constitution, and to emphasize not only change but also continuity. However, conditions in the armed forces did not provide the leisure for setting up courses of history lectures. The situation in 219 Pioneer Company, where Richard Samuel and I could set up a course of four lectures on British history, was rather exceptional. Indeed, one may ask to what extent an educational programme, however well conducted, can be able to change outlooks. Existing approaches to politics were deeply ingrained and often eluded questioning. Thus, it would be unusual for a soldier to be so impressed by something he heard in a lecture that he would reconsider fundamental approaches to political issues. After all, with the occasional course session and so many other matters occupying the soldier's mind, in-depth study was not feasible. Sometimes, existing attitudes might be reinforced.

All of these thoughts on the possible effect of Army Education on the Labour victory in 1945 draw exclusively on my papers and recollections from this period. I am not alone in wanting to puzzle through these questions. The General Election of that year has aroused considerable interest and has resulted in a number of publications.[62] The opening of some archives has also revealed a great deal about what was going on about army education behind the scenes, unknown to the ordinary instructor. From the beginning, there was criticism of aspects of army education by the Army Bureau of Current Affairs and by Conservatives going up to the highest level on the basis of the course being biased in a left-wing direction. The right-wing Conservative Member of Parliament and Under-Secretary for War, Sir Henry Page-Croft (Lord Croft), fully supported the provision of education (as well as entertainment) for the troops in the winter of 1940-41 to improve morale after the setbacks of the previous summer.[63] But both he and, more importantly, Prime Minister Winston Churchill were seriously disturbed by the apparent left-wing tendencies of the educational programmes. "In the eyes of Page-Croft, to question whether something was right[wing] inevitably was to stoke up discontent."[64] But questioning and frank discussion by the troops were essential in any educational activities involving current affairs and citizenship. Churchill voiced strong opposition to the setting up of the Army Bureau of Current Affairs in 1941,[65] and in October 1942 he asked that the ABCA courses should be wound up as quickly as possible, but was overruled.[66]

The continuation of army education in these sensitive socio-political areas owed a great deal to the steady support given by Sir James Griggs, Permanent Under-Secretary at the War Office who in an unusual move served as Secretary of State for War after February 1942. His support was joined by that of Adjutant-General Sir Ronald Adam, who felt a great concern and understanding for the welfare of the troops, the extent of which would have surprised most of us serving in the ranks.[67] Interestingly, objections to what ABCA was doing occasionally came from the Labour side. Ernest Bevin, Minister of Labour in the war time coalition, objected to an ABCA poster depicting a pre-war child with rickets standing amid scenes of poverty, with the kind of new and modern health centre that should be the aim in post-war Britain superimposed on this image. Bevin complained to the Prime Minister on the grounds that it would undermine morale by suggesting that some of the country's children still lived in such squalor.[68]

To what extent were ABCA and the BWP in the hands of left-wing organizers and lecturers? Undoubtedly the Labour Party now reaped the benefit of having taken a far greater interest in adult education in time of peace than the Conservatives. The Workers' Educational Association had for years been doing excellent work among those who wanted to enhance their knowledge. It was only natural that in many cases Army Education officers and NCOs, as well as civilian lecturers, should be drawn from the ranks of the Workers Education Association. In addition, the League of Nations Union had seen education as one of its main activities in the inter-war years; as a school-boy I had been one of the beneficiaries of a fascinating course on current European affairs in London just before Christmas 1938. While the Union was not affiliated to any political party, and while a Conservative, Lord James Cecil (J. Edward Hubert Gasscoyne, fourth Marquess of Salisbury; advocated a national government) had been one of its leading personalities, the internationalism of the organization at the time made appealed more to Socialists and Liberals than to Conservatives.[69] The Central Advisory Council (CAC) consisting of civilian adult education organizations, which supplied lecturers for army education, was thus bound to have at its disposal a supply of more speakers tending to Labour and Liberals, than to the Conservatives. And not surprisingly, Army Education officers who came from the Workers' Educational Association, frequently commissioned speakers from their left-wing network. Major Gilbert Hall, the AEC officer whom I heard lecture at an army education conference in 1942 or 1943, would have been a case in point. He and Major George Wigg appeared to advocate a commissar system into the Army. Hall was unusual in not following the King's Regulation that forbade servicemen to communicate unauthorized personal views. He caused exasperation in the War Office for his tendency to solicit "unsuitable" lecturers like Communist Member of Parliament D. N. Pritt. Even among left-wingers, the degree of his activism pushed beyond the limits of what was appropriate for an AEC officer. Because of his rather extreme left-wing communist teaching, he was transferred to Gibraltar and Egypt, but eventually was asked to resign his commission.[70]

As to the higher appointments in army education, Croft had some misgivings about W. E. Williams becoming director of the newly set up Army Bureau of Current Affairs. Williams, executive member of the Workers' Educational Association, "enjoyed a radical reputation."[71] But he was considered to be particularly well qualified through his experience in popular education to supervise the new organization. However, suspicions Croft voiced in 1943 that J. B. Bickersteth, Director of Army Education, was an ardent Left-Winger and was using his official position to promote state control are completely unjustified. Bickersteth was a man of integrity. In a completely different context, in connection with Hart House at the University of Toronto to which he devoted his life's work, he told an interviewer that he was "Conservative in England, usually Liberal in Canada, conservatively minded and patriotic."[72]

It is true that some left-wing AEC officers stand out, like Gilbert Hall and his ally George Wigg. The latter eventually became Paymaster-General in Harold Wilson's first Labour Government. Also, a relatively high number of AEC officers entered Parliament in 1945, and all six were Labour.[73] But one must not assume that the Army Education Corps as a whole was left wing. As to my own Northamptonshire unit, which may or may not have been typical, I cannot recall any of the four regulars (Alan Rawsthorne was a temporary supernumerary with us) voicing Labour views. Of the four (a Regimental Sergeant Major and three Sergeants), two struck me as a traditionalist and rather conservative in their outlook, one could have been a liberal, and the fourth one may well have been non-party.

In general, S. P. MacKenzie in his *Politics and Military Morale* comes to similar conclusions as I about the effect of Army Education on the 1945 general election. MacKenzie regarded it as "questionable whether the socio-political attitudes soldiers adopted during the war can be attributed to the influence of Army education."[74] The various education programmes were only accepted by the troops so long as they matched their "general interests and outlook." The author also emphasizes the soldier's negative reaction to the disciplinary role of the sergeants major, who to him represented the authorities; these he in turn associated with the major coalition partner, the Conservatives.[75] As Duff Cooper MP suggested, the exercise of the franchise gave the soldier an opportunity of expressing his opinion of the sergeant major.[76] However, the historian Jeremy A. Crang stated that from 1940, efforts had been made to give remedial classes for illiterates.[77] There had been a special network of Basic Educational Centres that were staffed by the Army Education Centre, AEC, even if its organization was probably somewhat patchy, using the *English Parade* booklet (8681 words long). ABCA and the *BWP* had increased the critical thinking in place of prejudice. The troops had shown the same political instinct as the civilian population in their feeling that the Conservative Party had failed the nation, that it was time for change, and that Labour would provide a better future by enacting a kind of collectivist politics which the experience of war had popularized. Even so, in general Conservative politicians tended to blame the activities of Army Education for their defeat.

Endnotes

1   Frank Eyck papers, *The British Way and Purpose*, (Consolidated edition of BWP booklets 1-18 prepared by the Directorate of Army Education).

2   Frank Eyck papers, Richard Samuel to Frank Eyck, 12th June 1944.

3   Oswald Spengler, *Untergang des Abendlandes*, (Wien: Braumüller, 1923 2nd ed.).

4   Frank Eyck papers, Lecture notes, February 1944.

5   Anthony Burgess is a cousin of the spy Guy Burgess.

6   See S. O. Mackenzie, *Political Morale*, (Oxford: Current Affairs and Citizenship Education in the British Army 1941-1942), p. 186.

7   Ibid, pp. 137-144, esp. the last four pages.

8   The Congress of Vienna 1815/14, attended by representatives of Austria, Russia, and the German States of the Deutsche Bund. Present were the Czar of Russia's deputized by Graf Nesselrode, the Emperor of Austria-Hungary and Fürst Metternich, the King of Prussia represented by Graf von Hardenberg and Freiherr Wilhelm von Humboldt and Representatives of other German States, for England stood Lord Castlereagh, and for France the re-emerged Prince, now President Tallerand. They sat during the day, and with their Ladies "the Congress danced" in the evening.

9   The Axis, i.e. the Alliance between Germany and Italy of 1936.

10 Paul Mackenzie, *S. P. MacKenzie*, (Oxford: Clarendon Press, 1992), p. 432.

11 Ibid, p. 436.

12 Ibid, p. 1.

13 Ibid, booklet 2, chapter IV.

14 Ibid, booklet 7.

15 A. D. Lindsay, *What more is needed of the citizen?* (Booklet 12), p. 363.

16 Frank Eyck papers, John Taylor, letters to Frank Eyck.

17 See John McCabe, *Alan Rawsthorne, Portrait of a Composer*, (Oxford University Press, 1999).

18 Frank Eyck papers, Sgt Frank Eyck, *Suggestions for a basic BWP Course*, 13803601 A. E. C. Northants Sub District, (undated, possibly March 1942) 5 pages, 3090 words, used here with minor editing.

19 Harold Nicolson, *Current Affairs No 21*. Author of the official biography of George V. 1962.

20 Ramsey MacDonald (1866-1937), Labour P.M. 1924, 1929; in an all party government 1931-1935.

21 Stanley Baldwin 1867-1947, Conservative P.M. 1923-1924, 1924-1929, 1931-1935; Lord President of the Council in the National Government, 1935-1937, introduced a moderate level of re-armament, and handled Edward VIII's abdication crisis in 1936 with dignity. Besides Mrs. Simpson's unacceptability as a divorcee, Edward VIII had fascist leaning, see Martin Pugh, *Hurrah for the Blackshirts*, (London: Jonathan Cape. 2005).

22 Herbert Henry Asquith, an ardent Gladstonian, Liberal P.M. 1908-1916, part of the coalition Government during WWI until 1916, returned to parliament 1920, and devoted himself to the Irish question.

23 See Erich Eyck, *Gladstone*, (London: George Allen & Unwin Ltd, 1938), p. 256ff.

24 See Erich Eyck, *Die Pitt's und die Fox'*, (Zürich-Erlenbach: Eugen Rentsch, 1946), p. 270ff.

25 Frank Eyck papers, Ken Green to Frank Eyck, 15th March 1942.

26 Frank Eyck papers, Ken Green to Frank Eyck, 26th May 1943.

27 Frank Eyck papers, Maxwell Garnett, to Erich Eyck 3rd, 10th July 1944.

28 Frank Eyck papers, Bikersteth's testimonial, 16th February 1949.

29 Lewis Carroll, a mathematician, Author of *Alice in Wonderland,* 1876.

30 I am grateful to my colleague Donald Smith for drawing my attention to this work.

31 John Terraine, ed. with an introduction by John Bickersteth, *The Bickersteth Diaries 1914-1918*, (London: Leo Cooper, 1995).

32 Ian Montagnes, *An Uncommon Fellowship. The story of Hart House* (Toronto, 1969). For details, I am indebted to Robert Spencer of the University of Toronto for his help with the story of Hart House. Burgon Bickersteth correspondence 1933-1942 on visits to Germany, University of Toronto Archives. See also MA thesis by Brian Watson, (Ottawa: Carleton University, 2003), *Nazis in Hart House: Burgeon Bickersteth and the Rise of European Fascism.*

33 Faulhaber, Kardinal Michael von, *Judentum ,Christentum, Germanentum, Adventspredigten*, (München 2M, Neuturm Str. 2a-4: Verlag der Graphishen

Kunstanstalt A. Huber, 1933).

34 Frank Eyck papers, Army Education handwritten notes 4 pages, undated probably 1942.

35 Martin Pugh, *Hurrah for the Blackshirts, Fascists and Fascism between the Wars*, (London: Jonathan Cape, 2005).

36 Herbert Morrison, *Herbert Morrison. Autobiography*, (London: Oldham Press, 1960).

37 Frank Eyck to Heinz Alexander (brother of Paul Alexander, my bother-in-law), 12th December 1943.

38 Defence Regulations 18B existed in draft form in 1939, became legal under the Emergency Power (Defence) Act, and was abolished as soon as the war ended in 1945.

39 Frank Eyck papers, Tom and Molly Sutcliffe to Frank Eyck, exchange of letters until Toms death 18th April 1972, Obituary in Methodist Recorder, April 1972

40 Hugh Montefiore, *On being a Jewish Christian,* (London, Sydney, Auckland: Hodder & Stoughton, 1998). Frank Eyck papers, Robert B. McFarland to Frank Eyck 29th August 2001, enclosed his essay, *Elective Divinities*: *Religiöse Konversionen im Exil und die Apologia pro vita sua, als Beitrag zur Exilliteratur* (Utah USA: Birmingham Young University Press Provo, 2001). Frank Eyck to Robert Mcfarland, 18th September 2001. Wallace P. Sillanpoa and Robert G. Weisbord, *The Zolli Conversion: Background and Motives*. London: Routledge, Judaism No. 150 Vol. 38 No. 2, Spring 1989. Wallace P. Sillanpoa and Robert G. Weisbord, "The Baptized Rabbi of Rome: The Zolli Case," *Judaism* (No. 149 Vol. 38 Winter 1989), pp. 74-91.

41 Frank Eyck papers, Tom, and Molly Sutcliffe to Frank Eyck, 24th November 1970.

42 Frank Eyck papers, Richard Samuel to Frank Eyck, 18th May 1944.

43 Frank Eyck papers, Frank Eyck second report, *On Basic Citizenship, some further suggestions* 14 pages 8415 words, undated probably second part of June 1944, given with little editing.

44 Frank Eyck papers, Samuel Hoare (1880-1959), Conservative MP 1910-1944; *DNB,* p. 487-490.

45 John Simon, (1873-1954), *DNB*, p. 892-894, a great jurist; Liberal MP 1906-1918, 1922-1940 Chancellor of Exchequer under Chamberlain; as

Lord Chancellor he initiated law reform.

46 Gustav Stolper, *This Age of Fable. The Political and Economic World we Live in,* (New York: Reynal & Hitchkock, 1941), pp. 448ff. In 1947 Gustav Stolper was a member of the official American mission to Germany under the American President Herbert Hoover and a major contributor to its recommendations of easing the economic situation of the defeated enemy. Gustav Stolper died at the end of that year.

47 Toni Stolper, *Ein Leben im Brennpunkten unserer Zeit,* (Tübingen: Rainer Wunderlich, 1960).

48 Pearl Harbour, the destruction of the USA Pacific Fleet by the Japanese, 7th December 1941.

49 Gustav Stolper, *This Age of Fable,* p. 70.

50 Ibid, p. 133.

51 Ibid, p. 133.

52 Ibid, chapter XI, Of British Degeneracy, esp. pp. 221ff.

53 Toni Stolper, *Ein Leben im Brennpunkt unsere Zeit,* p. 411ff.

54 Frank Eyck papers, Maxwell Garnett to Erich Eyck, 10th July 1944. Richard Samuel to Frank Eyck, 13th July 1944, about constant change of personnel.

55 Frank Eyck papers, Gilbert Murray to Erich Eyck, 5th July 1944.

56 Frank Eyck papers, Reginald Coupland to Erich Eyck, 13th August 1944.

57 Frank Eyck papers, Walter Oakeshott to Frank Eyck, 29th November 1943.

58 Frank Eyck papers, Heinz Alexander to Frank Eyck, 12th and 23rd December 1943, 7th March 1944.

59 Anthony Burgess, *Little Wilson and Big God,* (New York: Grove Weidenfeld, 1991), Part Four, especially pp. 239-312.

60 *Concise Dictionary of National Biography,* Vol. II. p. 429.

61 Clement Attlee, *The Social Worker,* (London: G. Bell, 1920), *The Will and the Way of Socialism,* (London: Methuen, 1935); his Autobiography, *As it happened,* (New York: Viking Press, 1954).

62 Paul Addison, *The Road to 1945,* (London: Jonathan Cape 1975), p. 146.

63 Ibid, p. 150.

64 Paul Addison, *Churchill on the Home Front,* (London: Pimlico, 1993), p. 346.

D. S. Birn, *The League of Nations Union, 1918-1945,* (Oxford: Clarendon Press, 1981), see also *Concise Dictionary of National Biography.* Maxwell

Garnett, *The world needs the Church's help*, (London: League of Nations Union, 1926), a speech delivered 19th April 1926 in the Central Hall, Westminster.

65 Paul Addison, *The Road to 1945*, pp. 150-151.

66 Jeremy A. Crang, *The British Army and the People's War 1939-1945*, (Manchester: University Press, 2000), pp. 123-4.

67 Ronald Adam, *Education in the Home Forces*, pp. 85-127, 98.

68 D. S. Birn, *The League of Nations Union, 1918-1945*, see also *Concise Dictionary of National Biography* Vol. II. pp. 199. Maxwell Garnett, *The world needs the Church's help*.

69 Jeremy A.Crang, *The British Army and the People's War*, p. 118.

70 See Mackenzie, *Politics and Military Morale*, pp. 111-112, 154, 165-170.

71 Jeremy A. Crang, *The British Army and the People's War 1939-1945*, p. 118.

72 Ian Montagnes. *An Uncommon Fellowship. The Story of Hart House*, (Toronto: University of Toronto Press, 1969), p. 122. I maintain that Bickersteth, on his frequent visits during the 1930s to Germany, did not fall for the "smoke screen" the Nazis were expert in putting over foreigners.

73 Mackenzie, *Politics and Military* Morale, pp. 185-186.

74 Ibid, p. 185.

75 Ibid, p. 188.

76 Duff Cooper, *Old Men Forget*, (New York: Dutton, 1954), p.359.

77 Jeremy A. Crang, *The British Army and the People's War 1939-1945*, pp. 126-129.

Chapter 6

CHAPTER 7

Psychological Warfare of the British Army, 1944-1945

As a result of being recommended for specialist employment, I was tested as a radio monitor at the head office of the British Broadcasting Corporation either later in June or early in July 1944. The BBC Broadcasting House was located right in the West End of London. The *Vergeltungswaffen*, the flying bombs, were unrelenting. Londoners listened in case the warbling noise of these colloquially called "doodlebugs" stopped overhead, hopefully not precisely over where one happened to be at the time. The writer Peter de Mendelsohn, also a German refugee, Deputy Controller of the Press Branch of the Public Relations/Information Services Control Group (PR/ISC),[1] conducted my test. He was one of the few refugees that received a commission. I still remember one question I could not answer: what was "monitoring" in German? Mercifully he told me it was "*abhören*." I was also tested in French because the monitoring of the French radio stations under German control was important at that time. Fortunately, my French passed muster, though it was pretty rusty by this time, eight years after leaving the Collège Français, partly because it was under the competition of English which tended to *anglicize* my French. A little later, when I had presumably been accepted for my new assignment, I visited the very extensive BBC radio-monitoring unit at Caversham as part of my training. The station was not far from London, which employed a good number of German and other refugees. I do not know whether we were all bilingual; I was certainly supposed to be and in general the others were, too.

Rome had fallen into the allied hands two days before the massive invasion of Normandy on D-Day, 6th June 1944, under the command of Field Marshal Montgomery. The Advanced Guard of the army was already in Normandy when I was posted to the Publicity and Psychological Warfare (P&PW) Branch at 21 Army Group Headquarters with the Main Guard of Montgomery's army. The group had its own monitoring unit and was situated near Portsmouth, Devon at that time. The Rear Guard of the army had yet to engage. Psychological Warfare was originally an American term, the British equivalent was the Political Warfare Executive (PWE), but in the interests of working with the Americans and of standardization, 21 Army Group adopted the term Psychological Warfare.

If I remember correctly, we were told at an intelligence briefing about serious disaffection in the German army. About 20th July 1944 we heard of the Generals' failed plot to kill Hitler that was lead by Oberst Graf Claus Schenk von Stauffenberg.[2] Although this attempt to eliminate Hitler was by no means the only one (there had been 42 attempts), this assassination attempt had immediate become widely public within Germany.[3] At first there was great general confusion. Then swift persecution of the conspirators and their families ensued. It was brutal. This was followed by the arbitrarily staged grim trials at the People's Court, the Volksgerichtshof. In fact, the attack on Hitler strengthened the regime. Goebbels as the Reich's Plenipotentiary for the Total War Effort and his propaganda machine made full use of this miscarriage. From the British side this news could initially only be transmitted on "Black" radio, through clandestine stations, as it otherwise would have given away their knowledge of the secret German code.[4] The German intelligence would soon realize that the source for certain information could only have been accessible to the British though their knowledge of Enigma.

In August, the bulk of Montgomery's Main Guard was moved to Normandy. My unit crossed the channel on D+60, 5th

August 1944, when things were thankfully mostly safe. It was a beautiful day and we spent much of the day on deck sunning ourselves. After disembarkation we saw the terrible destruction from friendly fire on many places in Normandy, including Caen. The damage even caused some protests from the French and Belgian Cardinals and Bishops. Goebbels certainty did not miss using this crisis to propagate more propaganda through the German occupied French stations, saying that Normandy's destruction demonstrated the cynical indifference of the British to French lives. We were installed in an orchard under canvas. One day a parcel arrived from my mother. Somewhat ironically, it contained apples from our garden at Boars Hill. However, at least the apples my mother sent me were ripe, whereas the ones hanging just above our tents were not.

For a while I worked as a clerk in the branch office, whose activities on the publicity side included looking after military correspondents. The officer in charge of the branch, Brigadier Neville, seemed to have had a particular aptitude for this task.[5] But my time was mostly spent in our converted ambulance that contained the radio monitoring equipment. Initially, we listened to German-occupied France, monitoring the broadcasts of French "radio traitors," the collaborators sending anti-Allied propaganda from a station under German control (e.g. Jean-Hérold Paquis from Radio Paris). I found these Frenchmen were speaking rather fast, I could just about keep up with them. We made notes in our van, using recording facilities for anything that struck us as particularly noteworthy, and were told that the Intelligence Branch at Head Quarters scrutinized our reports carefully for any interesting evidence, such as signs of German morale or of anything that might reveal intentions.

In 1952, Richard H. S. Crossman gave a lecture about the complex history of his years with Psychological Warfare.[6] He was by then a Labour Member of Parliament. As a young man he had a brilliant academic career reading Plato and Marx as fellow on New College Oxford. During a pre-war year in

Germany he made contact with and investigated both, the German Communist and National Socialist Parties. Soon he decided on a political career. He was elected to the Oxford City Council and leader of a Labour Group, and became assistant editor of the left-wing New Statesman.

In 1940, he was made head of the secret Department of Propaganda for Enemy Countries, European Part German Branch, administered outside London but under the Ministry of Information. He was stationed "in the Country" in Bedfordshire north of London at Woburn Abbey, which the Foreign Office looked to with a certain amount of suspicion. In the army, he somehow acquired the nickname double-Crossman. In May 1943, he was sent to Algiers to solve an unsatisfactory situation on the Anglo-American PWE front. I first saw him when he visited the Political & Psychological Warfare office in Normandy coming from Psychological Warfare Division at SHAEF, the Supreme Headquarters Allied Expedition Force, at General Eisenhower's headquarters. At the time Crossman was the chief British political warrior under the supreme command of Sir Robert Bruce Lockhart, initiator and then Director-General of Political Warfare Executive, PWE, from 1942-1945.[7] He had already served in this field during the First World War. The co-operation with Montgomery and General Bradley, on the American side, did not always run smoothly, when for instance news was aired too quickly or even without authorization. Both generals objected strongly to undue haste in broadcasting information as this could easily interfere with the strategic plans of their armies.[8]

One day Crossman appeared in army uniform, but without signs of rank and explained to us in detail the task at hand. It was made clear to us that our unit could not work on its own, but was serving as a handmaiden to the military and political authorities, who had to be consulted. Their consent had to be assured for any step we made. There was no substitute for military action; the aim of our Intelligence work was to try to subvert the enemy, demoralize, deceive, and anticipate the enemy's intentions.

Propaganda, already practiced effectively by the enemy, had always been part of war and was not a new idea, but the methods and technical possibilities had changed greatly. There was white or overt propaganda which the BBC engaged in, and black or covert propaganda – with its shades of grey – that was our unit's domain. The BBC used facts truthfully, if discerningly, so that anybody listening on either side of the conflict could ascertain them. Truth was found to be the better weapon, but it too had to be handled with great care, and it had to be believable, which even truth sometimes is not. Officially, black propaganda did not exist. Its information was conveyed through leaflets and radio messages, presenting a mixture of fact and credible fiction, purporting to come from an organization inside the enemy or her occupied countries. Leaflets were designed for strategic deception. Radio was more conducive for tactical delusion. Both media of communication had to have some truth in them, but contained inaccuracies for which the British Government would not take responsibility. They were meant to soften up the German soldiers' morale, gave an invitation to surrender, and create general discouragement among soldiers and civilians. Where I was stationed we were asked to supply the raw material for black propaganda. Crossman explained further that

> Intelligence had another use. As we studied the enemy's propaganda, we were able to deduce from it the directive on which it was based. From that we could deduce the enemy's estimate of his own civilians, and the soldiers' morale could be elicited. There is no disguising from the expert analyst what the Führer estimates to be the morale of his own countrymen, because totalitarian propaganda is carried out rigorously to rule. Therefore it is a perfectly

simple job to reconstruct the enemy appreciation and directive week by week. It was one of my jobs to write the enemy directive in this way.[9]

In an earlier lecture given in 1950, Sir Robert Bruce Lockhart had come to similar conclusions: "Of new techniques [in propaganda] the most valuable, perhaps, was the deduction of enemy intentions from enemy propaganda."[10] To help us to assess the importance of what we heard over the radio, we received regular intelligence briefings, which were of a high standard. It was my privilege in Oxford during the second half of the 1950's to meet E. T. (later Sir Edgar) Williams, the Warden of Rhodes House, who had briefly worked with the United Nations before Oxford called him back.[11] Williams had risen rapidly in the war-time army and, as a Brigadier, he was in charge of Intelligence at 21 Army Group under Montgomery where his brief and irenic Intelligence assessments and clear expression proved invaluable to senior offices. Montgomery immediately discerned his qualities and, perhaps uniquely, accorded him full respect. Williams showed me much kindness. He later confided in me that the task of anticipating and forestalling the enemy's intention – out-thinking the Germans – "caused him much anxiety." When I was researching the Oxford spy ring in the winter of 1987-88, I consulted him and he gave me information based on personal knowledge. I noticed the extensive use of academics for training military personnel on specialist employment. The success that, for instance, Ultra had at Bletchley Park in decrypting German messages, through their secret code Enigma, owed much to the input of academics.[12] Ultra was initially by Polish mathematicians who designed it originally at the end of the 1920s for commercial purposes; at the beginning of the war they had to flee via France to England. The system remained secret for a considerable period until well after the end of hostilities. The British did not hesitate to use academics, while the Nazi Germans always looked at intellectuals with suspicion.

We recorded anything that struck us as particularly interesting or that seemed aberrant. I reported my findings to my immediate superior, Major Leo Long of the Intelligence Corps. I still remember him sitting outside at a table with his colleague Major Gordon Shepherd who was, I believe, on the publicity side and later in the British Control Commission in Austria.[13] The experience must have helped him when after the war he established his own publishing firm, Brooks-Shepherd, and wrote several books on intelligence. Major Long struck me as a highly intelligent, alert, and incisive person. I had confidence in him and entrusted him with the sensitive information of my origin and my real name.

Thus, it came as a great shock to me when I opened the London Times of 2nd November 1981 to see a photo of Leo Long on the front page after he had been publicly revealed as a Soviet spy.[14] I was stunned by the change that had come over Long, which could not be explained simply in terms of aging. The bright and alert Long of the Normandy campaign had lost his zest and sparkle. He had been recruited as a spy for the Soviet Union while an undergraduate at Cambridge, between 1935 and 1938, probably by the art historian Anthony Blunt, who became a Fellow of Trinity College. Politically intellectual young people at that time tended to be attracted by the ideas of the far Left. Unlike Blunt and other members of the Cambridge espionage circle, such as Kim Philby, Guy Burgess, and Donald Maclean, Long did not come from a family within the "establishment," but from a working-class background; John Cairncross, the fifth man, also came from a less privileged family. In those days, there existed no security vetting for people who gained employment in sensitive government positions, as all of them did. Loyalty to the home country was taken for granted. Long and Cairncross entered Cambridge on Trinity College scholarships. In becoming Communists and also spies for the Soviet Union, these men were not out for financial gain, though some of them were blackmailed into becoming spies to cover their homosexuality. They became Communists for idealistic reasons, believing that Communism and the Soviet Union provided the best defence against Nazi Germany and Fascist Italy. Disenchanted with the British Parliamentary government, they were blind to the similarities between Nazi and Soviet dictatorship. They even accepted the cynical pact Stalin and Hitler concluded in August 1939, including the partitioning of Poland, blaming Chamberlain for it, and allegedly that Chamberlain had tried to enmesh the two dictators into war against each other.[15] They failed to see that the fundamental clash was not between Left and the Right but between democracy and dictatorship of any stripe.

During the war, Long abused his official position in British military intelligence, MI4, to pass on sensitive secrets to the Soviet Union. This branch of the War Office Intelligence was dealing with the deployment of German forces and processed thousands of decrypted signals transmitted by the Wehrmacht and Luftwaffe. Later on Long was transferred to 21 Army Group Headquarters, where I served under him. After the war, he served as Major General in charge of the Intelligence Division of the British Control Commission in the British Zone. A senior intelligence officer, who knew Leo Long, told me – after the espionage revelations were made – that he had regarded him as "agreeable, clever, disillusioned, amusing, and cynical." Even if they escaped prosecution, all in the circle paid a price during their life of treachery, waking up to constant anxiety, regret, and remorse. Long found escape in his cynicism, and others succumbed by taking to heavy drinking. The public revelation of their deceit hit at least some of them very hard. Tipped off by Kim Philby then somewhere in Washington DC, Donald Maclean and Guy Burgess absconded to Moscow in May 1951. Their activities compromised British security, strained relations between the United States and Britain, and may well have strengthened Soviet resolve toward a course of confrontation with the West.[16]

There was a postscript to the story of Leo Long for me. In 1970, I attended the International Historical Congress in Moscow. As I had served between 1951 and 1956 with the BBC as a news sub-editor on broadcasts to the East European countries that were liable to be jammed by the Soviet Union and its allies, I took the precaution of notifying the Canadian authorities about my trip. I also arranged to visit the Moscow embassies of the three countries with which I was connected, Canada, Great Britain, and Germany. To my surprise, I was allocated an interpreter in Moscow, although colleagues far more senior than I had to manage without one. The services provided were, in fact, very useful to me, for right at Moscow airport my electric shaver started buzzing and the handle of my case came off. Both problems were easily solved. But mainly it helped me not to get lost in cities with which I was not familiar. The lady interpreter, who studied English at Moscow University and spoke excellent English, showed me around and took me to a service in the Orthodox Cathedral at my request. Naturally, I wondered to what I owed the honor bestowed on me by the Soviet authorities and assumed that this was due to my having worked for the BBC. The interpreter frequently referred to her having to make phone calls, which presumably were made to her control in order to inform the authorities about my movements. I used this line of communication to pass messages to the Kremlin to defuse international tensions during height of the Cold War. But the atmosphere was depressing so that even after an excursion to the beautiful city of St. Petersburg, I left communist Russia a day earlier than planned to spend it taking a deep breath of freedom in Helsinki. Alas, there I could also observe youths hanging out by the train station acting like drug addicts. On my return home, the Royal Canadian Mounted Police looked at my passport which carried an endorsement pointing out that I was a very important person! Since 1981

I wondered whether Leo Long passed on my name to the Soviet authorities.

I was not in France long after D-Day before I had a welcome break from monitoring. Major Paul Bretherton of the Intelligence Corps, the pre-war correspondent of the London newspaper the News Chronicle in Berlin asked me to conduct interrogations of some German prisoner-of-war camp. This occurred in about the second half of August during or just after the battle of the Falaise gap in Normandy. While driving me there, he told me under strict secrecy about the existence of a clandestine and covert Allied radio station which called itself Soldatensender Calais. At that time, the French Channel port was still in German hands. At the end of August, however, when the Germans had lost Calais, the sender was relocated and renamed Soldatensender West.[17] With its broadcasts, the station tried to undermine German morale. It was my task to obtain information from the prisoners useful for that purpose. I had to obtain details about the units in which they had served to authenticate our broadcasts, and try to elicit any disreputable information. For example, by discovering relationships of German officers with French women, or by exposing a high-ranking German officer who was starting to fatten his art collection from French sources, while the ordinary soldiers festered in the mud and rat infested trenches. Major Bretherton was friendly to me and we had an interesting conversation during the journey.[18] In Brussels he had been together with Sefton Delmer, and later took over the Radio Section of Information Control in Berlin in 1945. I also met him once in peacetime at the BBC where he led a guided tour of foreign journalists.

On arriving at the prisoner-of-war encampment with another interrogator we set up our tent next to the camp but had to move quickly when we discovered we had picked a wasp nest for our site. Entering the prisoner-of-war compound was an extraordinary experience for me. For the first time after seven years, I was to be in touch with "official" Germans again. I remembered how in September 1937 a customs officer had strip-searched me on my final departure from Germany. I remembered the demeanor of the Hitler youth boys before my emigration, and having read about fanaticism, particularly of the younger troops, I was prepared for great difficulties in my interviews. It felt strange as a refugee from Germany to have been given the task of interrogating German prisoners. What a remarkable reversal of fortune! How would I react to these prisoners-of-war? I could not tell beforehand. Soon I found myself walking about among the POWs behind barbed wire, who were out in the open during the warm season. If the POWs I interrogated were surprised about a British soldier addressing them in fluent German, they did not show it. How they came to be there, having been taken prisoner or having deserted, they did not let on. Generally, many of them were found to have leaflets or Passierscheine on them.[19] They were far readier to talk than I anticipated; many apparently desired to put aside their Nazi past quickly. Although I associated the German army and their uniform with the Nazi regime, now that these soldiers had been captured and disarmed I could not harbour any feeling of dislike or hatred for them. It might have been different if I had to deal with unrepentant Nazis. I chatted to them quite informally. They were presumably glad to be out of the war, unlike other German troops determined to fight until the bitter end, such as some Waffen-SS. Even though these men might have been instrumental in the Nazi regime that persecuted my people, I talked to them as human beings. The men were hopeful that they would be able to make a fresh start. I was struck by how quickly they had stripped themselves of any Nazi ideology, and how, in a spirit of optimism, they tended to underrate the difficulties that Germans was bound to face after the end of the war. I do not know how successful we were in obtaining information; as a soldier I was doing a limited job and did not see the end result. I do not know how much of the intelligence I provided was used by Soldatensender

Calais or its successor Soldatensender West. I hoped that I had asked the right questions and that the prisoners, if they knew, gave me correct answers. I cannot remember discovering any stunning information from the soldiers I spoke with.

As the rules did not permit us to keep personal notes or diaries, there is little available documentation to help me write about this episode. For a considerable period after the war, there existed even restraints on public discussion about covert activities. Officially allied covert propaganda did not exist; material related to it was even ordered to be destroyed at the end of the war.[20] In the 1947 volume of Sir Robert Bruce Lockhart informative memoirs concerning his role in PWE,[21] he was careful not to mention any details about covert operations. This limitation was not observed by Daniel Lerner in his book Sykewar: Psychological Warfare against Nazi Germany, D-Day to VE-Day.[22] Lerner was an American who played a prominent part in allied psychological warfare operations against Nazi Germany. In 1962 Sefton Delmer followed with his autobiography, Black Boomerang, where he deals with British black and grey propaganda.[23] Since that time, a number of important works have illuminated many details about what the British originally called "political warfare" and the Americans termed "psychological warfare." The Oxford historian Charles Cruickshank based his work on the topic almost entirely on available official British papers from Government departments.[24] With admirable clarity he sketched the often tortuous development of this branch of the service. Soon afterwards Professor Michael Balfour published his monumental volume Propaganda in War, 1939-1945.[25] Balfour was Assistant Director in the British PWE and thereafter in the Psychological Warfare Division of SHAEF, from 1942 to the end of the war. The Black Game by Ellic Howe followed several years later. Howe was in charge of the black printing unit of PWE.[26] As a gentleman scholar, Howe had acquired detailed knowledge on all aspects of printing, its history, technology, and art. He also knew the notable people who worked in the different fields of this trade.

The *Daily Express* journalist Sefton Delmer was the brain behind much of British covert propaganda, including *Soldatensender Calais* for which I did my prisoner-of-war interrogation. Delmer was born in 1904 of Australian parents in Berlin, where his father was a member of the English language faculty at the university.[27] Soon after his birth he was registered as a British citizen by the British Consul-General in Berlin. While his father was interned, the young Sefton Delmer continued to attend a local grammar school, *Gymnasium.* When the family was repatriated in 1917, he went on to St. Paul's School in London and won a scholarship to Lincoln College, Oxford, where he read Modern History. His father returned to Germany after the war. A chance encounter with Lord Beaverbrook in 1927 in Berlin led to young Sefton Delmer joining the *Daily Express*, becoming its Berlin correspondent the following year and Chief European Correspondent in 1937.[28]

He was well qualified for intelligence work against Germany. He wrote in his autobiography:

I did speak German like a German. . . . I knew something of the mentality of Germans at war from having been at school as a lone English boy in starving Berlin during the first war. I had travelled around Germany with Hitler and his retinue during the Nazi struggle for power. I was personally acquainted with Göring, Goebbels, Hess, Himmler and many other Nazi leaders. I knew the way their minds worked. Also I had spent much time in the Balkans since the war began and watched German agents at work there. [29]

But there were a few hurdles to be cleared before Delmer

was allowed to contribute to the war effort of his own country, as he was suspected of being a German agent:

> The very fact of my having been born in Berlin militated against me. My acquaintance with the Nazis was held to be not a qualification, but a ground for distrust. Stool-pigeons had been sent to test me. I remembered how on my return to London from Poland in October 1939 a young stranger had contacted me and sounded me out on the best way of getting in touch with the Fascists. Colleagues had been instigated to watch and report on my "secret Nazi activities". MI5 officers got into oh-so-casual conversation with me on leave trains and tried to catch me out as a German agent.
>
> The whole thing had been as idiotic and as wounding to my pride as the same suspicions had been to that of my father twenty-three years earlier, when he and we, his family, much to our and everyone else's surprise had been allowed to leave Germany and return to Britain in May 1917.[30]

For a German refugee from the Nazis, it was interesting to me to read how British suspicions also applied to people of British stock. It may be worthwhile to add that antagonism of the British was more strongly directed against those who had left than to those who had stayed in Germany.[31]

At any rate, soon after his return to Britain following his escape from France in the summer of 1940, Delmer was cleared to broadcast on the BBC German service. That was the beginning of his involvement in wartime propaganda and other covert activities. It did not take long for him to play a leading part in the secret propaganda activities against Germany conducted initially from the stables of the estate of the Duke of Bedford at Woburn Abbey. The only record of the place's existence was a London mailing address. He soon had his own intelligence section on the estate at RAG, the "Rookery" in the house of Absey Guise.

On 10th May 1941, the Deputy Führer Rudolf Hess, an expert pilot, though mentally unstable, flew a Messerschmitt ME-110 from Augsburg, Bavaria, to Glasgow, Scotland, in a self-imposed mission to negotiate a peace settlement with Britain. Twelve days later on May 23rd 1941 Delmer started a black transmission from England. It had the deliberately mysterious name of Gustav Siegfried Eins, which left listeners guessing what it might stand for: Generalstab 1, (General Staff 1) or, as one of the jokers suggested, Gurkensalat 1 (Cucumber Salad 1). The idea, in Delmer's words, was to produce a programme "that undermines Hitler, not by opposing him, but by pretending to be all for him and his war" and that would also "get across all manner of subversive rumour stories under a cover of nationalist patriotic clichés."[32] The nameless leader was simply introduced as Der Chef, the boss. Delmer had heard this title used for Hitler by members of his entourage when he covered his travels as a journalist in 1932 and 1933.[33] Delmer's Chef was not a party member, but a well-informed patriot with German nationalist leanings. Der Chef was made to sound like a Prussian officer, often using coarse and obscene language as well as pornography, who was frequently upset by the corruption and lawlessness in the Nazi party. A friend of my wife Rosemarie remembers listening to this programme and recalls one of Der Chef's indignant outbursts: "Old King Fred would have chased off the Nazi-pack with his crook-stick." Here Der Chef was talking about King Frederic II of Prussia, Frederic the Great. Der Chef read the news every day in the late afternoon from seven minutes to the full hour until well into the night. Every program was followed by popular German music carefully jazzed up.

In his autobiography, Delmer provides a detailed critique of the way the flight of Rudolf Hess to Scotland was handled by the British authorities who ordered him to be imprisoned. Both, Hitler and Churchill declared him to be half insane:

> We behaved as though Hess was some dangerous Trojan horse planted in our midst, a booby trap that might explode in our faces at any moment.[34]

Delmer, who was well aware of Hitler's fears in this matter, exploited the Hess affair to the limit, in spite of the hesitations the British authorities displayed. Der Chef claimed to have sent a previous message warning that "this obscenity of a dilettante Deputy Führer was about to do something idiotic." He claimed that he had ordered his comrades to lie low in order to escape the eventual witch-hunt. Der Chef went on saying that Hess was not the worst of the lot. He had been a good comrade in the days of the Free Corps after the First World War. This was followed by an attack on the "cranks, megalomaniacs, string pullers and parlour Bolsheviks who call themselves our leaders." Everything was done to give Gustav Siegfried Eins the air of an authentic German station going so far as to denounce Churchill as a "flat-footed bastard of a drunken old Jew."[35] This broadcast was very popular and was widely accepted as genuine.[36] According to later interrogations on German prisoners of war, Gustav Siegfried Eins with its carefully jazzed up renditions of well-known German songs was often regularly listened to by half the army personnel in all European theatres.

The German invasion of the Soviet Union on 22nd June 1941 provided further propaganda opportunities for Gustav Siegfried Eins. At a high level conference of British officials just before the invasion, Delmer was asked what line Der Chef would take when it actually happened. Delmer replied that Der Chef was going to demand that Hitler would now conduct a cleaning-up campaign against the Bolsheviks (communists) in the Nazi party, whom he called the Parteikommune, which delighted his listeners.[37]

Der Chef was played by a German refugee, Paul Sanders, a writer of detective stories, who had served in the Pioneer Corps as a corporal. His Adjutant was Johannes Reinholz, a German journalist who had fled to Britain with his Jewish wife just as the war broke out.[38] The members of Delmer's team at RAG had collected a great deal of intelligence and other information that was gathered very methodically in card indexes, thus allowing the programmes to achieve an authentic air in content and expression. For some reason, however, Delmer decided on 18th November 1943 to end the programme which had started on 8th June 1941, Der Chef was finally caught and eliminated by the Gestapo, with the appropriate on-air sound effects.[39]

Delmer was always ready to meet the requests of any of the three services, the BBC, the PWE, and the Royal Navy Intelligence. He was willing to pursue any special propaganda line to help them with delicate operations. He worked particularly closely with Lt.-Commander Donald McLachlan, a senior intelligence officer of the Royal Navy, who knew Nazi Germany intimately from serving in the Berlin office of The Times before the war. It was McLachlan, as foreign editor of The Economist, who commissioned me to report on the German Social Democratic Party conference at Dortmund in 1952. He certainly knew more about personalities in the Social Democrat leadership and about the general political situation in the Federal Republic than I did, but he was very kind to me, a young writer. I was most impressed by his eminent intelligence and political grasp, but unfortunately I did not know about his war work at that time. McLachlan helped Delmer with intelligence information and, in turn, the black propaganda outfit always responded to naval needs.

Indeed, it was through Delmer's contacts with the Royal Navy that he was able to start a new station, Kurzwellensender Atlantik, which "was aimed specifically at German submarine crews and worked in close conjunction with the Admiralty as a weapon in the Battle of the Atlantic. The sender posed as a station run more or less officially for their entertainment."[40] Thanks to ample intelligence information (McLachlan had connections with Bletchley Park), diligent research, and the occasional inspired guess about future German plans, the station managed to build up a reputation for knowing what was going on inside the German services. This was borne out by the interrogation of a senior Luftwaffe commander after his capture who said. "[it was] no good my attempting to keep anything secret from you fellows. You know it all." Actually, Atlantik was not quite as omniscient as the officer believed but in this particular instance it had been helped by a number of coincidences.[41] Generally the station did everything to undermine morale among the U-boat crews. Soon Delmer's team was supplemented by German prisoners of war. The success he had in exploiting the high death-rate of U-boat crews to subvert the German navy's resolve in the Atlantic encouraged Delmer to start softening up the German forces in France in preparation for the invasion of Europe.[42]

In October 1943 Delmer launched the new station, Soldatensender Calais, for which I provided my prisoner-of-war interrogation. Thanks to a giant transmitter called Aspidistra, this station had the ability to carry information on medium wave of 500 to 600 kilowatt, while most stations were operated by 7 ½ kilowatt. Aspidistra was designed and engineered in Camden, New Jersey. Churchill very quickly authorized its financing, and after long technical, departmental, and legal considerations it was built in England at Crowborough, Sussex. It needed a two floor underground building covered by turf and trees to operate it. It was ready for testing and first employment on 8th November 1942;[43] it worked without a hitch. The transmitter enabled the station to quickly change frequencies and take over German wavebands when their stations went off the air because of allied air raids. Through sending out phoney instructions, Soldatensender Calais was able to cause confusion among the German population during air raids. The resulting disorder caused the official German radio to cease issuing any directions to the population, thus aggravating communication problems. The station made its announcements in German, one of them reads translated:

Here speaks the Soldiers Radio Calais broadcasting on wave-bands 360 metres, 410 and 492 metres. Coupled with it the German short wave radio Atlantic, Kurzwellensender Atlantik, on wavebands 30.7 and 48.3. We bring music and news for comrades in the command areas West and Norway. We shall now play dance music.[44]

The station managed to insert worrying items into its "official" German news bulletins pirated from the official German news agency, Deutsches Nachrichtenbüro, DNB. This was accomplished through a tele-printer (Hellschreiber), which had fallen into the hands of the British authorities. The radio was also able from a variety of sources to give fairly accurate information: for example, about extent of the damage received by cities that had just been bombed by the Allies. It was derived from reports given by air-crews and supplemented by accurate street-maps. The programme encouraged sabotage and malingering, and even it was if not fully successful in bringing these about, at the very least it helped to create an atmosphere of mistrust among Germans. This led to more prying by the German authorities, which in turn creating increased tension among the troops and the population. Besides constant criticism of the Nazi party, though not of Hitler, everything was done to lull the Germans troops on the Western front into a false sense of security, similar to that of the French in the first winter of the war. As part of this propaganda line, the station asserted that the German High Command regarded France as a minor theatre of war.[45] Soldatensender Calais discouraged the German troops in the West from displaying too much enthusiasm, as that might only result in their being posted to the eastern front![46]

Delmer thought Soldatensender Calais to be in the category of grey propaganda, that is between black and white:

> No doubt many of our German listeners realised we can't really be German. Nevertheless they accepted us gratefully, because we don't make that 'Boom, boom, boom' V noise of the BBC [V for victory, the first bar of Beethoven's fifth symphony], which betrays them to the Gestapo, and because we sound like ordinary Germans, not a lot of émigrés.[47]

There exists plenty of confirmation that Soldatensender Calais had a considerable resonance among Germans. The station worried Goebbels,[48] and captured documents reveal that it was causing noteworthy anxiety to the Bavarian Ministry of the Interior as reflected in a letter addressed to the Munich Chief of Himmler's SD, Security Service in March 1944.[49]

The pros and cons of psychological warfare have been debated at some length. The field of propaganda could not be left to Nazis, especially as it played such a decisive part in placing them into power and keeping them there. Thus the penetration of the Nazi monopoly of the information media in their territory had a high priority. How was Nazi propaganda with its distortions of the truth to be countered? In one way. the best response was not through a countermeasure adopting a cavalier attitude to the facts, but through telling the unvarnished truth, even where unpalatable to the Allies. In the case of Britain this was done officially and overtly through the news services of the BBC, which established a solid reputation for integrity, even with many Germans who dared to listen to them at the potential cost of their live. As Michael Balfour put it: "the BBC managed to break the virtual monopoly of the Reich Ministry of Propaganda over German ears and to force it into the continual rational dialogue to which it had never before been effectively subjected."[50] The reputation of integrity the BBC had built up during the war was a strong asset for the British occupation of Germany and for the British run newspapers then produced for the civilian population. The BBC announced itself as the body responsible for the transmission of news, in the case of the German Service through its call sign Hier spricht London (Here London is Speaking).

The problem was that the Nazi regime had made listening to enemy radio a capital crime. A listener to the BBC could not claim that he or she did not know he or she was hearing a British, and thus an enemy, radio station. This was different in the case of covert Allied radio transmissions, which could genuinely be mistaken for German stations and thus provided some kind of an excuse for those who were caught in the act. Furthermore, covert stations did not have to stick to the truth as closely as official stations as their accountability was not as crucial. Their promises or hints about the future were not hemmed in by the official Allied Policy of unconditional surrender that hamstrung white propaganda. The general aim was to undermine German belief in a final Nazi victory, which only became possible with greater allied successes on the battlefield. Clearly psychological warfare depended for its effectiveness on military performance and was only supplementary to it. Delmer reiterated this point to his mixed staff of British-born people, German refugees, and German and Austrian prisoners of war at the end of their work in April 1945:

> The share of psychological warfare in the defeat of Hitler is only a very small one indeed. The defeat of Hitler is the work of the fighting services. Our role has been only purely subsidiary.[51]

Psychological warfare attempted to destabilize German forces by sowing dissension between the German population and the Nazi party, while carefully leaving Hitler himself out of any criticism. For example, Delmar and his group pointed out any discrepancies between the treatment of the privileged Nazi leadership and the rank and file soldiers and civilians, especially when it pertained to inadequate food rations.[52] Covert propaganda used radio programmes and such forgeries as ration cards, forged stamps, and leave passes. On the overt side, the act of air dropping the Passierscheine (permits) promising formal safe-conduct from the Allied authorities for German soldiers who surrendered was one of the most successful operations.

While I personally view black and grey propaganda in general as positive, as a logical supplement to military, naval, and air operations, the absence of accountability raises some ethical problems.[53] Delmer himself admits in his autobiography that he exploited the deaths of German soldiers cynically and that this was "one of our many operations against the Germans of which I feel a little ashamed." In order to encourage German soldiers to flee to neutral countries, he used intercepted radio telegrams containing information about deaths in military hospitals to assure families that their loved one was safe in a neutral country. However, when looking back, Delmer mentions this as the only instance where he feels shame.[54]

Were there, or should there have been, any ethical limits to psychological warfare against the Germans during the war? There are two passages in the "Standing Directive for Psychological Warfare against members of the German Armed Forces" of June 1944 that perhaps give some indication of an ethical guide in place. In the first section "Scope and Purpose of this Directive", point 4, it is stated:

> It is recognised that in the execution of Psychological Warfare it is a fundamental principle not to antagonise the audience. Direct denunciation or direct offence against known susceptibilities will therefore be avoided in all Psychological Warfare against the

enemy armed forces.[55]

Elsewhere the directive laid down that

all psychological warfare will give the impression of Anglo-American reliability, reticence, soldierly dignity, and decency." [56]

To what extent did psychological warfare actually conform to the spirit of the directive, which presumably summed up the existing policy? Delmer mentions, without comment, another episode:

One of our aims was to involve German Officers in the conspiracy against Hitler; we wanted the Gestapo and the SD, Sicherheitsdienst, to suspect them of complicity. Among those whom we successfully implicated in this way was the German Naval Attaché in Stockholm. He was recalled from his post and arrested – much to the annoyance of his British opposite number who had found him useful! When the German Officer subsequently returned to Stockholm, he complained bitterly of the shabby trick the Soldatensender had played on him.[57]

Delmer also exploited the death of a famous fighter pilot, Colonel Werner Mölders, when an aircraft carrying him crashed accidentally in November 1941. Prisoner-of-war interrogation elicited that Mölders had been a devout Roman Catholic. "Delmer's Gustav Siegfried Eins station was soon proclaiming that his aircraft had been shot down by 'Himmler's Bolshevik scum' in accordance with the Party's prevailing anti-religious campaign."[58] Leaflets was produced that contained a letter allegedly written by Mölders to a Roman Catholic dignitary "subtly drawing attention to the Party's anti-religious attitude."[59] They were dropped in the neighbourhood of German nightfighter stations. His mother, when asked, thought it was a forgery, but it was nevertheless so successful that the letter affirming Mölders' deep faith was read from many Roman Catholic and Protestant pulpits, and led consequently a number of clergymen being arrested.[60]

There are bound to be differences over the latitude of action against the enemy population permitted in times of war.[61] I would now say that the accusation against the German Naval Attaché crossed the ethical line, and was a grave act of injustice against a random person that exposed him to imprisonment, and potentially even torture and death. It was not precisely a demonstration of Anglo-American soldierly decency in the sense of the official directive. From a practical point of view, this dirty trick antagonised a German official who was obviously not a Nazi hard-liner, and therefore a potential ally, who in fact had been found "useful" by his British counterpart. In the case of the Mölders affair, a number of clergymen were arrested merely because of Delmer's inventiveness.

Quite apart from their immorality, these kinds of random accusations, if they happened by chance to hit on an actual or potential conspirator, could in fact endanger an entire conspiracy. It might even draw the attention of the Gestapo to a person they had not so far suspected or against whom they had not yet built up what they would have regarded as a sufficiently strong case. Because of the network of operative and extreme necessity of secrecy involved in a conspiratorial plot, that the chance of incriminating an actual participant who had hitherto remained beyond suspicion was a very real one.[62] I personally do not think that the legitimate end of destabilizing Germany justified the means of exposing innocent people to the drastic treatment meted out to people suspected of enmity to the regime.

I cannot say conclusively how I would have reacted to the whole scheme if I had been involved on the programme side of covert propaganda, instead of merely interrogating for it. But probably I would have been opposed to tactics of this kind and would have declined to participate. In my refusal, I would also have been motivated by the knowledge that we had anti-Nazi German friends who might have been endangered by these tactics. Cruickshank states in his book The Fourth Army that there was little hope covert propaganda could produce any decisive result;[63] the repressive machinery of the Nazi regime was far too powerful to allow any popular movement to act against it.[64] Crossman concluded and there was general agreement in retrospect that black propaganda was "fun" for those who produced and dispensed it, but that the best talents should be used in white propaganda in future conflicts.

On one day after returning to Army Group Headquarters, I was monitoring Radio Paris and to my great delight I heard some English voices. They belonged to two correspondents who had penetrated to the French capital when the Germans retreated. Actually, they were there without the permission of the allied authorities, ahead of the official liberation that took place on 23rd August. Indeed, Asa Briggs relayed in The History of Broadcasting in the United Kingdom that the two war correspondents concerned were later suspended by the authorities for broadcasting before official facilities had been established for them.[65] To my good fortune, Briggs (Lord Briggs as of 1976) later was my tutor at Worcester College, Oxford, after the war.

For me, it brought a great relief that I was now switched to German broadcasts as I could follow them more easily. Among the speakers I heard was the minister for propaganda and enlightenment, Josef Goebbels. To my surprise he sounded very reasonable and even "God-fearing." He came over as a gentle speaker, who complained about the way Germans had been wronged and were being badly treated by other nations, who completely misunderstood them. If one had not known about the terrible brutalities which the Germans were perpetrating, one could easily have been deceived, as obviously millions of Germans were.

For months there had been negotiations and discussions between the relevant British government departments about the Normandy invasion and its impact on the French people. The advance northwards was fascinating. Understandably, the Normans could not have been too enthusiastic about the Allies' decision to land on their part of France and making it initially the main battleground. Even if the Allies tried to minimize the ensuing destruction, French casualties or other damage was sure to happen. In his lecture in 1950, Sir Bruce Lockhart touched on this question of bombing French targets:

> In March and April 1944, the preliminary bombing essential to the D-Day landing caused great anxiety to the [British] Government, lest inevitable French losses might embitter Anglo-French relations for years to come. I had to report daily to the Prime Minister on the reaction of the French people. Then M. Marin – a former Minister and a leader of the Conseil de Résistance arrived and assured the Foreign Office that France could take it if this time we were really coming. In point of fact, . . . French losses were less than a tenth of the estimates of the Ministry of Home Security.[66]

As we moved north to parts of France in which the British were still remembered as Allies during the First World War, the reception of the civilian population got friendlier particularly at Amiens, where we took a short pause of a week or so. There I enjoyed the hospitality of a French family who was even so kind as to write to my parents after my departure and to tell them I was well. From September 1944 and through the rest of winter, the Main Guard of the army were headquartered in Brussels, which had been liberated in early September. The reception from the population here was particularly warm. However, in Brussels there was one episode I will long ponder about. The Belgian Resistance was refusing an order from the British military authorities to surrender their arms. I was wholeheartedly in agreement with the principle that all illegal or unlicensed weapons had to be brought under control. An armed riot squad, that I was ordered to join, was formed at headquarters to deal with any trouble that might be caused by any continued non-compliance with British orders on the part of the Belgian resistance. I was not particularly happy with the prospect of being ordered to fire on Belgians, whom British fighting units had just liberated. The major in command was very understanding when I talked to him about my concern. He believed that the Belgian resistance would give in, as they indeed did. I mention this incident, because it shows how in grave times one can easily be put into situations where any action involves an unsettling comprise. In this case the alternative would have been either to obey or disobey. In the first instance, I might have to live with the experience of possibly wounding or killing Belgians who were not enemies. In the second, by refusing an order I would have faced a term in a military prison and dishonourable discharge from the army, with all the consequences this would have brought.

Sometime in the middle of October 1944, I took a brief leave to England. I found among my papers a small TOC H Pass (Talbot House) referring to a weekend at the Northampton Branch on 13th October.[67] Entered on my pass as "Private. TH" – the military liked acronyms – the Talbot House is a movement originating in 1915 during the First World War. Close to the trenches of Ypres, Belgium, where the men constantly faced danger and death, stood Talbot House at Poperinge. At Talbot House they found inner peace, and formed the most unlikely friendships. Under the guidance of Padre Tubby Clayton a soldier's club had been formed that expanded into many branches, and later incorporated peacetime activities. Men were encouraged to mingle and make friends,

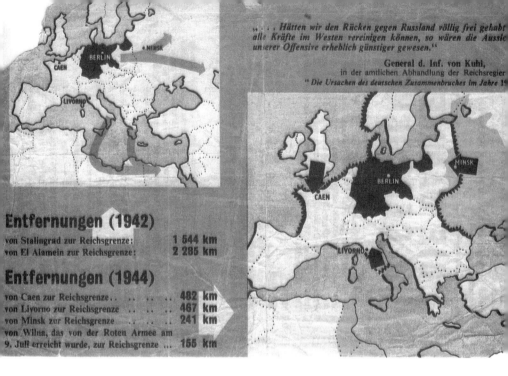

",... Hätten wir den Rücken gegen Russland völlig gehabt
alle Kräfte im Westen vereinigen können, so wären die Aussic
unserer Offensive erheblich günstiger gewesen."

General d. Inf. von Kuhl,
in der amtlichen Abhandlung der Reichsregier
" Die Ursachen des deutschen Zusammenbruches im Jahre 19

Entfernungen (1942)

von Stalingrad zur Reichsgrenze:	1 544 km
von El Alamein zur Reichsgrenze:	2 285 km

Entfernungen (1944)

von Caen zur Reichsgrenze..	482 km
von Livorno zur Reichsgrenze	467 km
von Minsk zur Reichsgrenze	241 km
von Wilna, das von der Roten Armee am 9. Juli erreicht wurde, zur Reichsgrenze ...	155 km

Leaflet printed by the British. Translation on page 273
Reverse side shown on next page.

ignoring the normal rules of rank and status, and were given
spiritual help. Today their aims are equally valid: "the principles
of friendship, of lessening the prejudices that divide people,
to look at the needs of others as their own, to find one's own
conviction, to influence public opinion so that conflict may
be lessened . . . that truth may prevail." Their spirit certainly
appealed and comforted me.

My next special assignment – this time as Corporal – was
my posting from Brussels to No. 18 Leaflet Unit in the
Netherlands,[68] close to the frontline near Venlo on the West
Bank of the Maas River not far from the border with Germany.
I was in charge of one the forward units that Psychological
Warfare through Second Army Headquarters operated on
the Continent. Amplifier Units were place close to the enemy
formations, about 1000 or sometimes even 300 feet away,
attempting to talk to them by means of loudspeakers. Leaflet
Units advised on drawing up of leaflets. The example shown

Dr. Eyck Rd. of History
Calgary U.

Deutsche Kriegsgefangene in den ersten 8 Wochen der Sommeroffensive 1918	**114 000**
Deutsche Kriegsgefangene in den ersten 8 Wochen der Sommeroffensive 1944	**162 000**

DIE DÄMME SIND GEBROCHEN!

Süden:

32 000 deiner Kameraden gerieten im Verlauf der Abwehr-kämpfe seit dem 12. Mai 1944 in Gefangenschaft. Unter den ganz oder grösstenteils aufgeriebenen Divisionen befinden sich die 1. Fallschirmjäger-Division, 20. Luftwaffe-Felddivision, 29. Panzergrenadier-Division, 44. Panzergrenadier-Division, 71. Infanterie-Division, 94. Infanterie-Division, 362. Infanterie-Division, 715. Infanterie-Division.

Westen:

52 000 deiner Kameraden gerieten im Verlauf der Abwehr-kämpfe seit dem 6. Juni 1944 in Gefangenschaft. Unter den ganz oder grösstenteils aufgeriebenen Divisionen befinden sich die 77. Infanterie-Division, 91. Infanterie-Division, 243. Infanterie-Division, 352. Infanterie-Division, 709. Infanterie-Division, 716. Infanterie-Division.

Osten:

78 000 deiner Kameraden gerieten im Verlauf der Abwehr-kämpfe seit dem 23. Juni 1944 in Gefangenschaft. Unter den auf-geriebenen Division befinden sich die 4. Infanterie-Division, 6. Luftwaffe-Felddivision, 197. Infanterie-Division, 206. Infanterie-Division, 246. Infanterie-Division — nicht gerechnet die Divisionen, die im Raum von Minsk zur Übergabe gezwungen wurden.

162 000 — *in den ersten 8 Wochen der Sommeroffensive.*
162 000 *deutsche Soldaten, die eine Zukunft haben.*
162 000 *deutsche Soldaten, die wissen, dass sie die Heimat nach dem Krieg wiedersehn.*

... jeden Gefangenen sind aber mehrere deiner Kameraden ... wer verwundet, gefallen oder — was ärger ist — für den ... ihres Lebens zu Krüppeln geworden. Heute steht es ... : Deutschland hat den Krieg verloren. Frage dich ... du unter diesen Umständen mit dem Einsatz dei... ...ens noch erreichen kannst.

here refers to the Dutch dikes being dynamited by the retreating German army and thereby flooding low laying Dutch land. [69]

The Leaflet Units were the smallest in the whole of the British army, consisting of a German-speaking corporal and a driver with a small truck. The Amplifier Units were slightly larger. Normally Amplifier and Leaflet Units operated in pairs. If the local military formation thought the moment propitious, the corporal would be called upon to give help in advising about the contents of leaflets that the artillery would shoot over to the German lines. This was a technique developed in the war theatre of North Africa where it proved very successful with the Italians. The techniques were developed further to the point that, right after D-Day, leaflets as well as special miniature daily newspapers in German, called Nachrichten für die Truppe, (News for the Troops) with a print order of two million were delivered. The RAF preferred to send these over to the German lines by firing them in shells, while the Americans preferred air drops from balloons.[70] The paper was much appreciated by the recipients and at times – to the chagrin of Goebbels – arrived more regularly than his own German paper.

The corporal, who would participate in the operations of the relevant Amplifier Unit, had to move close to the German lines and try to persuade the German troops to surrender. Some success in speeding up surrender was achieved, but at the cost of an occasional casualties. The pair of units to which I belonged spent some time near the front in the Roermond region west of the Maas River, but we were soon withdrawn. On 26th November I had again been taken to my assignment by Major Bretherton and reported to Major R. H. E. Heycock, the general staff officer for Psychological Warfare at HQ, 2nd Army.[71] I was glad to meet Heycock again in civilian life in 1949, when he was an official of the British Broadcasting Corporation. At that time, I had just joined the BBC as an editorial assistant to the German programme weekly, Hier spricht London. In the army I was impressed by his warm and friendly manner and by the conscientious and efficient way he went about his business, qualities he also brought to bear on his civilian tasks.

While I was stationed at Weert, in the Dutch province of Limburg, I was billeted by a local family with whose relative, a Catholic priest, I struck up a friendship; we even corresponded afterwards. We communicated with our Dutch allies in the language of our common enemy. We could understand Dutch, if spoken slowly, which did not apply to the old grandmother, who spoke very quickly. In turn the Dutch could understand our German if spoken with great deliberation. The reception was friendly throughout. I was struck and saddened by the suffering of the local population, who had very little to eat. The situation in this respect seemed to be considerably worse than that prevailing in Brussels.

We stood by, but were not called upon to undertake any particular assignment, either on the leaflet or the amplifier side. Of some interest to me, an entry in the war diary kept by Major Heycock notes that I passed his office on December 7th with the sergeant from the Amplifier Unit on my way from the 12th Corps HQ (Main) back to 21 Army Group in Brussels.[72] A week or so later, on 16th December the Germans started their last offensive, in the Ardennes, which – particularly because it was unexpected – was quite worrying for a time. Fortunately, this too ended in failure for the German side. I remained in Brussels until February 1945, when I was sent back to England to be trained for the occupation of Germany.

Endnotes

1 The British Control Commission for Germany, CCG (BE) directed by Major General Bishop, two subsections were PR, (Public Relations) and ISC (Information Services Control) to supervise the media, i.e. press, radio, film, book publishing. Those leading the sections were named Controllers. This arrangement marked the transition from the military government of 21 Army Group to the consolidation phase.

2 Freiherr von Schlabrendorff, *Offiziere gegen Hitler*, (Zürich: Europa Verlag, 1946). Rudolf Pechel, *Deutscher Widerstand 1933-1945*. (Zürich-Erlenbach: Eugen Rentsch Verlag, 1947). Rudolf Lill und Heinrich Oberreuter, eds, *Portrait des Widerstandes, Biographisch-Bibliograpisches Kirchenlexikon*. (Düsseldorf/Wien: Verlag Traugott Bautz, 1984).

3 Henry O. Melone, *Adam Trott zu Solz, Deutscher Wiederstand 1933-1945*. (Berlin: Siedler Verlag, 1989), pp. 213ff. Roger Moorhause, *Killing Hitler*, (New York: Bantom Press, 2000).

4 Sefton Delmer. *Black Boomerang*, (London: Viking Adult, 1961), pp. 692-693. Asa Briggs, *The War of Words, The History of Broadcasting in the United Kingdom*, (Oxford University Press, 1970), vol. III. pp. 692-693.

5 Frank Eyck to Klaus Wagner, 14th November 1993.

6 R .H. S (Richard Howard Stafford) Crossman, "Psychological Warfare," *The Journal of the Royal Service Institution* (Vol. 97, August 1952, No. 587), pp. 319-332. Janet Morgan, ed., *The Backbench Diaries of Richard Crossman*. (London: Hamish Hamilton, 1981). Ellic Howe, *The Black Game*, (London: Michael Joseph Fortuna, 1982), pp. 54-57.

7 Sir Robert Lockhart, "Political Warfare," *The Journal of the Royal Service Institution*, vol. 45, May 1950, No. 95), pp. 195-206.

8 Asa Briggs, *The War of Words, D-Day and After*, (Oxford University Press, 1970), pp. 666-667.

9 R. H. S. Crossman, *Psychological Warfare*. Ellic Howe, *The Black Game*, pp. 54-57. Robert Bruce Lockhart, *Political Warfare*.

10 Robert Bruce Lockhart, *Political Warfare*. Robert Cecil, "The Cambridge Comintern," in Christopher Andrews and David Dilks, eds., *The Missing*

Dimensions. Government and Intelligence in the Twentieth Century, (Chicago: University of Illinois Press, 1985), pp. 169-198. Peter Wright, *The Spycatcher, The Candid Autobiography of Senior Intelligence Officer,* (Toronto, Penguin, 1987), pp. 218-222. Simon Penrose and Simon Freeman, eds., *Conspiracy of Silence. The Secret Life of Anthony Blunt.* (New York: Ferrar Strauss & Gioux, 1987). These books are particularly useful because the author knew the main actors personally and professionally.

11 Frank Eyck to Klaus Wagner, 19th January 1996.

12 Wladyslaw Wikozaczuk, *Enigma, How the German Machine Cipher was Broken and How It Was Read by The Allies in WWII.* (London: Arms and Amour Press, 1984).

13 Klaus Wagner to Frank Eyck, 16th January 1995.

14 *The London Times,* 4th Nov. 1981, p. 10g. Tom Bower & André Deutsch, "The pledge betrayed." (New York: Doubleday, 1981).

15 Robert Cecil, *The Cambridge Comintern,* pp. 197-198.

16 Ibid

17 Michael Leonard Graham Balfour, *Propaganda in War, 1939-1945.* (London: Routledge & Kegan Paul, 1979), pp. 98-99, 198, 467.

18 Klaus Wagner to Frank Eyck, 14th November 1993, Frank Eyck to Klaus Wagner, 26th January 1994.

19 PW northwest Theatre S from Canadian Intelligence Corps September 1945 4/PWD CP OLD/1 p. 7. Leaflets and *Passierscheine* (i.e. invitations to surrender or desert). They were printed by the Allies and dropped over German lines.

20 Ellic Howe, *The Black Game,* pp. 6-8.

21 Robert Bruce Lockhart, *Comes the Reckoning.* (London: Putnam, 1947). Also *Memoirs of a British Agen,* (London: Macmillan, 1932).

22 Daniel A Sykewar, *Psychological Warfare against Nazi Germany, D-Day to VE-Day,* (Cambridge, MA: M.I.T. Press, 1971), revised paperback edition with an introduction by the author and a second one by William G. Griffith. The original edition was published much earlier.

23 Sefton Delmer, *Black Boomerang.* (London: Viking Adult, 1962).

24 C. G. Cruickshank to Frank Eyck, July 1977. *The Fourth Army, Psychological Warfare 1938-1945,* (London: Davis-Poynter, 1977). Also, *Deception in*

World War II, (Oxford University Press 1979).

25 Michael Leonard G. Balfour, *Propaganda in War, Organisations, Politics and Publics in Britain and Germany.* (London: Routledge & Kegan Paul, 1979).

26 Ellic Howe, *The Black Game.* He proved his skill, when on request by the FO within a day he managed to have printed the 1941 New Years Greeting cards, addressed to prominent Nazi leaders on French formatted paper and envelops and, sent via Swedish mail to Germany with forged stamps to the addressees; the text was suggested by the officer in charge: "Cursed be he that removeth his neighbour's landmark" (Deuteronomy 27:17). The recipients were furious but never discovered the origin of this communication.

27 Sefton Delmer, *Black Boomerang*, pp. 23-24.

28 This summary of Sefton Delmer's earlier life is taken from Ellic Howe, *The Black Game*, pp. 98-99. For Comparison between Crossman and Delmer, see Ibid, p. 95.

29 Delmer, *Black Boomerang*, p. 14.

30 Ibid, pp. 14-15.

31 Tom Bower and André Deutsch, *Blind Eye to Murder.* (New York: Doubleday, 1981), p. 149. In Frank Eyck papers, Klaus Wagner, draft of his dissertation, chapter 8, *Das Problem der Emigranten – Die Rolle der Hitler Flüchtlinge bei der Planung und Umsetzungspresse politischer Prozesse.*

32 Delmer, *Black Boomerang*, p. 41.

33 Ibid, p. 42.

34 Ibid, p. 52.

35 Ibid, p. 46.

36 Ibid, p. 45.

37 Ibid, pp. 63-64.

38 Ibid, p. 49.

39 Ellic Howe, *The Black Game*, p 125.

40 Balfour, *Propaganda in War*, p. 98.

41 Delmer, *Black Boomerang*, pp. 100-01.

42 Ibid, p. 102.

43 Ellic Howe, *The Black Game*, pp. 156-164.

44 Ibid, p. 108.

45 Ibid, p. 154.

46 Ibid, p. 119.

47 Ibid, p. 118.

48 Ibid, pp. 109-10.

49 Ibid, pp. 113-5.

50 Balfour, *Propaganda*, p. 96.

51 Ibid, p. 218.

52 Rosemarie related a story told by her father of his Nazi colleagues at the Deutsche Bank. Using an offer of extra food rationing cards, her father's colleague tried to extract information from him about members of the Dahlem congregation; an offer he declined.

53 Frank Eyck "Politics, Technology and Innovation in the 20th Century" in Tim Travers and Chris Archer, eds., *Men at War*, (Chicago, University of Illinois Press, 1982), pp. 140-141.

54 Ibid, pp. 134-35.

55 Daniel Lerner, *The Sykewar, D-Day to VE-Day*, p. 350.

56 Ibid, p. 361.

57 Delmer, *Black Boomerang*, p. 175.

58 Ellic Howe, *Black Game*, p. 208.

59 Ibid, p. 208.

60 Ibid, p. 209.

61 A black stations, like *Gustav Siegfried Eins* did not hesitate to use the methods of Goebbels. Asa Briggs, *The BBC: The First Fifty Years*, (Oxford University Press, 1985), p. 223.

62 See amongst other works Peter Hoffmann, *The History of the German Resistance 1933-1945*, (trans. from the German version by Richard Barry, Montreal: McGill-Queen's University Press, 1996).

63 Charles Cruickshank, *The Fourth Army*, pp. 184-186.

64 FO memo 898/101, ff. 34, also Hansard/Commons, Vol. 372, col. 1536.

65 Asa Briggs, War of Words, p. 675.

66 Robert Bruce Lockhart, *Political Warfare*, p. 200.

67 Toc House Movement, http://www.greatwar.co.uk/westfront/ypsalient/toch/tochmovt.htm.

68 The National Archive Kew, Ref. HO 405/12352 258266 part II, summary of army activity, 1st May 1946.

69 Shortly after Irving Hexham's father had died, who had served during the Second World War in the British Army, Irving's brother found this leaflet with the note to me while sorting through his father's papers; it will, however, be returned to Irving Hexham.

70 Lockhart, *Political Warfare*, p. 196. Crossman, *Psychological Warfare*, p. 321.

71 I owe these details to Klaus Wagner.

72 Again I express my gratitude to Klaus Wagner for the fruits of his research.

Translation of leaflet on page 264

". . . had they had their back completely free and been able to unite all forces in the West, the prospect for our offensive would have been much more advantages.". . .General d. Inf. von Kuhl

In the official protocol of the imperial Government: "The reason for the German collapse in the year 1918"

Distances (1942)
· from Stalingrad to the border of the German Reich, 1 544 km
· from El Alamein to the border of the German Reich, 2 285 km

Distances (1944)
· from Caen to the border of the German Reich, 482 km
· from Livorno to the border of the German Reich, 467 km
· from Minsk to the border of the German Reich, 241 km
· from Wilna, that has been reached by the Red Army on July 9th, to the border of the German Reich, 158 km

Translation of leaflet on page 265

German prisoners of war in the first 8 weeks of the summer offensive 1918, 114 000
German prisoners of war in the first 8 weeks of the summer offensive in 1944, 162 000

The Dykes are broken!

In the South:
32 000 of your comrades became prisoner during the defence battles since May 12th, 1944. Among the partially or totally destroyed divisions were the 1st Infantry Division, 20th Air Force-Field Division, 29th Armored Grenadier Division, 44th Armored Grenadier Division, 71st Infantry Division, 94th Infantry Division. 362nd Infantry Divison, and the 715th Infantry Division.

In the West:

52 000 of your comrades became prisoners during the defence battles since July 6th, 1944. Among the completely or partially destroyed divisions were the 77th Infantry Division, 91st Infantry Division, 243rd Infantry Division, 352th Infantry Division, 709th Infantry Division, and the 716th Infantry Division.

In the East:

78 000 of your comrades became prisoners during the defence battles since June 23rd, 1944. Among the destroyed Divisions were, 4th Infantry Division, 6th Air Force Field Division, 197th Infantry Division, 206th Infantry Division, 246th Infantry Division.

162 000 in the first 3 weeks of the summer offensive.
162 000 German soldiers who have a future.
162 000 German soldiers who know they will see their country after the war.

For each prisoner there are several comrades who were severely wounded or killed - what is worse - they will be cripples for the rest of their lives. Today it is certain - Germany has lost the war. Ask yourself, what in these circumstances could you still achieve by risking your life.

CHAPTER 8

British Occupation, Information Control, Germany 1945-1946

F OR SEVERAL MONTHS NOW, the fortune of war had turned in the Allies' favour, and plans for the occupation of Germany had been on many people's minds. They were vaguely discussed since 1941. More serious preparations were undertaken from 1943 on by those in charge of the Foreign Office in Britain and, as far as possible, in coordination with her Allies.[1] Winning the war certainly had priority, and Churchill concentrated on it with all his power, political acumen, and strategic gifts; however, winning the peace was never kept out of sight.

The entry on the 13th January 1945 in the War Diary of Major R. H. F. Heycock mentions a conference at 21 Gp, Army Group at Main Headquarters in Neerpelt, near Brussels, with Lieutenant Colonel G. R. de Beer and Information Control personnel on planning for German occupation.[2] Following the meeting, Heycock requested to see me and two others:

> Interview with Sgts. Martin, Egon Pollitt, [an Austrian refugee, a refined well-educated person], Spalding, [who had been a lecturer in a German department of a British university and later was Professor in Bangor, Gweynedd, Wales] and Cpl. Frank Alexander [Eyck]. Discussion re forward Information Control Units as and when needed. It was also agreed that Amplifier and Leaflet Units [in which all three of us served] should be transferred to Information Control when psychological warfare activities were concluded. It was agreed that Psychol. Warfare and Inform. Control staff at Army level should be a joint one.

Sgt. Frank Alexander, January 1945. Cobham.

Keith Spalding, on 7th February 1945 was given the order:

> You are in charge of a party consisting of yourself and
> Cpl. Alexander, Cpl. Pollitt and Pte. Hefti: You will
> proceed to Ostend today and report to Port Comd.
> for transit to the U.K. – On arrival in the U.K. you
> will proceed at once to Cobham. You will report to
> Adjutant, Pain's Hill Park.

This transfer led me to the training course on Information
Control in Cobham, Surrey. Here an attempt was made to
prepare for the control of the German media. This course was
attended by about eighty army personnel who, like myself, were
mainly German refugees.[3] I remember it as one of the best, or
perhaps the best course I ever attended, my studies in Oxford
including. Some of the lecturers were obviously specially invited,
such as the historian, Prof. F. L. Carsten from the University
of London. What was impressive, were both the quality of the
lectures and the range of the subjects. They covered local history,
politics, economics, psychology, and the religious division of
Germany. We were also given a Manual for the Control of
German Information Services published by the planning staff
of the Psychological Warfare Division (PWD) of SHAEF
under the direction of the American Brigadier Robert McClure
with detailed direction for action during the first half year of
1945.[4] The course was fascinating, and indeed granted a rare
experience, as no attempt was made to impose any particular
point of view on us. Besides, we had not exactly been spoiled
in the army with intellectual stimulation.[5] I was glad to still
have my lecture notes on army service, and consulted them
probably for the first time since my demobilization in 1946.
The highlights were the papers read by a psychologist, the
Intelligence Corps Lieutenant Colonel R. L. Sedgwick, who had
been on the white side of the Psychological Warfare Executive.[6]
One term he used about German psychology always stuck

in my mind was: "Anticipation neurosis, a condition whereby strong emotions are shaped by the memory of the past and combined with an excessive fear of the unknown. The German people were partial to an excessive anxiety about the future, which helped to explain the particular ferocity of German nationalism, resulting in what he called "strength from fear." This being a psychological weakness of the German people, the Nazis exploited it to the full.

The stratagem was to close all information media (with rare exceptions), to control the German information media (i.e. newspapers, radio, and book publishing); they should be taken over, followed soon by issuing licences.[7] This was to be an important part of the policy that the British Military Government ordered to be implemented on occupying their zone of Germany, alongside the Russians and the Americans, and later the French. However, a certain divergence in execution between the different occupying powers was thought to be acceptable. Lt. Col. Sedgwick said that occupation policy should be based on "irresistible power combined with discrimination" between Nazis and non-Nazis. Coupled with a practical sense of justice, this would cause anticipation neurosis to recede.

He suggested that a maximum of tact and firmness should be employed. He named five main elements of German psychology, which he developed in detail: 1. Mysticism and idealism. 2. Respect for authority. 3. Imitativeness. 4. Ambivalence. 5. Introspection. Sedgwick also dealt with German re-education, a major plank of Western policy, along with denazification, re-establishment of the rule of law and order, and re-building of democratic institutions. While demanding the complete re-education of the German people, he quickly added "the whole world is in need of re-education." He spoke of the terrifying responsibility of our task ahead, stating that, after all that had happened, it was difficult to achieve the necessary "right frame of mind. The work had to be done by people of good will." Sedgwick felt it was essential to understand some of the diplomatic, social, and economic conditions that had made the German masses responsive to stirring slogans, but that this did not excuse from its actions. For Sedgwick, it was necessary to understand this, so that the correct psychological treatment could be followed. By his account, National Socialism had been made possible largely by the growing general accessibility of radio, which helped to condition and hypnotise the masses.

Sedgwick continued with a whole series of comments on the correct course to cure Germany from the national character the Nazis had shaped: The cure was to be administered without passion or righteous indignation. It was important to establish order, persistently and consistently. Get the Germans back to their self-respect, so that they can take their place with other nations. The education of Germans can only be carried out by Germans, precise, orderly, and definite. They could be relied upon to do it themselves, if encouraged in this. Germans would have to be impressed by the fact that we know what we want, and that we can be successful. A variety of opinions will be fatal; in the early stages, there is to be no argument. Our case has to be stated clearly without conditions. There should be factual statements of the cause of the war and the conduct of the German Army and the SS. We should describe facts, and present documents without comment. Let the facts speak for themselves. There should be documentaries of towns bombed by the Germans. At the same time, let us emphasise all that is good and noble in their history, including their contributions to the body of learning. The implication should be: this is the real Germany that we once loved and have lost. A way must be found out of the vicious circle of damnation; a new orientation of German thought must be accompanied by a spiritual revival on the allied side. The world is crazy on the subject of planning. There cannot be a permanent renaissance without spiritual certainty all around. We should emphasise the rule of law and the individual's values on a Christian basis, and cooperation as good neighbours in the world outside.

We should follow a policy of right through determination, as from our kind of force justice is born. Democracy is to be the pattern to follow for the suffering world.

Turning to the German denominational division, Segwick believed that while many Roman Catholics had been taken in by Hitler, on the whole this had not happened to good Catholics. The elite of the church wanted a victory of the Allies. However, so far as he knew, no official protest of the German Catholic Church was ever made about the Nazi persecution of Poles; this was all the more remarkable as the Catholic Centre party had always been friendly to their Polish co-religionists. Sedgwick was critical of German Protestantism: History would show how attenuated the Christian element in German Protestantism had become. Protestant resistance to the Nazis had been less strong than that of Catholics, with the exception of groups like the Bibelforscher and Quakers; he did not mention the Confessing Church and he felt that all Protestant Pastors had to be regarded with suspicion. As another mark against them, the German Lutherans were not democratic, unlike the Scandinavians,.

Sedgwick, a highly educated man, had become a Catholic in 1922 and studied at the Bonn University, where he acquired a profound knowledge of German history and politics. At PWE, on the white side of propaganda, he had used Cardinal von Galen's sermons, interpreting them to British advantage "by fair means and by foul." The Cardinal had defied Hitler, but was also a great patriot and critically outspoken about the British occupation policy. Called the Lion of Münster, he very much disapproved of Sedgwick's cynical interpretation of his sermons and told him so when they met.[8] During the British occupation, Sedgwick became a leading official in the religious affairs branch of the British Control Commission in Germany. On request of Field Marshal Sir Gerald Templer,[9] Sedgwick organized a Bishops' Conference in the British Zone at Lübeck. The bishops expressed great dismay over the transfer of Pomerania and Silesia to the Soviet Union. As a result of the Conference,

Archbishop Frings of Cologne and von Galen made a trip to Rome in February of 1946 that they called "more like the second Pauline voyage to Rome." Their goal was to plead with the Holy See somehow intercede and speak against the exchange of East German territories to Soviet control.[10] In August 1945, Sedgwick aided in what was known as the first post-war Bishops Conference at Fulda, in Hessen, a traditional annual event at the tomb of St. Boniface. Sedgwick diplomatically secured the privacy of the bishops, who were accustomed to closed meetings, against the protest of the American officer.[11]

However, others at Colbham strategically planning the occupation of German were severe in their approach. Colonel Elgin echoed some of the sentiments of Lord (Robert Gilbert) Vansittart, who had been adviser in the Foreign Office and became chief diplomatic adviser to His Majesty the King after 1937.[12] Vansittart had warned and vigorously campaigned against the Nazis before the war began and openly expressed his hatred for Germans in general.[13] Elgin covered a number of aspects of the German situation including transportation, which was practically non-existent. He stated that priorities of Allied forces were as follows. First, he stated that the needs of the forces of occupation took priority over everything else. Second, he requested the delivery of urgent relief supplies to feed the "Huns," his word for the Germans, sufficiently to prevent revolt and the outbreak of disease. Third, prisoners of war needed to be discharged, which after the end of the war amounted to four million POWs in the British zone alone. Displaced persons such as non-German slave-laborers from the Nazi period would also need to be repatriated. Last, all remaining supplies, if there were any, would be left for the Germans. No German was allowed to move without Military Government permission. The whole industrial potential of the country was to cease. Synthetic rubber and oil plants were to be destroyed, as they had war potential and presented competition with the British victors did not want.

Germany had to be self-sufficient after a year of occupation. It was the opinion of economic experts that rehabilitation would take place within a year. The War Material Commission in London would list in fine detail all the war material that was to be blown sky-high, converted, or retained. Nothing would be imported into the British zone of Germany, except supplies needed for the occupying forces and those needed to provide urgent relief: for example, material for the German railway system. The Germans were not allowed to trade with neutral parties or the Allies. Elgin reported interestingly enough that the Russians had withdrawn from the European transport organization so that it would not function. The organization could therefore only deal with Western Europe.

Finally, Major O'Grady of the Military Government branch at 21 Army Group, spoke about restoration of law and order, elimination of Nazism and establishment and preservation of suitable civil administration.[14] The proposed military government was tasked with wiping out all discriminatory laws of the Nazis – such as those against the Jews – and destroying the legal architecture of the Nazi party's rule. Democratic trade unions would be permitted. Initially all schools would be closed, to be reopened as soon as possible.

These were the plans. [15] After the often-heated discussions about theory, the trusteeship clause, a new League Charter, and indirect rule by a small occupation force, we had now come to test the feasibility of our ideas. Allied cooperation in Germany was going to be put into practice.[16]

The reality was often quite different.[17] At the end of April, I was back on the continent.[18] The command structure developed as follows.[19] Information Control 21 Army Group and its Headquarter Military Government Detachment in Kiel commanded Information Control, which commanded my information control unit, the eighth. This unit was again subdivided into radio, press, publication, and film/entertainment sections; the press section, with a staff of twenty to twenty-five personnel was to be stationed in Hamburg,[20] Lübeck,[21] and Flensburg.[22] Each unit was staffed by a small number of British officers and NCOs; a car with a driver was supplied for their use.

Meanwhile we followed the advancing British Army on the Rhine. Under the leadership of Lieutenant Colonel Henry B. Garland, we scouted out a workable rotary press and a big supply of paper in Lengerich, a small township in Westphalia about half-way between badly bombed-out Münster and Osnabrück. The press was in working order and was operated by a helpful German anti-Nazi. Most of the paper was unfortunately of the wrong kind, but a small amount of newsprint allowed us to publish, free of charge and printed on both sides, a one-page "daily" German language news-sheet for distribution to the civilian population. It gave the latest facts about the war, but the number of copies and the frequency of issues that could be produced depended entirely on the available news print. We had to rely on paper contingents we could find and requisition. Only slowly did paper production start, mainly by the big paper-mill Feldmühle AG. But supply remained severely limited for years. Gradually, like in all other later publications, we were able to report about the dark side of the Nazi regime. All of it was eagerly seized, read, and shared within the German population.

While moving into Germany my unit received intelligence information through military channels that the Russians were not fully cooperating with the Western authorities during their advances into Germany.[23] Perhaps there had been too much euphoria in the West about our Russian Allies. The contribution of the Russian people to victory over the Nazis was not in doubt, any more than the courage and suffering of the Russian population. But did the Soviet Government have the same agenda for Germany as Britain and the United States? Did democracy mean the same to Stalin as it did to Churchill and Roosevelt? During the war, it had been almost taboo to even raise the question whether the Soviet Union was a democracy. But gradually reality sunk in. How could the Allied Control Commission function as the virtual government of Germany while there were fundamental ideological disagreements between East and West? Were the occupying powers – initially three until the French joined – going to follow uniform lines of policy through four unique occupation zones? Could the ideological gap be bridged between Britain and USA on the one hand and the Soviet Union and the other? How could the Allies in this situation speak in one voice to the Germans? This was something the instructors in the information control course had identified as of prime importance! Certainly, we hoped, a stage had not yet been reached in which all cooperation between West and East had ceased. But it was clear to us well before the German armistice on 8th May 1945 that a situation presenting enormous problems, even to a harmonious alliance, was going to be even more difficult in the absence of allied agreement.

Hitler and Goebbels had committed suicide on 30th April 1945.[24] Shortly before, Hitler had appointed Großadmiral Dönitz to head the so-called German Government in Flensburg-Mürwig. Dönitz and his staff had retreated from Plön, south of the North-East Canals, on 3rd May, when he initiated negotiations for surrender.[25] Admiral von Friedeburg arrived the following day with other German plenipotentiaries to negotiate unconditional surrender at Field Marshal Montgomery's Headquarters at Bleckede, a small town on slightly higher ground on the bank of the Elbe River in the Lüneburger Heide, not far from Hamburg. I saw the place in 1980 while visiting friends who have an estate in the vicinity. It was silent, forlorn in time – the drama and tragedy of the time almost forgotten. At 8:15 p.m. on 4th May 1945, SHAEF announced:

> Field Marshal Montgomery has reported to the Supreme Allied Command that all enemy forces in

Holland, Northwest Germany and Denmark have surrendered. The US Ninth Army breaks up the German Ninth and Twelfth Army. The US Seventh Army takes Innsbruck, Salzburg and Berchtesgarden, which is still smoking after an RAF raid. Fieldmarschal von Kleist gives himself up to the US Third Army near Straubing.

On the 5th May, Admiral von Friedeburg arrives at General Eisenhower's HQ in Rheims. General Blaskowitz, the German C-in-C of the Netherlands, surrenders at a ceremony in the small Dutch town of Wagennungen in the presence of Prince Bernhard. The British victory salvo is fired at 3pm from Montgomery's HQ

The On 7th May British troops enter Utrecht to a tumultuous reception.

The final unconditional surrender with cease-fire order for all operations was signed at General Eisenhower's Headquarters in the small red schoolhouse of Rheims, France, on 7th May at 2:41 a.m., to be effective one minute after midnight on 8th May, VE-Day. Signatories were the German Chief-of-staff, General Jodl and Admiral von Friedeburg and on the Allied side by General Eisenhower, Field Marshal Montgomery, and Marshal Zhukov. The final capitulation conditions were declared at 6:00 p.m. on 5th June when the French General de Lattre de Tassigny could also add his signature. They were drawn up in English, Russian, French, and German with authenticity only for the first three languages.

Shortly before his suicide, Hitler had declared the City of Hamburg to be a fortress. The Burgomaster Rudolf Peterson, however, negotiated independently to seek surrender of the city to the British Army, granted by General Wolz on 3rd May[26] According to the British war diary:

The 8th Information Control Unit had reached Hamburg on 4th May and at 14:30. Lt. Col Lieven and Major Findlay took over the Hamburg Radio Station intact. At the same time a small assault detachment under Lt. Geoffrey Perry[27] and three other military personnel occupied the [other] Radio station at Rothenbaumchaussee with its transmitters, editorial offices and printing presses all fully operational, and Perry broadcast. "This is radio Hamburg, a station of the Allied Military Government!" [This announcement was] followed on by the British news in the evening, from the same microphone that Lord Haw Haw, the British fascist in Goebbels' service had used a few days earlier for his NS Propaganda. [28]

Lt. Geoffrey Perry, a German Jewish refugee, was one of the few officers with journalistic experience. He had been interned in 1940, volunteered for the pioneer corps, and was of the few who were commissioned. He had worked for the New York Times and the Daily Mirror. After the war, he built a publishing house in London with international connections. In 1994, through my correspondence with the very thorough historical researcher Klaus Wagner, we renewed contact with each other. With great enthusiasm Geoffrey invited my wife and I to a very memorable weekend à quatre, full of heartfelt hospitality at their summerhouse in West Palm Beach, Florida, on our way to a holiday in the Bahamas. In the post-war occupation of Germany, he was ordered to establish and help to build and supervise the press in Flensburg. When collecting firewood in the woods near Flensburg together with Captain Lickorish, who supervised the Danish-German paper, the Flensborg Avis, Perry encountered "a down-at-heel character whose voice, in response to an innocent question, sounded like [and was] that of the infamous William Joyce."[29] Believing that Joyce might reach for his gun or take poison, Perry fired at him

Before going to press, 1945

shooting low, wounding Joyce in his right thigh; actually, Joyce was unarmed and looking for his passport. Joyce was subsequently tried in Britain, found guilty, and hanged for treason. [30]

Meanwhile I was with Lt. Col. Garland and together we drove from Lengerich to Hamburg while the German surrender was signed.[31] I still remember the journey quite distinctly, including the historical explanation Garland gave me. The destruction witnessed on route and at Hamburg was something I shall never forget. Total chaos had followed "Hitler's Total War."[32] One could not feel any Schadenfreude; the situation was far too serious for that. But though millions of innocent people suffered in the process, in the end historical or divine justice caught up with those who had perpetrated massive crimes against humanity.

When I left German soil in 1937 from Hamburg it would have been impossible to conceive that I would return to that very city with British troops. Nor could I have imagined in 1937 that I would return to help control the first news-sheet produced there by the British Army for the German civilians.[33] All newspapers were banned except the one we set up. We commandeered the building, offices, and printing presses of the Girardet Newspaper at the Gänsemarkt, from where the local newspaper the Hamburger Anzeiger had been published. We also took over some of their editorial staff to work under our direction. The first issue of the Hamburger Nachrichten der Militärregierung came out on VE-day, Victory in Europe, 9th May. Captain Bennan, a somewhat crude Canadian man, could not speak German so I took over the newspaper.

With the help of the German staff we started a three-times-a week "daily" news-sheet turning out 285 000 issues of one page printed on both sides, the Hamburger Nachrichten Blatt der Miltärregierung and Die Mitteilungen, and a twice-a-week "weekly" paper of a million copies. Frequently the number of copies had to be reduced because of an insufficient supply of newsprint. To begin with, these news sheets were delivered free-of-charge to the civilian population and prisoners-of-war camps. There was an enormous demand for them, with long line-ups of people eager to receive the latest news. We practiced strict separation between news and comment, which is still an article of faith to me. At first, we gave priority to straight news and printed general information and orders; later, we often followed these with reports on the Nazis and their crimes as they were uncovered (for instance, concentration camps). We gave full coverage of the Nuremberg and Bergen-Belsen trials. Our editorial job was done with integrity.

When things were a little more settled there arose, however, a controversy among the British editors, some of them wanted to develop a paper more in line with the popular- or boulevard-press of Britain. They did not like the reports on "that cultural stuff," such as German literature that had been prohibited by the Nazis or articles on Einstein, Thomas Mann, Stephan Zweig, Mahler, and many others.[34] In exile, Thomas Mann had written his three-volume novel Joseph and his Brothers. We, however, preferred to promote the positive side of German culture and tradition whenever we could. After years of reading nothing but what the Nazis wanted them to read, our intention was to allow our readers to develop their own independent judgement.

To this Major Barnetson gave his full support.[35] The sincerity of his support was unquestionable when it came to granting licences to Rudolf Augstein and his outspoken magazine, Der Spiegel, a publication that Barnetson knew full well would be troublesome. Even so, he also allowed Dr. Gerd Bucerius to publish Die Welt, a paper of a high standard. In 1987, for financial reason, the latter was unfortunately taken over by the Frankfurter Allgemeine Zeitung. But Der Spiegel, though often controversial, still exists and is appreciated today. Barnetson stated that:

> We wanted papers of a wide horizon, papers of weight, authority and intellectual dimension, not as dull as *The Times* or as righteous as *The Guardian*.

He was the chief press officer in charge of the publication branch. During the winter of 1944/45 under his guidance an eight page tabloid newspaper produced in Brussels had been widely distributed while the troops advanced. In Cologne, Düsseldorf, Essen, and Hanover a veritable chain of overt news-sheets had already been printed and distributed, but they had difficulties receiving and printing accurate information and soon folded.[36] I worked under Barnetson and remember him with great affection. He was one of the British officers to whom I taught German. I can still see us sitting outside in something like a wood probably during the time at PWE. I used *Heute Abend* (Today's Evening) and for many years still had a copy of the book with his name inside.

Barnetson was always friendly, a humble man who did not give himself airs, an attitude that was not always conveyed by some of the other officers to the likes of us in the lower ranks. As he had to approve the publication of books he actually asked me to read a novel by the somewhat controversial Ernst Jünger to advise him on the question whether printing permission should be granted; I can't remember which book it was I read. In 1972, the Queen bestowed a knighthood on Barnetson.[37] Quite by chance, I met one of the directors of the United Newspaper in 1978 while I was staying in London in the National Club, which I was transferred to because accommodations at the Royal Society were fully booked. Lord Barnetson was chairman of the United Newspaper at the time, and this chance encounter allowed me to see Barnetson again and have a good chat with him. He died in 1981 having been one of the great men of Fleet Street. So in some cases, though probably not in many, Information Control had been able to attract men of exceptional ability.

As to the staff of the Girardet Newspaper, we just walked into the office, and told some of the staff to carry on. I have a vague recollection that we knew of several experienced journalists in Hamburg at the time but kept off them, because we believed them to have been involved too much in Nazi-journalism. Naturally, we were cautious at first, because we did not always know enough about the views of our German colleagues and the part they had played during the Nazi regime.[38] But gradually, good relations were established with those that stayed. They accepted our directions without questioning. It was more often a matter of voicing suggestions than giving orders. There was never any opposition to what we were trying to do: stop the misuse of newspapers for the sake of propaganda, recreate decent journalistic standards, and, particularly, separate news and comment. After years of dictatorship and censorship, our German colleagues were keen to find out what had been hidden from them and to learn from the mistakes of the past.

I fulfilled something like the functions of chief editor, Chef vom Dienst, often as a kind of news editor, sifting through the tapes that came in over the tele-printer.[39] The news was received from the Allied Press Service.[40] This service improved when we also established contact with Reuter, the British News agency. For the international news, Seften Delmer started to organize the No. 10 German News Service, GNS, on 5th August 1945. Besides this, there existed a British supervised supplementary local German news service. After mid-December 1945, we received additional news from the *Deutsche Presse Dienst*, DPD, under the supervision of PS/ISC (Press Service/Information Service Control). By August 1945, in most parts of the British Zone the tele-printers were wired up between London and the British occupied zone, and within the British zone.

In a limited capacity, I was assisted by Hans Sommerhäuser, the previous editor-in-chief of the Hamburger Anzeiger, a friendly person, certainly not a great thinker but obviously happy to be kept on.[41] Klatt, another German journalist, who was with Girardet before, worked for us on the local, primarily non-political news. Some of the secretaries may also have been with Girardet. Ilse Wiegand, slightly younger than myself, and with whom I became friendly, had written occasional articles under the old regime. Another secretary later became Mrs. Garland. We met the Garland's years later in Exeter where her husband was professor and department head for German literature, and I taught in the history department. The atmosphere in the editorial office was generally quite relaxed. In the offices I served, we could count on the cooperation of the German staff.

While on my first leave post VE-Day at my parents' home, I wrote a long letter on 23rd August 1945. The leave gave me time to collect my thoughts about the tumultuous time I had experienced and observed. I have drawn from this letter throughout these recollections and I think it appropriate to present it here with only minor editorial changes.

One might accuse the Germans of want in patriotism, cringing, or lacking character. I have read in some British newspapers that the Germans were now adopting a very clever ploy of submission to orders to be in a better situation for the next war. I did not agree with the latter view. Anybody who had seen Germany in 1945 was appalled by the gigantic extent of the destruction there has been through long periods of Allied bombing. I had seen British towns. I had passed through Caen and Falaise. But the complete rubbing out of towns was reserved for Germany.

In Wesel, a small city on the Rhine close to the Dutch border, and Münster, an Episcopal city in Westphalia, the scale of destruction was at least that of Caen, the symbol of a dead city. In the whole of the British zone I very much doubt whether there was a town left which was only 'slightly damaged'. One had to go pretty far north, right up to the Danish border, and pretty low in population, to find places that were intact. One of these was Flensburg, above the Western end of the Flensburger Förde. Hamburg still had a population of something like one and a quarter to one and a half million. Parts of the city did not exist anymore. It was just a pile of rubble. It was difficult to imagine where and how people live. But one could still enjoy a walk along the Alster, an inland lake in the centre of the city, and Hamburg, in spite of all the destruction, is still a nice city. After several weeks one got so used to the sight of destruction, one hardly saw it any more. Clearing had not started, and, I suppose, with the then present lack of provision for transportation could only be tackled slowly. There was no beginning yet of any new building, and the problem of accommodation was a most pressing one facing the allied military authorities, and was equal to the desperate food situation. A tremendous attempt had been made in the British zone to grow enough food to feed the population during the coming winter. The want for heating material was badly felt that winter.

There existed another difficulty. Thousands of German soldiers, in fact one and a quarter million had landed in Schleswig-Holstein, and were taken into prisoners-of-war camps. As quickly as possible they were released under the scheme "Barleycorn."[42] There was an enormous movement of population, in addition to the presence of non-German displaced persons, who had been used as slave labourers. Two million fugitives and 200 000 displaced persons had to find some sort of existence. There had been a veritable stampede from East Prussia, Pomerania, Mecklenburg and Silesia ahead of the Russian troops pressing from the East. The food rations were very much lower than during the war. There was often no gas or electricity. There was shortage of clothing. Many returning soldiers had only their uniform to wear. Collections had been made for the concentration camp victims. It was by no means certain that people in the British zone would be able to survive without outside help. The influx included also the many ethnic Germans expelled from Czechoslovakia and Poland. The overcrowding of any available accommodation and the great diversity of people sharing it did not always run smoothly. The British and the American zones were regarded as a safe haven from Communist rule. This popularity, however, increased the problems of feeding the people and providing the necessary energy resources. Germans in the Western occupation zones were dependent on the good will and help of the occupiers. In the West, whatever the local variations, treatment of Germans was probably best in the British and worst in the French zone. The British and Americans had had time to prepare for occupation. Also, only the French, among the three Western occupiers, had themselves partly been occupied by the Germans and partly been governed by a regime collaborating with the Nazis. They did not have the opportunity to prepare for occupation, as illustrated by the training I was given; the French were not able to enjoy this advantage, as they had only recently been fully liberated.

During this time of reflection, I pondered the intentions of the occupying force. Did the British occupation policy follow more the line of my psychologist colonel-instructor sympathetic to the Germans or that of the other colonel that spoke about the "Huns"? Certainly in the long term, the occupation policy had to and did show understanding for the German civilian population. Even if at first there existed some harshness, perhaps partly due to the fact that we expected to be faced by an underground resistance, the so-called Werwolf movement, which did not materialize. Ken Green who also had feared guerrilla activity wrote to me 5th March 1945 that:

> The German forces were receiving such battering that organised resistance is due to stop in the near future. . . . Though Germany is your fatherland – I am going to risk your displeasure so far as to say that I hope the Allies do the job conscientiously and properly this time, to remove even the chance of a

powerful Germany arising. . . . The British – prone as they are to extend a helping hand to the beaten, at any time may falter in their trust, and the Americans may develop the same faltering by writing off by virtue of the general remoteness of the combatant areas from the USA. But I should think the Russians can be relied upon to extract their 'just pound of flesh' . . . I hope of course that both the British and the Yanks will efficiently carry out their duties.

Captain Arthur Geoffrey Dickens, the erudite historian of the Reformation, described in his elegantly written Lübeck Diary the devastation of the town.[43] He had been in charge of the British press there with his NCO Dr. Pollitt. Dickens also reported about gangster bands and armed displaced persons threatening and robbing civilians that were soon stopped. But he criticized the British military, in June, for giving orders to blow up shipyards and destroyed industrial plants.[44] He considered these acts on many levels as counter productive.

Going back to my own experience, I recollect that while at first we were ordered to always carry our weapons, we soon went about unarmed.[45] I certainly felt quite safe walking about that way. Initially, there was also the non-fraternization policy, which prohibited any personal contact with German citizens. The reason for this was partly political and partly to avoid the spread of infectious diseases, like typhus, dysentery, tuberculosis, and VD (venereal diseases); they had all reached epidemic proportions in the starving population. In November, the official food rations were reduced to 1350 daily calories, only to be raised in March 1946 to 1500 daily calories.[46] However, by September 1945, the fraternization order was relaxed.[47] Indeed one can say that the view the British troops took of the civilian population improved as they got to know the Germans, who basically adopted a positive attitude to the occupiers.

In Hamburg, I lived and ate in various sergeants' messes, of which one at least was on Rothenbaumchaussee.[48] When I suggested the surplus food might be given to German people, Captain Bennan got very upset and voiced: "I'll stop your demob [demobilisation]." I later found out that he was profitably involved in the black market, and may have suspected me as a rival marketer. For the Germans, their currency, the Reichsmark, had only limited value, e.g. enough to buy the very small official food rations. Cigarettes, alcohol, prized personal possessions were the main currency. Every British soldier had a free issue of cigarettes and could purchase another quantity duty free; also the military group with which my unit was associated seemed somehow to have acquired a large amount of alcohol in the form of Steinhäger, a strong type of brandy. Both at times came in handy in the barter-economy. I received hospitality from Germans, whom I was able to help with cigarettes; which they in turn could trade for food. In this post-war period, Germans were understandably preoccupied with their survival. They had to cope with damaged, quite restricted accommodations, which could at any time be requisitioned by the authorities, the Wohnungsamt. Many of them were recent refugees or expellees themselves, and it is not surprising that, in a time of extreme shortages, relations between the original population and the more recent arrivals were not always amiable. There was the worry about soldier-husbands or soldier-sons from whom there was no news; some were eventually discovered to be prisoners-of-war and, in spite of official effort, there was often a long waiting period before they could come home. In the streets one saw many amputees. Food, fuel, and clothing, with other necessities of life, were in desperately short supply.

The month of July brought many more changes. According to the Allied Agreement in Yalta of the previous year, Russian troops completed the occupation of West Mecklenburg, including the cities of Schwerin and Wismar.[49] When news of this plan with detailed maps reached our office, they were published.

However, on 9th June an internal order made sure that no newspapers would be distributed to any place close to the now confirmed border of the Russian zone, as this closure might cause a further disastrous stampede westwards of frightened civilians. Friends of my wife, Rosemarie, from the Prussian nobility were nevertheless tipped off. They later told us about their flight with their small children to the West by night in a freight train with some of their precious possessions hidden under loads of grain. The frontier was closed, a day later. When the wall had fallen in 1989 and the two Germanys started to reunite, her friend's family had the opportunity to regain their estate in Mecklenburg, but the manor house, the land, and the woods had been so mismanaged that their agriculturally active grandson had to decline the offer.

According to Allied agreement, on 4th July 1945 the division of Berlin into four Sectors was carried out by the American, British, French and Russian military. The city had previously been conquered and solely occupied by the Russian Army. The Potsdam Conference had started and took place in Cecilien Hof, Crown Prince Wilhelm's old summer residence. It was supposed to elicit preliminary agreements for a new start in central Europe. Its decrees were supposed to be preliminary and not intended as a peace treaty; that was still to come later. The German people were hopeful, and had greeted Churchill and Roosevelt with spontaneous enthusiasm. The Conference lasted from 17th July to 2nd August, and ended in a communiqué that was published some time later. It confirmed Germany's division into four zones under four military governments. Exchanges of territories that had already taken place in the previous month were now confirmed. On 17th August, Berlin became the official seat of the Allied Headquarters. All in all, from the German point of view the agreements brought further disappointments and worries to an already difficult situation. [50]

While still on my post-VE leave, we learned on 9th August 1945 about the bombardment of Hiroshima and Nagasaki. These atomic bombs caused a quick end to the War in the Pacific, and the Japanese Emperor broadcast the unconditional surrender on 14th August. I remember going to London to celebrate VJ day (Victory Japan) on 15th August with the jubilant crowd in front of Buckingham palace. [51]

During this rare pause amid the wood of Boars Hill, I asked myself, how did I see my own position? I could never call myself a German again. When I had entered Germany, I came as a British soldier. I never intended to settle anew in Germany. Having made a clean break, having parted with the past as far as one could, I looked on Germany only as something outside myself. Intellectually, I was interested to see how the Germans would take defeat. Yet, I was fully aware of Germany's importance for Europe. I was entirely in sympathy with the general principles of the British policy in Germany. No promises had been made to the Germans, and life was still pretty tough for them. Their houses might have been requisitioned at short notice. I myself had to walk into houses to have to look around. I noticed how the heart of the woman in the house stopped when we arrived, for she realised that if we liked the house, we would seek permission to move in, and she would have to leave without the possibility of taking more than a few personal belongings with her. Anybody could be arrested for any political suspicion; there was no claim to trial in court. There was no news of the many hundreds of thousands of soldiers and Hitler Youth Boys who stood on the Eastern Front. Children had been evacuated to Thuringia and to Saxony, and no news came from them either. All property may have been lost, if it was in Eastern Pomerania or Silesia. Few Germans were without the most serious worries.

The British military did not treat the Germans gently: they were quite firm, exacting obedience to orders. But they aimed at the creation of order, and in this they succeeded to a large extent. A German who had a clean political past had nothing to fear of the British authorities, and for the great masses of the population in the British zone, the arrival of the British was, strangely enough, a welcome event. In fact, if there had not been a policy of non-fraternization at the time, quite a wave of enthusiasm would have arisen. It was probably wise to appear in the role of the conqueror rather than the liberator, as otherwise it might have been easier for Nazis to integrate themselves and more opportunists would have risen on the crest of the wave. For the anti-Nazi minority, of course, this policy of conquest was a pity. Their enthusiasm was not channelled. Subject to the lethargy of an official body, they were not being put in a position of importance.

The highest Nazis were arrested immediately, as soon as they could be caught despite their various disguises. Lesser Nazis were allowed to remain in positions of authority only as long as they could not be replaced. The process of turning them out was continuing all the time. There was plenty of evidence, in fact, too much. In this situation, denunciation was as rife as ever. As soon as people realized that I spoke German, I was flooded with information. Captain A. G. Dickens, who was Commanding Officer in Lübeck until September 1945, mentioned in his Lübeck Diary, "16 000 denazification cases in his district alone."[52] It was suggested that a distinction be made between people who joined the Nazi party prior to 1933 and those who joined up to 1937, the closing date for joining. The reason for this distinction was that some may have felt compelled to join to avoid the crippling professional disadvantages, which is well remembered by my wife Rosemarie.[53] Dickens thought the later date to be more conclusive. In my opinion the earlier date was more revealing as there was then no compulsion to become a party member, nor did fear of the party yet play a part, which was very much the case during the reign at the later date.[54]

Ironically, the reason the British occupation forces had so little difficulty in asserting authority may be explained by the success of the German and, in particular, the Nazi teaching:

Montgomery was almost looked at as their war hero. This reverence might explain why there was no sabotage in the British zone. I believed these views were representative of those of my colleagues in Information Control; including those who were forced to emigrate from Nazi Germany. That British soldiers such as myself felt safe going without arms a strong indication of the tremendous achievement of British Military Government.

Would this have been the same in other countries? Was the hopelessness of resistance, now that the war was over, the key to this puzzle? Why did a great nationalistic nation form no resistance movement, at least not in the British zone? An explanation of the different structure of morale in Germany was provided by the fact that the retreating German soldiers received little encouragement from the civilian population during the last stages of the war. The orderly attitude of the German people, if one looks at it from the positive point of view, their servility, if one looks at it from the negative point of view, was mainly due to Nazi teaching that might is right and that the duty of every citizen is unlimited obedience to the power-that-be. Furthermore, the Nazis succeeded in their propaganda in scaring the German of the Russians – and rightly so! Last, their racial teaching stated that the British were blood brothers. All these factors combined to give the British a favourable start.

I further pondered about of the future of Germany's people? What about "re-education"? I found this to be a rather pompous term.[55] In this short survey, I concentrated on the facts of the situation, on the material side of it, on what we found. Schoolchildren could be taught the new outlook. But all grown-ups were too occupied with the fight for survival to have a lot of energy left to engage in political thinking. The German public was very receptive in the first weeks after the end of the war, but they obviously could not live on propaganda and thin air. The most important aim in those first weeks was the maintenance of law and order in Germany, and the provision of the bare necessities of life. Re-education involved the stirring up of political thought, and in many ways that needed to be avoided at the time. People cannot engage deeply in political thought when they were dangerously near to starvation, yet a redefinition of the political thought of Germany was needed if the country was to restore itself.

Germany was in a chaotic position, all the great centres had been entirely or partially been destroyed, communications and industry were disrupted, the male population was scattered all over the continent (some prisoners perhaps never to return), and the country was divided into four zones. Would breaking up the country between the conquerors be the solution of the fear of another German militaristic resurgence? It did not seem likely to me, after what I had seen that the Germans would ever want to restore again the mystical German greatness. Perhaps the only way to make Germany harmless once and for all was by destroying her physically, but there were other solutions. And while the danger of militaristic Nazi Germany may have past, what effect would this conflict visit upon Europe? Was the standard of living in Germany bound to drop to mere subsistence for years to come; when the community would no longer be able to support a widely educated class and the German population would be a vast proletariat? Nobody could deny that Germany was one of the pillars of the Europe of old. Was Europe dead?

By virtue of its geographical position as well as her joint military occupation, the German problem was a European one. Many Europeans thought it desirable to lead the German people back to a civilized and humanitarian way of thinking.[56] In my report *British Policy in Europe, the British Army of the Rhine* I gave a further analysis and historical background of Britain's new responsibility to see that Germany echo the principles that Britain represented.[57] I stated that it was to Britain's lasting credit that she decided to adopt a humane, though obviously firm, policy toward Germany and refused to take savage revenge.

I found it doubtful whether other countries in Western European would have been able to show the same political maturity and restraint, for these countries experienced the cruelty of being occupied by a people convinced that they were a "master-race." I felt convinced that these countries would benefit from this wisdom, and if they could free themselves of any reason of fear, they should be able to adopt a more conciliatory attitude to the German people as a whole. But they must feel that the British occupation will be bound to go on for a considerable time, and that a British return to 'splendid isolation' was out of the question. Britain is at present deeply committed in Europe. The following presents the elaboration of these ideas within my report:[58]

For the first time after a century of absence, Britian again had a continental foothold. Hanover is once more under the rule of the King of England, only this time not as a friendly kingdom but as part of an occupation zone. In 1837 the British public were relieved to see the end of the continental commitment. Schleswig and Holstein, those provinces which Palmerston regarded as a British interest,[59] though he refrained from going to war over them in 1864, are now equally under British rule. Britain owes her greatness to her dual role as a European and a world power. After the last war, as after every previous European conflict in which she had taken part, Britain severed all continental obligations with all possible speed. In 1918 there was a good deal of well-founded hope that the continent of Europe would be able to master its own problem. Then the explosion of tragic conflicts had released entirely new political energy through the wide principle of self-determination. The end of the Hohenzollern and Habsburg rules was hailed as the beginning of a new era. Today in 1945, it was impossible to feel that it was safe to allow the continent to try any further experiment. It is to Britain that the task falls of creating new life out of chaos.

The British authorities have recognized that by helping the Germans to survive the winter they will stabilise the situation. So far no support has come from the East; it might be more profitable if the British zone would face west. After the last war the victorious Allies lost the peace trying to compromise on German policy. They failed because they tried to reconcile suppression and conciliation. It would be tragic if the same were to happen again. In 1918, the nations concerned were Britain, France, and the United States. Now the issues lie primarily between Britain, Russia, and the United States. It is hard to see how a country can be run satisfactorily as a single unit by men of such widely different political, national, economic, and social backgrounds as the representatives of the Western democracies and Russia. Would it be better if the East and the West agreed to differ, and openly tackle the problems in their own manner? It is essential that harmonious relations should continue.

It is to be hoped that the zone, which is the first to be integrated into the framework of European civilisation, will set an example that will be followed by the others. The British occupation of Northwest Germany demands far more than a military or administrative task, it has become a mission. What is at stake is the life and death of Western civilization in Europe. If there is a strong belief in Britain, in the value of our political ideas, there is no doubt that the Scandinavian and the Low Countries could be infused with the hope of a better future. Fantastic ideas of world unity or the federations of a continent are more unattainable than ever. But a cultural understanding in Northwest Europe, together with economic cooperation, is practicable. It might appeal to France to join in.

At the end of my report I emphasized: "It is important to explain this to the British public as the continued existence of European civilisation is indispensable to a survival of Britain as we know and love her."

In my daily life in Hamburg, even at the time of the fraternization order, I was gradually able to find out something about the remaining Jewish people in Hamburg.[60] I contacted the Jewish Refugees Committee at Bloomsbury House London, and in their answer they stated that they were still trying to establish contact with many Jews who had lived in Hamburg. I also tried to contact my old friends in Germany. I remembered Franz Suchan.[61] He was originally a friend of my sister Irene. He and his fiancée Erika had often visited my parents' home from 1931 on and, though I was much younger than Franz, these visits were the start of a very close lifelong friendship. I remembered that he had worked for Schliemann's Ölwerke, a Hamburg firm, when I last met him, before my emigration. I initially traced the Suchan's through visiting his firm, who in turn contacted Franz's father in Harburg, so I learned that they all had survived, but Franz was not yet home. The welcome result of my visit for Erika was that the salary payments for Franz, which had been suspended, were resumed to her right after appeared at the firm. The owners obviously misinterpreted the three stripes and crown on my upper sleeve, apparently believing that I was a senior officer. When Erika visited me with her two small children in the British office at the Gänsemarkt, Captain Bennan took offence, saying: "Get your Frat out of here!"[62]

Erika did not precisely know where her husband was. In fact his final station before he was captured was near Lengerich! Franz had become a prisoner of war of the Americans. I had contact with Burgomaster Peterson, because I acted as a courier for his daughter, the wife of *The Economist* and *The Observer* journalist E. F Schumacher (author of *Small is Beautiful*) in London. I took some steps to speed up Franz Suchan's release, and I remember vaguely that I approached Peterson. When I heard that Franz was about to be released, I somehow managed to organize a jeep driven by a military driver so I could go to see him. I went to his parents' home in Harburg and eventually tracked him down in Quickborn, Schleswig Holstein, not far from Hamburg. A strong anti-Nazi, he had at first been a member of the Democratische Studentenbund, but had in the meantime joined the Sozialdemokratische Partei. In due course he became Chairman of the district Council and Magistrate, Oberkreisdirektor and Landrat, in the North Sea Port of Husum where he and his family lived in the *Schloß*, the castle. As member of the SPD he was elected Deputy for Schleswig-Holstein in the 1949 German Federal Republic election.

I received a lot of hospitality from the Suchans for the remainder of my time in Germany and later on. He often invited me to stay with him and his family, and I was happy to accept their kindness. We had much in common politically and spiritually. I could discuss the questions of the day quite openly with them in an atmosphere of mutual confidence. Franz was exceptional among Germans in 1945-46 in the optimism he showed about the future, and in the energy he displayed. Thus, it was not surprising that after some major assignments as plenipotentiary of Schleswig Holstein in the Two-Zone-Economic Government in Frankfurt and later in the Three-Zone Government of Bonn, he rose to be President of the Berlin State Bank and became a member of the Bundesbank Council.[63] Through the Suchans, I was able to find out how things looked from the point of view of German civilians. At one of my visits to Husum, I got to meet the future leader of the SPD, Kurt Schumacher, who with the support of the British resisted several attempts of the Communist party to amalgamate the two parties. Sadly Franz died in a traffic accident in 1971.

At the end of June, I was transferred to the editorial office in Flensburg.[64] A lot had happened there before my arrival. On 1st May Großadmiral Dönitz with his Headquarters in Flensburg-Mürwick at the Naval School, had taken over what was left of the German government. Then on the 9th May he acknowledged and announced the unconditional surrender in a broadcasted speech and in the *Flensburger Nachrichtenblatt*.

Lt. Geoffrey Perry had been ordered to establish the British press in Flensburg. He arrived with his vanguard on the 9th May, but he encountered resistance when entering the editorial office and had to draw back; however, with military assistance he soon confiscated the press office in the Nikolaistraße. The 10th May was Ascension Day, an official holiday, so no papers would be published. Punctually on May 11th, 40 000 copies Nr.1 of the *Flensburger Nachrichten-Blatt of the Allied Militärregierung* had been composed, edited, printed, and handed out to the civilian population. It was also exhibited and eagerly read from the glass cases outside the editorial office. The Flensburger Nachrichtenblatt had ceased to appear, while the radio station, the Reichssender – now illegal – was still used by Dönitz until 14th May.[65] The British Military Government, well aware of this act of disobedience, had given orders to "do nothing to challenge the authority of Admiral Dönitz, but as far as possible ignore his existence and that of his government." On 23rd May, Dönitz and his staff of 420 officers and 5000 troops were arrested and asked to get ready for further transportation to imprisonment.[66] They were allowed to bring some private belongings, of which Dönitz managed to pack six suitcases, only one of them could be taken on the plane, while the others would be sent on. While in the airport in a private place, Admiral von Friedeburg committed suicide using his own weapon. According to Hitler's command, Schleswig had been the last retreat for the rump government of Dönitz.[67] It was also where a large number of Nazi-ministers and officers had sought refuge. Heinrich Himmler, in disguise, fled and tried to hide with his staff in a farm house, but he was captured the same day. Although strip searched, he still killed himself by taking poison.

As at other press centres of the British Military Government, the numbers of issues published depended on the availability of newsprint. Until the middle of June, the *Flensburger Nachrichten-Blatt* appeared three times a week.[68] To begin with, it was offered free. A few weeks later there was a charge of 10 Pfennige. The number of copies varied between 13 000 and 35 000, eventually averaging at 140 000. Kiel, the nearest larger city was very badly bombed and no printing facilities were at hand there, so the Kieler Kurier, a "weekly" paper issued twice a week was also edited and printed in Flensburg, and then sent over to Kiel.

The latter soon reached 200 000 copies. In this way there was always one paper available during ordinary weekdays. The numbers of copies permitted and distributed were calculated on the area's population allowing a quota of 1:5. For this, the necessary paper amounted to 3000 tonnes per month. The news sheets consisted of two pages printed on both sides. According to directives the first page had to "present news objectively, avoiding tendentious writing and distinguished from comment so there would be no confusion produced by editorials."[69] From August on, editorials were permitted on the second page. The third page brought international and local news with a report-run-over from other pages. There was a constant lack of space. The fourth page had to be shared between letters to the editor and advertisements. But by order of Information Control: "no letter will be published which attacks or implies criticism of the Military Government or occupying Forces."[70] This order also applied to German officials elected by the Military Government. And in the pre-licence period, editors could not publish under their own names, as the British Press Unit alone had the editorial responsibility and had to give its approval.[71]

On his supervisory visit in Flensburg, Major Barnetson found that

> The German-Danish paper the *Flensborg Avis* had not followed orders and was still actively publishing as before the armistice. The proprietor claimed that since his journal was designed to serve the Danish minority, he felt he was exempt from the regulations.[72]

However, he and his staff were allowed to carry on, but to their dismay, they were ordered to only publish a limited number of issues in the Danish language disallowing any German text or German inserts. There was to be no exporting of the paper to Denmark. This was later waived, and they were also allowed to buy newsprint in Denmark, which was costly because of an unfavourable exchange rate.

By the time Captain Jack Zubick and I arrived at the Flensburg, we found the editorial office of the *Flensburger Nachrichten-Blatt* to be well-organized.[73] Zubick, a liberal and social man came from the business world of Calgary, Alberta. Although he had only limited German at his disposal, and virtually no journalistic experience, he got on well with the German staff. Perry, who with his great energy had done a lot of work here, was soon transferred, so that Zubick and I, with some other officers continued the work at the *Flensburger Nachrichten-Blatt* and the *Kieler Kurier*.[74] A great deal of work was left to me, as most of the other officers neither knew German nor had background knowledge of German life.

I was very happy with the opportunities I had in the last two years of my army service. I was able to observe history in the making and received several opportunities to shoulder considerable responsibility. Reflecting on my near total lack of professional qualifications, this was quite remarkable. It was a long time before I had this level of responsibility and authority once I left the military.[75] In both the PWE and at Information Control Offices, there was a number of German refugee NCOs among the staff, but hardly any prospect of promotion. However, rare exceptions existed, like of Peter de Mendelsohn, Captain Geoffrey Perry, and F. E. Jellineck who came from an Austrian family of scholars.[76] Quite understandably, the British officers wanted to remain in command. Fundamentally, it was difficult for the British, with their strong sense of patriotism and their long tradition of orderly government, to understand the émigré who wanted to fight his own country, although in the end that

Flensburg editorial office, Stg. Frank Alexander, 1945-46

was reservedly accepted by the Foreign Office. Perhaps they feared that some of the refugees might use their positions in the army of occupation to exercise revenge for crimes committed against their families. This I never witnessed. Any tendency of that kind among my colleagues, even those who had suffered far more than I, and had lost their nearest kin, would have gone against the ethos of the any of the members of the army units that I had known. The refugees, I knew, would not have approved of vindictiveness. When I received an answer to some material I had sent to Wolfgang Schieder, son of Theodor (both were Professors of History at Köln University), he complimented me on my positive attitude and my

actively taking part in rebuilding up the country
that had expelled you. Owing to the many visits in
Israel I know that such attitude was by no means
self-evident.[77]

I am not able to say which attitude applied to the US army.
Certainly those who served in the US Army were frequently
granted citizenship, and a greater number (in fact well over a
thousand) of bilingual German refugees were used for presswork
and censorship.[78]

Our offices were busy, constantly pragmatic decisions had
to be taken, about what to use and what to omit, and how to
present things. I cannot remember any guidelines that I felt
were restricting the editorial work, but some principles applied:
to help with the process of re-education and denazification, to
tell people about the atrocities of the Nazi regime, to deflate
rumours, and to explain something about democracy, to help the
Germans to see their situation in an international perspective,
to gradually start building a parliamentary constitutional state,
a Rechtsstaat, after the English model, and to pass over or at
least play down differences between the Western Allies and
the Soviet Union.

The Danish minority question resurfaced was always present,
but it was ignored for the most part and only drew attention
from time to time.[79] The British, though well aware of it, did
not touch the question in any of their militarily controlled
newspapers, we never wrote a single word about it, although
many requests and applications from the Danish minority were
received. From the British point of view, there existed enough
news, and more important problems needed our attention.
Officially, I was neutral in the border question during my time
of service in Flensburg. Alas, quite a few Danish Germans only
spoke German. Applications for permission to print a Danish
German-language paper in both languages were denied, but in
the end a licence for a paper in each language was granted on 20th

June 1946 as it could no longer be avoided. Foreign policy issues concerning the Danish-German border had started to cause controversies between Britain and Denmark in London, and in the newly formed provincial government the border question was openly discussed. Given the guidelines to be followed, it was permissible at the paper to give historical facts about the border but the editor had to desist from "initiating propaganda for detachment of South Schleswig from Germany."[80] That said, neither the *Flensburger Nachrichten-Blatt* nor the *Flensborg Avis* would have succeeded in stirring up the undesirable border question, as neither attracted a significant enough Danish readership.

Personally, I had little sympathy for reopening an issue that had been settled by the plebiscite of 1920. In this I found myself in agreement with three friends who were certainly not rabid nationalists: Franz Suchan, and the two journalists with whom I worked, Gerhard Becker and Will Rasner. Franz Suchan's widow Erika told me that her husband had developed good contacts within the Danish government that helped to dissuade the Danes from strongly pursuing the border question. The Suchans were fully aware of the appalling voting record of at least part of Schleswig-Holstein in the latter stages of the Weimar Republic.[81] One of the arguments used to dissuade the Danes from pursuing matters further may well have been to point out to them that they would have little joy with a German population within their border, a population that had shown a vigorous German nationalism and had supported National Socialism. I accepted the argument of my German friends that there was a lot of *Speckdänentum* (Bacon-Danish attitude, a reference to economic opportunism) among the ethnic Germans in their support for a change of the frontier in favor of the Danes. I also remember my mother's experience of the plebiscite of 1921 in Upper Silesia when some Germans voted for Poland, not having enough confidence in the future of their own country.

Even if we did not print anything about the border question, decisions had to be made about suggestions that infringed on military regulations. When Theodor Seltzer,[82] nominated Landespräsident of Schleswig-Holstein, presented a plan to revive and licence a paper presenting agricultural interests at Rensburg, a town just north of the North-East Canal, I was asked on 29th June 1946 to help in the negotiation.[83] It may be mentioned that Seltzer was also the owner of the Seltzer publishing house that was under military control at that time. To follow his plan would have seriously reduced the circulation of the *Flensburger Nachrichten-Blatt*. As stated in the official report, "the *Flensburger Nachrichten-Blatt* is particularly good in using its influence concerning the Schleswig border question, and as it was desirable to support this work," the Seltzer project had to be denied for the time being.[84]

Attending to the daily tasks usually included the ceremony of showing the officer in charge the lay-out of the paper before we went to press; Zubick was deliberate in this, trying to avoid mistakes. But obviously somebody like Garland could have made more of that than Bannon or Zubick. I got on quite well with Zubick; he was certainly friendly towards me, and also got on well with the German staff. After demobilization, I saw him walking about in London from the top of a London bus on which I was riding and jumped off and talked to him. He was sociable, and rather critical of the other officers, saying that he had asked for me to be commissioned. As a Canadian he was likely much more open to a move like this, but that the other officers had prevented this. His own view of himself as a Biederman (a man of integrity) did not quite tally with the way his colleagues viewed him. I was told by them that Zubick was involved in practically every black market there was. He was, I believe, a married man. After he left the unit, the other officers viciously directed their dislike of him on his secretary, with whom he had carried on a friendship. They fired her by stamping her as a former Nazi, perhaps the worse form of slander in post-war Germany! This was a petty act, and quite unjust. However, I do not know how much it mattered to the lady, who came from a good family and later got married to a German in the Flensburg area.

The most senior German journalist taken over from the previous regime was Gerhard Becker, at least ten years older than myself. He was a friendly, well mannered, somewhat shy man who had been taken in by the Nazi propaganda. He was really quite an unlikely person to have been a Nazi, which shows how successful the party had been in recruiting Germans from a wide range of backgrounds. Like most Germans at the time, Becker was eager to learn what had really been happening in the world during the Nazi regime. He was our main German journalistic resource, and soon I had a close professional and personal contact with him. He often invited me to his home where I met his wife and family. To my consternation and great regret, he was barred from the profession for a while because he had been a member of the NSDAP. I do not recall whether the Germans or the British barred him, Zubeck would have been unlikely to have done so. I thought the action against Becker was unfair and said so, and, I may well have intervened in his favour.

While naturally it would have been better if there had not been so many Mitläufer (fellow travellers), I did not think it was right to use party membership in itself as ground for exclusion from the journalistic profession.

In any case, from a practical point of view, one might find oneself in the position of hardly having anybody suitable to employ. I came to the conclusion that every case had to be looked at on its own merits, which naturally made all judgements subjective. Eventually Becker was able to return to the *Flensburger Nachrichten-Blatt* and its successor the *Flensburger Tageblatt* attending to news.

For our editorial work we recruited Will Rasner, who had been an officer in the Wehrmacht. He was roughly my age.

He took to journalism like a duck to water, and I became very friendly with him. He also invited me to his home where I met his wife Erika and their small daughters. I remember that I again read German literature with them, particularly Rilke's *Kornett*.[85] At the office we could gradually cover a wider range of topics with editorials, but still under review by IC.[86] The editorials could be signed and appeared on the second page. We wrote about the difficulty of supplying coal, raw material, and food, the scarcity and facility of dwelling-places, transportation, and the general calamity of the people. We also had to work hard to refute the extensive rumours about these topics had to be dealt with. We also reported on the active work of the Churches, the relationships among state and church and education, and the general education towards truth. Rasner and I both enjoyed working on many editorials together, and we developed a useful German-English cooperation.

Will Rasner remained perhaps my closest personal friend from my information control period. Yet his excellent work in Flensberg was merely a preamble to the work he would accomplish with in fostering inter-European cooperation at the *Europäische Verteidigungsgemeinschaft* (European Defence Community) starting in May 1952. In this position he took part in close collaboration with Konrad Adenauer. I met him periodically while he rose in the world. In 1953, he was elected *Christliche Demokratische Union* (CDU) deputy for Scheswig-Hostein. He soon became *Geschäftsführer der CDU Fraktion im Bunderstag* (Chief Whip) under Dr. Konrad Adenauer, the first Chanceller of the newly constituted Federal Republic of September 1949. Will had the rare gift to carry out his duties with absolute honesty and to be fair and unfailing in executing the arrangements between the parliamentary parties without which a parliamentary democracy is not able to work well. He was fighting for the independence of parliament versus the government of the day.[87] After his early death in 1971, we regularly visited his widow, who lives in Bonn. For my wife and me she is a very special person.

From a journalistic point of view, the military control period in Flensburg and in Hamburg was very personally satisfying for me because I found a real niche professionally and made lasting the friendships of great quality.[88]

Occasionally we received visits by officers from Hamburg. One of them was Captain Sington, whom I had already met at the Amplifier Units; he had come to see whether everything was as it should be.[89] As a tank-officer, he had taken part in the liberation of the Concentration Camp of Bergen Belsen; the shock of what he saw there may explain why this highly intelligent and interesting man was extremely intense in his conversations and somewhat nervous. He had objected to a transfer order on the grounds that his unit was still urgently and with undeniable priority needed by the "camp": "conditions there are still bad." Later he would contribute to *Die Welt*, a valued and important paper.[90]

I later learned that Klaus (Sir Ken) Adam, a classmate from school and friend from my time at his mother's boarding house in croft Gardens, became a RAF Captain with a top-scoring single-seater fighter squadron.[91] He had flown many missions in Hawker Typhoons, and was now put in charge of 10 000 Luftwaffen prisoners in Wunsdorf near Hanover. He was asked to form these prisoners into labour units to construct the airfield – the airfield that in 1948-1949 became one of the principal bases for supplying Berlin.[92] Ken remembers:

It was a strange experience, but funnily I became quite popular with the POWs even though they knew about my background [as a Jewish and a RAF officer]. I took the whole of the officer staff, still in uniform, to Bergen-Belsen concentration camp two or three weeks after Belsen had been liberated, and it's some thing I will never forget. The inmates, by the time, were living in the SS barracks, but they were almost

proud to show us around, proud of the horrors they
had lived through. I did not see a single German
who was not emotionally shattered by what they saw.
Two days later one tried to commit suicide. It would
have been easier to hate them, but I could not. Only
if somebody would have behaved arrogantly towards
me would I have shot him. After that they more
or less administered themselves, and did some very
good work.

In my report *British Policy in Europe, British Army of the
Rhine*, I observed that occupation may be the only thing that
kept Germany from total chaos:

It is enormous. Today, the last thing the German population
in the British zone would want is a withdrawal of the British
occupation forces. It is surprising that perhaps the most violent
nationalistic and militaristic nation in Europe should almost
welcome the arrival of the enemy in the moment of defeat.
It is only the British soldier who today stands between the
population and civil war. The German civilians in the British
zone reacted very positively towards us, and appeared to look
at us not only as an assurance against the Russians but also
against any worsening of the general conditions.[93]

Here it may be interesting to note that on one of my walks
in the summer of 1946 I met a young navy cadet at Mürwick at
the entrance to the navy school, just outside Flensburg. Not so
long ago he had fought against us with apparent conviction. He
now stated that he had never been treated as well as under the
English. Nearly word for word I noted down what he said:

In the instance when the Military Government will be
replaced by a German administration the great hour
of test will have come. May this hour still be spared

us for a long time to come! At first we will have to
let the democratic world of thought mature in us, to
be confident in its ideology and become able to act
on the basis of this conviction. Help us, you, who as
our enemies have now become our friends." [94]

Gradually the German cultural life emerged again and was
much appreciated by the public. From 24th September 1945
on the Flenburger Nachrichten-Blatt reported concerts "in St.
Nikolai: a Bach Cantata and organ recital by Bach and Reger
are well attended by Germans and British alike, to comfort
and console." Dickens, in his Lübeck Diary, gives detailed
description of concerts performed in that city despite the
extensive bomb damage to almost every building.[95] He records
and ponders about a well-attended organ recital of Buxtehude
and J. C. Bach's cantata, "Bethink Thou, Man, thine End."
When looking into the Roman Catholic Church he found that
"eleven high masses were held on Sundays, with sermons and
prayers in English, Latvian, Lithuanian, Polish and Ukrainian
[besides I suppose in German].[96] An official said the "total
number of those assisting [(sic) and attending] on Sundays
often exceeds a thousand." In another part of his diary, Dickens
reports an interview with the Princess Wilhelmine of Prussia,
the widow of the ex-Crown-Prince who was killed in action
on the western front in 1940.[97] She represented the liberal,
progressive, and humanely engaged Prussia, an aspect that is
seldom mentioned today, when more often an easy cliché is
used about the Junker-class.
At Christmas 1945 in Flensburg, I used the welcome pause
to write about some of my thoughts and, as was my custom,
to send them to family and friends.[98]
How many of us would have been able to forecast a year
ago that we would be here? During the festivities we might –
amid the rush of modern everyday life – consider the somewhat
strange happenings of the last year. It is only too easy to forget

how thankful we should be that we managed to avoid defeat and won the war. This Christmas cannot be one of untempered joy, but perhaps we will see it in a truer perspective if we recall other possibilities we might have faced. We are better qualified to do this now than a few months ago, for we have in the meantime seen what the total defeat of a nation implies under condition of modern warfare. The loss of a war by a nation that had been fully mobilised carries with it a total collapse of all the normal things in life, whether you take savings, jobs, or some semblance of private morals. That this should be so is inherent in modern political and industrial trends. Countries are fully geared to war. Military conscription was one of the 'blessings' first practised by the Protestant King Gustavus Adolph of Sweden in the Thirty Years War and applied on a bigger scale by the atheists of the French Revolution.

Industry in wartime devotes itself practically exclusively to one purpose and it can thus be readily understood that the transaction from war to peace demands the same resources as the mobilisation of the industry for war. The requisite resources are certainly not available to the vanquished, and only partially so to the victors. Finally, in the political sphere, the coordination necessary for modern war, in varying degrees, according to the political structure of the country concerned, does neglect, or sometime even forcibly suppress the potential elements of an alternative government. A country like Germany carried this development to the utmost extreme. The Nazis did not merely order the physical blowing up of bridges which were essential for assuring food supplies for the civilian population, but for years they also did their best to sever all intellectual connections with the outside world. They saw to it that it would take a long time to bridge the gulf that separated the German nation from the outside world.

A nation, so defeated, is therefore neither politically nor industrially in a position to find its way back from war to peace, to re-establish some semblance of pre-war life. Chaos is the natural consequence of defeat in modern war. Strangely it is only the former enemies who are in a position to restore something like normal conditions. The victorious powers may adopt one of three courses of action. They can do nothing, which, if carried to its logical extreme, amounts to the toleration of an intolerable state of affairs. Secondly they can intervene in favour of the defeated nation by helping them in their reconstruction. Thirdly, they can practice revenge. Every one of these policies has been adopted and practised by various statesmen and nations since the German defeat. From the moral point of view, the British people are, however, not free agents.

Let us just remember for a few moments that the parts might have been played the other way round. Defeat was at one time, not only possible, but probable. We know now what the Germans would have done, had they occupied Britain. We all have different explanations for our victory, according to our outlook on life. To some of us, the success of the Allies may have been due to the overwhelming material superiority. Others may ascribe it largely to the superior fighting quality of our men. Others again may feel that our victory must be primarily attributed to the achievement of Anglo-American science. We are all especially interested in one particular aspect of the question. But some of us feel that some higher power came to our rescue. That whilst we are by no means perfect, we did represent something worth defending.

Few of us would deny today that a British defeat in 1940 would have been disaster for Europe, not only for ourselves. I for one firmly believe that our greatest driving force was the fact that we were fighting for certain ideals. Right does not always triumph quickly for the Higher Powers do not reckon in days, months, years or even a lifetime. But let me assert openly at this time, at Christmas, that I do believe in the eventual victory of good over evil. To me the deliverance in 1940 and our victory this year is evidence of the existence in life of a something more than purely material things, and the presence of a higher purpose in human life, than mere living. Above all let us thank whoever we recognise as our Higher Master, though we suffered great losses, we can look forward to a better future; and that we did not have the experience, not merely the natural agonies of defeat, but also of the brutality of our former enemy in our land.

Besides being engaged by the daily editing before the paper went to press, I sought contact with my old friends in Berlin, which was my primary reason for visiting the city. I recorded the events of that weekend on 31st March 1946 to present some of my impressions of Berlin post-war: [99]

In the days before the disastrous situation at the end of the war and the British occupation, one used to catch a train from Hamburg to Berlin, which took three to four hours. This, of course, is slightly different today. I did the hundred-odd miles by train from Flensburg starting at 10 o'clock in the morning and got to Hamburg at 1 o'clock. I had lunch at Hamburg at the Unit mess, left Hamburg-Altona at 3:15pm in the afternoon by military Diesel-Train to reach Hannover shortly after 6pm, was transported to a transit camp, and left for Berlin on the military (leave) train at 9pm. Before we got to the train, a volunteer was required for each of a warrant officer and a sergeant. As you probably realise it is entirely against army principles to volunteer for any job. I, however, thought that the duty might be interesting, which it proved to be. The warrant officer and I were shown into a first-class compartment, which was marked TCO. We decided that this meant Traffic Control Officer. We were then told that we had to deal with the Russians at the border. And we were next offered a first-class-meal in the *Mittropa-Speisewagen*, an elegant restaurant car, which I was only too gladly accepted though two meals, the one in Hanover and this one, followed too close on each other, and afterward made me doubt the wisdom of my decision. It was, however, a matter of honour not to refuse an opportunity to travel in a *Mittropa-Speisewagen* after nine years. After pleasure-duty, we duly reached the frontier between the British and the Russian zone at 11:30 p.m., had the train guard posted, and proceeded to get out of the train when it stopped on the Russian side of the border. The [Russian] armed guards were on the train, but the warrant officer and I were unarmed and we met the Russians [on the station platform], who carried weapons. I did not get further than saying *"Guten Abend"* (good evening!) and the rest of the negotiation was left to the German railway-officials. The Russian officer merely noted down the details of the train, the German official then signalled and with [the traditional decisive] suggestive manner and said *"Abfahren!"* (Depart!), the Russian repeated the word *"Abfahren!"* and we did not hesitate to get back on the train and carry on with our journey. It may be added in passing that we conducted negotiations with the Russian allies in the language of our former enemy.

[Having been in charge of the train had the advantage that nobody looked into my luggage that contained meat-cans. I had traded them in against cigarettes with the help of friends in Schleswig to bring to my Berlin friends, who thanked me profusely for them, as there the food-supply was far from adequate. For obvious reasons, as it might have stamped me as a black marketer, this remark does not appear in the letter, but in later years I often referred to this story orally.]

We both then went to sleep in our first-class carriage. The journey took 8 ½ hours in all and it is, of course, unfortunate that the most interesting part of the journey is done in the hours of darkness, though there may be a reason for that. I woke up when we were passing through Wannsee around 5 o'clock in the morning. The *"Stadtbahn,"* the electric city train had already started running.

Among the families I managed to trace are the Rau's. The address I was given was incorrect and had not led to any success previously. But I knew it was the first turning after the Station Heerstraße, going along the Heerstraße, from the Reichskanzlerplatz; I found the road was Boyenallee. No 7 was unfortunately bombed out. In the house next door I found a woman who told me Dr. Rau had died at Christmas, that Frau Rau was living at Boyenallee 5. I went to the latter place but Frau Rau was out. I left a message and called again the following morning. The meeting was terribly sad, for her daughter Renate had had TB, and was also dead; she left a child. Her son Rüdiger lives with his wife in Rathenow near Berlin. When Frau Rau saw who I was, after a moment's pause because of my name change, she, of course, was glad to get contact with the outside world again, but during the first meeting tears were constantly in her eyes, and in mine, too. She told me that she and her husband had hidden Staatssekretär Fritz Kempner, a high civil servant, for a week after the miscarried plot of 20th July 1944. I remember that we some times met him on our walks in Tiergarten. For the Raus it went without saying to help an old and trusted friend. Kempner stayed at their home, leaving in the morning, only to return when it was dark by crawling into one of the ground floor rooms through a window. Every morning he left before the maid returned to the house, as she might have talked, innocently or otherwise. The position proved hopeless and Kempner decided to give himself up.

As a marginal comment, it should be stated that Frau Rau said that from what she knew about the preparations of the plot that they were quite amateurish, *laienhaft*. The conspirators did not even have false papers. She did not have a lot of confidence in the ability of the conspirators to make good, should the plot have been successful. And it seems that she risked everything for a cause she did not truly believe in, which she could back only as a hopeless way of getting rid of the Nazis, and in which she got involved through the ties of a long-standing friendship of her and her husband's with Kempner. She told me that the conspirators had no contact with the working-classes, that Kempner was highly theoretical in his outlook on government, that the existence of a written list of the new 'government' proved how little ability the conspirators had to adapt themselves. Frau Rau visited Kempner in Prison before his execution. During denazification, Mr. Rau had lost his job as a civil servant in spite of the help they had given to Kempner. When I think of the participants of the 20th of July 1944 and on Frau Rau's courage, I do so in deep humility.

I went to see Frau Rau again the following day when she was far more settled. She was in fact quite the old one. I told her how much I hoped that she would be able to spend some time with my parents at Chilswell House... She mentioned that she was writing a novel. We talked about old times, and she wanted to know about my parents, Lore and Irene and their families. With all the unhappiness she had suffered I was reluctant to make too much of our happiness. But when I noticed how settled she was I showed her pictures of all of us which I carried with me at all times.

Like most people in Berlin, Frau Rau has lost more or less everything. The house was bombed and most of their furniture with it. She still has the furniture of one room. Her husband had been denazified and did not want to live any more. This also meant that she lost her claim to her pension. She has now had the matter raised again, in view of the help they had given to Kempner, and she hopes that she will receive a pension after all. When her claim to her pension has been settled, she would like to go and live in the neighbourhood of Frankfurt/Main, if possible, as her son-in-law who married again, is living there. What was so impressive with Frau Rau, as well with many of the other people I saw, was the objectivity with which they still managed to judge things, and we also talked about happier times.[100]

Years later, while visiting her grand daughter, since married in England, Frau Rau indeed visited my parents and my wife and I in Exeter. She had just been at Stonehenge, which was then not yet a tourist trap. I also saw her in Frankfurt before her death. Fortunately I found more old friends in Berlin:

I had arrived early in the morning, my first call was to the Schmidt family, when the time got a little more civilised. They were now living in Schmargendorf, Breite Straße in the British sector, (to which Bahnhof [station] Heerstraße, also belongs,) five minutes on foot from the mess at Warnemünderstraße, where I was staying. They were expecting me; I had indeed been in contact with them for several months. The joy of seeing them again was tremendous. Fate had separated us for nine years. Wolfgang and I had served in armies on opposite sides during the war. His parents had been in Berlin all the time and gone through a bombing whose intensity was easily understood when one walked about. Wolfgang's sister and his fiancée had been in Berlin during the initial occupation, when they had to hide in the attic. They all had to go through terrible things, many directly at our hand, and others at the hands of our Allies. Yet when I walked into their home, there was nothing to separate us. We talked with each other as if our friendship had never been interrupted.

During my 3 ½ day stay in Berlin, I went to their flat every night and we discussed at leisure many topics, some more up-to-date than others, some political, others historical, others again religious, philosophical, economic, etc. They all joined in, Dr. Schmidt with all his wide and varied industrial and financial experience as Director of the Deutsche Bank, and yet with an ethical outlook on life deeply rooted in Christianity, a man whose desk never prevented his contact with people at large, a man who has deep understanding for the working classes; his wife, Frau Dr. Schmidt very often quiet, but following every stage of the argument, and revealing by an occasional remark how important her contribution to the family was; Wolfgang who had kept much of the boyish balance and humour, yet eminently practical and still a full believer; then Rosemarie, who has inherited even more than Wolfgang everything that was special of the parents, a girl with deep insight and intelligence.

For both sides this contact was a joyful event. This could be felt. Before we sat down for our meal, Dr. Schmidt said a simple prayer in which he thanked God for the mercy of leading me back into their family circle after these years of separation. This was a moment I shall not forget. Never has the meaning of civilisation been clearer to me. We had all, on both sides of the frontiers, acted according to a moral standard, which enabled us to meet again without feeling that any of the experience of the preceding years separated us. We were all 'good Europeans.' Our political views were not of the passing opportunism, but the result of deep-rooted beliefs. Thus we did not blame each other for anything the other did, although we were never able to communicate with each other and confer on a common course of action. The independent standard of decency enabled us to make the right decisions in the various strange circumstances in which we found ourselves.

From a material point of view, the fate of the Schmidts mirrors the development in the Russian zone. Berlin surrounded by the Russian zone, of course, depended on it, whatever the sector may be. The Russians did not believe that banks were necessary, so they closed them, and grabbed everything on the premises, shares, and the property in the 'safe deposit boxes' among other things. Some of the shares they burned, but others they kept, which I felt might eventually lead to some rather absurd situation, such as Russian officials or their agent appearing at a board meeting of a firm in one of the western zones, and saying 'We are share holders.' If Dr. Schmidt had been in one of the Western zones, he would certainly have found himself deservedly in a position of great influence. Men of administrative experience with a 'clean shirt' were hard to find, but in the Russian zone neither his industrial experience nor his allegiance to the Confessing Church were much of a recommendation.

Soon, however, he was a member of the committee under the chairmanship of Bishop Dibelius that began to address the questions of a Christian society and of Christian socialism, of socialistic as well as of individualistic economy – a type of think tank.[101] There was also a plan for him to become Secretary to Robert Pferdmenges, a member of the Rheinisch-Westfälische coal and steel syndicate, a Paladin of the Ruhr economy.[102] As Secretary, he would work on the economic reconstructing of Germany under Konrad Adenauer, at that time Mayor of Cologne, a position he had held before 1933. Adenauer had been dismissed by the Nazis, was arrested by them several times, and had to hide himself for a while. He had found refuge in the Benedictine monastery of Maria Laach in the Eifel. In 1945, Adenauer was again installed as Burgomaster of Cologne, but then for some obscure reason he was dismissed as "incompetent" by the British officer in charge, not allowed to enter Cologne or to be politically active. Meanwhile, with many other important economic experts, Pferdmenges and this group of Ruhr industrialists found themselves in British internment without ever getting an explanation; so that the plan came to naught. Ironically, this turn of fortune had the advantage that these high-powered people got to know each other better than they other wise might have done. Despite these occurrences, Dr. Schmidt was later tasked under Allied High Command orders with the *Entflechtung der Vereinigten Stahl Werke*, that is, to break-up the interwoven United Steel Works because the occupational powers considered it too powerful a monopoly.

Reflecting on these events in the early 1950s, Rosemarie recalls a most memorable evening spent with her parents at Pferdmenge's house high above the Tegernsee in the Bavarian Alps enjoying the equally memorable Rhine wine, Schloß Johannisberg Fürst Metternich Spätlese (ice wine). The conversation revolved plans that worked and plans that did not. The wine reminding everybody of Metternich having been one of the leading politicians at the Congress of Vienna 1814-1815 who had been instrumental in building the German Confederation.

Not every controversy surrounding Germany reconstruction centred around politics and economics. Another interesting issue arose while with the Schmidts at Breitestraße in March 1946, as recorded here:

One of the many questions we discussed was one which is very controversial in Germany today, that of Pastor Martin Niemöller. The Schmidt family who had been in close contact with Niemöller came out strongly in his favour. Vigorous attacks have been levelled against him in some quarters on the grounds that he fought the Nazis on a very narrow church-basis. The Schmidt family believed that Niemöller's resistance sprang from the deepest religious motives and they respected him as one of the great religious opponents of Nazism. When I asked whether they believe that the rumour concerning Niemöller volunteering to serve in the German Wehrmacht (the German Military) was correct, this was not denied. We then discussed this possible fact and they agreed that it was by no means easy to condemn him out of hand . . . In my own mind, I felt all the more uncertain on this subject because other friends such as the Suchans had been expressing the opposite point of view.

A fortunate correspondence with one of Martin Niemöller's sons, Dr. Heinz-Hermann Niemöller, cleared up this question, and his letter of 10th April 2006 is translated here:

Re "reporting for war service": this was indeed offered by my father on 7th September 1939, shortly after the beginning of the war. It is important to assess the prerequisite for this reporting. Since the end of his law suit [1938] my father was held unlawfully in strict solitary confinement in the bunker, a separate building, of the concentration camp in Sachsenhausen, Berlin. This stone-built unit was like a prison within a prison, surrounded by its own walls, a place of torture and execution. There was practically no prospect of being set free, certainly not without the permission of the dictator (which has been proved historically correct). It has to be considered that my father as a former U-boat Officer had old friends in the Navy and the Army, some of them indeed personally pledged for his release. Many patriotically minded conservatives (to which my father at that time considered himself belonging) were of the opinion that they could and even ought to serve their country although they were strong opponents to National Socialism. These facts might have made it easier for my father to register his report. Another decisive motive for my father to serve again in the navy is mentioned in a letter of my mother: Through attaining the prospect to enter into an 'honourable' calling, with the help of friends, and underlined friends, he might get out of the horrible conditions of imprisonment at the concentration camp. A further motive to register for the navy – which even then was thought to be the wrong decision by several other friends – is to be found in a letter to my mother of 15th September 1939. It can be inferred from this letter that the decision and the offer to register for active service was taken and realised on 7th September after her visit in the KZ. Evidently my mother had suggested that he enter this report. She certainly had not arbitrarily offered this suggestion but, I am sure, she had done so on the advice of my father's defence counsel, the lawyer Dr. Hans Koch. At the beginning of the war Dr. Koch, a retired officer, had been recalled and served at the army's armament office (Heeresrüstungsamt) in Berlin. Because of his involvement in the active military resistance and his participation in the plot of the 20th July 1944 he was eliminated (*mördered*) without trial. That [my father's] attempt for renewed participation in active military service was immediately denied by General Keitel appears nevertheless consistent from today's point of view. Anyhow Martin Niemöller did not make any further attempts in this direction.[103]

At the end of the war Niemöller and a group of prominent fellow prisoners from Dachau, where he had been transferred to in 1941, and their guards had been taken to Southern Tyrol, where they were found by American troops.[104] Consequently, the prisoners were freed and their guards detained. It is not surprising that a person like Niemöller had become somewhat controversial when he got too accepting and involved with the Soviet Union and her communist ideas.[105] The idea of a state-planned economy attracted a wide range of people in many countries at that time. However, he was certainly a saintly man even if not perfect. When Niemöller was invited in 1964 to speak at our Methodist Church in Exeter, Devon, our minister knowing that we spoke German asked us whether we would be willing to billet him, which we were very happy to do. He was delighted to find so unexpectedly an old member of his Dahlem congregation. We spent a wonderfully intensive evening with him.[106] When Rosemarie asked him what the most difficult thing was during his time in Dachau, he answered: to love the torturer (*Schergen*) who tormented and killed his fellow prisoners. It had taken him a long time through prayer and meditation to reach this type of love, the agape that passes all understanding. Next morning when he said prayer the powerful mystery and blessing of prayer was palpable and stayed ingrained in our memory.

That weekend in Berlin in 1946 produced yet more interesting memories that I recorded:

I had another remarkable experience. It was a visit to the Collège Français (the French gymnasium). The original school building on the *Reichstagsufer* was bombed out, and the school has now been put in the backyard of another school close to the Spittelmarkt, on a road called Niederwall. The first person I met there was a lady, in a very queer dress, which I had never seen before to whom I spoke in German, who answered me in French and asked whether I was English. I found out later that this lady had been put at the disposal of the Collège by the French occupation authorities. This contact with the French was one of the many points, which Professor Levinstein, now head of the college, was glad about. That Levinstein survived the Nazis, of course, was pure luck. The main reason was his mixed marriage (*Mischehe*, a marriage between an Aryan and a Jewish person) but even that would not have prevented his deportation and possible death, had the war lasted any longer. However, having narrowly escaped this danger for many years, he was fresh, full of vigour, and did not show the least sign of nervousness. We spoke about present, past, and future for two hours. The bell announcing breaks and lessons, as in times of old, went more than once. He talked about his many activities, about the contacts with the French occupation authorities, and their helpfulness, about the books they put at his disposal, about his plan to have practically all subjects, even mathematics and the sciences, taught once more in French. When I asked him about the position of Professor Heinrich, he said that the burden for Prof. Heinrich to teach in French would be too much for teacher and pupils, and that an exception would have to be made in his case.

The years of enforced inactivity in the latter phase of the Nazi-regime did not leave Levinstein idle. He started writing a book which I believe was a mixture between autobiography and a history of culture. He had become very prominent in various cultural activities and seemed to have found considerable scope intellectually. He told me quite a lot about the other masters too, some of his negative comments I later could not corroborate. Among the people who I respected and had confidence in, Director Roethig seems to have been a rare example of somebody who did not come up to Levinstein's expectation. This controversy is already discussed in the second chapter of this writing. During the war, the younger pupils had been evacuated, and their schooling continued in Silesia, but before the end of the war they had moved to Sülzburg in Bayern where again Mr. and Mrs. Roethig's supervised the school.

I always had the highest regards for *Studienrat* Ernst Lindenborn, and my faith in him was not deceived.[107] Lindenborn was pursued by the Nazis for his political views owing to the denunciation by a "charming" colleague. I did not ask for details, but he was apparently forbidden to teach for some time. During the war he studied theology and became, according to Huguenot tradition, a Calvinist minister advising and helping numerous people of his scattered congregation at the French cathedral in the Centre of Berlin. He blessed many marriages, christened the children of his former students, and gave comfort to all, particularly to the bereaved. After the building of the Collège Français was bombed out, he looked after its pupils in the ruins of the French cathedral. When this became impossible he gave lessons to the remaining students in the Zoo bunker until 1st May when the bunker was turned into a military hospital. He told me that he still had and often used the historical tables I gave him as a school-boy. During the battle for Berlin, his wife was killed by the conquering Russian troops. I was enormously impressed how balanced he was in spite of everything he suffered. About his own sad experience he only spoke when pressed to do so, and pointed out that we had suffered far worse. His example proves the importance, above all, of sincere faith that can form a dignified character of this kind. [In 1948, at the beginning of the Berlin blockade and the British and US Airlift, Lindenborn left the French Gymnasium to become director of the College of Pedagogy (Pädagogische Hochschule). For his wide-ranging work as a teacher, writer, and pastor, he received the Grosse Verdienstkreuz, the highest Order of Merit of the German Federal Republic. He died in 1964.]

The fourth and last group of people I went to see were the parents of Gerald Fränkel. Gerd was then in Kenya. I still remembered the house: I got out of the Stadtbahn at the Station Townhall Schöneberg and walked to the house in Eberstarße a minute from the station. Gerd's parents were still living in exactly the same place. That part of the street was mysteriously intact. We have indeed been blessed with good fortune in the fate of our friends. I need not tell you how surprised the Fränkels were to see me walk into their home. I was able to discuss things with them at the same table we used to play board games (Gesellschaftsspiele), and asked each other questions about history and music. I might add that the Fränkel's survived the double danger of Jewish persecution and allied bombing. In overcoming the former they were again helped by the circumstance of a Mischehe. Madame Fränkel told me that the ordinary German behaved very well to them, and shopkeepers gave them extra-rations when they saw that their ration-card was stamped with a "J" (for Jew). It was certainly exceptional, when denunciations were unfortunately quite rampant.

This is the tale of people I went to see in Berlin.[108] Primarily I wanted to find out what had happened to our friends and to re-establish contact after years of separation. I was very glad I went. My family and I were blessed with friends of real character and decency. I was privileged to be the deliverer of a message from the West, for the people in the Eastern Zone felt their isolation very strongly. From my own point of view, meeting the Schmidts, Frau Rau,

Lindenborn and Fränkels again brought to conclusion a long and often hard period of intellectual development. For years, all the things that I had learned to love about Germany were taken from us. In this visit to Berlin, I felt that, at last, my family, my fellow refugees and I could believe in what was good in out German heritage. Criminals no longer claimed to speak in the name of the German people and tell us what a real German is. This journey gave me the insight to form a synthesis of my German childhood with my later British upbringing, which before I was unable to achieve. The contact I had with those who represent a better Germany within the framework of European co-operation gave me tremendous strength. The idea of unmitigated hatred was always a great strain.

The following part of my letter to my parents 31st March 1946 was in German and is translated and condensed here:

In this way, it was easier to give the purely factual account of my impressions of Berlin. Arriving at the Charlottenburg Station in the British Sector several military vehicles stood ready to bring us to the different Berlin Units. I was lucky my driver was willing to first of all show me the city, and several times we drove along the Kaiser Allee and the Kaiserdamm and in the distance saw the Siegessäule. The driver pointed out that this is not the present Victory Column. The amazing thing of Berlin is that the streets still somehow exist, that one can drive through the city, that she somehow has kept her image. Also, the public transport system functions well. Some streetcars take their old routes with little change, so that one vaguely gets the impression that Berlin coexists out of streetcars, city-trains, underground railway, sidewalks and just a few houses, as the destruction of apartment buildings is frightful and monstrous. One may well ask: where do the people live?

Just as an example: I carefully looked at our old area around the Lützow Platz. This area is completely destroyed. The houses in the Luther Staße 40, and Magdeburger Str. 5, known to all of us in the family, are ruins. Only part of the facades is left. The houses of neighbouring streets are wiped out in the same way. The whole area is a dead. The Hercules monument is a heap of rubble, and so is the bridge, which is now replaced by a temporary American military one. The old West [district] simply does not exist any more.

To ask whether I felt depressed? Somehow one has got used to this colossal destruction on the continent. It is nothing new anymore. The Tiergarten looks bare, has lost almost all of its trees which were used for firewood, instead of the park's grass there are now many little vegetable plots. The best known streetcar, the number 76, still runs, but only from Hundekehle to the Zoo. No. 75 cruises between Reichskanzler Platz and Kurfürstendamm, the 57 leaves from the Roseneck. In a way one is reminded of past times, but they will not come back. The streetcars run orderly and punctually unless there is an unexpected cut of electricity, then for the rest of the journey one proceeds on foot. In Berlin one has to save electricity but not according to an advertised plan as in Hamburg where public transportation simply does not run at certain hours. On the Kurfürstendamm, only a few houses are habitable. The Gedächtniskirche is badly damaged, only one tower had remained. The West of Berlin had been turned into a slum, and the inner city gives the similar picture of destruction.

At the moment it is not possible to prophesy what will become of Berlin. Her economic situation is bleak, which mirrors in extreme form the situation for the whole of Germany. Berlin is artificially kept alive so that the Allied Powers can maintain their administrative head offices. Berlin has to be supplied with food as this is a question of international prestige. Further shortening of rations could lead to unrest. Dismantlement has been carried out on a wide scale. The machines of firms like Siemens are rusting on abandoned railway tracts in the eastern part of the city. Berlin has stopped producing, has therefore nothing to give in exchange. Life in Berlin is extremely expensive. She now mainly lives by the black market . . . In the shops prices for the smallest things are fantastic.

One question is often asked, what are the consequences arising from the division of the city into the four sectors with the different occupation powers. Officially Berlin is governed by the Allied City Commandant with the help of the Russian selected magistrate under the burgomaster Dr. Werner. The magistrate only seems to have the executive power, although the public often does not appreciate this, because of the contrary public commands from the Allied Headquarters. In spite of Allied Occupation, Berlin is dependent on the Russian zone, as economically and industrially one cannot separate the city from her surroundings. Therefore the Russian point of view is decisive, even if the Western Allies can soften certain hardships. The civilian as well as the soldier can go from one zone to the other without difficulties. Only sign-boards remind one that one is leaving one sector and entering another, and civilians naturally can go into the countryside around Berlin, as there exist neither a guarded border between the sectors within the city, nor on the ring around Berlin that separates her from the province. So Berlin is de facto behind a curtain, but not yet an iron one. And Berlin is naturally the watchtower of the Russian zone.

On my return back to Flensburg the British direct control of newspapers was gradually softened. For some time we still carried on with pre-publication censorship, but soon went over to post-publication scrutiny.[109] After long and careful considerations, the

Flenbruger Nachrichten-Blatt der Militärrregierung ceased to exist. A celebration in the Blue Hall took place on 4ᵗʰ April 1946. The Commander of the local Military Government, Lt. Col Lindsay-Young, accompanied by the chief Officers of the No.8 IC Unit Lt. Col Johnson, handed the licence for *Flensburger Tageblatt*, Landeszeitung für die Kreise Flensburg, Schleswig und Südtondern to the three licencees, Director Ludwig Iversen, Tax counsellor Thomas Anderson, and Master painter Hans Harloff. All three belonged to different political parties. Previously the paper had been owned by Flensburg citizens but from 1933 on was gradually expropriated by the government. Now with the help of the British Control Commission, the paper was returned into civilian hands as a newspaper of a free press. The spokesperson thanked the British Control Commissioner and was looking forward to publishing a paper that would give news objectively and truthfully, standing above parties and keeping in close contact with her readers, fully aware that this new freedom also entailed responsibility.

Will Rasner gave a survey of the recent history, and included his cordial thanks for the exemplary cooperation between the English and German editorial staff under the guidance of Major Barnetson and Zubick, Captain Perry, and Staff Sergeant Alexander. Major Zubick in his address looked back over nine months of constructive journalistic work and expressed the sincere thanks from the English side. The very first edition of the *Flensburger Tageblatt* on 6ᵗʰ April gave a full report of all the speeches. Dr. Hanno Schmidt the new chief editor pointed out that "in the hope needed for reconstruction neither optimism nor pessimism apply but courage, necessary in spite of the misery and distress that everybody feels very personally."[110]

For this important day, the editorial signed by Will Rasner, but prepared with my input, started with a quote from Goethe's Italian Journey in 1787.[111] Quoted and translated it bore the title:

"Deutschland mein geliebtes Vaterland"
(Germany my beloved Country).[112]

> Approaching from Amalfi in the South, we now reached a height,
> and the magnificent view of Naples was spread out in front of us
> in its splendor, the mile-long rows of houses on the flat shore of
> the Gulf, the foothills, promontories, cliffs, than the islands, and
> behind the sea. A shocking song, more a lusty noise, and joyful
> outcry from a boy coming up behind us, startled and annoyed
> me. I frowned at him, he had not heard a bad word from us; he
> was a good-natured lad, who did not move for a while. Then he
> gently touched my shoulder, and with an outstretched arm and
> pointing index finger raised between us he said;
>
> Signor, perdonate! Questa è mia patria. (Sir, pardon me!
> This is my country.) . . . And this was second time I was
> surprised. Something like tears formed in my eyes, in me, a
> poor Northerner.

It is an historical fact that Germany has been defeated
on the battle fields of Europe, on the seas of the world,
and in the air. The material consequences of the defeat
are pushing to the limits of what is bearable. Defeated
was also the contaminated and distorted German spirit,
which in the period behind us, had adopted this high-flying
name. A realisation has now taken hold of and among the
German people that in the recent past their conduct, desire,
thinking and planning had been led astray. The reasons
are to be found in the failure of character – primarily of
the leading personalities – but also to a great part of the
general population, who lacked the will to resist, and, if
resisting, failed to master the skill and courage to carry it
through.[113] An exaggerated nationalistic pride propagated
by that regime that did not tolerate anything besides an
egocentrically deluded attitude of the perceived welfare for
the German people. The over-estimation of their own 'racial'

characteristics and mental values led to pogroms and acts of violence with the consequence that, in the end, needed a coalition of the world to overpower.

Now Germany is in distress, and in this situation every one of her citizens has to draw his or her own conclusion. The foreign countries, insofar as they at present occupy German soil, and exercise control of public life, will, when appropriate, judge their former adversary according to their reaction at a time of great affliction. The moment of recognition and acceptance into the community of free and independent people will depend on her development that will be carefully observed. This scrupulously followed observation includes, without doubt, the unfolding of her national sentiment, her national pride.

National sentiment, what does it mean? It means to love one's homeland in days of fortune as well as in days of distress and wretchedness. It means to respect all members of one's own country as father, mother, brother, sister and children. It means to own up to it in every situation, also when belonging to that country provides difficulties. And it also has to be stated that it means to be prepared to pledge life and property for *just* causes of the homeland against reckless or arbitrary aggression.

Having national pride does not exclude an appreciation of members of another state and to recognise them as friends, or simply just fellow human beings. That attitude is moreover a healthy presupposition so that pride is not to turn into its pathological exaggeration. Any country that owns a sense of national dignity must make it impossible to infringe on the eternal laws of humanity.

The leaders of Nationalsozialism have always talked about educating their people to enhance their national pride; looking at a great number of the Germans and their attitude today, one sees, how empty those phrases were, which proclaimed only a verbose statement of success.

At present great parts of the population, and in particular the youth, want to emigrate, "as here [at home] one will not soon find any green pastures." Relatives abroad are in great demand, and a person considers himself lucky if he or she can state "I am *really* an American." 'World-citizenship' seems to be a new religion, now that the German garment has become threadbare.

Culprits and criminals shall receive the punishment they deserve – a healthy national sentiment even demands this – but now, this effort often deteriorates into dirty and anonymous denunciations *vis à vis* the previous adversary, when he would be thankful for an openly and honestly delivered hint. For those kinds of machinations, however, he only has contempt, as this will be the reaction from any decent person facing such demeanour.

To dirty one's own nest, and the despicable attempt to denigrate the concept 'Germany,' that is frequently expressed by Germans, have no longer anything to do with the knowledge of guilt and faults, but simply pollute this noble concept. This behaviour by some Germans is without example in history, and such reaction seems to be unthinkable in other countries.

It is the aim of the occupying authorities to help in starting the reconstruction and restoration of democracy in Germany, that through her importance, her industriousness and her abilities of her people she should regain her appropriate place among the people of the earth. In order to carry out this plan in the present difficult situation, and to be successful in this task, a precondition is needed to pay respect and reverence, also to show charity, loyalty and faithfulness towards a Germany purged through death and misery. Thus she may rise out of the rubble and chaos of an opportunistic, self-provoked, and often more than inhuman war.

Besides eradicating the *excessive* national pride burdened

by war-guilt,[114] all those working toward the broad aim of reconstruction have the duty to awaken a new national sentiment that will fit into the framework of international co-operation. Again and again it cannot be sufficiently emphasised, that undignified abandonment of the homeland in the hour of need, would mean failing the test, and could not bring the beginning of a fruitful reform and reconstruction for which, besides a lot of other things, an inner decency is required.

In all areas of life German researchers, German scholars with their inquisitive mind, German thoroughness, enterprise, and industriousness have created ageless values, efforts that are well able to build a foundation for a sound national feeling. Even the horrifying criminal acts will not invalidate the thoughts, the works and influence of a man like Johann Wolfgang von Goethe. With his world-embracing spirit he once commented, on the theme discussed here, during a conversation with Heinrich Luden: "Don't ever think that I am indifferent to the great ideas of freedom, people and fatherland. Nay, these ideas are within us, they are part of our nature, and nobody is able to throw them off. Besides, Germany remains close to my heart."[115]

After granting the licences there was now less possibility for British influence; however, a watchful eye was held when anti-democratic ideas, tendentious rumours or when inappropriate German inner-political questions were raised.[116] Most of the time it was sufficient to give an oral warning, but in extreme cases the licence was withdrawn.

Sometime in May 1946 after the transfer of the *Flensburger Tageblatt* into German hands, I was ordered back to Hamburg.[117] I worked in an office pleasantly located in Mittelweg. Cultural life in the city gradually picked up during my stay, and I remember going to excellent musical concerts, and getting to know the conductor Eugen Jochum.

Many of our military personnel had applied for demobilization, and release was gradually granted. Replacing these people with qualified Germans often proved difficult, as most of the German journalists had been party members. One had to make compromises. It came down to judging the individual applicant and hoping for the best. In the Hamburg office I dealt with representatives from various newspapers. Covering a wide area, we went through the different stages of supervision of the licenced press, starting with pre-censorship and then going on to post-censorship. In the meantime new political parties had been formed.[118] With their preference for regions the CDU (Christian-Democratic Union), KPD (Communist Party of Germany) and SDP (Social Democratic Party) found themselves represented in the licensed papers affiliated to each of the parties. The Control Commission took care to watch the output, so that the license holder's papers would not become purely party-political papers, but only presented the different party's ideas in an objective way. They were now papers that tried to stand above party controversies (being *überparteilich*), like the *Flensburger Tageblatt*. An attempt was made to give the different party programmes equal opportunity and, because of limited paper supply, there was a strict but fair distribution quota calculated for each of them.

Normally this went quite smoothly.[119] But with the journalist Dr. Günther Sawatzki representing the *Hamburger Allgemeine* it was different. He practically exploded (metaphorically) in my office and told me a few hometruths (the content of which I don't remember). He was certainly vehemently critical of the whole situation in Hamburg and presumably the state of the press. As it was refreshing to encounter a German who was not submissive, I became very friendly with him, was invited to his home and met his wife. I took him with me when I went in a very comfortably chauffeur-driven car on an inspection tour of licensed newspapers in Schleswig-Holstein during the early summer of 1946. We took our bathing clothes with us and swam in every lake and river we could find. It cannot have been too early in the season for otherwise it would not have been warm enough to swim, thus I would expect we went in June or possibly late May. Franz Suchan, however, in a letter on 14th October 1946 was highly critical of the *Hamburger Allgemeine*, and said that Sawatzki did not have a good reputation among the middle-class journalists. I last saw Sawatzki many years later when he was Chief Editor of the *Kölner Stadtanzeiger*. We always had excellent conversations.

I do not recall whether I found anything adverse during my inspection tours. We had tried to keep law and order, and in this we mainly succeeded. We were keen to handle the relationship with our Russian allies with caution and discretion. We did not want to weaken our own position, but were not quite comfortable in it. As there now existed local German governments we could no longer publicly ignore the border question with Denmark that was openly discussed in the Provincial Diet, so we carefully tried to defuse it. The Nuremberg trials of the German war criminals presented another questionable and precarious topic. However well an article might be written, no journalist would succeed to convince the reader that all the judges taking part, including the Soviets, were convinced democrats. We had aimed at inviting the German journalist to independent thinking, instead of functioning like automatons, and had encouraged their giving equal voice to all parties so the reader could form his own judgement. At the same time we wanted to ensure that in the German publishing houses there would not be any Nazis sitting behind the typewriters. At Zero Hour [a familiar term for the new beginning after the signing of the armistice] the challenge was to work together with the acceptable German colleagues to contribute and to rebuild the country. At least in the British zone, the Germans generally were not ashamed that their country was occupied. This was an attitude that greatly facilitated our work, which was quite different from the situation in 1918. To a great extent citizens considered themselves as victims of the Nazi regime.

Although I had been offered to stay on in Information Control, I preferred to apply for release from active service and was demobilized on 16th July 1946.[120] I had not changed my views as to where my future lay by the time of my departure; I would live in Britain and not Germany.[121] Nonetheless, reaching the end of my service in Germany, I would have put my views somewhat more gently than a year previously. Particularly through the friendship with the Suchans and Rasners, though our situation in the Nazi period had been different, I found that we had much in common on the basis of our shared moral and political values. I was sorry to leave them behind.

Chapter 8

Endnotes

1 Adolf Birke and Eva Mayring, *Britische Besatzung in Deutschland*, Aktenerschließung, 1987, pp. 34ff.

2 War Diary, 20th May 1997, PW Main HQ Second Army, Army Form C 2118. Klaus Wagner to Frank Eyck, 20th May 1997, sent me copy of the War Diary's relevant pages, 16th September 1945, and kindly gave his permission to quote and to otherwise use the correspondence between us.

3 Frank Eyck papers, *Exercise Book*, Cobham, Surry. Here an attempt is made to summarize the various lectures using much of the lecturers own words.

4 PRO, WO. 219-974, and FO, 898-402. Wolf Gehrmann, *Britsiche Presse und Informations-politik in Schleswig-Holstein 1945-1949*, PhD diss. privately published, Kiel 1993, p. 36.

5 Frank Eyck papers, Exercise Book, Cobham, Surry.

6 Heinrich Portmann, *Cardinal von Galen, the Lion of Münster*, translated and with an introduction by R. L. Sedgwick (London: Jarrold, 1957), Introduction pp. 11-29.

7 POT. WO, 219-974, and FO, 898-402.

8 Heinrich Portmann, *Cardinal von Galen*, Introduction by R. L. Sedgwick.

9 Ibid, pp. 20-23.

10 Ibid, pp. 23-28.

11 R.L. Sedgwick organized the first post war Bishops' Conference. Albert E. J. Holländer, *Offiziere und Prälaten, Beitrag zur Bischofs Konferenz, August 1945*, in Mitteilungen des Österreichischen Staatsarchivs, vol. 25, 185-206.

12 Gregory Kameniecki. MA thesis, *Vansittart and the German Menace*, Calgary, Alberta, May 1987. On Vasitttart see also: *National Dictionary of Biography*, 1951-1960, pp. 1005-1006.

13 Frank Eyck Exercise Book, Cobham, Surrey.

14 Ibid.

15 Klaus Wagner to Frank Eyck, 20th February 1996.

16 Frank Eyck papers, 1945 otherwise undated report, *British Policy in Europe*, (British Army of the Rhine).

17 Adolf Birke and Eva Mayring, eds., *Britische Besatzung in Deutschland*, see essay by Lothar Kettenacker, *Britische Besatzungspolitik im Spannungsverhältnis*

von Planung und Realität, (London: Deutsche Historische Institut, 1987), pp. 17-33.

18 Frank Eyck, my talk, *Germany, Defeat and Reconstruction, a personal view*, (for HIST 493. 23, 28th March 2003), also Frank Eyck to Klaus Wagner, 16th December 1992.

19 Wolf Gehrmann, *Dissertation*, p. 53.

20 Hamburg, a Hansa-City, founded as an Arch-Bishopric in 834 AD.

21 Lübeck, a Hansa-City, founded in 1143.

22 Flensburg founded in 1284, Jubilee-edition of *Flensburger Tageblatt* 1984, *700 Yeas Flensburg.*

23 Taken from my talk of 28th March 2003.

24 On 30th April 1945, Hitler, after marrying Eva Braun, shot her and himself, Goebbels did so too, after at first killing his children and his wife. However, according to the autopsy report of Hitler's remains, he had taken poison; see *Flensburger Nachrichten Blatt,* 7th June 1945.

25 see http://www.bbc.co.uk/ww2peopleswar/user/67/u1256867.shtmt, (January 17th, 2005).

26 Kurt Detlev Möller last chapter, *Geschichte der Kapitulation von Hamburg*, (Hamburg Hoffmann und Campe, 1947).

27 Ibid, The AJR Information, January 1998, by Ronald Channing, p. 8.

28 Christopher Herrendörfer, *Wiedersehen am Rothenbaum, Die Befreiung des Reichssender Hamburg*, (Nordwestdeutscher Rundfunk, Rothenbaumchaussee 132, 8th April 1996).

29 Francis Selwyn, *Hitler's Englishman: The Crime of Lord Haw Haw*, (London: Penguin Books Ltd., 1987), pp. 162-163.

30 Ibid.

31 Frank Eyck papers, Frank Eyck to Klaus Wagner, 16th December 1992.

32 Refers to Goebbels' speech, 18th February 1943 with the question: "Do you want the total war?" (Wollt Ihr den totalen Krieg? Which was answered by an orchestrated enthusiastic YES).

33 Frank Eyck papers, Frank Eyck, while on leave, letter to family and friends, 23rd August 1945, 5 pages, 2592 words.

34 Arthur Geoffrey Dickens, *Lübeck Diary*, (London: Victor Gollancz, 1947), pp. 252-253.

35 Lord Barnetson, *The Rebuilding of the German Press 1945-49*, (Cardiff:

University of Cardiff, Journalism Studies Review,1978.), No. 3, p. 7-11. Also Frank Eyck papers, Lord Barnetson, (1917-1981), Obituary.

36 A. G. Dickens, *Lübeck Diary*, pp. 225-252. Frank Eyck papers, Klaus Wagner's Dissertation draft No 1, 4 and 5, p. 166; *Information Control*, pp. 121ff.

37 Frank Eyck papers, Frank Eyck to Lord Barnetson, William, London, 13th January 1972. Lord Barnetson to Frank Eyck, 18th January 1972 and 22nd June 1978 in answer to my work at the International Centre for Post-graduate Studies in Dubrovnik, 1973-1979.

38 Frank Eyck *Worcester College (Oxford) Record 1995*, p. 75.

39 Frank Eyck papers, Frank Eyck, my talk, 28th May 2003.

40 W. Gehrmann, Dissertation, pp. 125-127.

41 Frank Eyck papers, Frank Eyck, my talk, 28th May 2003. Also taken from my letter to the family and friends, 23rd August 1945.

42 A reference to the broadside ballad: *A Hay and Cry after Sir John Barleycorn.*

43 Arthur Geoffrey Dickens, *Lübeck Diary*, p. 252. Dickens main works: *The Lollards and the Protestants in the Diocese of York 1509-1559, The German Reformation*, 1964, *The German Nation and Martin Luther*, 1974.

44 A. G. Dickens, *Lübeck Diary*, pp. 339-430.

45 Frank Eyck papers, Frank Eyck letter, 23rd August 1945.

46 A. G. Dickens, *Lübeck Diary*, pp. 282ff, on Burgomaster Perterson's speech about his concern for the coming winter.

47 Ibid. pp. 308 and 330.

48 Frank Eyck papers, Frank Eyck to Klaus Wagner, 16th December 1992.

49 Frank Eyck papers, Frank Eyck, *Note to the Bundersarchiv*, 1995, p. 4.

50 Frank Eyck papers, Frank Eyck to Klaus Wagner, 16th December 1992. Also, Rosemarie remembers how disappointed and disheartened everyone was.

51 Frank Eyck papers, Frank Eyck to Klaus Wagner, 16th December 1992.

52 A. G. Dicken, *Lübeck Diary,* pp. 325 and 330.

53 Rosemarie told me, that some time in the spring of 1937 she and her friends were asked to join the BDM (Bund deutscher Mädchen), the Nazi organization for girls, that would automatically at a later date have led them into the NSDAP, and this being their last opportunity for joining. Their answer was "no thank you, good thing you won't bother us any more."

Actually, when the father, a high civil servant, of one of her friends, had difficulties because of his daughter's refusal, she tried to join the BDM, but was not able to do so.

54 Frank Eyck papers, Frank Eyck to Klaus Wagner, 2nd January 1993.

55 See also Adolf M. Birke, *Nation ohne Haus, Deutschland 1945-1961*, (Deutsche Geschichte, Berlin: Siedler), Kapitel III, Umerziehung, pp. 82-96.

56 Frank Eyck papers, Frank Eyck to Klaus Wagner, 30th July 1995.

57 Frank Eyck papers, Frank Alexander (Eyck) report, *British policy in Europe, British Army on the Rhine*, (early summer 1945), 6 pages.

58 From here on I give the above mentioned report verbatim.

59 Henry Temple 3rd Viscount Palmerston (1784-1865) and member of the 1830 reform cabinet, and Benjamin Disraeli 1st Earl of Beaconsfield (1804-1881), on opposite sides of the 19th century House of Parliament.

60 Frank Eyck papers, Jewish Refugee Committee Bloomsbury House to Sergeant Alexander (Frank Eyck), 20th June 1945.

61 Frank Eyck papers, Frank Eyck to Klaus Wagner, 16th December 1992. Also Frank Eyck's report, *British policy in Europe, British Army on the Rhine*, 1945.

62 Frat, this being a degrading term for a woman, derived from fraternization.

63 Adolf M. Birke, *Nation ohne Haus*, (Kapitel, Wirtschaft und Währung), pp. 126-156. At the end of 1946 it became possible to start pursuing and following an economic political agreement between the Zones of the American and the British Military Governments (*Zweizonesien)* that was soon joined by the French administration (*Dreizonesien)*. With the Marshall Aid of 1947 and the influence of Ludwig Erhard's soziale Marktwirtschft, as opposed to Planwirtschaft, the economic situation became increasingly successful from 1948 on, i.e. after the currency reform with the exchange rate of 10 RM to 1 DM. See also Konrad Adenauer, *Erinnerungen 1945-1963 Fragmente*, (Paderborn: Siedler Verlag 1961), chap. 3-7. Aldolf Birke and Eva Mayring, eds., *Britische Besatzung in Deutschland, Aktenerschliessung und Forschung*, 1987.

64 Frank Eyck papers, Frank Eyck to Klaus Wagner, 16th December 1992.

65 PWE Political Warfare Directive (Europeans Theatre) for the week beginning 12th May 1945, On the German Rump-"Government" of Admiral Dönitz.

66 Frank Eyck papers, copies of the *Flensburger Nachrichten-Blatt der Militärregierung*, 24th and 25th May 1945.

67 Ibid

68 Ibid

69 PRO FO 1056/20 "Standing Directive No.1" 20.7.1045.

70 Ibid

71 For regulations and statistical informations see Wolf Gehrmann, Dissertation.

72 Lord Barnetson, William, "The rebuilding of the German Press 1945-1949," *Journalism* (No. 3, June 1978).

73 Frank Eyck papers, Frank Eyck to Klaus Wagner, 16th December 1992.

74 Ibid.

75 Frank Eyck papers, Frank Eyck to Klaus Wagner, 2nd January 1992.

76 Frank Eyck papers, Frank Eyck to Klaus Wagner, 14th November 1995.

77 Frank Eyck papers, Wolfgang Schieder to Frank Eyck, 29th May 1995.

78 Klaus Wagner dissertation draft, Kapitel, 8, *Das Problem der Emigranten*, p. 354.

79 Frank Eyck papers, Frank Eyck to Klaus Wagner, 2nd January 1992.

80 PRO FO 1049/405 PR/ISC-Director General Bishop and Christopher Steel/ Political division, 17th August 1946.

81 Frank Eyck papers, Franz Suchan to Frank Eyck, 14th October 1946, mentions the election results: Flensburg with a pro-Danish majority, Schleswig a strong CSU majority and Holstein a strong SPD majority, which however, did not interfere with Suchans personal communal supervisory duties.

82 Wolf Gehrmann, Dissertation, 1993, pp. 323-332.

83 Allied Zeitungsverlag Schleswig-Holstein, "Akten Protokolle 1946-48" Aktennotiz Hagemann, "Gespräch Seltzer", 29th June 1946.

84 AZSH Akten Protokolle, 1946-48. Aktennotiz Hagemann "Gespräch Sergeant Alexander," 1st July 1946.

85 Frank Eyck papers, This and some part of the next paragraph are taken from my talk in Flensburg, 28th March 1995.

86 Wolf Gehrmann, Dissertation, pp. 114 ff.

87 Frank Eyck papers, this is a short summary of Will Rasner's achievements taken from his obituaries.

88 Frank Eyck papers, Frank Eyck to Klaus Wagner, 16th December 1992.

89 Ibid.

90 Frank Eyck papers, Klaus Wagner to Frank Eyck, 16th January 1995, and F. Eyck to K. Wagner, 19th February 1995.

91 Ken Adam interview with Christopher Frayling, *The Art of Production Design*, (London: Faber and Faber, 1988), p. 39.

92 W. P. H. Davison, translated by Hans Steindorff, *The Blockade von Berlin*, (Frankfurt/Main: Alfred Metzner Verlag, 1960). (FAZ 23rd March 1960)

93 Frank Eyck papers, Frank Eyck memorandum, *British politics in Europe* 1945, verbatim to the end of note 572.

94 Frank Eyck papers, Frank Eyck, used the Marine's response in his *Vortrag zur Eröffnung des Schleswig-Holsteinische Zeitungsverlags* in Kiel, 28th March 1995.

95 A. G. Dickens, *Lübeck Diary*, pp. 310ff.

96 Ibid, p. 282.

97 Idid, pp. 311 ff.

98 Frank Eyck papers, Frank Eyck memorandum, *Christmas 1945*, verbatim.

99 Frank Eyck papers, Frank Eyck to family and friends, 31st March 1946, a report of 8 pages, 4554 words.

100 Frank Eyck papers, Frank Eyck, notes for a talk 28th October 1997 at the Munich Institut für Zeitgeschichte.

101 Frank Eyck papers, report by Erhard Schmidt for committee of Bishop Dibelius on Christian society.

102 Adolf M. Birke and Eva A, Mayring, eds., *Britische Besaztungspolitik in Deutschland*, Aktenerschliessung und Forschung, 1987, pp. 72 ff. Also part of what Rosemarie remembers.

103 Frank Eyck papers, Heinz-Hermann Niemöller to Rosemarie, 10th April and 20th May 2006.

104 Frank Eyck papers, Klaus Gottstein to Rosemarie, 27th March 2006.

105 Frank Eyck papers, Frank Eyck, Summary for the *Bundersarchiv*, 1995.

106 Niemöller told us about his audience with Pope Pius XII, that as soon as his name was announced, in an unusual display of joy the Pope embraced his guest saying that during the war he had prayed for him and the other prisoner–priests; Niemöller himself, however delighted, felt somewhat guilty about the division of the church through the Reformation.

107 The story of Ernst Lindenborn is partly taken from Frank Eyck's letter of

31st March 1946, and partly from Christian Velder, *300 Jahre Französisches Gymnasium*, pp. 449ff.

108 Aldolf M. Birke, *Nation ohne Haus*, pp. 183-206.

109 W Gehrmann, Dissertation, pp. 297 ff.

110 *Flensburger Tageblatt*, 6th April 1946, p. 3.

111 Johann Wolfgang von Goethe, *Italienische Reise,* Bd.II. p. 259.

112 Since 1995, Frank had looked for this article and was always told it would be difficult, meaning impossible, to find. But in 2006, I (Rosemarie) found a possible answer to this quest through the chronological electronical listing of newspapers in the Catalogue of the Lübeck City Library. With the kind help of my friend Irving Hexham the *Flensburger Tageblatt, Landeszeitung für die Kreise Flensburg, Schleswig und Südtondern, Veröffentlicht unter Zulassungsnummer 35 der Miltärregierung, Jahrgang 1946,* No. 1 and the following numbers, the actual papers arrived by ordinary mail. These very aged pages were spread out for a few days on her kitchen table and to her delight I found the long-sought article and other 'news'which gave insights into the events of the time.

113 Roger Moorhouse, *Killing Hitler, the Plot, the Assassins, and the Dictator who Cheated Death,* (New York: Batam Books, 2006).

114 Peter Godman, *Hitler and the Vatican, Inside the Secret Archives that reveal the New Story of the Nazis and the Church.* (New York: Free Press, a Division of Simon Schuster Inc. 2004), Appendix I, pp. 172ff. *Die Welt* (newspaper), Ehre, Freiheit, Vaterland, 150 Jahre Deutsche Burchenschaft. Nr. 134, page III, 12th June 1965.

115 Heinrich Luden, 1778-1847, *Rückblick über mein Leben,* (Berlin: K, Curtius 1916), Goethe über Deutschlands Zukunft, das Faust-Gespräch, German Book, Book XII, p. 119, Jena, Goethe zu Heinrich Luden, "Glauben Sie nicht, daß ich gleichgültig wäre gegen die großen Ideen Freiheit, Volk, Vaterland. Nein, diese Ideen sind in uns, sie sind ein Teil unseres Wesens, und niemand vermag sie von sich zu werfen. Auch liegt mir Deutschland warm am Herzen."

116 Wolf Gehrmann, Dissertation, pp. 373f.

117 Frank Eyck papers, Frank Eyck to Klaus Wagner, 16th Dec 1992

118 Wolf Gehrmann, Dissertation, pp. 372 ff.

119 Frank Eyck papers, Frank Eyck to Klaus Wagner, 16th December 1992

120   Frank Eyck papers, Army book entry application, demobilization, 16th July 1946, army leave expired 10th September 1946, when I was registered in the Reserve.

121 Worcester College (Oxford) Record, 1995, p. 77.

Chapter 8

CHAPTER 9

Homecoming Civilian Life

WHILE I WAS STILL IN THE army, I was fortunate enough to gain admittance to Worcester College Oxford by Provost Lys as a commoner, which is the Oxford term for an undergraduate.[1] I still accredit my entry into Worcester College to the recommendation of G. P. Gooch and a supporting testimonial of the High Master of St. Paul's as well as on the strength of my school certificate. Coming home to England, I could look forward to having a bed at my parents' guest-house on Boars Hill. I longed for the beginning of the autumn term in October 1946 to finally begin my studies and settling into an old, romantic two-room apartment at the College. My choice was to read Philosophy, Politics and Economics (PPE), known as Modern Greats. In July 1946, I applied for a war service grant to the Ministry of Education for the Further Education and Training Scheme.

This was their answer to me:[2]

1) For assistance under the above Scheme in order to enable you to pursue a full-time course at Worcester College Oxford leading to an Honours Degree in Philosophy, Politics and Economics I am directed by the Minister of Education to state that it has been decided to grant you the under mentioned award: a) approved fees, which will be paid by the Minister to the Institution which you attend, b) maintenance-grant at the rate of £29 per annum [sic], which will be paid to you terminally beginning of the autumn term 1946. 2) The award is tenable, subject to satisfactory attendance, conduct and progress, until the

end of the summer term 1949 or for such shorter period as may be determined in the light of the reports on your progress...

I am, dear Sir, your obedient servant,

L.C. Duke

The grant starting in the autumn term 1946 was already raised for that term to £33. There were a few more clauses, and I was asked to reapply, and report annually which allowed me to receive this grant till my last term in 1949. Besides helping out at my mother's guest-house during the summer, I was keen to finally acquire British citizenship after many previous tries. On 20th July, I wrote to the Hon. Wilson Harris, whose liberal principles had brought him the editorship of the Daily News, where he had also acted as diplomatic correspondent.[3] In 1923, he had joined the staff of the League of Nations and between 1939 and 1945 served as an independent and highly respected MP at the House of Commons.

Dear Sir,

I wish to draw your attention as a Member of Parliament to my experiences since release from the British army on the Rhine. I believe they affect the public interest.

I came to Britain as a refugee at the age of 14 in 1936, went to St. Paul's school and had almost 6 years of service in the British army during and after the war. I was accepted for Worcester College Oxford on recommendation and am now on Foreign Service leave before taking up study in Modern Greats (PPE) next term. The following is my experience since passing through the dispersal centre at Guildford on the 16th inst.:

1) At Guildford I received notice headed "discharge of aliens" on which it was stated that I had to report to the

police on arrival at Oxford. At the same time I was given, along with everybody else, a slip stating that I was still under military law during release leave, and was not allowed to write articles for the press, etc. When I asked how military and "alien" status was to be reconciled, nobody was able to give me a satisfactory answer.

2) On reporting to the Oxford Police Station as instructed I was informed that I was technically an "enemy alien." Various references were made to the internment of German refugees earlier in the war. I was told to report to the Abingdon, Berks[hire], Police Station.

3) On 18th July I called at the Inter Services Naturalisat[ion]. Board, War Office, Demob[ilization] 4 to enquire on the state of my application for Naturalization which had gone forward with my Commanding Officer's recommendation whilst with the BAOR three months ago. I saw the Lt.Col. of the department concerned and was merely told by him that the application would take 6 months. He did not consult my file. He did not explain why the application had to take a fixed time. In the course of the conversation he told me that he could not understand why I wanted to hide my German nationality. He could not understand somebody who denied his country. [Or that] I had been "allowed" to serve in the British army. – So for what was actually said by the Colonel, I could not help but gain the impression that this officer felt that I had been a traitor to the country in which I was born, namely Germany, and that I really should never have been allowed to serve in the British Army.

4) Finally I reported to the Abingdon Police Station. There I had a long conversation with an ordinary policeman who showed me the Britain which I had served for six years.

These are the facts of the situation. I need not assure you, Sir, that these experiences spoiled the fun of my demobilization. What had happened to me brings out the complete absurdity of the reversion to the status of an "enemy alien" after doing nothing else for 6 years but being a member of the army which had first the job of fighting Germany and then of occupying it. After being a member of Home Force during the time whilst Britain was in danger of invasion, and a member of the British Liberation Army during the campaign in North-West Europe, after going through non-fraternization with the Germans as a British soldier, after carrying out very difficult duties with regard to the direct and indirect control of the German Press as a representative of Britain up to the very last day of my departure a week ago, I am suddenly told by policemen and officers in Britain that I am just a German and an "enemy alien", and that many of them just cannot understand what I have done.

I fail to see either why the question of a reversion to "alien" status should be raised at all during one's release leave, or why there should be any need for elaborate machinery for the naturalization of men who served in the British army for years and whose record is clear so that their Commanding Officer had felt able to recommend them for naturalization – such as in my case. Furthermore I believe that the duality of military and alien status is contrary to common sense and full of possible snags.

On the broader and higher plane, Sir, I feel that the treatment is completely out of harmony with the British spirit which I have endeavoured to serve and to explain to our former enemy. I believe that the regulations which have shown so much misunderstanding of our position have been drawn up by minor officials. I appeal to you, Sir, as a Member of Parliament, to take up these matters, because I believe in British democracy.

May I ask you, Sir, to treat this matter confidentially,

and to leave my name out of it, if possible? I can, however, vouch for all he facts I have given. I am, Sir, your obedient servant,

Frank Alexander

Mr. Harris' answer of 23rd July reads: [4]

Dear Sir,
The story you tell me describes quite intolerable behaviour on the part of the British officials, and I will take an early opportunity to talking to the Home Secretary on the whole question. I am not quite sure whether you are concerned with the general question or desire me to take some particular step in your own case. Perhaps you would let me have a line regarding that.
Yours faithfully,

J. Wilson Harris

On 27th October I received a further letter by him telling me that he just obtained a reply form the Home Office which he enclosed:

We have received application from several thousand of aliens who have served, or are serving, in H.M. Forces, and they are being dealt with as quickly as possible in order of length of service. I find that Mr. Alexander, who had over five years' service to his credit, will be asked to attend for an interview before the Inter-Service Naturalization Board on a date in December.

Since 1940 I had tried to apply for British citizenship. At first, granting British nationality had failed because I was still a minor, then none could be given during the duration of the war. There are over thirty documents in the National Archive cataloguing my attempt to become a

British citizen: including my personal applications starting in 1939, answers and official notes dealing with this question, even a clearing from MI5, and my "declaration that I would not intend to make an application . . . for retention of German nationality."[5] Paying the requested fee of £10, I received the Naturalization Certificate on 5th March 1947 and was able to swear the Oath of Allegiance to His Majesty King George the Sixth on 19th March 1947. Fairly soon, on 12th April 1947, with just one application, I also regained my original family name.

We had many discussions with my mother's guests who were mostly Jewish refugees at Chilswell House. The conversations circled often about the Nazi regime, the war years, and the peace efforts. When Ludwig Heuss, the son of Theodor Heuss, visited us one of these often lively exchanges turned a little too critical about all things German of the recent past.[6] My mother felt that some of her guests had gone too far and simply said: "Mr. Heuss is Aryan", which caused the excessive criticism to be silenced.[7] Ludwig told us privately that the Heuss and Elsas family had shared a long-time friendship from their Swabian home town days. Following the 20th July 1944 plot, Fritz Elsas, First Burgomaster of Berlin had been taken into the Concentration Camp Sachsenhausen.[8] He was tortured, and after a one-day hearing he was shot on 4th January 1945,[9] because he had shared with his colleague, Carl Friedrich Gördeler, the Chief Burgomaster, the comfort of his home; Gördeler suffered the same fate.[10] According to the Nazi principle of *Sippenhaft* (the persecution, detention, and sometimes killing based merely on kinship) Elsas' wife, Marie, and Hanne, their daughter, had been taken to the Women's prison in Berlin Moabit. In April 1945, just before the end of the war, Ludwig, dressed in military uniform, persuaded a woman official at the Prison to make out a discharge certificate for Mrs. Elsas and her daughter Hanne without reference to the main office.[11] As soon as the news of their release came out, the Nazis wanted to arrest them again, but the situation in Berlin was so chaotic that they did not succeed. After the war, full of hope but deeply scarred, Hanne and Ludwig rebuilt their lives. They were the first post-war couple to get married in St. Annen, the village church in Berlin Dahlem, the suburb in which they lived.

Having so recently returned from Germany and having had some insight into the nation's prevailing sense of frustration, I put my thoughts in writing and I recollect part of them here:[12]

Casting one's minds back over the narrow span of a year, that time now apparently so distant when millions of people in Europe still had faith in the future, a better future, there is now the complete standstill, an economic paralysis and impasse in a country, which had formed an important part of the civilisation of the ancient European Continent; it has confounded the hopes of men of good will . . . Two irreconcilable policies are followed side-by-side at present: a constructive line and a violent destructive one. The obvious inability of the Allies to deal fairly and squarely with the country they once fought together is a triumph of the cynics and a challenge to the believer. The British public, too, at first apathetic about the German problem, is gradually becoming alive to the tragedy of the situation.

People in Britain who take a serious interest in Germany are agreed on the aim of the policy for that country, however much they may disagree about the method of achieving the goal. They want to have a Germany integrated onto the framework of European civilisation. They are anxious to avoid that this very important member of the European community should ever again threaten the peace of the world. But they are alive to the possibility that a threat may develop in quite a new manner, unless the situation is handled competently. Germany broke the peace in 1939 by firing the first shot into Poland. In a few years Germany may become either too weak or too strong. The latter may be discounted, but through the complete breakdown of law and order she may become a plague which would infect the whole of the continent, and would not stop on the other side of the channel.

Never in modern history [European] has a victory settlement failed as utterly as that of Potsdam of 2nd August 1945. Comparatively speaking the Treaty of Versailles (1919) was an object lesson in peace making. For it, at least it gave Europe 20 years of peace. The much-maligned monarchs and noble diplomats of reaction at the Congress of Vienna seem like prophets when one thinks of today's notorious 'Big Three' and looks at the newspaper headlines. The earlier agreement created in the Concert of Powers, a framework for European relations which lasted longer than the Geneva League, and was more effective than the UNO is today. The retort of the complacent may be that Potsdam gave only a provisional arrangement. It is true that the proper peace settlement is yet to come. But it is hard to see how a proper peace settlement could undo many of decisions made at Potsdam. Would the Poles be prepared to yield an inch of Eastern Pomerania and Silesia, after expelling millions of Germans, and for months are now trying to settle their own nationals there? Would the Russians, to whom the Potsdam agreement confirmed a position of unassailable independence in Central and Eastern Europe, suddenly be prepared to surrender part of their position? Would they who have for a year shown themselves utterly unaware of the necessity of co-operation in Europe suddenly change? The Russians will not be prompted by any anxiety to lessen the tension on the European continent but by tactical considerations. Indirectly they have created an impossible situation by their refusal to co-operate and by their territorial policy towards Poland. The observer is therefore forced to draw the conclusion that the Russian Government does not by any means view with concern the creation of a "Western Desert" on their border with the British and American occupied territory.

It is hard to see how the British and Russian concept of a solution for Germany can be bridged, as there are no common aims, such as a desire to create stable conditions in the heart of Europe or the yearning for a lasting settlement. There are no shared political ideas, as for instance about the meaning of the term 'democracy' and 'fascism.' Potsdam was based on the illusion of the unity of Allied aims. As a result the Anglo-Americans were prevented by this formal allegiance to the Allied Control Council from carrying out a fully effective policy in their own zone. A series of half measures added merely to the confusion, to further chaos. In every one of the four zones the various Military Governments introduced some usage of their mother country – enough to make the transition to amalgamation extremely difficult, but not sufficiently so as to let the different zones develop into fully grown organisms. Differences between the three Western zones on constitutional development, on basic conception of the role the German people would play, are great enough. The gap between East and West is infinitely greater.

At present, whatever is done by any of the occupying powers is not contributing in the slightest to a solution of the Germans question. Occupation as such without a policy is no answer to a problem, for it is, in its very nature, a temporary phase, and can only achieve a positive purpose if it becomes part of a co-ordinated policy . . . Without any agreed plan the occupation only serves to cover up the hopelessness of the situation for a limited time. The bankruptcy of it remains; but officially this is not admitted. It may be linked to inflation which is a fact in Germany today, and which is strictly controlled by the occupying powers; alas the underlying causes remain. Whatever the merit of this attitude, it is in itself no solution. All that the Allies are doing in Germany is preventing the complete breakdown of law and order. This they are in a position to do owing to their military presence and power . . . But they are merely putting off the decision and leaving everything till the day of reckoning. In the meantime, the task of occupation is daily becoming more unprofitable and distasteful. Money, food, and essential supplies have to be pumped into the occupied country to prevent the outbreak of civil disorder.

The question of the 'Western Allies' attitude to the Russians should be decided, one way or another, and without delay. Allied unity in Germany, if humanly possible, is a consummation devoutly wished, but it can only be achieved on our terms. Once it has been decided whether we have a plan for a single Germany or for a Western Germany, if the Russian attitude became irrelevant, a clear policy based on principles has to be formulated. This plan should be the result of a wide ranging discussion with the neighbouring countries, France, the Low Countries and possibly the Scandinavian countries with the aim of a constructive protection of a vital cell [sic] of European civilisation. There are different ways of clothing this purpose in words. It may be called re-education, or integration of Germany into the framework of European civilisation.[13] The occupation should ensure that what may be called 'Allied Germany' has no inside trade barriers. Great effort should be made to overcome the obstacles to German trade with her neighbours and the world at large. As the victorious nations do not want to have to 'carry' Germany, all the dismantling of peace industries should cease. 'Allied Germany' should receive a Government of its own, nominated pending elections and the growth of a free parliament. The occupation should go on to ensure that it carries out the general policy by the Allies. The German Government should be licensed on condition that it observes a Charter of Rights for her people.

This Charter should proclaim the basic liberties of democratic citizens, such as Habeas Corpus, Freedom of Speech and sanctity of private property. Although shortages in Germany make the power of requisitioning essential, the power should not be used arbitrarily. The German officials should be made to feel that they are under the law, and the 'insolence of office' should be curbed. It is generally believed that Germany should avoid over-centralisation and acquire a federal system.

In the British zone, the Military Government at present still goes to Kreis-[municipal] level while in the American zone the lower functions of local administration have reverted to the Germans. The army should merely keep order and 'contact' among the Allies. There ought to be a complete separation between Army and civilian service. As in India, the office of the Commander-in-Chief and the Civilian Governor are not to be in the same hand. A civil service should be selected and formed by Germans, small, specialised and competent. Salaries ought to be high enough to attract the best people.

Contact with the outside world by way of political, religious and philosophical societies should receive every encouragement. This would be an appeal to the soul of Germany. In trying to enlist the co-operation of the German people it is not sufficient to draw up a budget. A nation that has received intoxicating propaganda for years has to be gradually nursed back to normal. Every effort should be made, including sacrifice, to implement this policy. For instance, lack of paper due to shortage of foreign currency has been allowed to hamper our re-education programme in the past. Financial generosity here would have its reward. Primarily, securing food for the Germans presents a link in a long chain to success. If the Germans are too weak to work, they have to be carried by the occupying nations. This would constitute reparations from the victors to the vanquished. If German miners are hungry, Europe will freeze, and [their] industry will be paralysed. We have yet to show to the Germans that democracy is not merely freedom to starve, freedom to freeze and freedom to be unemployed.

My obvious disappointment in the developments in Germany found an echo when the previously optimistic Franz Suchan wrote to me during the winter of 1946-1947 after first thanking me for the food packages I had sent:[14]

Allowing for the general conditions we are relatively well off, thankful to be together, even if we freeze, and in the evening when it becomes dark are going to bed early or sit around a miserable oil-lamp (*Ölfunsel*). But this cannot be compared to the much worse conditions in the refugee camps and in the big cities.

Before Easter he reported:

We just overcame the coal crisis, and are about to enter a difficult food crisis. It is indeed so bad that we feel things cannot go on like this. Though here in our region we got through fairly well, as in the district of Husum we did not have anybody who froze to death. It is, however, proof of the horrifying situation that this is considered a success . . .

Erika added to the letter that they and the children missed my weekend visits, and that during the winter months the cultural life in Husum was frozen (*eingefroren*), so that in the evening they resorted to a borrowed radio and books if available.

I received other, sometimes much more desperate letters.[15] In Berlin the situation was the worst. All I could do was to send food packages to my friends from whom I received stirring thank-you letters.[16] Unfortunately, with the increasing danger of the Cold War, a much more wretched time was waiting ahead. Noel Annon in his book, *Changing Enemies*, published in 1995 gives detailed insight into the situation, when he writes:

> People forget these days how strong those illusions [about the Soviet Union] still were in 1945 . . . I had no doubt, that the British policy in Germany was right. It was based on fear of Communism, which could lead once again to a German-Soviet alliance, . . . and also on the fear that America would quit Europe two years after the Yalta agreement.

Fortunately the USA did not do so. During the Blockade, Berlin would hardly have survived had the Western Allies under General Clay not provided the *Luftbrücke* (Air-Bridge) from 1947-1949 to the city.[17] Often risking their own safety, American and British planes regularly flew provisions to supply the city during a Soviet blockade. In the Airport of Berlin Tempelhof there stands now a monument in memory of their heroic efforts. As the tension grew more and more unpleasant, checkpoints were added at the border, the Berlin Wall was erected in 1961, and the minefields along the border-fence, equal to a death-strip, running between East and West Germany, led to much suffering and hardship for the people in the East, and their deep estrangement with those in the West.

In peaceful green England, after the Matriculation ceremony on 12th October 1946, I began my studies with a deep feeling of thankfulness and concerned thoughts for my friends in Germany.[18] During the first year, my parents still lived close by on Boars Hill before they permanently moved into a suite of their apartment house in 12 Lindfield Gdns., Hampstead, London that became the family home.

I found the company of my fellow undergraduates congenial, most of them being of a similar vintage, having gone through military service. This led to a more mature attitude to university life than the usual inexperienced commoner who came straight out of school. Studies at Cambridge or Oxford University are based on the tutorial-system, still very much appreciated and fiercely adhered to today.[19] The English Red brick and Scottish University have their own different systems of teaching. In North America and on the continent of Europe, the lecture and seminar system is the custom which caters to larger numbers of students at the same time. In Oxbridge there are three terms of eight weeks per year, students are obliged to attend a minimum number of classes, four hours per week (in the arts). The undergraduates meet their Don individually every week. At that time, they submit an essay on their subject under study. The tutor then criticizes their work and suggests books to be read. This allows much greater freedom. Tests are less frequent and vacations are longer. Oral examinations carry a great deal of weight. It is not customary for students to work at paying jobs during term time. During term, students live like "gentlemen" in their individual colleges, each person has two rooms to himself with a butler to take care of the needs of eight students. There are, however, rules and regulations accompanied by frequent student complaints. At midnight the College gate is locked. Those who arrive after that hour (unless they know where to climb the wall) must awaken the porter who turns in a report to the Dean.

Initially, I read Modern Greats, which had the significant advantage of placing me under the tutelage of Asa Briggs in Economics. After a term, I preferred to read Modern History and learned a lot from Paul Roberts in interpreting constitutional documents. Henry Vere Fitzroy Somerset gave me a taste for medieval History (on which I again worked late in life). He wrote an encouraging recommendation in 1949 calling me "a real student, genuinely interested in his subject, experienced in addressing an audience. He would interest and stimulate his pupils if elected lecturer."[20] Both Asa Briggs and Vere Somerset were very sociable and gave freely of their time. However, I was occasionally despondent about the chance of ever being fully accepted by the English as one of them, and I remember Somerset referring to a fellow student, the honourable Richard Kepple, son of the Earl of Albermarle, as "that Dutchman" (who had come over with William the Conqueror). In one sense it was reassuring to be in good company, if even that distinguished family, half jokingly, was not fully accepted after nearly a millennium; in an another it was a worrying thought that my descendants would have to wait even longer than that! The Provost, John Cecil Masterman, I only knew casually during my undergraduate days, but he took a great deal of interest in me during the years I was at the BBC in London from 1949-1956.[21] While on my first sabbatical from Calgary at Oxford in 1972-1973, I had tea with him in his home in Beaumont Street, and was deeply impressed by his wisdom, his interest in others, and his humility. He told me the fascinating story of his being nearly prosecuted under the Official Secrets Act for publishing his official report on his activity during the war in *The Double Cross System*. In his autobiography *On Chariot Wheel* he also gives a lot of space to the difference of espionage during war, as opposed to in peacetime, the latter directed mainly to industrial spying. Masterman held that the importance of spies is on the downgrade, due to the growth of technological devices and inventions. The account I wrote on my experience in the army is dedicated to him.

I was a frequent visitor at the chaplain's residence, and still remember with gratitude the hospitality and friendship extended to me by the (now Very) Reverend R. L. P. Milburn

M. A. Frank Eyck 1949

and his wife. With the blessing of the chaplain, a few of us undergraduates read Compline, the last canonical prayer at the end of the day, in the College chapel at ten o'clock in the evening.[22] Sometimes he would join in, to give us encouragement. Altogether I my time at Worcester College was a very happy one.

As for modern European history, I was instructed by Lionel Butler, a scholar and junior lecturer at All Souls' College who later developed a flourishing Medieval History department at the University of St. Andrews.[23] On 14th February 1949 he wrote a testimonial that was helpful in obtaining my first job:

Mr. F. Eyck has been a pupil of mine in European History since April 1948. He has always been a hard and conscientious worker, and his writing style has steadily improved and matured. His essays and arguments are shapely and well-balanced and never loaded down with superfluity of unnecessary facts . . . I believe him to have the qualities which would make him a scholarly and discerning historian . . . He has a convincing power of presentation. Finally he is a man of firm integrity, reliable and sociable, and I have been happy working with him.

For my political affiliation, I decided to join the Young Conservatives, and took part in the Speakers' Classes, arranged in conjunction with the University of Oxford, by giving a talk about "Germany and Society Planning." Among others, I let Captain J. B. Cartland know about this talk.[24] I had met him first when he was in charge of No. 16 Amplifier Unit, the only one that during my time suffered casualties through German fire. The feeling among some of the Amplifier/Leaflet Unit personnel was that he probably went in too close to the German troops, to spur surrender by verbal appeal. He had also been at Worcester College, and became Appointment Secretary of the Oxford University employment office. He gave me a positive reply and attended my talk. As a bonus to my army service, I think it was he who, after graduation in 1949, drew my attention to the BBC job. The competition for the job was fierce and it is not unlikely that I would have not received the posting without him. Tragically, Cartland was later on murdered while on holiday in France, with one of his sons being suspected of killing him. I do not think the matter was ever cleared up. Truth is sometimes stranger than fiction.

At the BBC, I edited the German weekly programme *Hier spricht London* (HSL or Here Speaks London),[25] half of which came under the German Service, where Christopher Dilke was one of the two assistant heads. He struck me as a person of great ability. His elder brother, Sir John Dilke, Baronet, with whom I worked in the Foreign Service News Department from 1951 on, became a good friend. For several years, this job gave me the chance to visit and observe the development of Western Germany, which I followed with great interest. Sometimes it was only to negotiate with the publisher in Köln-Deutz during the printing strike in Britain, but mostly to observe the remarkable changes of Continental Europe.

After the devastating war and the even further crippling winter of 1946-1947, a plan was devised in June 1947 by the USA Secretary of State George Marshall to strengthen Europe after the war. The Marshall plan entailed $20 billion in relief funds to help Western Germany to rebuild its industry and get on its feet. (The plan was also offered to the Soviet Union, but Stalin, suspicious of ulterior motives, refused to participate.) Western European countries were determined to establish security within their own borders and with each other. On 17th March 1948, the European Council, the treaty of the Western European Union, was signed in Brussels. A year later, the Council of Europe was constituted

Press Card

and started holding its meetings in Strasbourg, to deal with the wide issues of human rights. Inside Western Germany, the country was greatly helped by the Marshall Plan and the currency reform on June 1948, initiated by Ludwig Erhard to replace the worthless Reichsmark with the new Deutschmark, at an exchange rate of 1 DM for 10 Reichsmark, and an initial offering of 20 DM for everyperson.[26] It was a very successful move, although very hard for many people. Before there was nearly nothing to buy for your money; now goods suddenly appeared, but money was very scarce for most people. On 23rd May 1949, the Federal Republic of Western Germany was born with Chancellor Konrad Adenauer, a Catholic from the Rhineland.[27] As leader of the CDU, which comprised both Catholics and Protestants, the religious division lost its sharp edge. He led a coalition of the CDU, his own party and the FDP the party of Theodor Heuss, who became the first President.[28] Heuss was the main architect of the Basic Law, the German constitution, which through its far-sightedness has stood the test of time. Heuss, a Swabian from the south west of Germany, was a highly cultured man and had great warmth; he introduced a relaxed atmosphere into the presidency, while insisting on high standards in government in every respect. Ludwig Erhard became Finance Minister and sought to implement a social market economy as opposed to state controlled planned economy. After long negotiations and even opposition by the Western Allies, fearing financial instability, the Equalization of Burden, the *Lastenausgleich*, became law in 1952.[29] Adhering to the principle of social justice, a tax was levied against Germans who had preserved more of their assets than they had lost. A year later, in 1953, the law of *Wiedergutmachung*, Financial Restitution, was instituted to make material amends for the atrocities committed in Nazi Germany.[30] Adenauer acknowledged a "moral and material indemnity for the immeasurable suffering that was brought against Jews and Jewish descendants, Gypsies, homosexuals, and communists in Germany and in occupied territories at the time of Nazionalsocialism." While years of discrimination, denigration, and the happenings in the concentration camps could not be undone, financial restitution was something that could be done. It was an act of greatness and – as it was carried out as soon as feasible – it helped many refugees. During my mother's widowhood, the most important item of her income was a German pension in compensation of my father's deprivation of his livelihood.[31]

In June 1950, I was asked to find out what had happened to the British licensed press and the licensees, as well as generally to give a report on the newspaper situation in the British Zone, particularly in Hamburg and Schleswig-Holstein. The trip would also allow me to gather some world news items for our publications, Aviso[32] and *Hier spricht London*. Much of the information that follows is drawn from that report.[33] The anti-British feeling had reached a "rather high level," supported by Foreign Minister Ernest Bevin's[34] somewhat unfortunate remark in the House of Commons that "the Hitler revolutions did not change the German character, it expressed it."[35] This did not, however, seem to affect the BBC publicity work. The Germans thought that the British European service was government controlled but they did not seem to see anything strange in running down the "Engländer" (by which they seem to mean mainly Bevin) while being on perfectly friendly terms with British representatives. There was no doubt that a lot of the shouting was done by people who were keen to establish their own position, as staffs were frequently changed. The question of who was a Nazi was difficult to decide. I suggested that neither unfavourable information nor anti-British reputation should deter BBC publicity from sending out material. Inside publishing houses and between editorial staff there were so many divisions that, I felt, it would even be a good thing to deal with the borderline cases to strengthen the position of the elements friendly to democracy.

It would help if journalists and public men knew more about HSL. Its future was linked mainly to the popular English lessons more suitable for adults rather than schools; here circulation would have benefited from the use of lists of organizations. It was then too early to say whether experienced and interested distributors like Mr. Schulz in Flensburg would bring results. It might have benefited the corporation to give him some titular office in connections with HSL distribution in the British Zone. I knew also, that Mr. Schulz would have been pleased if we subscribed to his journal. Any *Aviso* reproduction was still suffering from newsprint difficulties. Occasionally something might be able to get into the editorial section of current papers. The offices of the big newspapers were, however, now flooded with material. Our material would have to be particularly attractively written and brief. Publicity work is very much a matter of constant personal contact, and I thought we might gain from having a BBC representative on the spot.

With the gradual reduction of the Control Commission Government Staff (CCG) "projection of Britain" would have to depend more and more on non-official bodies. All this was no reflection on the excellent work done by various bodies, Independent German Studies (ISD) Hamburg, and the British Centres like *die Brücke* (the Bridge). The structure of the press in the British Zone was at the time also undergoing important changes, primarily due to the decisive impact of business and financial considerations.

Everywhere the work of the Military Government and its licensing was under attack – sometimes openly, sometimes in disguise – the political consequences of which were not predictable. The British aim had been to replace the old publishers and journalists, who were all too some extent tainted by the Nazi regime, with new men to whom fell the task of creating a democratic press. All or most objectives were now in danger. If the intention had been to get rid of the old publishers like Girardet, Broscheck, and so on, thorough arrangements should have been made about their publishing and printing companies. They were not expropriated or forced to sell. Now the licensees were to a large extent at their mercy. The licensees of the *Lübecker Nachrichten*, apparently a very decent paper, and in some way the successor of the Military Government paper, had thought it advisable to take back the old 'Nazi' publisher, Kohlmann, though in a slightly less prominent position: They had "come to terms." (This was confirmed by the editor, Schramm.)

Where licensees were not amenable to pressure, or persuasion, the old publishers have used more rigorous methods. The Düsseldorf branch of Girardet was now printing on the same press as the SPD paper, *Rhein-Echo* and *Düsseldorfer Nachrichten*, their own paper. Both came out at the same time, which on the technical and especially the advertising side, created an awkward situation. Similarly the Droste Verlag, who printed the *Rheinische Post*, had started their own paper, *Der Mittag*; however, they appeared at different times. Competitors working in the same building presented a serious problem. In the long run there was no doubt that the financial and business experience of the old publishers would win the day. This had already been shown in Hamburg, where the situation was somewhat different. Technically Girardet had been reduced to a print facility only; nonetheless, special connections existed with one of the papers, namely the *Hamburger Freie Presse* (originally FDP), that gave it more influence in the news then had been intended. Two of their other licensed papers, the *Hamburger Allgemeine* (formerly CDU) and the Niederdeutsche Zeitung had been absorbed by the *Hamburger Freie Presse*, as they had been in financial difficulties.

The editorially much respected *Hamburger Allgemeine* was involved in a scandal. While in the last two months of independent existence, staff's salaries were no longer paid, Beyrich, the licensee, had helped himself to a considerable sum of money. I was told by Lüth, the Pressechef (editor in chief) of the Hansastadt, that the case was under judgment as there were several questions to whether the procedure adopted by Beyrich was in breach of bankruptcy regulations. Developments of this kind reflected adversely not only on the licensed press but also on the parties because Beyrich was a prominent personality in the Hamburg CDU. Unfortunately, this case was not the only one. It had a strange parallel in Kiel, where the leader of the Schleswig-Hostein CDU, Schroeter and other CDU leaders were involved. It is a sad chapter for the "democratic" press. While the licensees originally worked together with the old Nazi publisher, Heinrichs, and had made an effort to whitewash him politically, they, or some of them, had changed their tactics and tried to get Heinrichs. These licensees attempted to have classify Heinrichs as a Nazi and have him removed from printing through denazification. The climax of this conflict occurred when an anonymous letter was received by the local denazification panel, denouncing Heinrichs as a Nazi. It was found that the letter had been typed on licensee Schroeter's typewriter. Schroeter was incidentally a member of the Bundestag in Bonn, and had become Deputy Whip. I understood, however, that at the time his Bundestag immunity had indeed been lifted.

Generally, it was too early to see the effect on the reorganization of the German press due to the lifting of military controls. Competition was still stiff and borderline areas were much contested. It was, yet, already clear that the objectives that licensing had in mind had to a large extent not been realized. Many of the old publishers had come back, finance being a primary factor. The licensees had often been weak or corrupt. Many of the barriers to keep out Nazi or semi-Nazi journalists seemed to have broken down (see Sambacher *Die Zeit*). Whether the press would be sufficiently independent and resist pressure from publishers and their undue outside influence was hard to judge in the short time of my investigation. The relationship between publisher and journalists often appeared to be strained, so that some journalists had little confidence in the integrity of their own firm. The *Heimatzeitungen* (local papers) did not seem to have had the success expected. Many party papers and *Heimatzeitungen* have disappeared. Only the SPD and KPD, presumably with the help of party funds, had been able to survive, though with reduced circulation.

A year later, I had the chance to write about the

confusing situation of Western Germany's parties.[36] Particularly worthy of examine were the Neo-Nazis who found a political place with some of these parties.[37] My article in the Contemporary Review runs over six pages, of which I only mention the most important developments. Although old Nazis could be found everywhere, they were also in the two major parties on the right, like the CDU and FDP, who formed the backbone of the Bonn coalition.[38] Nazis were even more prominent in the Right splinter parties. The Bonn leaders had only limited control on the periphery of their domain. Even the trusted method of federalism as a safeguard against autocracy and central government could have unforeseen consequences. In the long run, former Nazi Party members with administrative experience could not be totally excluded from all posts in public life. The outlawing of too many of them could act as a boomerang, for a common fate quite often is a bond of unity for a minority, and the Nazis started small. The only hope was that the former Nazis, whenever they are not too deeply involved by having participated in terrible crimes, would have seen the error of their former ways. After all, there is a deep truth in the Christian teaching about sinners who repent. But many of the sinners had not repented. Surely, it was not necessary for senior political posts to go to men who made such grave errors, to put it mildly, in the political field.

The main two fringe parties were the Refugee Parties BHE, *Bund der Heimatlosen und Entrechteten*, which might be translated into Union of the Homeless and Deprived, and the SRP, *Socialistische Reich Partei*. These groups were more like a movement than a party. The BHE formed surprising coalitions, in Schleswig-Holstein with the CDU and the FDP, while in Lower Saxony it became a partner to the SDP. The *Socialistische Reich Party* (SRP) achieved remarkable results in Lower Saxony with

11% in the Landtag, (the provincial Diet). A certain notorious Nazi, Major-General Remer was one of their leading personages. Stationed in Berlin, he played a prominent part in the Generals' foiled plot of 20th July 1944, and personally ordered the execution of its principle participants. Some survivors of the plot now stood accused of unpatriotic conduct and had to defend themselves in open court in Schleswig–Holstein against Hedler, another neo-Nazi leader. In the pronounced nationalistic publications of the SRP, one only found phrases and slogans of the unity of the Reich. The SRP did not hide the fact that they considered themselves to be the successors of the Nazi Party, except when it was a question of evading police measures. As in the days of the NSDAP, recruitment took place among the unemployed and the refugees, of whom there were unfortunately many. A private army, since banned, of hired thugs had been formed to "protect" meetings. It was mainly to the credit of the Minister of the Interior, Robert Lehr, who took the, otherwise regrettable, measures to curb their activities. I assumed more would be done when the newly created Constitutional Court began to operate.

As to the opposition party, the SPD, under Schumacher, was free from any Nazi connection.[39] It was found to be surprisingly nationalistic, and in Lower Saxony in alliance with the SRP. It expressed the understandable, but at that moment impractical, desire for a united Germany. Further, there was the idea of West Germany's contribution to the European Defence Community, EDC, which was supported by the government but vigorously objected too by the SPD. Both CDU and SPD were locked in the narrowness of their doctrinaire background, and the dislike between their leaders, Adenauer and Schumacher, was well known. But some prominent personalities in both parties wished to see more collaboration. The terrible thing was that the basic dilemma of the Weimar Republic now confronted her successor.

Among the millions of West Germans, one in every five [40] persons had lost their home in Silesia, Pomerania, or Poland, or had fled from the Russian occupied zone. There presence was an unavoidable problem, and it was tempting see them merely as a problem and not as people, to think about them in an almost impersonal and statistical way. When one attended meetings like the "Silesian Home Rally" in Cologne, the irrational element in the meeting was hard to comprehend. Co-operation between the old inhabitants and the newcomers was often very poor, and the latter would not accept the fact, however regrettable, that they lost their homes. There was a mystical, semi-religious and completely unworldly atmosphere at their gatherings. They only wanted to live in the past. This will always be a curse to the émigré, but an even worse one if one fails to draw the necessary conclusion from a given situation.

Despite the understandable criticism of the three great democratic parties towards the Western Allies, it may be said that basically they were all sound Westerners. Even the thought of active collaboration with the Communists was unimaginable for them. This did not apply to the radicals on the Left and to the Right like the SRP. The Nazi-Soviet pact of 1939 could not easily be forgotten. From where did the SRP get its funds? It would not be surprising if the Communists helped. The SRP certainly furthered the Communist aim of disruption. In this situation, it was vital that the Western world co-operated to the utmost, and just as important, West Berlin had to be held at all costs.

In September 1952, I was commissioned by chief editor McLachlan of The Economist to watch and report on an important SPD party rally in Dortmund.[41] About my observations I gave a private and confidential talk at Chatham

House, London, on 15th October, by invitation only:

The week previous to the British Labour Party conference at Marecombe, Lancashire and the German Social Democrats had their meeting at Dortmund. The eyes of Europe were on these important conferences, as they would determine their parties' position in the East-West struggle. In Britain the struggle took place in the open. But in Germany very little could be gathered about the future balance within the party from what was said on the floor of the conference nor from the summaries of the speeches in the newspapers, and it could only be hinted at in the interpretation of the periodical press. I attempted to give the inside story, referring to the Bonn Treaties dealing with the end of occupation status, release of prisoners of war from Moscow and Rearmament of the Federal Republic.

Would the SPD, when and if in power, pursue the Schumacher foreign policy, i.e. follow their bitter opposition to the Schuman Declaration and Rearmament?[42] In this declaration Schuman, France's Foreign Minister, and Adenauer aimed at peace in Europe. The carefully designed document stated that in the long run, the aim was to create a federal Europe, but for the present it suggested to start small. A customs union between France and Germany should be formed beginning with the coal and steel industries under an independent and elected common High Authority. This would be bound to create a peaceful relationship between France and Western Germany, and be of economic benefit to both countries, so that later on other countries might want to join with similar agreements.

When Dr. Kurt Schumacher had died in August 1952, Erich Ollenhauer, his faithful lieutenant for many years, became party leader. To understand Ollenhauer one must first assess Schumacher, who had fought and lost an arm in the First World War. I had met him privately soon after the last war at the Suchans while still serving in the British army. One could not help but be impressed by Schumacher. There was a man who stood for that part of the German people who had actually fought Hitler. In the bitter struggle with his jailers in several concentration camps he had further sacrificed his health. Schumacher could have had his freedom if he had signed the necessary promises which the Nazis wanted to extort from him. He never gave them. He, as senior SPD leader with an untarnished reputation, soon established his predominance within the party. As the result of the treatment at those camps, however, he could not face the difficult problems of post-war Germany with the detachment and cool judgement necessary. He had not only sacrificed his physical health but also some of his balance of mind. One can even go further, that in fighting the Nazis he had not failed to catch some of their poison. That Schumacher, a passionate unbending politician, often was dictatorial, impetuous and irresponsible, that he was in his way a kind of militarist, was undoubtedly largely due to his terrible experiences. He, once in a debate, denigrated Adenauer as 'Chancellor of the Allies,' and contributed too many unnecessary difficulties and problems on the post-war German political scene. But it should not be forgotten that he represented one very sound aspect of his country, the abhorrence felt by that part of the German people about the crimes of the Nazi regime. When the funeral cortège bearing Schumacher's mortal remains made its slow and dignified way from Bonn to Hanover, hundreds of thousands of Germans watched in silence by the roadside honouring a man who had never compromised with evil, a man whose courage had not failed.

In Britain Schumacher was often only seen from the point of view of his opposition to Bonn, but this should be balanced against his long anti-Nazi tradition, which was also part of Ollenhauer's legacy. There could never be any doubt as to Schumacher's hostility to the Communists, however much he emphasized the unity of Germany, even after 1949 when the German Democratic Republic in the East and the Federal Republic of Germany in the West had been established. Although the situation of the peoples in the Eastern State became increasingly saddening, there was no compromise in sight as long as the Communist regime would last. Schumacher early on recognized the danger of a Socialist-Communist amalgamation, and to his everlasting credit fought vigorously against it. But no two leaders are the same. Where Schumacher was brilliant and fiery with all the spontaneities that go with it, Ollenhauer was solid and sound in his approach, mistrusting inspiration. Instead of a leader with a nervous temperament, the party had a leader with strong nerves, apparently backed by good health. It will be recalled that he was in London with the SPD in exile during the war.

Schumacher's leadership had left a deep gulf within the party, between its Headquarter and many of the various groups of interests on which the success of every party depends. He had largely worked in isolation, a thing Ollenhauer could not do even if he wanted to. He had to rely on the talent and goodwill of former dissidents' like the Burgomasters' group, and that will be to the credit of the party. At Dortmund superficially, endorsement of Schumacher's policy might be taken as a continuation of the status quo, some commentators took that view. I, however, thought that a remarkable thing had happened, Ollenhauer had widely been able to reunite the party, and received the support of the three vital personalities, Reuter Burgomaster of Berlin, Brauer of Hamburg and Kaisen of Bremen. The two mayors of the North Sea ports knew very well that the refusal of the Social Democrats to take part in the German rearrangement, as a contribution to the European

Defence Community, could never be the basis of an actual policy. But Reuter told me that, if asked, he would not sign it. All three were shrewd enough to play a waiting game, for it was very doubtful whether the SPD opposition to the treaties would, in fact, ever become a practical question. There was a general assumption that the treaty would have been ratified well before the next election, and all the arguments against the treaties would soon be out of date. But, just for argument's sake, it might be worthwhile to look at them.

Under Schumacher, the SPD had maintained that the Federal Republic was not fully sovereign, only a provisional grouping of *Länder* (Provinces), pending the inclusion of Eastern Germany, and therefore she could not conclude international treaties of long duration. Further the Bonn treaties appear to be based on the perpetuation of the division of Germany into two halves. This the SPD could never accept, as they considered themselves to be the trustees for the people in the East, while in their opinion the capitalist and Catholic Bonn government did not seem to be to sorry about this separation from the more socialist and Protestant East.

Concerning rearmament they maintained that this would release reactionary forces with which the young democracy would not be strong enough to cope, as she also lacked the economic strength necessary for it. Genuine equality of status would have to be given before Western Germany could take part in Western defence. And the Western Powers would have to share with her on the basis of equal risk. A surprising statement could be heard that Western Germany was constantly asked to contribute in advance. At heart there was the SPD's underlying attitude of a complete disbelief in the effectiveness of armies, and a vague belief there must be other ways. Some of these arguments even contradict each other, and it would be impossible to base a government policy on them. If Western Germany was going to take part in Western defence, a decision had to be taken now, and Western Germany's constitutional theories mattered nothing in the grave international context. Ollenhauer did not supply an answer to these problems in his speech – he did not have one.

As to finding a political partner, the various party coalitions often were opposite in the Länder to those in the Government, which did not look like unquestioning faith to party doctrine. Ollenhauer made it quite clear that the decision to accept the treaties was entirely up to the recognized organs of the constitution, and that pressure on them or a general strike etc. would be entirely unconstitutional. He was very restrained in the manner in which he spoke about matters of foreign policy, where he steered clear of neutrality and extreme nationalism – which Schumacher always found difficult. I talked to all three burgomasters. Overshadowed by Reuter and Brauer, Kaisen may be the least known one, but in many respects he was the most foresighted one of the three. Kaisen seems to have something rare in Germany those days, a detachment and a long view based on experience, and maturity coupled with respect for wide sections of the community across party lines. This did not apply to Reuter and Brauer who were far more controversial if more brilliant figures. Kaisen stressed that Ollenhauer would be more conciliatory, and that he had succeeded to a remarkable degree in keeping the extremists silenced. As they could not expect to get an absolute majority, the door had been left open for a coalition with one of the other parties. This Ollenhauer admitted to me personally, as did everybody else.

He was concerned that two points, off the record, should become known to the proper quarters in London. First, the SPD considered the continuation of four-power talks important (without really believing in their success). For these talks would, in his opinion, never disappear from the agenda (the Russians would see to this), and if they were not agreed to voluntarily by the Western Powers, they eventually would take place, but under less favourable conditions for the West through pressure from German public opinion. Second, the SPD views gravely the creation of the European six-power group without England and Scandinavia. Ollenhauer would have liked to see a form of co-operation which included the latter two countries, and, of course, Federal Germany. When I raised a query about the SPD's desires to take part in forming this group, he stressed that her pro Western co-operation could be taken for granted. He felt that, in due course, there would be a useful collaboration between the Federal Germany and England. He clearly recognized the limits of the federal absorption inherent in the British position, and therefore advocated multilateral treaties à la NATO.

At the end of the conference the SPD link with the Weimar Republic was demonstrated when the chairman announced that he had arranged for the former president of the Reichstag, Paul Loebe, to say a few words. There was a hush of silence as the old man of nearly eighty mounted the rostrum. In Lincoln-like simple words he expressed all that was best in the SPD movement emphasizing the fundamental decency and respect for others, a sense of obligation for the community and the hope that these virtues were still the ideals of the party.

In concluding, I found that there were far more points of contact for the West, and for Britain in particular, with the German Social Democrats than would appear on the surface. At heart they were neither nationalistic nor unreasonably negative. The transition from the Schumacher policy would only be concluded after the next election; the election could bring the change from a negative opposition to a more positive contribution, or even a possible share in the work of government. This change, however, would put a great strain on the rank and file, who might consider themselves betrayed. The inconsistency of the party policy would be exploited to the full by their opponents, but if the SPD could succeed in its goal of sharing power once more, as it did during the Weimar Republic, its dangerous 'appearance and reality' would at last be over.

The expected German election took place on 6th September 1953. I was again sent to watch, and on 15th October, I had the honour to give a further report at Chatham House, London:[43]

It took me some time to get an explanation for the new and rather complicated German electoral system that gives everybody two votes. Finally, a day after the election, an official of the Federal Information Office in Bonn – who at least undoubtedly knew the procedure – said it would take too long to explain the system to me. He searched in his office for a pamphlet which would explain everything but could not find it and said he would send it to me, which he did. This is what the pamphlet said: Every *Land* [Province] would send twice as many deputies to the Lower House as it has constituencies. To start with, they were shared equally between the first and second vote. The first, a 'direct' vote went to the constituency candidate for one seat each in the Lower House, the *Bundestag*. With the second, an 'indirect' vote, each citizen also voted for his preferred party; which may or may not be the party of the directly elected candidate. From all the parties thus voted for, a proportion of the total *Land*-votes (constituency votes) would decide how many deputies, and of which parties will be sent to the Lower House. If any of parties elected fell under the 5% clause, this will reduce the number of deputies elected by the second vote. Thus the second vote did not guarantee the allowable number of deputies. The Upper House, the *Bundesrat*, is not an elected body; each Land would send a fixed number of deputies, depending on the number of inhabitants and the result of the general election, i.e. the party or coalition in power. The system certainly was interesting and a sincere effort to keep alive the ideas of constituency members without sacrificing comparative fairness between parties, and yet without encouraging splinter parties. Parties that did not reach 5% of the total votes could not get a seat. In this way it was hoped to avoid the many pitfalls and splinter-parties of the Weimar Republic.

The pollsters had predicted a narrow coalition majority for Adenauer assuming that the behaviour of the West German elector had not changed from his or her attitude of 1949. The election campaign was quietly conducted, although it was maintained in some quarters that the campaign displayed mutual recrimination and personal abuse. From my observation, it did not do so unduly. Generally, the speakers expressed their respective plan clearly: for and against the Bonn treaties, foreign policy being the main issue; for and against free enterprise. The poll of 86% was incredibly high.

Adenauer and Ollenhauer, I had heard both, put their respective case forward clearly. The contrast between the two party leaders was very interesting. Ollenhauer did not create a bad impression on the public, by any means, but he had not yet developed into a great public figure, which Adenauer had. The overwhelming victory of the CDU undoubtedly did not only imply a preference for the government's policy, but also a preference for the pilot at the helm of the state. At 77, Adenauer did not shirk the endless travel through the Federal Republic, tirelessly addressing the electors everywhere. He had a great charm of personality, immediately gaining contact with his audience by saying a friendly word or cracking a joke. He had a delight for the fray, which showed in the hint of pleasure that came over his face as he, during an argument, resolutely moved to the kill. He spoke to his electors simply – never once using a complicated word or turn of phrase – he chatted to them, never shouted, he did not have to stress that he was the chancellor, he was never afraid of talking to his listeners as an equal. He was not a born orator, but he had solved the secret of the successful democratic leader.

Compared to him Ollenhauer was at a disadvantage. He is much more pedestrian in his approach. I had heard him speak last year in Dortmund, and even earlier, I doubt whether he is capable of the Adenauer technique. Ollenhauer, though, is a competent speaker; he is good at holding together the big battalions of this own troops, he makes the most of all that holds a working class party together, using all recognizable class arguments, which, however, at this meeting received limited applause. The only occasion on which he got a big hand was when he attacked Adenauer – a reflection of the extent to which leaders succeed in personifying causes.

I went to some smaller meetings too, getting to know quite a few pubs in the country. At the German Party meeting in Hamburg the speakers curiously combined extreme nationalism with a strong attack on the occupying powers and the returned emigrants – like the socialist burgomaster Brauer, who supported both Adenauer's policy of Western integration and the Treaties. I wanted to find out whether the smaller parties were unsound, for they are subject to strong regional variations. I went to the DRP, a radical right party suspected of being a Neo-Nazi party, which might be libellous if I said so. They were not prepared to reveal themselves in their true colours, for then they would be banned like the SRP. In the Schleswig-Holstein, the CDU Ministerpäsident Lübke succeeded in creating something like a two-party system through a series of manoeuvres though more or less eliminating the minor coalition parties. Apparently with Adenauer's agreement, Lübke formed his government with the help of the BHE.

The result of the Bundestag elections took everybody by surprise. The CDU/CSU received 246 seats and the SPD 151, leaving 88 seats for the splinter parties. How to explain this enormous majority of the CDU and their Bavarian partner the CSU? The government could point to a record achievement:

to a recovery of German prestige abroad, to economic recovery, to financial stability, to the execution of an unprecedented building programme. The Social Democrats, who had kept about their previous number of seats, were unable to put forward a clear alternative policy. They generally opposed Adenauer's foreign policy. They had increasingly emphasised their claim to be the true representatives of the working classes. But now that the trade union in Germany was above party attachment, the movement was no longer their domain. They alienated those decisive sections that either were no longer working class, or considered it wrong to stress class division. The defeat of the SPD was not only a defeat of policy, but also of personality. Ollenhauer, though a man of some ability, had to compete with an outstanding personality like Adenauer. If the late Mayor Reuter of Berlin had led the SPD, the result might have been different.

The Christian Democrats were only to a limited extent dependent on their coalition partners. The BHE was expected to join the government, but only polled 5.9 % and 27 seats. If they dropped any further they might have excluded themselves. It shows, however, how well integrated the displaced Germans had become. The Communists, who in 1949 had secured 5.7% and 15 deputies, were reduced to 2.2% and no seats. The FDP with 10% and 48 deputies is the only other party left with any stature. Parties, both to the extreme Left and extreme Right had become a quantité négligable.

Dr. Adenauer's government would be in an enormously strengthened position in the *Bundestag*, and the Constitutional Court in Karlsruhe was likely to be reformed. Even if they decided that the Allied treaties involve a change in the basic law, and thus required a 2/3 majority, this is not likely to create a problem in the *Bundestag*. The Upper House, the *Bundesrat*, that previously lacked a clear majority, had definitely turned the scale in Adenauer's favour.

In foreign policy the socialist governments in Belgium

and France had given assurances about their vote in favour of the allied treaties. Like the Americans, we in Britain welcomed the emergence of a stable democratic government in Western Germany, and hoped that more stability would again ensue in France and Italy. Surely any weakness in the West only played into the hand of the Communists. Furthermore, no practical alternative had been found for the EDC. It is doubtful whether taking the Federal Government into NATO would set at rest the fears of the EDC critics.

The SPD slowly changed, but remained in opposition. The party had to wait until the election of 1969 to win enough seats to become the majority party. Willy Brandt, Mayor of West Berlin, became Chancellor and formed a coalition with the FDP. By that time four governments headed by Konrad Adenauer had been elected, followed by the government of Ludwig Erhard (CDU/FDP) and then the government of Kurt Kiesinger (CDU/SPD).

It is necessary to highlight an event that magnified the understanding developing between Western nations, President de Gaulle's visit to Germany in 1962.[44] He created a powerful impression on the German people with his message of reconciliation. After all that the Germans had done to the French in two World Wars, de Gaulle was prepared to forgive in the name of the French people. The resulting close relationship between the two countries that ended the century-old "hereditary enmity" (*Erbfeindschaft*) is an example, and a model, to many other parts of the world that seem unable to overcome mutual hatred.

In Eastern Europe, the German and Czech uprising of 1953 was brutally crushed by the Soviets. The construction of the forbidding and deadly Berlin Wall in 1961 was a somewhat later manifestation of the hatred and unrelenting control of the Soviets. It was a measure to keep its own citizen inside the country. From a raised platform near the Brandenburg Gate, we could look over that wall onto the Potsdamer square, the busiest square of Berlin in old times; it was now barren, stacked with anti-tank blocks and watchtowers manned by armed soldiers. On the Western side of the wall the occasional cross was raised in memory of people who had dared to escape and paid with their lives. The Wall lasted twenty-eight years, when the Communist regime in the Gorbachev-era imploded. It was finally dismantled by the East and West German people alike, during the courageous East German uprising in November 1989.

Two years earlier, my old school in Berlin had invited us to a reunion for the *Abiturienten*, school-finalists of 1936 and 1937, at the same time Berlin was celebrating her 750th anniversary. Additionally, the city had invited the expatriates of this group to a week's stay with their spouses. Moreover, in an intimate ceremony honored us with a gold memorial coin. Both events were full of lively and often very serious discussions. The only unpleasantness was our waiting for hours in the bus outside Potsdam, where papers were checked and armoured police walked around us with their sharp dogs. Now things have changed drastically, and for the better; on a later visit to Berlin, we no longer noticed any division driving from Berlin to Potsdam. Charles Cahn, my old school friend, invited me to give a talk, which I delivered on 21st April 1991, on this momentous event to the Benevolent Society in Montreal.

At the fall of the Berlin Wall, Helmut Kohl with his CDU/FDP coalition, had been chancellor in Western Germany for seven years (1982-1989); he now continued to govern the united Germany from 1990-1998. He was very quick to seize the sudden change and secured an international understanding with Gorbachev in Moscow, Margaret Thatcher in London, and, which was easier, with his old friend and alley François Mitterrand in Paris to contractually unite the two Germanys in May 1990. Helmut Kohl officially accepted the Oder-Neiße Border with Poland as final. He was committed to European integration and soon led the old East German *Länder* into the European Union. Economically, he generously exchanged the Eastern currency of one East German Mark to one Deutschmark which was by no means easy on the well established DM. But the hardest part was uniting the people, to help those in the Eastern *Länder* to adjust to the Western way of life once the first enthusiasm had calmed down. For forty-four years, Westerners and Easterners had lead completely different lives. The latter's political thought pattern was suddenly no longer valid, and the economic system they knew completely collapsed. Not all was bad, besides the now dysfunctional communist ideas. In their educational system, German classical literature and history, and even a richer appreciation for the Prussian past, was better represented than in the West. The necessary adjustment of the two sides to each other turned out to be extremely difficult, rather long, and painful for both. Even now, there is no final resolution between East and West; still, I remain confident that with ample patience it will succeed, as it must.

Another and quite different inquiry into the German past leads to a question that surfaced again and again; it is that of the involvement of the German Army[45] in Nazi atrocities.[46] It has and will still take Germany quite some time to come to grips with the traumatic past from which there is no hiding. Take the example of famous writer Günther Grass, who as late as 2006 finally admitted that in 1944, when things were already chaotic, he had been recruited into the ill-reputed Waffen SS.[47]

While the army was widely considered at the time to be a refuge from Nazi involvement. This was the reason why our good friend Hans von Herwarth von Bitterfeld had joined the army as he had some Jewish blood from his mother's side of the family.[48]

On 20th July 1944, he had just returned from the front,

exhausted, when Elisabeth, his wife, answered the telephone. Oberst von Stauffenberg was on the line and he wanted to talk to Hans, but by then he was fast asleep and his wife did not want to wake him up. They soon learned that they had escaped the consequences of the failed plot against Hitler. During my research on G. P. Gooch, I met another survivor of the army's plot: the officer Fabian von Schlabrendorff, a fine man; he was a descendant from the trusted adviser of the Coburg dynasty and the British royal family through Baron C. F. von Stockmar. I later heard through a mutual friend that Schlabrendorff, as a believing Protestant, worried whether the attempted tyrannicide could be theologically justified. Altogether it should be remembered that a not insignificant number of Germans suffered the ultimate penalty for their opposition to the Nazi regime, it is incredibly sad that the executions by the Nazis following the fail putsch went on right to the end of the regime.

Yet, the army nevertheless often did succumb to taking part in Nazi crimes. Now, in the information media, in scholarship, in school education, and in public life, the nettle has been grasped. When I was in Munich in October 2003,[49] I viewed the exhibition, *Crimes of the Wehrmacht*, which acknowledged the army's dark deeds during the Nazi period. This was not an easy exhibition to visit; moreover, it is even more difficult to truly take in and think about because it once again brings the darkness of Germany's past to light. Yet, I believe the task of bringing forth the truth of the past must continue for there is a danger in allowing a-historical or even anti-historical younger generation simply disregard German history as entirely bad. Not only does this disregard for history permit Germany's youth to forget how the nation had fallen into fascism, but it also leaves them ignorant of the noble acts that attempted to redeem her, such as Restitution payments and the Equalization of Burden.

At home, after I had graduated (Oxford parlance "I had

come down") with honours in 1949, and started working for
the BBC. I continue to be active with the Young Conservatives
in Hampstead. On October 15th-17th,1954, I organized
and chaired a weekend school at the Montpelier Hotel at
Brighton.[50] The programme was billed as "The Tory Answers"
and it sought to form clear responses to several topics. The
topics covered were Principles (Neil Shield, M.C.), Good
Citizenship (Henry Brooke, MP), the Welfare State (Julian
Tobin, second session Basil Webb), Industrial Relations
(Dr. Angus S. Roy, B.Sc.), Slogans (Malcolm Agnew), and
the Commonwealth – our Imperial Heritage (Ronald Russell
MP). Interspersed there were lively and helpful questioning
periods. Henry Brooke, MP, commented in a letter to me,
"I should congratulate you most warmly on the planning of
[the weekend school], it went from strength to strength and I
hope that everybody enjoyed it as much as I did. It should be a
feather in the cap of the Hampstead Young Conservatives."[51]

Of my contemporaries who stayed in Britain, I would
like to mention Karl Leyser, an old friend from St. Paul's days.[52]
He received a first class degree, and became a well-known
medievalist, fellow of Magdalen College, and Chichele Professor
of Medieval History. We had just started a correspondence on
my manuscript titled *Religion and Politics in German History*,
and in response to the scope of my project, he stated on 28th
August 1990 that he was stunned by my enterprise:

> And to cast back our concept of 'Politics' into the
> tenth century demands much more empathy with
> mentalités as, say, the Annales School defines these
> terms. And religion? The very meaning of the
> 'religion' [53] in a single text must be wrestled with and
> hammered out passage by passage.

Grateful to him for having pointed at the changing concept
and interpretation of both terms, I was disappointed that there

East Choir of Speyer Cathedral,
drawing by President Theodor Heuss

was no follow up of our scholarly correspondence. To the sorrow and sadness of his wife Henrietta, also a renowned medieval historian, and the great regret among scholars and myself, he suddenly died on 27th May 1991.

It took several more years to come to the end of this my enterprise, which required many useful discussions with my German scholar friends Josef Becker, Adolf Birke,[54] and Rudolf Lill,[55] as well as a visiting Professorship at the University of Würzburg in 1982,[56] and a year's fellowship at the Calgary Institute for the Humanities 1985-1986.[57] During this time, I was relieved of most of my teaching duties, offered easy access to research material, and fostered stimulating exchange of thoughts with other scholars. The only gladly undertaken duty was to conduct a seminar and give a talk on the subject of my investigation that in itself was furthering my understanding. My book, dedicated to my wife Rosemarie, was published by the Macmillan Press in 1998.

This long awaited moment we celebrated with Lord and Lady Judd who invited us to a dinner in the House of Lords;[58] Christine being, my faithful "student" from Exeter days. We continued with a delightful and intimate weekend in their Rose Cottage at Thackthwaite, Cumbria. Frank Judd had an illustrious career in politics, starting as Labour Minister of Parliament for Portsmouth West, Devon (1966-1979), followed by many other important parliamentary appointments. He has always been deeply concerned about and actively involved in eliminating the inequality in society at home and oversees. Two years earlier, the Queen had bestowed a knighthood on him. The Judds and I often met on my frequent visits to England, sometimes with our families. In return, they often paid us the honor of visiting us in Calgary. Christine, besides raising her family and giving practical and moral support to her husband, developed her own career as a history teacher.

Another fellow student was Edward Charles Gurney, Lord

Boyle of Handsworth (Life-Peer in 1970), who was educated at Eton and read history at Christ Church Oxford. He went down in 1948 with a third class degree that, in light of his long illustrious career in the House of Parliament, seemed to misrepresent his intelligence. Espousing most liberal causes, he was against capital punishment, strongly supported the United Nations, advanced homosexual reform, and opposed racial prejudice. For many years served as a Conservative Minister of Education bringing Primary and University education into one department. After leaving the civil service, he was a very successful Vice Chancellor of Leeds University. His gift for administration, understanding of money and diplomacy greatly benefited the "red brick" institution. He was equally knowledgeable in music holding his own against professionals. When I learned of his passing on 28th September 1981, I wrote to his sister Mrs. Ann Gold:

> Perhaps you will consider a rather belated contribution about Lord Boyle from Western Canada. No undergraduate at Oxford after the Second World War who watched Edward Boyle as President of the Oxford Union will have been surprised about his successful career as a Member of Parliament and cabinet minister. We met fleetingly in London on a conservative education policy committee in the mid-sixties and for the last time at the Commonwealth University Congress in Canada in 1978. During walks on the British Columbia campus in Vancouver Lord Boyle talked to me about his time in politics. He was quite frank without being indiscreet, fair-minded yet never uncritical, while he accepted the necessity of party politics. I had the impression that he could never quite discard the cross-bench mind. He had a rare personal warmth and impressed me as a model public servant, of absolute integrity, always

putting the general interest before self.

Some of us contemporaries were dispersed over the Commonwealth. Thanks to email and my last book, old contacts blossomed late in our lives. I received fascinating letters from John May in Kingston, Tasmania,[59] and John Suggit in South Africa.[60] We all remembered attending Compline in the College Chapel. Now, they are both retired Canons. John May and his wife, Mary, had spent their working lives in Australia. They had three short periods serving in parishes, but he mainly taught in institutions. Mary, who had discovered my book because of her own interest in history, taught at a girls' school for some years. They had both given lectures on the popes. John had taught at the Royal Military College, Duntroon, New Zealand, and at the Theological Colleges of the University of Hobart, Tasmania, and New South Wales, Australia. They now live in a retirement home near Hobart. They were delighted to receive a generous compensation from the government of New Zealand as he had been a prisoner of war by the Japanese, but, like us, were no longer sure whether they should travel very far.

John Suggit was also an active priest and theologian mainly in Gelandale, in the Diocese of Port Elisabeth, South Africa. He wrote a guide to the gospel of St. John, called *Down to Earth and Up to Heaven*. His book *The Word of God and the People of God* came out in 1994. Both couples liked to keep their interest in religious thought and institutions, but from the distance of mature and advanced age.

As soon as Ken Green and I were back in England we made sure to meet as often as possible at Oxford.[61] My parents also became very fond of him and our frequent meetings carried through to my time in London and Exeter. Ken had been invalided out of the Army owing to a long hospital stay with a bleeding stomach ulcer, but he recovered reasonably well. We consoled one another as neither of us had been commissioned in spite of several attempts, and started building up our post-war lives. Ken and Helen married in 1946, music playing an important role all their lives. For health reasons Ken could not develop his engineering career, he became a much liked and appreciated high-school teacher in mathematics and the sciences at Sevenoaks Grammar School, Kent. And Helen was a successfully and dearly loved primary school teacher at the Weald village-school where they also lived in the charming age-old Potkiln Cottage. We saw our careers and families blossom, often staying in each other's homes. They were among the few friends who visited us several times in the "Wild West" of Alberta. Sadly Ken died in 2003.

On the social side, I was delighted to renew contact with the Maxwell Garnett's who again showed me great kindness during many pleasant afternoon teas at their Oxford home. Their son John had also started to take PPE. Occasionally, we followed the progress of our careers. I was glad to congratulate John on becoming the Director of the Industrial Society since 1962. He was very much concerned about fairness in compensation for civil servants at a time of inflation. In a letter to The Times he states that "people are not helped in restraining themselves if the policy benefits those most able to afford restraint but penalises those at the lower end of the earning scale."[62]

As I mentioned earlier I stayed in contact with my German friends. My frequent visits to Köln and Bonn allowed me to see a lot of Wolfang and his wife, Dörte. I also sometimes saw his parents who by that time had moved to Düsseldorf. But I had not seen Rosemarie, the sister of Wolfgang who lived in another part of the country and had become a medical doctor. In the spring of 1955, it dawned on me to make up for this and we arranged a weekend in Küßnacht near Zürich, a convenient halfway point between my Italian holiday and her place of work in a Sanatorium at Münster am Stein, Rheinland Pfalz. As there had always been the feeling of mutual respect and friendship since childhood, we gradually found out that we had quite a lot more to say to each other, and love started to blossom. Both of us had some holidays remaining that year so we agreed to a joint vacation in Lynton, North Devon, adding several days in London. That summer England showed itself at its best. I soon asked the vital question, which was answered positively. We got engaged and with the generous help of her parents planned our wedding for 10th December 1955 in Düsseldorf at the Protestant Matthäi Church.

The civil marriage at the town's registrar office was witnessed by Wolfgang Schmidt and Franz Suchan, and the church ceremony was conducted by Will Praetorius, pastor of Rosemarie's parents' parish.[63] Praetorius was an old friend from their time in Berlin, where he had belonged to the Confessing Church and had suffered persecution from the Nazis. He was also a friend of Theodor and Elly Heuss, who had sheltered him during the Nazi regime when he was threatened and in danger of being "eliminated." The solemnization of our marriage was his last ministration before his retirement. We chose the reading of 1 Corinthian 16:14, "Let all your things be done in love (Eros and Agape)." The two families and friends shared the wedding festivity. The guests of honor were President Heuss,[64] and Hans Schäffer,[65] friends of both families. Schäffer had been Staatssecretär (Statesecretary) at the Treasury in the Weimar Republic. On our later visits to Düsseldorf, we always spent an inspiring afternoon with Praetorius and his wife, Gisela, who for several years was an MP in Bonn. Twice did we have the pleasure to visit Theodor Heuss, besides meeting him during his 1958 state visit to Britain and at a later date during the ceremony for his Honorary Doctorate from the University of Exeter.[66] His unfailing greeting at each meeting was:

December 10ʰ, 1944.
Wolfgang Schmidt, Rosemarie & Frank (Ullo) Eyck,
Franz Suchan.

May 10th, 1955.
Leaving the Matthäi Church.

"*Das ist doch gar nicht der Frank, das ist doch der Ullo!*" (That is not Frank, but it is Ullo); this being the more intimate form of my first name, Ulrich. In Bonn, besides a personal and political discussion, he was keen to share the Caspian caviar, a recent gift of a visiting Russian diplomat. The second time we saw him was after his retirement while he lived in Stuttgart. To our pleasant surprise, Toni Stolper was also present.[67] The Heuss and Stolper couple had been friends since

the 1920s, and now he and Toni had long been left widowed. Heuss talked about preparing his autobiography, among more serious things he planned to mention his last waltz he had danced with Rosemarie on our wedding day, because soon afterwards he badly injured his foot.[68] We also met his little nine-month-old grandson, whom he very much hoped to see grow up, so that the memory of his grandfather would be more than a postage stamp. Sadly, his wish wasn't granted to him.

Back in London, my job as a sub-editor at the BBC had become an increasingly boring routine. Although I had the honour of being elected Father of the Chapel, National Union of Journalists in 1956, an interesting and sometimes worrying position, it did not quite make up for lack of the stimulation I was seeking. But due to the 24 hours shift work that allowed alternatively two or three days off per week I had started research in the Round Tower at Windsor Castle on Prince Albert of Coburg. When I noticed an advertisement offering a Research Fellowship at the newly founded St. Antony's College at Oxford (1950).

Just before my thirty-fifth birthday, the cut off date, Rosemarie and I decided to apply.[69] William (Bill) Deakin, the warden from 1950-1968, wrote to me on 16th May 1956 that the College was glad to elect me to a Research Fellowship and offered a stipend of £700 per annum (1956-1958).[70] Bill Deakin had been an adventurous soldier during Second World War, parachuting into enemy lines in Yugoslavia, besides being an aide to Winston Churchill. James Joll, who had been my Tutor in Politics at New College, had in 1951 become Fellow and Sub-warden of St. Antony's. He gave me much good advice on my way into academia. With his guidance I used my previous research to write my first book *The Prince Consort, a political biography of Prince Albert*, which brought me a B.Litt.Oxon.[71] The College graciously provided Rosemarie and me with a two and a half room furnished flat in one of their neighbouring Victorian houses, and in spite of reduced pay, we felt well off.

Soon news of the Suez Crisis of July 1956 spread out, and disturbed everybody: Was Nasser a new Hitler? The president of Egypt, who had overthrown King Faruk, now nationalized the Suez Canal that was owned by British and French shareholders. Britain and France answered with armed intervention, which caused passionate reactions all over the commonwealth. The country was buzzing with fear of war, anxious and vehement controversies were expressed wherever you went. My father was glad not to find my name on *The Times* list opposing the government. However, under pressure from the USA President Eisenhower and the Russians, Britain and France had to compromise, and Prime Minister Anthony Eden resigned. After this crisis had calmed down, the Suez Canal was still blocked for a considerable time because of the bombing. New super tankers were built to transport the oil the long way around the Cape of Good Hope. A year later, I reported to the German weekly about the Iraq Revolution of 14th July 1958 when King Feisal was assassinated and Sadam Hussein began his ascent to power in the East.[72] Notwithstanding these events, we very much enjoyed these two stimulating years at Oxford.

Although the world for any length of time was never without challenges, disasters, natural or man made, crises or even wars, nor was my own life short of several serious health crises.[73] I became more observing, watchful, and contemplative rather than taking a minor part in political developments. I was, fortunately, always gainfully employed with work, lots of work that I mostly enjoyed. I stayed in contact with the College, and was awarded a Senior Fellowship in 1971. Whenever possible, it was always delightful to return to St. Antony's Gaudies, where I also gave the occasional talk. I developed and kept contact with German historians and with scholars in European history in Europe and North America. We'd meet personally or while attending conferences; sometimes I'd form these connection by giving talks or through reviewing their work. For many years, I contributed to The Economist and to G. P. Gooch's Contemporary Review. *Die Gegenwart* (the Present) regularly printed my comments on political developments with the introduction *Aus London wird uns geschrieben* (reports we receive from London).

After the Oxford years, I got a one-year temporary history lectureship at Liverpool University replacing a fellow who was on sabbatical leave. We found the atmosphere in Liverpool, despite the occasional thick yellow smog, very congenial and welcoming both at the University and in the town. There the department head had been David Quinn, who held the Andrew Geddes and John Rankin Chair in Modern History at the University of Liverpool.[74] He developed courses in Irish history, and was a fascinating and scrupulous researcher mainly of the English explorers, resulting in many publications. He and his wife Alison, a scholar and indexer in her own right, gave us great warmth, much help, and sound counsel. At the end of that year, and after several interviews, I got a permanent job as lecturer in modern German history at the University of Exeter, Devon. The campus lay on the beautifully treed Read estate, that had been a paper magnate's property just above the city.[75] Some years later, in 1968, I advanced to a senior lectureship with a salary of £1350 p.a. My courses covered Modern European History starting about 1500, Diplomatic Relations of the Great Powers 1815-1890 and the German Revolution 1848-1849.[76] In all this, I was generously supported by German and British Academic awards.[77] Over the years, I took part in various capacities in the University's growth and administration. I was an elected representative on the University Senate, became a member of the library committee, joined the Council and Senate Working Party on Teaching Accommodation, and served on the Arts Faculty Board and the History Panel for the Bachelor of Education. I was Secretary and then President of the Exeter Association of University

Teachers. In my specialized research, I concentrated on the Frankfurt Parliament 1848-1849. Besides with others, it led to a lively and helpful correspondence about source material with Dr. Rüdiger Moldenhauer at the German Bundesarchiv,[78] the result was my book published in 1968, which I dedicated to the memory of my father.[79] It also brought me the honor of being elected a Fellow of the Royal Historical Society, London, England. In the summer of 1967, in the Albany, the private residence of Edward Heath, I was part of a small circle of conservative academics to meet the shadow cabinet to discus the future of education.[80] I met and talked to Edward Heath again when he received an honorary Doctorate at the University of Calgary in 1991.[81] Close to the sea and Dartmoor we spent nine happy years in Exeter, where our two sons Andrew and George enriched our lives.

But by 1968 I had started to look around for further opportunities in other British universities; they were slow in reacting to references. We vaguely started to talk about Canada, when on 23rd March I received a letter from Professor William Norton Medlicott who through his work on Bismarck was a scholar-friend of my father's.[82] Earlier on in his career, Medlicott had taught at the University of Exeter and had become Stevenson professor of international history at the London School of Economics. He asked me whether I might be interested in a post at the newly founded University of Calgary, which had received its charter the previous year. Enclosed in the letter was a descriptive note from the Calgary Professor Frederick Heymann whose career and life had been shaped more by the history and conflict of our time than anything else.[83] Born in Berlin, he had become a teacher of Eastern European History and the Reformation, particularly the Hussites as his special interest. He had also been a refugee from Nazi Germany, and via the USA had come to the University of Calgary. He was a great admirer of my father and his work. Sharing many common interests he became a valued friend until his death in 1983.

Very quickly a confidential, lively, and helpful correspondence developed about an offer for a professorship in history for the 1969-1970 semesters. I asked to first have a look at Western Canada, a part of the world completely new to me.[84] I consulted Robert Spencer, Professor of History at the University of Toronto, whom I had met the previous year at the History Conference in London, England.[85] He had given me an inviting description of Canadian academic life that had made us curious. He wrote to me that the vast distances could easily, if exhaustingly, be overcome by modern air travel, that Calgary was a small but rapidly growing comfortable city, and that the University's "youngish staff by no means suffered from the lack of funds, and is evidently able to operate without political interference." According to my brother-in-law, Paul Alexander, a Byzantinist in Berkeley, California,[86] the institution was "an up and coming University." Thus encouraged and interested in "pioneering." I offered my service.

Not long thereafter on 1st May, Rosemarie answered the telephone, somebody at the post office read out a telegram with the invitation to a full Professorship at the University of Calgary and a salary of Can $17 500 p.a. for the academic year 1968/69. This equalled £6785 at the current exchange rate.[87] There would be a two-year probationary period, and after that, tenure and further merit increments would be granted if I wanted to stay. We very much liked the invitation and I accepted the professorship in German history. This professorship soon branched out into European and even World history, including the Ottoman Empire with its Caliphate. After a whirlwind confidential correspondence about the agreement for the new post, it took slightly longer and some needed prompting from my friend Derek Mitchell to obtain the legal documents for landed immigrant status in Canada.[88]

My mother reacted in firm support to this move, which also helped my parents-in-law accept the vast distances that would soon separate us. At our farewell party in Exeter, we left many good friends behind. Bobby (Robert) Melbourn, a Baptist Minister and senior lecturer in department of Philosophy, mentioned that it was appropriate for the author of Prince Albert to move to Alberta.[89] Meeting James Joll at Oxford, he wished us well, though he was slightly saddened at our leaving England. Having said good-bye to family and friends in our final two months before departing, we sailed on 7th August 1968 from Liverpool. On the sailing deck, just before we sailed, we received a surprising heart-warming farewell from the friends we had made during our short year there. David Quinn and Alec Meyer,[90] department heads of medieval and modern history and Hans Liebeschütz,[91] a Medievalist, came to the departure of the Queen Elisabeth, her last crossing of the Atlantic, to give us their sincere and warm wishes for following the "well-trodden path" to the New World.

After seven long days at sea – the four of us in a boat full of teachers serving all levels of education – we moored in Montreal after a stopover at Quebec City, which made a pre-French Revolution impression on us. In this lively and beautiful city, still full of exhibits from the World Fair of the previous year, we looked around for two days, sensing something of the tension between the British- and French-speaking populations. Then we took the 2367 miles (3743 km), 48 hour long train journey. The train went one whole day alone along Lake Superior, looking at nothing but the lake and boreal forest rising up on the Canadian Shield that already showed signs of the coming autumn. Only very occasionally would a glimpse of a simple cottage break the constant sight of wood and water. Then the train crossed a perfectly flat landscape, the prairie, stopping at many perfectly flat prairie towns with their giant grain elevators next to the railway tracks. Slowly, we advanced to our final destination. I described our experience and first impressions in letters to my mother.[92]

On 18th August 1968, to the great surprise of our boys at age four and a half and three, we stopped travelling; we had arrived at Calgary, the train station a bustling dusty building site, next to the just proudly opened Husky Tower. Balancing kids and luggage over swinging boards we were heartily welcomed by the department head John Toews, of Mennonite origin. He and his wife Lillian were very helpful in finding our feet in a startlingly new world.

Three days later, we bought a middle range, split-level-entrance house, at 6 Varbay Place, for $37 000 CDN. At half-a-year old, it counted as the oldest in the district. On day four, we bought a new car and a used car for Rosemarie. (It proved a good thing that just half a year ago we both had passed out driving tests.) Beyond the end of our cul de sac of only four houses started the prairie. The wooden framed houses, well equipped to withstand the extreme temperatures easily ranging between -40 to +30°C, were often painted in bright colours, and very different from European stone or brick buildings. We were astounded by the amount of comfort, fittings and amenities inside, by their use or misuse. There is always central gas heating, which in England was practically non-existent outside from London. We bought beds, and our vendor kindly lent us some garden chairs and a table until our furniture arrived, which happened to be during the first blizzard in November. Calgary, a prosperous and rapidly expanding city, with a population then of about 350 000 inhabitants, was full of building sites; her latest city map was and is always out of date. In 2006, her population has reached one million.

In our suburb, Varsity Village, all of the street names obstinately started with "Var." Our house was a ten-minute drive to the University at the northwest end of the city; it was too far to walk, however, mainly because of construction blocking the way and wind blowing up the powdery glacial silt that after weeks was reasonably quickly tamed by some top soil and grass surrounding the new houses.

As far as I was concerned, I had every hope of being

happy in Calgary. My new colleagues were very friendly. There was work for me to do, particularly in connection with the extension of post-graduate studies in German history. The history department with a staff of seventeen, including chairman and the senior professors, was still growing. The number of students at the University was about 5200, and also increasing. Further faculties and departments would be added. The province of Alberta directed a lot of money into her three universities. With the natural resources in the province, agriculture, surface coal, forestry, gas, tourism, and above all oil, Alberta is still one of the richest provinces in the country.

Shortly after I arrived, the department moved into the fourteenth floor of another new building, the Education tower. The elevator only went to the thirteenth floor at that time, but I did not mind walking one flight of stairs. I was, nonetheless, concerned about what happened when the lift broke down, which I was led to belief was known to happen. Once moved in, I had a large new office with a wonderful view of the town including the Husky Tower, one of the highest buildings in Canada at that time, where we had a meal in the revolving restaurant. I remember thinking that the library building was spacious with a staff of ninety librarians and library assistants. I was also pleased to see that there were airmail editions of *The Times* and *The Economist* as well as *Die Welt*, and so on. The University placed emphasis on serious research, and this was encouraged financially in various ways. During the week I kept office hours, there was always a lot going on. Secretarial help in the department was good, and there were grants for research and travel available. I hoped to and did attend the American Historical Association in New York between Christmas and the New Year. Flights of this kind were not in any way considered out of the ordinary.

Living, like in Exeter, in a part of the country attractive to tourists, we had our first day-excursion by car to the mountain-town of Banff, some 80 miles from Calgary, soon after settling

Professor Frank Eyck about 1976.

in. I remember taking a walk and having a picnic by Lake Minewanka to the enjoyment of all four of us. The wide-open plains, the foothills, and the Rocky Mountains were overwhelming. It might seem amusing now, but we could not quite understand why we were constantly overtaken by other cars while going 60 miles/h.

We socialized often with neighbors and faculty. We would visit in people's homes, while there would be some large parties at the Dean of Arts and Science house or the University. I got to know members of other departments; unfortunately there was no staff club. We made new friends, particularly with those who had come about the same time as us, and who had a similar background. But nearly everybody, or at least their parents, has an immigration-story to tell. We even met and made friends with a few people born in Canada. I enjoyed the teaching, conversing with colleagues, and sharing in administrative responsibilities.

One of the charms of my appointment here was that with the North American structure being less hierarchical than that in Britain or Germany, I did not feel that I was superseding anybody. Indeed, I had been made very welcome and had already been elected to the Board (Executive Council) of the Arts and Science Faculty thanks to the support of the History Department. The younger members of the department were pleased to have me there as I could help them with their research and writing in an informal way. I was also there to help them address problems that they may have with academic life in general: for instance, their teaching. After all, we all have to start, so I felt that I could play a useful part in this way. I also learned a lot from them and found out matters about Canadian and American politics and history, which was quite new to me.

The department was growing truly international; this applied in varying degree to the university as a whole. Many matters were in a stage of flux so that a newcomer could still have a prominent role. When I started teaching, I noted that the students were for the most part polite and friendly and determined to get on with the job. They thanked me for my teaching, considered it interesting and stimulating, especially when I took smaller groups. During my active time at the university, however, it suffered two financial crises: one in 1971-1972,[93] and the other one in the year of my retirement in 1987.[94] They were both overcome, but the latter one was more aggravating with lots of cuts; people were even asked to give five days unpaid holiday to help out. But none of this interfered with my historical research.

Soon after our arrival in the "New World," our old friend George Peabody Gooch died at the age of 94. His son Bernard asked me to write his father's biography. It was a task I gladly took on and which led me to many far-flung interesting places and people over a decade of researching for it.[95] Gooch had been a man of independent means who used that opportunity to become a historian, a shrewd observer and commentator of current affairs, and above all a Good Samaritan deeply interested in people. He knew how to help in matters large and small. During my research for this task, beside from others, I received much encouragement form my previous tutor, the Provost of Worchester College, Lord Briggs.[96] The resulting book *G. P. Gooch, A Study in History and Politics* was published in 1982 and dedicated to our sons Andrew and George, the latter had been named after G. P. Gooch and my uncle Jorg (a German form of George).[97] At the same time, I edited a volume on the German Revolution 1848-49 (1972). Also, on the request of his widow and the help of his son, I edited the posthumous work of Fredrick Herz, *The German Public Mind in the 19th Century* (1975), which was translated into English by Eric Northcott, as the last of a three volume series.

In due course I served as Chairman of the Library Committee, and over the years on the General Faculty's Council (the GFC), and the Senate. To further my research, I was thankful to receive several grants from the Canada Council, a Killam Resident Fellowship at the University of Calgary, and a year's Resident Fellowship at the Institute of Humanities.[98]

As citizenship played such an important part in my life, we applied in the summer of 1974 for Canadian citizenship and on 30th July all four of us were granted citizenship in a simple but meaningful ceremony, followed by a welcoming letter from the Secretary of State, J. Hugh Faukner.[99] We retained our United Kingdom citizenship, and now after Britain joined the European Union, we also belong to that wider field of European citizens.

While on my first sabbatical 1972-1973 spent in Abingdon, close to Oxford, I received a letter from my home university requesting me to look into the budding Inter-University Postgraduate Centre in Dubrovnik, founded in 1971. It sounded very intriguing, and all four of us went to see ancient Ragusa so that I might investigate this new project in the age-old seaport known as the pearl of the Adriatic. I attended the second meeting of the Council Centre on 26th-27th April 1973. During the course of this trip, I was also holding a watching brief for the University of Oxford.[100] Both universities were soon unanimously invited to become members of the Centre and they accepted the invitation.

I found the spirit of the meeting excellent. Its enthusiasm was great without minimizing the difficulties. It consisted of non-communist European Universities as well as universities from the Americas, with Yugoslavia as the only Communist state represented. Most participants at the Council regarded the Centre as a modest bridge between Communist and non-communist countries. I gave a lecture in the course of Philosophy of Science and Humanism and in History and Ethics with the title "Different Approaches to History; Value Judgements and Objectivity of Research."[101] For the present we had decided not to touch the complex Israeli and Arab problems, but in November 1974 I joined in a case study of the Arab-Israeli conflict, which was only part of the course on "Theories and Development, Conflict and Peace." My proposal for a colloquium between representatives of the Christian, Jewish and Islamic faiths in the following years did not bear any fruit;[102] I only had positive answers from the Evangelical Episcopal Bishop of Jerusalem, the Right Reverend Faiq Haddad, and the Right Reverend Aql I. My friend Hugh Myers, when I told him about this, remembered in a 1992 letter to me that: [103]

> At that time of the Palestinian fighting (of 1949) at the end of the British mandate, there was a small society formed in London – which didn't last very long, and had the rather grand name of 'The Jewish Society for Human Service.' Some of its leading figures were cousins of cousins or cousins in-laws of my mother's – Norman Bentwich, Harold Rubinstein and Victor Gollancz – and I was very keen on it and sometimes addressed envelopes in the small office that V. G. provided on his publishing premises. Basically it was a group of Jews who wanted to show that they sympathized with the Arabs too, believed in conciliation, and wanted to help both Arab and Jewish victims of the fighting. Many of the most moving letters, with donations actually came from committed Christians, who sympathized with the whole enterprise.

Ancient Ragusa/Dubrovnik had been an independent city-state since the eleventh century. During the Ottoman Empire, the city fathers just paid a ransom as a sort of tax to the Empire to keep their distance and their peace. The city was conquered by Napoleon but not destroyed and, from the 1815 Vienna Congress on, formed part of the Habsburg Empire until after the First World War when Yugoslavia under Tito came into being. Its people, mainly Croats, with a chequered and not entirely pleasant history, were not happy with their role in Tito's Yugoslavia. This may well be one of the reasons that they directed their glances beyond the confines of Yugoslavia.

The University of Zagreb played a leading part in the assertion of the Croat language and contributed to liberalization of conditions. Much of the credit for launching the Centre and of watching over its tender growth belongs to both Professor Orjar Oyen of the University of Bergen, Norway, who as chairman ran the Centre on a shoestring, and to the deeply committed former rector of the University of Zagreb, Ivan Supek, a nuclear physicist. He turned to philosophy after disagreement with the Yugoslav Federal Commission for Nuclear Energy because of his unwillingness to build an atomic bomb. He joined many peace efforts, including his membership in the International Pugwash Committee. While taking part in the congress on the Philosophy of Science in London, Ontario, in the August of 1975,[104] he also visited the University of Calgary, and gave a lecture on Science and Philosophy in her distinguished lecture series and conducted a seminar followed by discussion.[105] Politically, the success of the Centre was a matter of prestige for the Yugoslavs, to keep an open door to the West. Those of us who were fortunate enough to take freedom of speech and freedom from arrest for granted had a rare opportunity there to open that door a little bit further to the troubled and oppressed.

The Centre itself was comfortably housed in a former teachers-training college, built during Austrian rule, and had started to assemble a library. As a rule, English and German were the lingua franca; sometimes Serbo-Croat was used but was accompanied by an interpreter. A lot of work went into developing courses for post-graduate studies. The topics include development theories; international law and international relations; philosophy of science and ethics; mathematics; engineering; man and the environment; communications;

social service; and Adriatic history, as the city had an archive that for some 200 years had hardly been used and had not yet been catalogued. The practical questions like student fees, transportation, and accommodation in this holiday area would all be manageable. Fundraising was certainly always a topic. The beautiful city, with an outward looking attitude, was ideally suited as the meeting place of ideologies. For seven years, I served as Vice-Chairman of Council attending meetings two to three times a year at Dubrovnik and sometimes closer to home in Germany or Eastern USA. By the end of the 1970s, the Centre was well established in spite of two earthquakes in 1979, one of which I missed by 24 hours. Over many years, the University of Calgary has remained a member of the Centre, has contributed financially, and has lent teaching faculty, who always came home happy and enchanted by the beauty of the place as well as the stimulation they received and gave. Amazingly, the Centre also survived the civil war and the violent break-up of Yugoslavia when Dubrovnik became part of the Republic of Croatia. The city had been severely damaged from fierce bombardment by Serb artillery fire in 1992, but was soon reconstructed.[106] She displays again her old beauty and the Centre celebrated their thirtieth anniversary in 2001.[107] Both, Ivan Supek and Orja Oyen are still actively involved.

Between Christmas of 1977 and the New Year, during the proverbial blizzard, we moved some distance from Calgary into the Foothills, to live in a rather roughed up but beautiful cedar house on a half-acre lot in the hamlet of Bragg Creek. My family adored the firs and aspens surrounding our new home and the small creek that gave the hamlet its name flowing gently past – most of the time. After considerable alterations the house became a comfortable home for the four of us, our dog and cats, and last not least my library. The latter and all the other help I received enabled me to finish my study in German History.

In our new community I soon got to know Fr. Pat O'Byrne who had instituted the Interfaith Association that brought some of the different Christian denominations and the Jewish congregation together through active social work and enterprises. He was semi-retired and lived in Bragg Creek, but he was still Vicar of Higher Education in the Roman Catholic Diocese of Calgary and looked after the local Mission of St. Bosco. His masses were quite special; they included as a sermon, a dialogue with the reader of the lessons. This engaged the members of the congregation into deeper thought than usual, and the message stayed with them throughout the week.

The question of religious education in Southern Alberta had for some time been of concern to Fr. Pat's brother, Bishop Paul O'Byrne. The Bishop's interest soon brought me into closer contact with Fr. Pat.[108] We discussed the feasibility of a Theological College at the University of Calgary (U of C) that would include the Jewish community and as many Christian denominations as possible.[109] In frequent meetings, other ideas like a Christian or an Ecumenical Christian College, including the necessary financing, were considered.[110] In the draft of the guidelines for a Christian College at the U of C it was suggested that the College would become a meeting place for various denominations, could bring together clergy and laity from both within and without the campus, and should be of a high academic standard.[111] It could provide a congenial setting for dialogue between Christians and members of other religions or of no particular faith. Besides formal courses, seeking accreditation with the University, interchangeable between the University and the College, there would be conferences and informal discussions in a common room open to faculty and students as well as anybody who might be ʰterested.

ʰe paper was sent to the Dean of Humanities, the Head of ʰs Studies Department of the U of C, to the Diocese, the leaders of the Anglican, Lutheran, Presbyterian, and United Church as well as both School Boards. In due course, most of them took part in the meetings or sent observers. I served in different capacities on the Roman Catholic Higher Education Committee and the Ecumenical Christian College Committee. I stayed actively involved until 1981 when I resigned, but retained my interest in further developments of the project. These committees also had planned the establishment of a Chair of Christian Thought in the Department of Religious Studies that was to benefit both the University and the Christian College.[112] A lot of consultations had taken place, and advice was sought from other Canadian Universities and the wide range of independent denominational Colleges; many of them were glad to share their experience. However, any realization of these plans proved to be difficult, and would certainly take a long time to bear fruit. But the outcome was quite different. However, the Chair of Christian Thought at the U of C was granted in 1984.

Two years later, under pressure from the educational needs of the Separate (Catholic) School Board teachers, the Roman Catholic Higher education Committee founded St. Mary's College. To begin, it found suitable accommodation in the Inter-faith Lacombe Centre in Midnapore, at that time still outside the south end of the City. At the same time it tried to negotiate affiliation with the U of C;[113] even though the University's Faculty of the Humanities had passed series of resolutions opposing "Affiliation agreements with religious colleges or seminaries." The department of Religious Studies strongly opposed affiliation, while the provincial cabinet supported the idea. But the final decision rested with the General Faculty Council whose majority argued against, though the faculty of Education, under certain conditions, was in favor of it.[114] The discussion carried on until 1991, when the U of C decided not to proceed.

After receiving a Charter (1985) and Provincial Legalization

George, Frank, Rosemarie, Andrew Eyck 1985

(1986), St Mary's College was established in 1987 and enjoyed the support of the existing Protestant Colleges. In 1991, it added a liberal Arts College, and became affiliated with St. Francis Xavier University of Nova Scotia. Since the year 2000, it has run full-time programs of study. Four years later, it was able to grant Bachelor of Arts degrees and calls itself St. Mary's University College, with nearly 600 students at present and eighty full or part time staff.[115] It enjoys electronic communication with the libraries of the U of C and the Alliance and Nazarene University College in downtown Calgary.[116] Although there is no official affiliation, the three academic institutions do attempt to coordinate when possible for the betterment of their students.

In the meantime my family had grown up. Only officially,

as my son George pointed out, did I retire from teaching in the history department in 1987. There was, however, an elaborate lunch given in my honour by the department with speeches referring to my life and work, conveying good wishes and giving me useful presents. In a quieter moment, Norman Wagner, the president of the University, said to me that he could not comprehend what it must mean and feel like when one's own government deprives his citizens of their rights and sense of belonging. Although now called Professor "emeritus," I certainly did not stop researching and served a further four years of part-time teaching and gave the occasional lecture. I kept my connections with my schools though membership with the Collegianer Verein of the French school, in Berlin, the Old Pauline Club, London, the Oxford University Society, Worchester and St. Antony's College. I have the honour to be mentioned in several dictionaries and works of reference,[117] where I was asked for my curriculum vitae and my personal philosophy.[118] To the International Biography Centre, Cambridge, England, I wrote:

> I believe that only acceptance for their acts by the persecutor, and in response in a spirit of reconciliation on the part of the victim, can be overcome the inter-ethnic and inter-religious hatred from which the world is still suffering.

As a baptized German-Jewish refugee I did what I could to help post Nazi Germans to come to terms with their history, in lectures and writing. I kept in touch with the Jewish people from whom I am descended through the lifelong membership of the Society of Friends of the Leo Baeck Institute, London England. In the first quarter of 1999, I gave a series of weekly lectures at the Calgary Jewish Centre on the history of Jewish-Christian relations. Pursuing further historical research I gave lectures on specific topics. These were talks at the University of Calgary and the Nazarene College in town. On 9th June 1998, in appreciation of my efforts, the Order of the University of Calgary was bestowed on me, an honor I was glad to accept.

Our home gave us ample room to offer hospitality to our friends, and, whenever possible, to our widely dispersed family. Fairly regularly we enjoyed celebrating my birthday. As it fell conveniently in the summer months, we could make full use of the grounds. On my eightieth birthday, like my father, who greeted my mother that special morning: *Liebste, ich hab's geschafft*, I was happy to now also say to Rosemarie: "Darling, I have managed it." The festivities started with my very independent cousin Vera Rosenheim, from Corpus Christi, Texas, now in her ninetieth year, the daughter of Hans Eyck, staying with us ten happy days, while her daughter and her husband Mark Wormser toured the Rocky Mountains. In the afternoon of the 12th July, Jean and Michael Alexander, Professor of history at the University of Chicago, Illinois, the youngest son of my sister Eleanor (living in Berkeley, California), arrived with Peter Reuter, Professor of public policy and criminology at the University of Maryland, son of Irene (living in Sydney, Australia). Jean, Michael's wife and a librarian, soon noted that it was quite an achievement to have so many Eyck's under one roof.

After drawn out breakfasts and lunches, walks along our creek and river or on the hill behind the house, the close family celebrated the actual birthday, Friday 13th July, with a dinner at the Bragg Creek Trattoria. The next day there was a reception with friends at the University Club, and on Sunday with local friends and neighbours and their children, offering a buffet at our house and garden. There were always speeches with thanks for a long life and its work. Andrew and George performed a roast. Sheila Gow with her beautiful alto voice sang the hundredth psalm. As often before, our close neighbours Emma and Hazel Forman, whom we saw growing up, performed an accomplished Scottish dance on the sunny grass. Among all of our guests there was neither a shortage of topics for conversation nor lack of general enjoyment of the occasion. There were lots of cards and congratulations from our local alderman Linda Fox-Mellway, our MLA Janis Tarchuk, and the Premier Ralph Klein, accompanied with the Alberta's coat of arms *"fortis et liber."*[119] I was moved and deeply thankful for a long life and the ample support from many sources.

Although I was forced to leave Germany while still a youth, her history had become my main field of research. I always stayed interested in her, and particularly in Flensburg where, in a minor way, I had been actively involved. I learned about a visit to the editorial office paid by Peter de Mendelssohn on 29th July 1946 shortly after my departure.[120] Mendelssohn reported that he found the editors vigorously debating the Danish question, one of them being a Dane, and that the recent elections had resulted in a Danish majority in this district. The discussion got so heated and noisy that nobody noticed when Mendelssohn quietly left the room. In his protocol he described them as "arrogant, self-serving, senseless and puffed up group of people which had not suffered much but nevertheless constantly complained, and tried to prove their democratic attitude." However, not so much later the Dane left the editorial staff. Franz Suchan wrote to me that:

> The Flensburger Tageblatt developed well, even within its basically welcome pro-German course, as the town lies so close to the border with Denmark, the paper is sometimes rather nationalistic.[121]

After the many even belligerent confrontations between the two sides, the Bonn-Copenhagen Declaration of 29th March 1955 solved the minority problem on the principle of counter-pledge and counter-security.[122] After wars, suppression of minorities, animosities and chicaneries, it was a long way until the dominating nationals accepted the minority not as a foreign body but as a cultural enrichment in their midst. "They have become neighbours without problems."

The *Flensburger Tageblatt* certainly survived the various storms, and is one of the few remaining newspapers from post-war era; it even flourishes today. Very soon after it reached independence, it came under the editorship of Georg Macknow, who was not born in the region, therefore kept his impartiality in the frequent local controversies.[123] Above all he was somebody with professional experience. He started serving the small towns by using headlines and articles of local interest on the front-page, while the rest of the paper was more or less the same as for all editions. He took care of interest groups like the farmers' association. The *Flensburger Tageblatt* paid attention to classified announcements; by and by it gave them more space, and it eventually took over other papers that had specialized in this and other fields. It now belongs to a big corporation that owns the large rotary press in Rensburg supplying the whole of Schleswig-Holstein, publishing several different newspapers. In January 1995, fifty years after receiving the licence, a young lady journalist, Iris Gorße-Kleiman, visited us on behalf of the Schleswig-Holstein Newspaper Publishing-House in our home in Bragg Creek.[124] Well prepared, Iris interviewed me extensively as one of the men of the first hour. It was enjoyable to visit the past with somebody young and interested. Soon her reportage appeared as an extra-publication of the *Flensburger Tageblatt*, which had a good reception among its readers.

The year 1995 offered many occasions to remember the end of Second World War. The German history institutes held conferences referring to "50 years and after." *Die Stunde Null* (the Zero Hour) involved many contemporaries, I had sent some of my relevant material to one of them, Sir Julian Bullard. [125] He was on his way to Germany when with great interest he read my papers, stating that he was only sorry that we had not met as undergraduates. It had not been long ago that we attended a most successful dinner of the Calgary branch of the Oxford society. It was one of those evenings when everybody found it difficult to part. Sir Julian, who had given the address, had enjoyed a prominent diplomatic career, serving in Austria at the time of "*The Third Man*,"[126] and in many Middle-East counties, as well as in Russia and twice in Bonn.

To our surprise and delight, it did not take long that an invitation to myself and Rosemarie arrived, and that preparations started for our week long visit to Flensburg, all expenses paid by the publishing house. We departed on 23rd March 1995 from Calgary. We were treated in a princely manor, and stayed in Glücksburg, a few minutes drive or a slightly longer walk to Flensburg in a splendid hotel overlooking the Fjord. The reason being, besides a celebration for the fiftieth anniversary of receiving the licence, was that on 28th March I was asked to give the formal address for the opening of the new editorial office in the city of Kiel, located right opposite the Provincial Diet Building.[127]

The festivity was attended by the politicians from Schleswig-Holstein, the Burgomaster of Kiel, dignitaries from the university and commerce as well as Party representatives, all carefully listening to my presentation. After a short historic overview of the local and general development, I was glad to say that the recovery of Western Germany happened much faster then myself or anybody else had expected. My remarks were well taken up, with considerable interest and without hostility. In the discussion no attempt was made to offset the Nazi crimes with allied bombing. Great sympathy was shown for me as a victim of persecution and an appreciation that I advocated a constructive attitude to Germans and Germany during my activity at the British military press control. For me, to give a public address in Germany was of particular benefit, to answer questions and discuss in German, my native language, was a return to my roots. The Lady Minister Heide Simonis, besides others, congratulated me on my talk. She was most impressed that my talk was aimed at mature thinkers, not the usual superficial, easily-digested speeches that generally characterized such events.[128] At the reception, an owner of the Kiel wharf confirmed, from his childhood experience in Hamburg, my impression that the British occupation was well received. On 4th May, with an introduction, nearly the whole of my talk appeared in Kieler Nachrichten. In my correspondence with the historian Alan Bullock, who wrote the first Hitler biography, he commented on 22nd January 1996:[129]

> There can be few cases in history of such recovery as Germany has made. From 1890 to the end of World War II, Germany made just about every mistake that was possible and ended with a crash which few other large nations have experienced. This was followed by fifty years in which they have not put a foot wrong, emerging as the strongest nation in Europe with the readiness to lead the move towards a more effective European union.

Late into the night Chef Editor of the Kiel office, Stephan Richter, drove us safely through a severe rainstorm back to Glücksburg. The storm, however, could not stop our conversation. He told us that he had been apprenticed to Gerhard Becker, who had since died, and who had told his trainees that he was ashamed of what he had written in the Nazi period. While Becker was editor, he strictly adhered to reporting news. Only once did he break this self-imposed rule; he wrote a comment on the murder of Israeli athletes during the Munich Olympics 1972.[130] This was confirmed by his daughter Jutta Becker-Iverson and his grandson Gerhard, with whom we met the following sunny afternoon.[131] Gerhard Becker had suffered deeply from the deception the Nazi propaganda.

On the first afternoon in Glücksburg we were visited by Renate Hensel, one of the Suchan daughters, who as a teenager had spent several weeks with us in our home in Exeter. She had since married, and with her pastor husband they braved another of those vicious North-German storms to reach us. Because of this, it turned out to be a rather shortened but nevertheless memorable reunion. On the other days of our visit, I attended an editorial meeting as of old. I also gave an interview to the Nordwest Deutschen Rundfunk; I was introduced as one of "the men of the first hour." We had tea with Klaus May, the manager of the Schleswig-Holstein Publishing House in Flensburg. We attended a debate at the Provincial Diet. Iris drove us to visit the Danish Royal Castle of the Glücksburg-Sonderburg branch. With Stephan Richter, late at night, we visited the large and very modern printing centre at Rensburg just when printing had started and the different papers were all coming out mechanically sorted and bundled up. I gave a lecture followed by discussion at the University of Flensburg: "The Germans and their History," and there were people in the audience who still remembered me from my work in 1945-1946.

The visit was most enjoyable. As human words and actions can cause destruction, so they equally can lead to reconstruction. In this way the visit had a healing effect on me. This healing was confirmed back home in Calgary when, during treatment, my massage therapist said, "Frank, you let go of something." Mind and body are connected more than generally thought. It is a wonderful thing when deep scars from past injustices – ignored and half forgotten – can be made to disappear.[132]

Frank Eyck,
Christmas, 1995

Endnotes

1   Frank Eyck papers, F. Lys to Frank Alexander (Eyck), 29th September 1945.

2   Frank Eyck papers, L.G. Duke to Frank Alexander (Eyck), July 1946, revised 14th December 1946.

3   Frank Eyck papers, Frank Alexander (Eyck) to the Hon. MP Wilson Harris, 20th July 1946. Harris also wrote, *The Daily Press, 1943* and *The Problem of Peace,* (both, Cambridge England: Cambridge University Press, 1944).

4   Frank Eyck papers, Wilson Harris to Frank Alexander (Eyck), 23rd October, and a note from the Home Office from 27th Oct. 1946.

5   Frank Eyck papers, Copies of the following documents of the British National Archive.

6   Frank Eyck papers, Frank Eyck to Rudolf Lill, 8th February 1984; Frank Eyck to Michael Neufeld, 24th May 2001.

7   For a younger generation it may be difficult to comprehend the enmity or at least the suspicion that had been sown between Aryans and Jews by the Nazis thorough their racial teaching.

8   Frank Eyck papers, Frank Eyck to Rudolf Lill, 8th February 1984. Before the war, on walks though the Tiergarten, my father and I sometimes met Staatssekretär a.D.(außer Diensten) Kempner and Burgomaster Elsas, while greetings were exchanged, we occasionally engaged in short conversations. Wilhelm Kosch, Biographisches Staatshandbuch, Bd. I .p. 287, the Elsas and Heuss families enjoyed a long-standing friendship.

9   Theodor Heuss, *Nachzeichnungen, Profile aus der Geschichte,* (Stuttgart: Rainer Wunderlich Verlag, Hermann Leins, 1964), pp. 299ff.

10 Ibid. p. 403.

11 Frank Eyck papers, Frank Eyck to Michael Neufeld, 24th May 2001. This letter also contains information on their conversation about Werner von Braun.

12 Frank Eyck papers, Germany, summer 1946, Taken from a memorandum of six pages and about 3123 words.

13 Hans Ulrich Wehler, *30th January 1933, Ein halbes Jahrhundert danach,* (Article on Politik und Zeitgeschichte Beilage zur Wochenzeitung *Das Parlament,* ISSN 0479-611 X, B 4-5/83, 29th Januar 1983), pp. 43-44.

14 Frank Eyck paper, Frank Eyck to Franz Suchan, 14th October, 9th November 1946, 8th February, 2nd April, 27th May, on 6th June 1947, an attempt was made for me to help out at the children's hostel of Herrmann Neuton Paulson on Süderoog, which did not come off.

15 Frank Eyck papers, Max Pick to Frank Alexander (Eyck), 10th April 1947.

16 Frank Eyck papers, letter mainly from the Schmidt and Suchan family, from 1946 onwards.

17 When Berlin was totally cut off from the outside, Britain and the USA had the will and the means to regularly fly into Tempelhof Airport, Berlin, to supply the city. The pilots often risked their lives in what, after all, was peace time.

18 Frank Eyck papers. The following is taken from Worcester College Records (Oxford), 1995, and a letter by Franz Suchan, 8th February 1947.

19 Frank Eyck during my travels on Greyhound Buses in the USA visiting family and friends, my article appeared in the, *Geneva Daily Times*, USA 22nd July 1948.

20 Frank Eyck papers, H. V. Fitzroy Somerset, April 1949, testimonial.

21 John Cecil Masterman, *The Double Cross System in the World War of 1939-1945*, (London: Yale University Press 1972).

22 Compline, the last of the canonical hours of prayer includes the hymn:
Before the ending of the day, Creator of the world we pray,
That with thy wonted favour thou wouldst be our guard and keeper now.
From all ill dreams defend our eyes, from nightly fears and fantasies;
Tread under foot our ghostly foe, that no pollution we may know.
O Father, that we ask be done, through Jesus Christ, thine only son;
Who, with the Holy Ghost and thee, doth live and reign eternally.

23 Frank Eyck papers, Lionel Butler, testimonial 14th February 1949. Dr. L. B. Butler, *The London Times*, Obituary 26th November 1981.

24 Frank Eyck papers, British War Diaries, 16th Leaflet unit (WO 171 13805). J. B. Cartland to Frank Eyck, 12th June 1947. Frank Eyck to Klaus Wagner, 16th December 1992, p. 3.

25 Ibid, p. 5-6.

26 Alfred C. Mierzejewski, *Ludwig Erhard, a Biography*, (Chapel Hill: University of Northern Carolina Press, 2006), pp. 27.

27 Adolf M. Birke, *Nation Ohne Haus, Deutschland 1945-1961*. John E. Rodes,

Germany a History, (New York: Holt, Rinehart and Winston, 1964), p. 568 ff, 645 ff.

28 A. M. Birke, *Nation ohne Haus*, pp. 116-119.

29 David Crew, *Germany's Victims,* (Austin: University of Texas, 1997).

30 Michael L. Hughes. *Shouldering the Burden of Defeat, West Germany and the Reconstruction of Social Justice,* (Chapel Hill: University of Northern Carolina Press 1999).

31 Frank Eyck, *Germany, Defeat and Reconstruction, a Personal View,* talk for History 493, 23, Department of History University of Calgary, 28th Mach 2003.

32 *Aviso, Informationsdienst der deutschen Gesellschaft für Publizistic und Kommunikationswissenschaft.*

33 Frank Eyck, report about the trip to Germany on behalf of the BBC German Service, 12th to 22nd June 1950, 4494 words. As the Press Card shows I went on another mission, 29th September - 29th October but did not keep a record.

34 Frank Eyck, Frank Ericson (my pen-name as the BBC would not permit the use of one's actual name for political articles.) Bevin's remark is quoted in my article in *Time and Tide*, August 1950, "Germany and the West."

35 Aldolf M. Birke und Eva Mayring, *Britische Besatzung in Deutschland*, Akten Erschließung und Forschungsfelder 1987, p. 38. Bevin is quoted: " . . . we must fight the battle for the soul of Germany. If we deprive ourselves of the forces for this purpose (and the adequate staff) we shall lose the battle." April 1948.

36 Adolf M. Birke, *Die Bundesrepublik Deutschland, Verfassung, Parlament und Parteien*, Enzyklopädie Deutscher Geschichte, Band 41, Kapitel A und B, Oldenburg 1997.

37 Frank Eyck article in the *Contemporary Review*, November 1951, *Neo-Nazies in Western Germany,* pp. 264-270.

38 Hans-Ulrich Wehler, *30th January 1933 – Ein halbes Jahrhundert danach.* Aus Politik und Zeitgeschichte, Beilage zur Wochenzeitung: *Das Parlament,* ISSN 0479-611 X, B 4-5/83 29th January 1983, pp. 44 ff. This includes an analysis of the different interpretations of Fascism, the idea of a national socialist Doppelstaat and Revisionismus.

39 Adolf M. Birke, *Nation ohne Haus 1945-1961*, pp. 99 ff.

40 John E. Rodes, *Germany, a History*, pp.631-633.

41 Frank Eyck papers, Frank Eyck, preliminary report on the SPD Dortmund Conference September 1952. Also, a private talk, personal and confidential and a discussion meeting at the Royal Institute of International Affairs, Chatham House; London, by invitation only, (8 pages, 4910 words), *The Dortmund Conference and the Future Policy of the Social Democratic Party*, 15th October 1952. Article in the *Contemporary Review*, November 1952: *Parties in Western Germany*, pp. 272-276.

42 Schuman, Declaration of 1953.

43 Frank Eyck papers, Frank Eyck, Royal Institute of International Affairs, Private discussion Meeting 15th October 1953 at Chatham House: *The Federal German Election and After*. This and some of the other documents were slightly modified by the editor, mainly by changing the tense, to fit into the different context, but as much as possible is given verbatim.

44 Frank Eyck papers, Frank Eyck, talk for History 493, 28th March 2003: *Germany Defeat and Reconstruction, a Personal View*, pp. 7-8.

45 Alexander Stahlberg, *Die Verdammte Pflicht, Erinnerungen 1932 – 1945*, (Berlin: Ullstein Verlag, 1987).

46 Christopher R. Browning, *Ordinary Men, Reserve Police Battalion 101 and the Final Solution in Poland*, (New York: Aaron Asher Books, 1992, Harper Collins Publishers).

Bernhard Schlink, *Der Vorleser*, (*The Reader*), (Berlin: Diogenes Verlag, 2000).

47 Günther Grass, *Crabwalk*, 2006. (translated by Winston Krichna, Orlando: Harcourt,

2002).His long silence about his short involvement in the SS shows who difficult it is to come to terms with the deep scars and the guilt that every German carries within him who lived through this period of history. One cannot escape the part played by one's country in good and bad days.

48 Our good Friends Hans von Herwardt von Bitterfeld, Ambassador to Moscow, at the time when agreements with the UDSR made and broken, London and Rome, had some Jewish blood from his mother's side of the family, is a striking example of this. About his experience in the Moscow Embassy he wrote, *Against Two Evils*, (London: Macmillan, 1981).

49 Frank Eyck papers, Frank Eyck talks to History 493, *Germany, Defeat and Reconstruction*, p. 7.

50 Frank Eyck papers, Frank Eyck, Invitation: *Come to Brighton with the Hampstead Young Conservatives 1954.*

51 Frank Eyck papers, Henry Brooke, MP to Frank Eyck, 18th October 1954.

52 Frank Eyck papers, Karl Leyser to Frank Eyck, 3rd June 1989, 28th August 1990. Karl Leyser, obituary, *The London Times,* 30th May 1992.

53 Concise Dictionary of Etymology, from Jack Worlton, *"religio"* etymologically stems from *religare*, re-'again' and *ligare* 'to bind'. Religion is that to which we are strongly bound. But we have many bonds, so there could be many religions. Religion has evolved in a belief and reverence for a Power regarded as the Creator of the Universe."

54 Adolf Birke held the prestigious chair in modern history at the university of Munich. We frequently met during my research trips, in Bayreuth (University) near Bamberg and vicinity, as well as in München and Halle/ Saale where his wife Sabine is professor in English literature.

55 Frank Eyck papers, correspondence with Professor Rudolf Lill, 1982-2003.

56 Lothar Bossle, Professor of Political Science, Würzburg University, whom I had met a year earlier, in Fulda during the German visit of John Paul II attending the pontifical mass at the grave of St. Bonifacius. Bossle kindly arranged this visiting professorship for me in 1982.

57 Frank Eyck papers, Killam Resident Fellowship (Calgary), January to April 1978; Harold Coward, Director of Calgary Institute for the Humanities, to Frank Eyck, 3rd March 1985. Frank Eyck's Statement of Proposed Research. Frank Eyck to Harold Coward, 15th August 1986, Harold Coward to Frank Eyck, 18th and 28th September 1986. 1981 May-June German Academic Exchange Service Award.

58 Frank Eyck papers, correspondence with Frank and Christine, Lord and Lady Judd 1966 to 2002. On Lord Judd see: Who is Who 1992, p. 1007.

59 Frank Eyck papers, John May to Frank Eyck, 20th April 2001, 18th May, 15th July 2001, Frank Eyck to John May, 5th May, 23rd July 2001.

60 Frank Eyck papers, John Suggit letter to Frank Eyck, Frank Eyck to John Suggit, May 2001.

61 Frank Eyck papers, Ken Green to Frank Eyck, 5th March 1945.

62 Frank Eyck papers, John Garnett, letter to *The Times,* 30th March 1973.

63 Will Praetorius, *Konturen der Erinnerung, Ein Lebensbericht,* (Düsseldorf: Presseverband der Evangelischen Kirche im Rheinland, 1969-70), p. 59.

64 Frank Eyck papers, Theodor Heuss to Erich Eyck, 24th November 1955; 18th January 1956.

65 Schäffer being Jewish immigrated to Sweden, where he became director of the Swedish Matchstick Company. His brother, who had been a close friend of my father-in-law, was killed on the German side in WWI; Rosemarie remembers his photo from her father's library.

66 Die Gegenwart, 1st November 1958, *Nur ein Anfang*, on the State visit of President Heuss, the article is unsigned, but written by Frank Eyck

67 Theodor Heuss, *Tagebuchbriefe, Briefwechsel mit Toni Stolper*, (widow of Gustav) 1955-1963, (ed. Eberhard Pikart, Tübingen und Stuttgart: Rainer Wunderlich Verlag, Hermann Leins, 1970).

68 Frank Eyck papers, Erich Eyck to Erhard and Helene Schmidt, 12th December 1958, in answer to his congratulation for Erich Eyck's 80th birthday: ". . . Über den Verlauf der Festlichkeiten werden Ihnen die Kinder berichten (this includes the state-visit of President Heuss in Britain) wenn sie Sie Weihnachten besuchen. Der deutsche Botschafter von Herwarth, der ein kleines Treffen im Freundeskreis für uns gab, nannte Rosemarie eine alte Bekannte, da ihr Bild auf dem Schreibtisch seiner Frau stehe, es ist natürlich 'Heuss's letzter Walzer.' "

69 St. Antony's College founded in 1950, as a gift of Antonin Besse of Aden, a merchant of French descent. The College developed into a flourishing centre of advanced study and research in the fields of modern history, philosophy, economics, and politics. It provides an international centre within the Oxford University where graduate students from all over the world can live and work together, directed by senior members of the University who are specialists in their particular field of interest. C. S. Nicholls, *The History of St. Antony's College Oxford 1950-2000*, (Wilshire: Anton Rowe Ltd, Chippenham, 2000).

70 Frank Eyck papers, Sir William Deakin, first warden of St. Antony's to Frank Eyck, 15th May 1956.

71 Frank Eyck, *The Prince Consort, a political biography of Prince Albert*, (Cambridge: Houghton Mifflin Company, 1959), dedicated to my father and teacher. The German translation carries the title *Prinzgemahl Albert von England*, (Erlenbach-Zürich and Stuttgart: Eugen Rentsch Verlag, 1961).

72 *Die Gegenwart*, 9th August 1958. England nach Feisal, this article appeared

unsigned.(n. 664)

73 Frank Eyck papers, Frank Eyck to Erika Rasner, 1ˢᵗ December 2002.

74 David Beers Quinn 1900-2002, *The Voyages and Colonising Enterprises of Sir Humphrey Gilbert* (1940), *The Roanoke Voyages 1584-1590* (1955), *The Patent Granted to Sir Walter 1584* (1955), *Ethnography of Northern America 1611* in the watercolour collection of John White (1964), *The English New England Voyages 1602-1608* (1983). He made much archival material available in document volumes. He was a giant among specialists in the history of discovery and exploration. Obituary, *The Guardian,* 6ᵗʰ April 2000.

75 Exeter started as a Roman town in 50 AD, became a walled city by 200 AD, and in the twelfth century after many turns of fortune a cathedral city. The Exeter University was founded in 1955.

76 Frank Eyck papers, Frank Eyck, Personal Details, 1968.

77 Frank Eyck papers, 1962 German Academic Service Award (Deutscher Akademischer Austausch Dienst) and 1963 British Academic Award, both for research on the Frankfurt Parliament 1848/49, see also Dictionary of International Biography.

78 Frank Eyck papers, Correspondence with the German Bundesarchiv mainly Dr Rüdiger Moldenhauer, 1963-1968.

79 Frank Eyck, *The Frankfurt Parliament 1848-1849*, (Toronto: Macmillan, New York: St. Martin's Press, 1968). The German translation by Thomas Eichstätt carries the title, *Deutschlands Große Hoffnung*, (München: Paul List Verlag),1973.

80 Frank Eyck papers, Edward Heath MBE, MP PM to Frank Eyck, 17ᵗʰ August 1965. Frank Eyck to Edward Heath, 26ᵗʰ June 1970, Edward Heath to Frank Eyck, 16ᵗʰ July, and December 1970.

81 Frank Eyck papers, Frank Eyck to Edward Heath MP, 24ᵗʰ May 1991. MP. E. Heath to F. Eyck, 30ᵗʰ May 1991.

82 Frank Eyck papers, William Norton Medlicott to Frank Eyck, 23ʳᵈ March 1968. William Norton Medlicott, (1900-1987), lecturer at Swansea, 1926-39, Professor of history at Exeter, 1939-53, London School of Economics 1939-53, special studies of international relations of the Bismarck era and diplomatic history in the twenieth century.

83 Frank Eyck papers, Friedrich (Friedel) Heymann note of 14ᵗʰ March 1968. Frederick Heymann (1901-1983) born in Berlin, Ph.D. Frankfurt/Main,

worked for Frankfurter Zeitung, published in German, Czechoslovak, and British newspapers, emigrated to the USA, taught at the Fieldston School in New York (1947-1956), spent a year at the Institute of Adavanced Studies in Princeton N.J., Professor of History, Calgary, Canada, until 1973, specialised in the Reformation, published, *John Zizka and the Hussite Revolution*, also article on *George of Bohemia, King of Heretics*. Friedel Heymann to Frank Eyck, 5th, 26th May and 26th June 1973.

84 Frank Eyck papers, Frank Eyck to Friedel Heymann, 26th March 1968. F. Heymann to F. Eyck, 26th April 1968.

85 Frank Eyck papers, Frank Eyck to Robert Spencer, 30th March 1968.

86 Frank Eyck papers, Paul Alexander to Frank Eyck, 20th April and 6th May 1968. Frank Eyck to Paul Alexander, 24th May 1968.

87 Average exchange rate 1968 £ 1= can$ 1.5792.

88 Frank Eyck papers, Derek Mitchell to Frank Eyck, 13th May 1968, Frank Eyck papers contain a lifelong correspondence about the development of our careers and family life.

89 Frank Eyck papers, Donald Hudson to Frank Eyck, 15th May 1977, 10th December 1977; Frank Eyck to Donald Hudson, 14th January 1975. W. Donald Hudson, *The Question is/ought Question*, Macmillan 1969.

90 Frank Eyck papers, Alec Meyers to Frank Eyck, 12th December 1969. Frank Eyck to Alec Meyers, 13th February 1970. A.Meyers to F. Eyck, 25th May 1972. A. Meyers, (1912-1980), English Historical Documents 1307-1485 (1969*); History of England in the Middle Ages*; in *The Pelican History of England*, Vol. IV, (1952). Obituary, *The Times*, 9th July 1980.

91 Hans Liebeschütz, 1883-1978, Medieval Historian and Philologist, *Medieval Humanism in the Life of John of Salisbury*, (London: Studies of the Warburg Institute, University of London, vol. 17, 1950). In Schriftenreihe wissenschaftlicher Abhandluingen des Leo Beack Instituts, *Das Judentum im deutschen Geschichtsbild von Hegel bis Max Weber*, (Tübingen: J. C. B. Mohr, Paul Siebeck, 1967), Leo Baeck Yearbook XII. Lehmann Hartmut und Otto Oexle eds, *Nationalsozialismus und Kulturwissenschaft,* Gespräch mit Wolfgang Liebeschütz (Sohn) und andere, *Nationalsozialismus in der Kulturwissenschaft,* (Tübingen: Vandenhoek & Ruprecht, Gespräche: Wissenschaftliche Emigration in England, 2004), Band 2, im Anhang pp.

413ff; Frank Eyck on Erich Eyck (1878-1963), Bd, 2 pp. 513ff,. My talk on Erich Eyck was only read at this meeting as I was unable to attend.

92 Frank Eyck papers, Frank Eyck, excerpts of my letters to my mother 8th September, 6th October, and 13th October, 1968.

93 Frank Eyck papers, Frank Eyck to Peter Lougheed, 20th May 1972, Peter Lougheed to Frank Eyck, 19th June 1972.

94 Frank Eyck papers, Frank Eyck to Irene and Reu Reuter, the Ides of March, 1987.

95 Frank Eyck papers, Frank Eyck to Charmian Brinsin, 26th January 1997.

96 Frank Eyck papers, Asa Briggs correspondence with Frank Eyck 1959-1982.

97 Frank Eyck, *G. P. Gooch: A Study in History and Politics*. 1982. P. G. Gooch, a Summary in *New Dictionary of National Biography*, Clarendon Press, Oxford 1999.

98 Frank Eyck papers, Killam Resident Fellowship (Calgary), January to April 1978.

99 Frank Eyck papers, J. Hugh Falkner to Ulrich F. J. (Frank) Eyck, August 1974.

100 Frank Eyck papers, Frank Eyck, confidential report on the Inter-University Centre of Post-Graduate Studies to the University of Calgary, Abingdon, Berkshire, 7th June 1973, 1st January 1979, 8th June 1979 and 18th April 1980 to Vice-President Academic Dr. Peter Krueger and 5th December 1979, to Dr J.B.Hyne, Dean, Faculty of Graduate Studies. Confidential Report to Ernest Enns, Department of Mathematics and Statistics U of C, 14th September 1992. The text is composed from these reports. The minutes are also in the hands of the present representative, the International of the Centre of University of Calgary and in Dubrovnik.

101 Frank Eyck papers, Frank Eyck to Ivan Supek, 9th September 1974. Ivan Supek to Frank Eyck, 13th December 1974, 3rd March 1975.

102 Frank Eyck paper, Frank Eyck to Bishop Faiq Haddad, Jerusalem, 20th November 1974.

103 Frank Eyck papers, Hugh Meyers to Frank Eyck, 6th December 1992; Frank Eyck papers contain a lifetime correspondence of this friendship.

104 Frank Eyck papers, Ivan Supek to Frank Eyck, 23rd August and 13th December 1974.

105 Frank Eyck papers, Preparation for the visit and lecture of Ivan Supek, September 1975, Ivan Supek to Frank Eyck, 23rd August 1974; F. Eyck to D. L. Mills, and associate Dean R. G. Weyant, 20th August, 23rd September 1974.

106 Frank Eyck papers, Frank Eyck, 14th September 1992 letter to Ernest Enns, Associate Vice-President Academic, and Vice-President A Peter Krüger, as well as International Centre of the U of C.

107 See Inter-University Centre Dubrovnik, www.iuc.hr/g.member.php.

108 Frank Eyck papers, unsigned memorandum, *Introduction*, 1979.

109 Frank Eyck papers, The Rev. Patrick (Pat) B. O'Byrne: confidential Memorandum, 7th June 1979.

110 Frank Eyck papers, Ernst McCullough, Excerpt from a talk given at the inaugural meeting to research the possibility of establishing a Christian interdenominational College in Calgary, 12th September 1979. Frank Eyck notes, 26th October 1979. R. C. Higher Education Committee, 8th and 12th November. Fr. John Kelly, c.s.b (congregation of St. Basil) on visit to Calgary, 16th November 1979. Further discussion paper unsigned. R. C. Higher Education Committee, 6th and 20th December 1979. Catholic College Committee, 10th and 17th January 1980. P. R. Barth, Medicine Hat Catholic Board of Education, to Frank Eyck, January 1980. Frank Eyck to P. B. Barth, 30th January 1980. Ecumenical Christian College Committee, 24th January, 20th February, 23rd April. Catholic Committee for Higher Education, 28th May, 5th June 1980.

111 Frank Eyck papers, Proposal for Christian College at the University of Calgary, 18th September 1979.

112 Frank Eyck papers, Draft, Policy of Christian Thought Chair, by Fr. Pat O'Byrne and Frank Eyck, 12th November 1979, Frank Eyck papers.

113 *Calgary Herald*, 27th December 1986, p. 5, copy in Frank Eyck papers.

114 Ibid.

115 For St. Mary's University College, see http://www.stmu.ab.ca/aboutUs/

116 Alliance and Nazarene University College renamed itself Ambrose University College in 2007 and now has a new campus in southwest Calgary as of 2008

117 *Man of Achievement, England*, (4th Ed., Cambridge University, 1974).

Dictionary of American Scholars, (8th Ed., Tempe, AZ, Jaques Cattell Press, 1982). *Dictionary of International Biography,* vol., 17, 1980, and Vol. 18, 2000, Cambridge, UK). *International Who is Who in Community Service,* (2nd Ed., 1976, 3rd Ed. 1978, Cambridge: IBC) *Who's Who in the West,* (15th Ed., 1977, Chicago) mention me as "Outstanding Scholar of the 20th century."

Frank Eyck papers, Frank Eyck, 12th September 2000, Mr. Grifford, at IBC refers to me as among "2000 ~ Outstanding Intellectuals of the 20th Century."

Frank Eyck papers, Official congratulations, 13th July 2001, by Premier of Alberta Ralph Klein, our MLA Janis Tarchuck, and Alderman Linda Fox-Mellway.

Peter de Mendelsohn Deputy Controller, Press, ISC Branch, Public Record Office Kew (Richmond) London FO 372/55516 (C11778/59/18)

Frank Eyck papers, Franz Suchan to Frank Eyck, 14th October 1946.

Die Zeit, article by Professor of History Karl Christian Lammers in Copenhagen, 31, April and 4th August 1995: Nachbarn ohne Problem, neighbors without problems] in memory of the 75th anniversary of the North-Schleswig plebiscite.

Wolf Gehrmann, Dissertation, Kiel 1993, *Britische Presse und Informationspolitik in Schleswig-Holstein 1945-1949*, pp. 389-390.

Flensburger Tageblatt, 25th and 29th March 1995.

Frank Eyck papers, Julian Bullard to Frank Eyck, 24th August 1993, 3rd May 1995.

The Third Man is the title of a popular film of 1949, of the time of the Russian occupation of Austria, reflecting the problems of the looming Cold War.

Flensburger Tageblatt, 29th März 1995, p. 4.

Minister Heide Simonis complimented me on my talk , added: *Es war eine Rede fuer Erwachsene und nicht wie ueblich fuer'n Kindergarten,* which I rather liked.

Frank Eyck papers, Sir Alan Bullock to Frank Eyck, 22nd January 1996. Alan Bullock, *Hitler, A Study in Tyranny,* (London: Book Book,1952).

Frank Eyck papers, Frank Eyck, talk for History 493, *Germany Defeat and Reconstruction.*

131 Frank Eyck papers, Gerda Becker to Frank Eyck 30th June 1995, Frank Eyck 10th July and 4th November 1995. Gerda Becker died 16th October 1995.

132 Frank Eyck papers, CBC Interview, *Mountain Top Music*, 9th November 1996, a survey of my life.

Acronyms

AA	Allied Army.
ABCA	Army Bureau of Current Affairs.
ACA	Allied Control Authority.
ACC	Allied Control Commission.
ADG	Allgemeiner Deutscher Gewerkschaftsbund.
AGB	Army Education Corps.
AG	Aktien Gesllschaft.
AHC	Allied High Commission, and Command.
AMPC	Auxiliary Military Pioneer Cops.
ATS	Auxiliary Territorial Service, women's Royal Army Corps.
BAOR	British Army on the Rhine.
BBC	British Broadcasting Corporation.
BHE	Bund der Heimalvertriebenen.
BWP	British Way and Purpose.
BPW	British Prisoner of War.
CAC	Central Advisory Council.
CCG(BE)	Control Commission for Germany (British Element.).
CDU	Christian Democratic Union.
CIC	Commander in Chef, (MI5 Military Intelligence).
CPGH	Communist Party of Great Britain.
CV	Centralverein Deutscher Staatsbürger Jüdischenn Glaubens.
DBR	Deutsche Bundes Republik (Federal Republic of Germany)
D-Day	6th June 1944.
DDR	Deutsche Demokratische Republik (German Democratic Republic).
DDP	Deutsche Demokratische Partei.

DDPR	Deputy Director of Public Relations.
DGB	Deutscher Gewerkschafts Bund.
DMG	Deputy of Military Government of USA.
DPR	Director of Public Relations.
DNB	Deutscher Nachrichten Dienst.
DPD	Deutshcer Presse Dienst.
EDC	European Defence Community.
EVG	Europäische Verteidigungsgemeinschaft.
FDP	Freie Demokratische Partei.
FO	Foreign Office (British).
GESTAPO	Geheime Staatspolizei.
GB	Great Britain.
GNS	German News Service.
HMG	His or Her Majesty Government.
HO	Home Office (British).
HSL	Hier spricht London.
HQ	Head Quarters.
ISD	Independent German Studies.
KPD	Kommunistische Partei Deutschlands.
Lt.	Lieutenant.
LT.Col	Lieutenant Colonel.
ME	Middle East.
MP	Member of Parliament.
NCC.	Non-combated Corps.
NCO	Non commissioned Officer.
NSDAP	Nationalsozialistische Demokratische Arbeiterpartei.
NSKK	Nazianlsozialistischer Kraftfahrer Korps.
PC	Pioneer Corps.
PM	Prime Minister.
POW	Prisoner of War.
PPE	Politics Philosophy Economics.
P&PW	Publicity and Psychological Warfare.
PPU	Peace Pledge Union.

PTW	Powered Two Wheeler.
PWD	Psychological Warfare Division.
PWE	Political Warfare Executive.
RAF	Royal Air Force.
RAG	Delmer's quarters, the Rookery at Absey Guise.
RAMC	Royal Army Medical Corps.
SD	Himmler's Sicherheits-Dienst.
SHAEF	Supreme Headquarters Allied Expeditionary Forces.
SOE	Special Operation Executive Section V.
SOGA	Control Office for Germany and Austria (in London).
SPD	Sozialdemokratische Partei Deutschlands.
SRP	Sozialistische Reichs-Partei.
SS	Hitler's paramilitärische Organisation, Schutz Staffel.
PR/ISC	Public Relations/ Information Service Control Group.
PR	Public Relations.
PRO	Public Record Office.
PTW	Powered Two Wheeler.
TCO	Traffic Control Officer.
UK	United Kingdom.
UNO (UN)	United Nations Organisation.
USA	United States of America.
USSR	Union of Soviet Socialist Republic.
VE	Victory Europe.
VJ	Victory Japan.
WOSB	War Office Selection Board.
Waffen SS	Military Arm of Himmler's Elite Corps.

Bibliography

Addison, Paul. *The Road to 1945*. London: Jonathan Cape, 1975.

——— . *Churchill on the Home Front*. London: Pimlico, 1993.

Adenauer, Konrad. *Erinnerungen 1945-1963. Fragmente*. Paderborn, Siedler,1961.

Andrew, Christopher, & David Dilke, eds., *The Missing Dimensions,Government and Intelligence Communities in the Twenties Century*. Chicago: University of Illinois Press, 1985.

Angell, Norman, and Dorothy Buxton. *You and the Refugees*. London: Penguin Special, Paperback, 1939.

Attlee, Clement. *The Social Worker*. London: G. Bell, 1920.

——— . *The Will and the Way of Socialism*. London: Methuen, 1935.

——— . *As it Happened*. New York: Viking Press, 1954.

Bach, Steven. *Leni, The life and Work of Leni Riefenstahl*. London: Faber & Faber, 2007.

Baeck, Leo. *Das Wesen des Judentums*. New York, 1974.

Balfour, Michael Leonard Graham. *Propaganda in Wars. Organisations, Politics and Publicity in Britain and German*. London: Routledge & Kegan Paul, 1979.

Barkow, Ben. *Alfred Wiener and the Making of the Holocaust Library*. Portland, OR: Vallentine Mitchell, 1997.

Barnetson, William, Lord. "The Rebuilding of the German Press 1945-46," *Journalism Studies Review,* (June 1978).

Bendt, Veronika. *Wegweiser durch das jüdische Leben in Berlin*. Berlin: Geschichte und Gegenwart, 1987.

Bentwich, Norman. *I Understand the Risks. The Story of the Refugees from Nazi-Oppression who Fought in the British Forces in the Second World War*. London: Victor Gollancz, 1950.

Bering, Dietz. *Der Name als Stigma. Antisemitismus im Deutschen Alltag*. Stuttgart, Klett-Cotta, 1987; translated by Neville Plaice, Ann Arbor: University of Michigan Press, 1992.

Bickersteth, John. *Bickersteth Diaries 1914-1918.* Introduction by John
Terraine. London: Leo Cooper, 1995.

Birke, Adolf, and Eva Mayring, eds., *Britische Besatzung in Deutschland,
Aktenerschließung und Forschungsfelder.* London: Deutsches Historisches
Institut, 1987.

——— . *Nation ohne Haus, Deutschland 1945-1961.* Berlin: Siedler
Taschenbücher, Goldhammer Verlag, Verlagsgruppe Bertelsmann, 1998.

——— . *Die Bundersrepublik Deutschland, Verfassung, Parlament und Parteien.*
Oldenburg: Encyklopädia Deutscher Geschichte, Band 41, Kapitel A und
B, 1997.

Briggs, Asa. *BBC: The First Fifty Years.* London: Oxford University Press. 1985.

——— . *The History of Broadcasting in the United Kingdom.* London: Oxford
University Press, 1979.

——— . *The War of Words, The History of Broadcasting in the United Kingdom,*
Vol. 3. London: Oxford University Press, 1970.

Birn, D. S. *The League of Nations Union 1918-1945.* Oxford: Clarendon Press,
1981.

Brinson, Charmian. "Im politischen Niemansland der Heimatlosen,
Staatenlosen, Konfessionslosen, Portemonaielosen. Otto Lehmann-
Russbüldt in British Exile, German-speaking Exiles in Great Britain." In
*München: The Yearbook of the Research Centre for German and Austrian Excile
Studies,* Vol. 1, 1996.

Bower, Tom, and André Deutsch. *The Pledge Betrayed.* New York: Doubleday,
1981.

Browning, Christopher. *Ordinary Men, Reserve Political Battalion 101 and the
Final Solution in Poland.* New York: Aaron Asher Books, Harper Collins,
1992.

Bullock, Alan. *Hitler. A Study in Tyranny.* London: Book Book, 1952.

Bunsen, Victoria de. *Charles Roden Buxton. A Memoir.* London: George Allen
& Unwin, 1948.

Burgess, Anthony. *Little Wilson Big God.* New York: Grove Weidenfels, 1987.

Chappell, Connery. *Isle of Barbed Wire.* London: Robert Hale, 1988.

Churchill, Winston. *War-time Speeches.* Washington, DC: Churchill Centre.

Clapham, J. H. *The Economic Development of Germany and France 1815-1914.*

London: Cambridge University Press, 1961.

Cooper, Duff. *Old Men Forget*. New York: Dutton, 1954.

Crang D. S. *The British Army and the People's War, 1939-1945*. Manchester: Manchester University Press, 2000.

Cresswell, Amos and Tow, Maxwell. *Dr. Franz Hildebrandt: Mr. Valiant-for-Truth*. Macon, GA: Smyth & Helwys Publishing, 2000.

Crew, David. *Germany's Victims*. Austin: University of Texas, 1997.

Crossman, Richard Howard Stafford. "Psychological Warfare." *The Journal of the Royal Service Institution* 47, no. 587 (August 1952).

Cruickshank, Charles. *The Fourth Army, Psychological Warfare 1939-1945*. London: Oxford University Press, 1979.

Dancy, John. *Walter Oakeshott. Adversity of Gifts*. Norwich: Michael Russell, 1995.

David, Anthony. *The Patron, a Life of Salman Schocken, a Complex Institution Builder, 1877-1959*. New York: Metropolitan Books, 2003.

Davison, W. P. H. *Die Blockade von Berlin*. Translated by Hans Steindorff. Frankfurt/Main: Alfred Meltzer Verlag, 1960.

Delmer, Sefton. *Black Boomerang*. London: Viking Adult, 1961.

Dibelius, Otto. *Ein Christ ist immer im Dienst*. Stuttgart: Kreuz Verlag, 1961.

Dickens, Arthur Geffrey. *Lübeck Diary*. London: Victor Gollancz, 1947.

Durzak, Manfred, ed., *Die Deutsche Exilliteratur 1933-1945*. Stuttgart: Philip Reclam jun., 1973.

Eckstein, Modris. *Limits of Reason, The German Democratic Press and the Collapse of the Weimar Democracy*. London: Oxford University Press, 1975.

Eliot, T. S. *Idea of a Christian Society*. London: Faber & Faber Ltd., 1939.

Eyck, Erich. *Die Arbeitslosigkeit und die Grundlagen der Arbeitslosen-Versicherung*. Frankfurt/Main: Sauerländer, 1899.

——— . "Der Vereinstag Deutscher Arbeitervereine 1863-1868." Ph.D. diss., Berlin University, 1904.

——— . *Die Krise der Deutschen Rechtsplege*. Berlin:Verlag für Kulturpolitik, 1926.

——— . *Gladstone*. Tranlslated by Gerhard Miall. London: Allen & Unwin Ltd., 1938. Originally published as *Gladstone (*Erlenbach-Zürich: Eugen Rentsch Verlag 1938).

———. *Bismarck*, 3 Vols. Erlenbach-Zürich: Eugen Rentsch Verlag , 1931, 1943, 1944.

———. *Die Pitt's and Die Fox*. Erlenbach-Zürich: Eugen Rentsch, 1946.

———. *Das Persönliche Regiment Wilhem II. Politische Geschichte des Deutschen Kaiserreiches von 1890 bis 1914*. Erlenbach-Zürich: Eugen Rentsch Verlag, 1948.

———. *History of the Weimar Republic*, 2 Vols. Translated by Harlan P. Hanson, and Robert G. L. Waite. Cambridge: Harvard University Press, 1962 & 1963. Originally published as *Geschichte der Weimar Republik* (Erlenbach-Zürich: Eugen Rentsch), 1956.

———. *Auf Deutschlands politischen Forum. Meine politische Lehrmeister*. Erlenbach-Zürich: Eugen Rentsch Verlag, 1963.

Eyck, Frank. *The Prince Consort, a Political Biography*. Cambridge: The Riverside Press, 1959.

———. *The Frankfurt Parliament 1848-1849*. London: Macmillan, 1968.

———. *The Revolution of 1848-49, Evidence and Commentary*. Series Editors: C. M. D. Crowder, L Kochan. Edinburg: Oliver & Boyd, 1972

———. *G. P.Gooch. A Study in History and Politics*. London: Macmillan, 1982.

———. *Religion and Politics in German History*. London: Macmillan, 1998.

Faulhaber, Michael Kardinal von. *Judentum, Christentum, Germanentum, Adventspredigten*. München: Verlag der Graphischen Kunstanstalt A. Huber, 1933.

Freeman, Simon, and Simon Penrose., eds. *Conspiracy of Silence. The secret Life of Anthony Blunt*. London: Graften Books, 1986.

Fest, Joachim C. *Hitler*. New York: Vintage Books, 1975.

Frayling, Christopher. *Ken Adam and The Art of Production Design*. New York: Faber & Faber, 1988.

Furness, N. A. "The Morale Imperative of Exile: Otto Lehmann-Russbüldt's Mediation for Victims of Nazi Persecution." In *Between Two Languages: German-speaking Exiles in Great Britain 1933-1945*. Edited by William Abbey, Charmian Brinson, Richard Dove, Marian Malet, and Jennifer Taylor. Stuttgart: Akademischer Verlag, 1995.

———. "Otto Lehmann-Russbüldt: The Forgotten Prophet of a Federal Europe." *England? Aber wo liegt es? Deutsche und Oesterreische Emigranten in Grosbritanien 1933-1945.* Ed. by Charmian Brinson, Richard Dove, Marian Malet and Jennifer Taylor. München: Iudicum, 1996.

Garnett, Maxwell. The World's Need of the Church's Help. *League of Nations Union, London: League of Nations Union.* Speech delivered 19th April 1926 in the Central Hall, Westminster.

Gehardt, Bruno. *Handbuch der Deutschen Geschichte.* Vol. IV, Stuttgart: Klett & Cotta.

Gehrmann, Wolf. "Britische Presse und Informationspolitik in Schleswig-Holstein 1945-1949." Ph.D. diss., Christian Albrechts University, 1993.

Gerteis, Klaus. *Sonnemann, Ein Beitrag zur Geschichte des demokratischen Nationalstaatsgedanken in Deutschlan,* vol.1, Frankfurt/Main: Waldemar Krämer, 1969.

Gillmann, Peter and Leni. *Collar the Lot! How Britain Interned and Expelled its War Time Refuge.* London: New York, Quarter Books, 1980.

Goethe, J. W. von. *Italienische Reise. Bd.II.* In *Goethe's sämtliche Werke.* Jubiläumsausgabe in 42 Bänden. Edited by Eduard Heinrich von der Hellen and Konrad Burdach. Stuttgart: Cotta, 1902-1907.

———. *Faust II*, Act 1. In *Goethe's sämtliche Werke.* Jubiläumsausgabe in 42 Bänden. Edited by Eduard Heinrich von der Hellen and Konrad Burdach. Stuttgart: Cotta, 1902-1907.

Gollwitzer, Helmut. . . . *und führen wohin du nicht willst.* München: Beck, 1952 and Gütersloher Verlag, 1994.

Grass, Günther. *Crabwalk.* Translated by Winston Krichna. Orlando: Harcourt, 2002.

Gräter, Karl-Heinz. "Theodor Barth's politische Gedankenwelt, Ein Beitrag zur Geschichte des entschiedenen Liberalismus." Ph.D. Diss., Julius Maximilian Universität, 1963.

Hanfstängl, Ernst. *The Missing Years.* London: Eyre & Spottiswood, 1957.

———. *Zwischen Weißem und Braunem Haus, Memoirs eines politischen Außenseiter.* München: Piper, 1957.

Harris, Wilson. *The Daily Press.* Cambridge: Cambridge University Press, 1943.

———. *The Problem of Peace.* Cambridge: Cambridge University Press, 1944.

Hecht, Ingeborg. *Als unsichtbare Mauern wuchsen. Eine Deutsche Familie unter den Nürnberger Rassegesetzen.* Hamburg: Hoffmann & Campe, 1984.

Heilborn, Ernst. *Zwischen Zwei Revolutionen.* Berlin: Elsner, 1927.

Herwarth von Bitterfeld, Hans von. *Against Two Evils.* London: Macmillan, 1981.

Heuss, Elli. *Ausblick vom Münsterturm.* Stuttgart: Rainer Wunderlich, 1961.

Heuss Theodor. *Der Mann, das Werk, die Zeit.* Stuttgart: Rainer Wunderlich, 1934 and 1947.

———. *Vorspiele des Lebens: Jugenderinnerungen.* Tübingen: Rainer Wunderlich, 1953.

———. *Nachzeichnungen, Profile aus der Geschichte.* Stuttgart: Rainer Wunderlich, 1964.

Heymann, Friedrich. *John Ziska and the Hussite Revolution.* Princeton, NJ: Princeton University Press, 1955.

Hindenburg, Paul von. *Aus meinem Leben.* Leipzig: Hirzel, Leipzig, 1929.

Hitler, Adolf. *Mein Kampf.* Translated by J. J. G. Alexander, and T. Gibson. Oxford: Clarenden Press 1976.

Holländer, Albert E. J. "Offiziere und Prälaten." Beitrag zur Bischofs Conferenz, Mitteilungen des Österreichischen Staatsarchivs, August 1945.

Hoffmann, Peter. *The History of the German Resistance 1933-1945.* Translated by Richard Berry. Montreal: McGill-Queen's University Press, 1996. Originally published as *Widerstand, Staatsstreich, Attentat. Der Kampf der Opposition gegen Hilter* (München: Piper, 1969).

Howe, Ellic. *The Black Game.* London: Michael Joseph, Fortuna, 1982.

Hudson, W. Donald. *The Question is/ought Question.* London: Macmillan, 1969.

Hughes, Michael L. *Shouldering the Burden of Defeat: West Germany and the Reconstruction of Social Justice.* Chapel Hill, NC: University of Northern Carolina Press, 1999.

Isay, Rudolf. *Aus meinem Leben.* Weinheim/Berg str. Chemie, 1960

Joung, Louis de. *German 5th Column in the Second World War.* London: Routledge & Kegan Paul, 1956.

Kettenacker, Lothar. "Britische Besatzungspolitik im Spannungsvehältnis von Planung und Realität." In Adolf Birke, and Eva Mayring, eds., *Britische Besatzung in Deutschland, Aktenerschießung und Forschungsfelder.* London: Deutsche Historische Institut, 1987.

Klaußmann, A. O., ed., *Kaiserreden. Reden und Erlasse, Briefe und Telegramme Kaiser Wihelms des Zweiten. Ein Charakterbild des Deutschen Kaiser.* Leipzig: J. J.Weber, 1902.

Kochan, Miriam. *Britain's Internees in the Second World War.* London-Basingstoke: Macmillan Press, 1983.

Koestler, Arthur. *The 13th Tribe, The Khazar Empire.* Chapter VIII, Race and Myth, New York: Random House, 1976.

Laqueur, Walter. *Generation Exodus.* Waltham, Mass.: Brandeis University Press, 2000.

Lehmann, Hartmut & Otto Gerhard Oexle, eds. *Nationalsozialismus in der Kulturwissenschaft.* Band 2, Göttingen: Vandenhoeck & Ruprecht 2004.

Lerner, Daniel. *Sykewar, Psychological Warfare against Nazi German. From D-Day to VE-Day.* Cambridge, Massachusetts: M.I.T. Press, 1971.

Lessing, Theodor. *Der Jüdische Selbsthaß.* Berlin: Zionistischer Bücher-Bund, 1930.

Levinstein, Kurt. *Zur Feier des 260th Jährigen Bestehens des Französischen Gymnasiums, Fondé 1689.* Berlin: Graphische Betrieb W. Büxenstein GmbH, 1949.

Liebeschütz, Hans. *Medieval Humanism in the Life of John of Salisbury.* London: Warburg Institute, University of London, 1950.

Lill, Rudolf, and Heinrich Oberreuter, eds., *"Portrait des Widerstandes." Biographisches–Bibliographisches Kirchenlexikon.* Düsseldorf/Wien: Traugott Bautz, 1984.

Lindenborn, Ernst. *Colligny.* Berlin: Quadriga Verlag, J. Severn, 1985.

Lockhart, Robert Bruce. "Political Warfare." *The Journal of the Royal Services Institutions* 45 (May 1950).

Lorant, Stephan. *I was Hitler's Prisoner.* London: Victor Gollancz, 1935.

Lowenthal, Ernst G. for Veit-Simon. *Juden in Preussen, Biographisches Verzeichnis. Ein representativer Querschnitt.* Edited by D. Reimer. Berlin: Bildarchiv Pressischer Kulturbesitz, 1981.

——— . *Herrmann Veit-Simon zum Gedächtnis, 8th May 1856 to 16th July 1941.* Berlin: privately printed, 1956.

McCabe, Alan. *Rawsthorne, Portrait of a Composer.* London: Oxford University Press, 1999.

Mackanzie, Paul. *S. P. MacKenzie.* Oxford: Clarendon Press, 1992.

Machtan, Lothar. *The Hidden Hitler.* New York: The Perseus Book Group, 2001.

Maehl, William H., and S. William., eds., "Erich Eyck." In *Essays on Eminent Europeans, Some 20th Century Historians.* Chicago: University of Chicago Press, 1961.

Maier, Mathilde. *All the Gardens of my Life.* New York: New York 1983. Originally published as *Alle Gärten meines Lebens* (Frankfurt/Main: Knecht, 1978).

Maier, Max Hermann. *Ein Frankfurter Rechtsanwalt wird Kaffepflanzer im Urwald von Brasilien.* Frankfurt/Main: Joseph Knecht, 1975.

——— . *In uns verwoben tief und wunderbar, Erinnerungen an Deutschland 1938-1975.* Frankfurt /Main: Joseph Knecht, 1972.

Manasse, Ernst Moritz. *Historical Miniatures.* New York, Viking Press, 1940.

Masterman, John Cecil. *The Double Cross System in the World War of 1939-1945.* New Haven and London, Yale University Press, 1972.

Melone, Henry O. *Adam Trott zu Solz, Werdegang eines Verschwörers 1909-1938.* Berlin: Siedler, 1947.

Meyer, Joseph and Erich Ütrecht. *Meyers Orts- und Verkehrs Lexikon des Deutschen Reichs: Mit 15 Stadtplänen, 19 Umgebungs- und Übersichtskarten, einer Verkehrkarte und vielen statistischen Beilagen.* Vol. II. Leipzig, Bibliographisches Institut, 1913.

Mielke, Siegfried. *Der Hansabund für Gewerbe, Handel und Industrie 1909-1914.* Göttingen: Vandenhaeck & Ruprecht, 1976.

McFarland, Robert, B. "Elective Divinities: Religious Conversion im Exil, and die *Apologia pro vita sua*, als Beitrag zur Exilliteratur." Provo, UT: Birmingham Young University Press Provo, 2001.

Mierzejewski, Alfred C. *Ludwig Erhard, A Biography.* Chapel Hill, NC: University of Northern Carolina Press, 2006.

Möller, Kurt, Detlev. *Geschichter der Kapituation von Hamburg.* Hamburg: Hoffmann und Campe,1947

Montagnes, Ian. "Uncommon Fellowship. The Story of Hart House." Master's thesis, University of Toronto, 1969.

Montefiore, Hugh. *On Being a Jewish Christian.* London: Hodder & Stoughton,

1998.

Moorhause, Roger. *Killing Hitler, the Plot, the Assassins, and the Dictator who Cheated Death*. New York: Bantam Books, 2006.

Morgan, Janet., ed., *The Backbench Diaries of Richard Crossman*. London: Hamish Hamilton, 1981.

Morrison, Herbert. *Herbert Morrison, an Autobiography*. London: Oldham Press, 1960.

Müller, Joseph, and Ulrich Chaussy. *The White Rose: Student Resistance Against Hilter, München 1942/43*. München: White Rose Foundation, 1991.

Nicholls, C. S. *The History of St. Antony's College Oxford 1950-2000*. Chippenham, Wiltshire: Anton Rowe Ltd., 2000.

Niemöller, Martin. *Vom U Boot zur Kanzel*, Autobiography, Berlin: M. Warneck, 1934.

Niewyk, Donald L. *Solving the Jewish Problem – Continuity and Change in German Antisemitsm 1871-1945*. Leo Baeck Year Book XXXV, published for the Institute in London: Jerusalem, NY: Secker & Warburg, 1990.

Oakeshott, Walter A. *Founded upon the Sea*. Cambridge: Cambridge University Press, 1942.

Ollmann, Helgo. *Die Rundfunk Situation in der Bundesrepublik Deutschland Vergangenheit, Gegenwart und Zukunft. Rundfunk im 3. Reich*. Retrieved in September 1997 from http://home.wtal.de/ollmann/ RUNDFUNKSITUATION/RUNDFUNKSITUATION.htm

Pauker, Arnold, *Der Jüdische Abwehrkampf gegen Antisemitismus und Nationalismus in den letzten Jahren der Weimar Republik*. Hamburg: Leibniz, 1969.

———— . *Searchlight on the Decline of the Weimar Republic*. London: Leo Baeck Yearbook XIII, published for the Institutes in London. Jerusalem, NY: Secker & Warburg, 1968.

———— ., ed,. *Deutsche Juden im Kampf um Recht und Freiheit*. Einführung von Reinhard Rürup, Berlin: Hentrich & Hentrich, 2004, Veröffentlichung des Leo Baeck Instituts.

Pechel, Rudolf. *Deutscher Widerstand 1933-1945*. Zürich-Erlenbach: Eugen Rentsch, 1947.

Perry, Warren. *A Biography of Professor Richard Samuel 1900-1983*. Melbourne,

Australia: University of Melbourne, 1997.

Praetosius, Will. *Konturen der Erinnerung. Ein Lebensbericht.* Düsseldorf: Presseverband der Evangeschichen Kirche im Rheinland, 1969-70.

Pugh, Martin. *Hurrah for the Blackshirts: Fascists and Fascism between the Wars.* London: Jonathan Cape, 2005.

Rathenau, Walther. *Staat und Judentum, Eine Polemik,* vol. 1, Gesammelte Schriften. Berlin: S. Fischer, 1918.

Richarz, Monika., ed. *Jüdisches Leben. Selbstzeugnisse zur Sozialgeschichte im Kaiserreich.* Stuttgart: Deutsche Verlagsanstalt Veröffentlichung des Leo Baeck Institutes, 1979.

———. *Jüdisches Leben in Deutschland 1918-1945.* Stuttgart: Deutsche Verlagsanstalt, Veröffentlichung des Leo Baeck Instituts, 1982.

Ricketts, Albert. "WWII The Peoples' War. Operation Oyster, Part 2." BBC program, 17th January 2005, http://www.bbc.co.uk/ww2peopleswar/ user/67/u1256867.shtml

Riegner, Gerhart. *Ne Jamais Désespérer, Soixante Années au Service du Peuple Juif et des Droits de l'Homme.* Paris: Cerf, l'histoire à juif, 1998.

Riggs, Bryan Mark. *Hitler's Jewish Soldiers.* Kansas City, KS: University Press Kansas, 1984.

Röder, Werner & Herbert A. Strauss, eds. *Biographisches Handbuch der deutschen Emigranten nach 1933, International Biographical Dictionary of Central European Emigrés 1933-1945.* 3 Vols. München: Saur, Vol. I.

Rodes, John E. *Germany, a History.* London: Holt, Rinehart, and Winston, 1964.

Röhl, John C. G. *Kaiser Hof und Staat. Wilhelm II und die deutsche Politik.* München: C.H. Beck, 1987.

Rosenstock, Werner. *The Refugees, some Facts and Britain's New Citizen.* In Manfred Durzak, ed., *Die Deutsche Exilliteratur 1933-1945.* Stuttgart: Philip Reclam jun., 1973.

Schlabrendorff, Freiherr Fabian von. *Offiziere gegen Hitle.* Zürich: Europa Verlag, 1953.

Schöneberner, Gerhard. *Der Gelbe Stern, Die Judenverfolgung in Europa 1933 bis 1945.* Hamburg: Rütten & Loening, 1960.

Schwarz, Max. *MdR Biographisches Handbuch der Reichstage.* Hannover: Verlag für Literatur und Zeitgeschichte GmbH, 1965.

Portmann, Heinrich. *Cardinal von Galen, the Lion of Münster.* Translated by Russell Luke Sedgwick. London: Jarrold, 1957.

Selwyn, Francis. *Hitler's Englishman: The Crime of Lord Haw Haw.* London: Penguin Books Ltd., 1987.

Sillanpoa, Wallace P., and Robert G. Weisbord. "The Baptized Rabbi of Rome: The Zolli Case." *Judaism* 38, no. 149 (Winter, 1989).

Simion, Heinrich. *Leopold Sonnemann, seine Jugendgeschichte bis zur Entstehung der Frankfurter Zeitung. Zum 29th October 1931.* Privately printed at the Frankfurter Societät-Druckerei, 1931.

Simpson, A. W. Brian. *The Highest Degree of Odious.* Oxford: Clarendon Press, 1992.

Spengler, Oswald. *Untergang des Abendlandes,* 3rd ed. München: C.H. Beck, 1923.

Stahlberg, Alexander, *Die Verdammte Pflicht, Erinnerungen 1932-1945*, Berlin: Ullstein Verlag, 1987.

Stent, Ronald. *A Bespattered Page.* London: André Deutsch, 1980.

Stolper, Gustav. *This Age of Fables. The Political and Economic World we Live in.* New York: Reynak & Hitchcock, 1941.

Stolper, Toni, *Ein Leben im Brennpounkt unsere Zeit*, Stuttgart: Rainer Wunderlich, 1970.

Trimborn, Jürgen. *Leni Riefenstah:. A Life.* Translated by Edna McCow. London: Faber & Faber, 2007.

Vierhaus, Rudolf., ed., *Das Tagebuch der Baronin Spitzemberg. Aufzeichnungen aus der Hofgesellschaft des Hohenzollernreiche.* Göttingen: Vandenhoeck & Ruprecht, 1960.

Velder, Christian. *300 Jahre Französisches Gymnasium Berlin.* Berlin: Nicolaische Verlagsbuchhandlung, 1989.

Vossberg-Rau, Editha. *Namenlose.* Stuttgart: Engelhorn, 1926.

Wikozaczuk, Wladyslaw. *Enigma: How the German Machine Cipher was Broken and How it was Read by the Allies in WWII.* London: Arms and Armour Press, 1984.

Wehler Hans Ulrich. "30th January [1933]. Ein halbes Jahrhundert dannach." Beilage zur Wochenzeitung in *Das Parlament*, January 1983.

Wehler, Ulrich, and Klaus Hildebrandt., eds., *Deutsche Historiker*, 9 Vols. Göttingen: Metropole Verlag., 1971.

Wright, Peter. *The Spycatcher. The Candid Autobiography of a Senior Intelligence Officer*. Toronto: Stoddart, 1987.

INDEX

97, 98, 99-103, 114, 116, 142, 166, 168, 172, 232, 234, 238, 436, 439, 449, 454, 463

Meyer, Alec, (historian), 410, 438

Meyer, Oskar, (member of the *Reichstag*), 59, 99

Milburn, Rev. Robert, L.P., 367

Mitchell, Sir Derek, (civil servant, fellow student of St. Paul's school), 119, 409

Mitterand, Francois, (French president, 1916-1996), 391

Mölders, Werner, (Colonel), 259-260

Moldenhauer, Rüdiger, (librarian), 408

Monk-Jones, Mrs, (wife of AM-J), 128-129

Monk-Jones, Arnold, (Headmaster), 128-129

Montgomery, (Field Marshal), 211, 238-240, 284-285, 300

Morrison, Herbert, (MP), 159, 163-165, 199, 201, 211-212

Mosley, Lady Diana, (wife of Sir Oswald), 146, 211-212

Mosley, Sir Oswald, (leader of the British Union of Fascists), 146, 154, 211-212

Murray, Gilbert, (Regius Professor of Greek), 179-180, 207, 221

Murray, Lady Mary, (wife of GM), 179-180

Myers, Hugh, (fellow student oft St. Paul's), 112-120, 417

Nasser, (President of Egypt), 406

Naumann, Friedrich, (1866-1919), (social theorist, publicist, politician), 51-52, 64

Nicholson, Harold, (publisher, writer), 198

Nietzsche, Friedrich, (philosopher), 192

Niemöller, Heinz Hermann, (MD), 106, 327

Niemöller, Martin (Protestant Pastor, Bishop of Hessen-Nassau), 89-91, 107, 171, 327-329, 349

Nussbaum, Arthur (1877-1964), (Prof. of international law), 18, 32, 44, 117

Nussbaum, Trude, née Eyck, (wife of AN), 18, 32, 117

Oakeshott, Walter, (Highmaster of St. Paul's school),122-123, 129-133, 135-137, 157, 178, 207

O'Byrne, Paul, (Catholic Bishop of Calgary), 420

O'Byrne, Fr. Pat, (Patrick, brother of PO), 4201

Ollenhauer, Erich, (German social democratic leader), 380-385, 387-389

Oyen, Orja, (social scientist, University of Bergen, Norway), 418-419

Paquis, Jean-Hérold, (journalist), 239

Pelteson, (MD), 26, 58, 77

Perry, Geoffrey, (Captain), publisher), 286, 306, 308, 336

Peterson, Rudolf, (Burgomaster of Hamburg), 285, 304

Pevsner, Nikolaus, (art-historian), 150-152, 170

Pferdmenges, Robert, (industrialist), 326

Philby, Kim, (British diplomat, Cambridge spy-ring), 243-244

Pineas, Herrmann, (1892-1988), (MD, husband of LE), 25-37, 39, 44

Pineas, Lilli, (daughter of JE and HE), née Eyck, 18, 24, 33, 35-37

Pitt, William, the younger, (1759-1806), 203

Pollitt, Egon, (Sergeant), 275, 277, 295

Praetorius, Will, (Protestant Pastor), 400

Quinn Alison, (wife of DQ), 407

Quinn, David, (historian, husband of AQ), 407, 410

Ramsey, A. H. M. (Captain), 148

Rasner, Erika, (wife of WR), 311, 343

Rasner, Will, (husband of ER, journalist, politician), 311, 313-314, 336, 343

Rathborn, Eleanor, (MP), 178

Rathenau, Walter, (189-1922), (minister of reconstruction, Weimar), 30

Rau, Editha, (widow of Vossberg; writer), 66, 321-323

Rawsthorne, Alan, (composer), 196, 229

Reuter, Dorothy, (daughter of FR and IR), 61

Reuter, Ernst, (social democratic politician; burgomaster of Berlin), 59, 78, 80, 94-95, 99, 382-384, 389

Reuter, Irene, (daughter of EE and HE) née Eyck, 39, 81, 94-